Stance

OXFORD STUDIES IN SOCIOLINGUISTICS

General Editors:

Nikolas Coupland
Adam Jaworski
Cardiff University

Recently Published in the Series:

Talking about Treatment: Recommendations for Breast Cancer Adjuvant Treatment
Felicia D. Roberts

Language in Time: The Rhythm and Tempo of Spoken Interaction
Peter Auer, Elizabeth-Kuhlen, Frank Müller

Whales, Candlelight, and Stuff Like That: General Extenders in English Discourse
Maryann Overstreet

A Place to Stand: Politics and Persuasion in a Working-Class Bar
Julie Lindquist

Sociolinguistics Variation: Critical Reflections
Edited by Carmen Fought

Prescribing under Pressure: Parent-Physician Conversations and Antibiotics
Tanya Stivers

Discourse and Practice: New Tools for Critical Discourse Analysis
Theo van Leeuwen

Beyond Yellow English: Toward a Linguistic Anthropology of Asian Pacific America
Edited by Angela Reyes and Adrienne Lo

Stance: Sociolinguistic Perspectives
Edited by Alexandra Jaffe

Investigating Variation: The Effects of Social Organization and Social Setting
Nancy C. Dorian

Stance

Sociolinguistic Perspectives

Edited by
Alexandra Jaffe

OXFORD
UNIVERSITY PRESS

2009

OXFORD
UNIVERSITY PRESS

Oxford University Press, Inc., publishes works that further
Oxford University's objective of excellence
in research, scholarship, and education.

Oxford   New York
Auckland   Cape Town   Dar es Salaam   Hong Kong   Karachi
Kuala Lumpur   Madrid   Melbourne   Mexico City   Nairobi
New Delhi   Shanghai   Taipei   Toronto

With offices in
Argentina   Austria   Brazil   Chile   Czech Republic   France Greece
Guatemala   Hungary   Italy   Japan   Poland   Portugal   Singapore
South Korea   Switzerland   Thailand   Turkey   Ukraine   Vietnam

Published by Oxford University Press, Inc.
198 Madison Avenue, New York, New York 10016

www.oup.com

Oxford is a registered trademark of Oxford University Press.

Library of Congress Cataloging-in-Publication Data
Stance: sociolinguistic perspectives / edited by Alexandra Jaffe.
    p.   cm.
Includes index.
ISBN 978-0-19-533164-6
1. Sociolinguistics.   2. Language and languages—Style.   3. Social interaction.
4. Dicourse analysis—social aspects.
I. Jaffe, Alexandra M. (Alexandra Mystra), 1960–
P40.S562 2009
306.44—dc22   2008034910

9 8 7 6 5 4 3 2 1
Printed in the United States of America
on acid-free paper

CONTENTS

CONTRIBUTORS

MARY BUCHOLTZ, Associate Professor of Linguistics, University of California at Santa Barbara

JUSTINE COUPLAND, Reader in Interactional Sociolinguistics, Centre for Language and Communication Research, Cardiff University

NIKOLAS COUPLAND, Professor and Chair at the Centre for Language and Communication Research, Cardiff University

JUDITH T. IRVINE, Professor and Chair of the Department of Anthropology, University of Michigan

ALEXANDRA JAFFE, Professor of Linguistics and Anthropology, California State University, Long Beach

ADAM JAWORSKI, Professor and Head, Centre for Language and Communication Research

BARBARA JOHNSTONE, Professor of Rhetoric and Linguistics, Carnegie Mellon University

SCOTT F. KIESLING, Associate Professor and Chair of the Department of Linguistics, University of Pittsburgh

JANET MCINTOSH, Assistant Professor of Anthropology, Brandeis University

ROBIN SHOAPS, Assistant Professor of Anthropology, University of Chicago

CRISPIN THURLOW, Associate Professor of Communication and Linguistics, University of Washington

Stance

Introduction

The Sociolinguistics of Stance

Alexandra Jaffe

This volume is a sociolinguistic exploration of one of the fundamental properties of communication: stancetaking. Stancetaking—taking up a position with respect to the form or the content of one's utterance—is central because speaker positionality is built into the act of communication. Although some forms of speech and writing are more stance-saturated than others, there is no such thing as a completely neutral position vis-à-vis one's linguistic productions, because neutrality is itself a stance. To take a simple example, when we choose a verb of saying to introduce speech represented as another's, our choices entail stances toward that speech, from neutrality ("said") to doubt ("alleged"); every choice is defined in contrast to other semantic options. By the same token, speech cannot be affectively neutral; we can indeed convey a stance of affective neutrality, but it will of necessity be read in relation to other possible emotional orientations we could have displayed.

Epistemic and affective stances are both socially situated and socially consequential, as will be explored below. Speech is always produced and interpreted within a sociolinguistic matrix: that is, speakers make sociolinguistically inflected choices and display orientations to the sociolinguistic meanings associated with forms of speech. Thus sociolinguistics has much to offer to the study of stancetaking.

The study of stance in the contemporary literature is wide-ranging and quite heterogeneous (see Englebretson 2007), and has a robust history in a number of analytic traditions, ranging from corpus-linguistic treatments of authorial stance as connected to particular academic genres, to critical discourse analyses of embedded stances in political, cultural, and persuasive texts, to studies of stancetaking as an interactional and discursive phenomenon, to the analysis of stance-saturated linguistic forms as they are used to reproduce (or challenge) social, political, and moral hierarchies in different cultural contexts. The aim of this volume is to map out the *sociolinguistics of stance,* bringing together analyses that allow us to explore both what the study of stance has to offer sociolinguistic theory, and to define the territory occupied by sociolinguistic approaches to stance as it overlaps with and is distinct from the territory occupied by other approaches. This introduction is therefore not intended to be an encyclopedic overview of research on stance in all of the research traditions in which it has been used; nor is it intended to be an exhaustive review of research on stance in sociolinguistics and linguistic anthropology. The goal is at once more modest and more focused: to identify dimensions of stance research that are particularly salient for sociolinguistics, and to situate the sociolinguistic focus on stance in relation to related concepts and currents of analysis within sociolinguistics and linguistic anthropology. With respect to these existing analytical traditions, I will argue that the concept of stance is a uniquely productive way of conceptualizing the processes of indexicalization that are the link between individual performance and social meaning.

Taken as a whole, the lines of research discussed below are concerned with *positionality*: how speakers and writers are necessarily engaged in positioning themselves vis-à-vis their words and texts (which are embedded in histories of linguistic and textual production), their interlocutors and audiences (both actual and virtual/projected/imagined), and with respect to a context that they simultaneously respond to and construct linguistically. One of the primary goals of a sociolinguistic approach to stance is to explore how the taking up of particular kinds of stances is habitually and conventionally associated with particular subject positions (social roles and identities; notions of personhood), and interpersonal and social relationships (including relations of power) more broadly. Secondly, a sociolinguistics of stance has a crucial role to play in theorizing the relationship between acts of stance and the sociocultural field: in particular the role these acts play in social (and sociolinguistic) reproduction and change.

As an emergent property of interaction, stance is not *transparent* in either the linguistic or the sociolinguistic, but must be inferred from the empirical study of interactions in social and historical context. A particular linguistic stance (or a set of stances taken over time) may index multiple selves and social identities; conversely, it may index a single social identity, a personal identity that endures over time (referred to in Johnstone, this volume, as an ethos of self) or a privileged, "core" self (McIntosh, this volume). Speaker stances are thus performances through which speakers may align or disalign themselves with and/or ironize stereotypical associations with particular linguistic forms; stances may thus express multiple or ambiguous meanings. This makes stance a crucial point of entry in analyses that focus on the complex ways in which speakers manage multiple identities (or multiple aspects of identity). The focus on process also foregrounds multiplicities in the audiences indexed by particular linguistic practices, and on the social dynamics and consequences of audience reception, uptake, and interpretation.

Locating the Sociolinguistics of Stance in the Broader Literature

Stance Terms and Definitions

A useful place to start is Du Bois's definition of stance as "a public act by a social actor, achieved dialogically through overt communicative means (language, gesture, and other symbolic forms), through which social actors simultaneously evaluate objects, position subjects (themselves and others), and align with other subjects, with respect to any salient dimension of the sociocultural field" (2007: 163). It is important to note that Du Bois's "stance objects" are not just material: in fact, "salient dimensions of the sociocultural field" can include language and stancetaking itself, a point to which we will return in some detail below.

Table 1.1 summarizes the various terms that have been used in the literature to describe different types of stancetaking, and represents a synthesis of my own and Jaworski and Thurlow's efforts to survey this terrain for this volume. The first segment of the table (A) shows the centrality of evaluation; the second two sections (B and C) illustrate the interconnectedness of evaluation and speaker/author self-positioning in pragmatic, systemic functional, anthropological, sociolinguistic, and critical discourse analytic traditions.

Evaluation and the Social

Evaluation as a broad category of focus is a nexus where the linguistic and social are implicated in a number of ways. First, evaluation of and through language takes place within and invokes moral and social orders, systems of accountability, responsibility, and causality (Clift 2006, Fox 2001, Harré and VanLangenhoeve 1991). As such, it can be "read" as an index of coherent individual or community value systems (Thompson and Hunston 2000: 5); conversely, it can be a site of political struggle and ideological contestation (Fox 2001, M.Goodwin 2006, Hodge and Kress 1988, Matoesian 2005, Modan 2006). Secondly, as Du Bois's definition of stance indicates, all acts of evaluation are simultaneously acts of alignment or disalignment (thus positioning) with other subjects. Goodwin's detailed analysis of these processes in girls' conversations illustrates how evaluation (or "assessment") of talk, objects, and other features of shared context is one of the key ways in which social actors take up stances and "make visible their current alignment with regard to others who are present or talked about" (2006: 191).

In this volume, the social and moral dimensions of evaluation are foregrounded in several chapters. In Coupland and Coupland's chapter, public and media discourses about obesity are both implicitly and explicitly evaluative, and position people as good or bad citizens within a moral discourse about weight, self-control, and health costs to the society at large. The textual strategies used in these texts impute stances of alignment with "expert" discourse and attribute stances of moral failure to the obese. Jaworski and Thurlow's analysis of the discursive construction of elite tourism (and tourists) in texts also shows how the descriptions of tourist consumables (including place) are always implicit evaluations that index systems of distinction (cf. Bourdieu 1981): it is partly by discursively identifying "bad" tourists that "elite" tourists define themselves. Readers are invited to align with the stances in particular texts, and by doing so, to align with a superordinate elitist stance that produces and reproduces social hierarchies. In Irvine's chapter, social (and possibly racial) hierarchies define who has the right to evaluate language. The evaluation of language is in turn connected with the moral order, and

TABLE 1.1 Stance Terms

	Term	Author
A. Evaluation		
of propositional content	**appraisal (judgment)**	Martin (2000)
	attitudinal stance	Halliday (1994)
	evaluation	Fairclough (2003)
	assessment	C. Goodwin (2006); M. H. Goodwin (2006)
	evaluation	Labov and Waletsky (1967)
	deontic attitude	Berman (2004)
of probability, usability of propositional content	**modalization**	Halliday (1994)
of form or style of the utterance or text	**style stance or manner**	Biber and Finegan (1989)
	accountive (second order) positioning	Harré and Vanlangenhove (1991)
	appraisal (appreciation)	Martin (2000)
of the degree of reliability of proposition	**epistemic stance**	Biber and Finegan (1989) Conrad and Biber (2000)
of the truth value of a proposition	**modality**	Fairclough (2003); Verscheuren (1999); Hodge and Kress (1988)
of the degree of affinity between speaker/addressee stance	**modality**	Fairclough (2003)
	stance differential	Dubois (2007)
of stances taken (own or others')	**second order stances**	Kockelman (2004)
B. Reflecting Speaker's/Author's Positionality		
	performative positioning	Harré and Van Langenhove (1991)
Commitment to propositional content (authorship)	**modality**	Stubbs (1996)
Knowledge of/belief in/ commitment to propositional content	**epistemic stance**	Biber and Finegan (1989)
	epistemological stance	C.Goodwin (1986)
	modalization	Halliday (1994)
Feelings about utterance or text	**affect**	Besnier (1993)
	Appraisal (affect)	Martin (2000)
	epistemological stance	C. Goodwin (1986)
Speaker/writer's opinion	**Appraisal**	Martin (2000)
Obligation/inclination	**modulation**	Halliday (1994)
Identity claims		
Claims to authority, responsibility	**assessment**	Heritage and Raymond (2005)
C. Attributing Position to Others		
	performative positioning **interpersonal stance**	Harré & Van Langenhove (1991)

has a constraining effect on the kinds of stances that different social actors can successfully take up. Shoaps shares this focus on the relationship of stance to the moral order, investigating how "moral irony" is used interactionally to criticize the stances taken by unspecified social actors and thereby indirectly index "shared community values." Jaffe's chapter on a Corsican bilingual school looks at the way that teachers use their evaluative role to project bilingual identity and community on their students.

Affective and Epistemic Stance: Social Dimensions

Both affective stances that represent emotional states of the speaker and epistemic stances that convey speakers' degrees of certainty about their propositions are socially grounded and consequential. First, affective display can do the work of evaluation, self-presentation, and positioning that is central to stancetaking. Second, displays of affect have a variety of social and moral indexicalities. They can index shared, culturally specific structures of feeling and norms for its expression and can thus be mobilized in the drawing of social boundaries that is central to the work of social differentiation and categorization (Besnier 1990). Displays of affective stance are resources through which individuals can lay claims to particular identities and statuses as well as evaluate others' claims and statuses. In this volume, McIntosh's chapter shows how epistemological uncertainty leads white Kenyans to give affectively complex and conflicted accounts of their beliefs. In doing so, they attempt to navigate a satisfactory form of self-identification and presentation that both distinguishes them from black Kenyans and accounts for cultural experience that crosses racial lines.

Epistemic stance is likewise culturally grounded, because claims to know are embedded in and index particular regimes of knowledge and authority. Epistemic stancetaking thus serves to establish the relative authority of interactants, and to situate the sources of that authority in a wider sociocultural field. Speakers may use epistemic stance in the pursuit of the social capital that accrues to being recognized as having authentic or authoritative knowledge (as in Johnstone's 2007 analysis of stances towards Pittsburghese) and/or to legitimate further acts of evaluation. In some cases, individuals may project a stance of privileged personal knowledge; in other instances, speakers may use generalizations to shift the location of epistemic authority from the individual to the societal level. As Scheibman points out, indexing societal discourses as shared and compelling through the use of generalizations can indirectly strengthen speakers' stances (2007: 132). Conversely, epistemic stance markers can be used to downgrade speaker authority and attribute/acknowledge other interactants' greater claims to hold relevant information (Rauniomaa 2007: 232).

Stance and Its Relation to Key Themes in the Sociolinguistic Literature

Self- and Other-Positioning

The examples above draw our attention to the way that social relationships are entailed by self-positioning—or individual stance. These entailments take several forms. First of all, because individual identities are defined within social formations, by taking up a position, individuals automatically invoke a constellation of associated social identities. In doing so, speakers project, assign, propose, constrain, define, or otherwise shape the subject positions of their interlocutors (see Harré and VanLangenhoeve 1991, Kockelman 2004, Matoesian 2005). An utterance framed as a performance, for example, positions receivers as an audience; a speaker who takes up an expert stance to give advice positions receivers as novices (or as otherwise needing or receptive to counsel). Similarly, speaker or author stance may construct or invoke proximal or distant, real or imagined audiences. In some cases, the interactional calibration of these socially paired roles is collaborative and consensual. In other cases, stance attributions are tools of control and ideological domination, and may be subject to questioning or contestation in what Harré and Vanlangenhove (1991) call "accountive positioning" (this dynamic is richly illustrated in C. Goodwin 2007 and M. H. Goodwin 1998, 2006). In Jaworski and Thurlow's chapter in this volume, readers of travelogues in prestige newspapers are invited to collude in the evaluative work of the authors, and thus to occupy a shared, elite status. Students in Jaffe's chapter are similarly positioned through teachers' structuring of participant roles as "connoisseurs" of esthetic features of texts in Corsican and thus, incorporated into their teachers' expert stances. In Coupland and Coupland's chapter, authors of articles in women's lifestyle magazines and geriatric doctors take up teaching roles and thus position readers and patients as learners. In some cases, these stance attributions (as well as claims to "know" readers' or patients' feelings and concerns) are collaborative and "donate" positive stances to their targets; in other instances, they have controlling, even patronizing functions. Moreover, as Scollon asserts, both stance and its social entailments are built into linguistic and communicative practice: in his discussion of conversational "maxims of stance" he makes the important point that that acts of interpersonal stancetaking are the necessary preconditions for the conduct of conversation; speakers cannot attend to topic until interactional stances have been established (1998: 71–75).

Second, many stances are "mobilized interactionally across turns," as Clift's analysis of how individuals index their epistemic authority relative to others using "interactional evidentials" shows (2006: 583; see also Heritage and Raymond 2005: 34). This draws our attention to the dialogic dimension of stance: that it is achieved and emergent in interaction, coconstructed with one's interlocutors (see Du Bois 2007; Gardner 2002; Kiesanen 2007; Ribeiro 2006; White 2003; Wu 2004). Constructing and negotiating stances is also clearly the object of much interactional work. In this respect, *uptake* of acts of stance can be critical. This uptake may take the form of audience/interlocutor stances of alignment, realignment, or disalignment (C. Goodwin 2007, Matoesian 2005): what Du Bois calls the "stance follow" (2007: 161). Stance follows also include whether or not interactants take up actions made relevant by the speaker's prior talk (Schegloff 2001: 241). At a basic level, all alignment moves (whether positive or negative) *recognize* the stance taken by a speaker and are thus (constitutive) traces of those stances. Uptake with alignment may also be one of the ways in which stance is implicated in the production of more enduring ideologies or "stands" (Jaworski and Thurlow, this volume) and, in turn, play a role in the "fixing" of indexical relationships between talk and social identities and categories. Three chapters in this volume take us in this direction (Jaworski and Thurlow, Jaffe, and Coupland and Coupland) by showing examples in which stance uptake and alignment is a relatively explicit objective of a broader social project which aims to incorporate audiences into "naturalized" textual and social stances.

In other instances, uptake may creatively transform, recast, or potentially undermine speakers' original stance claims. Advice (and thus the stance of legitimate advice giver) can be ignored, sources of authority contested, jokes taken as insults, and so forth. This dynamic can be seen in Marjorie Goodwin's work on stance in girls' playground games, in which peer group uptake (or recognition) of stance performances can be the primary goal of individual players (1998, 2006). Unratified stance claims in contexts in which positive uptake of stance is either a target or "felicity condition" (Austin 1965) of interaction may significantly undermine not just an individual's social position in the moment, but also may impede her future ability to make similar stance claims in the future. In this sense, stances taken in the present not only retrospectively frame other interactants' speech but have prospective implications (see C. Goodwin 2006, Kärkkäinen 2007, Rauniomaa 2007). In Irvine's chapter in this volume, Mr. Taylor suffers in just this way: his stance projections are unratified and his future position compromised.

Finally, all of these examples underscore the fact that personal stance is always achieved through comparison and contrast with other relevant persons and categories. Stance saturates talk about others, in which speakers engage in both explicit and implicit forms of social categorization and evaluation, attribute intentionality, affect, knowledge, agency to themselves and others, and lay claim to particular social and/or moral identities.

In this volume, we see the interplay between personal stance and the uptake and attribution of stances (the social-relational) in several chapters. Jaworski and Thurlow's chapter shows how an elite tourist stance is built both through discursive opposition with common tourists and through alignment with insider knowledge and consumables associated with luxury. Coupland and Coupland show that in their discourse, doctors working with elderly patients simultaneously take up expert stances and define patients as more or less virtuous in their attitudes and behaviors related to their own health and ageing. Shoaps also explores the role of indirect stancetaking in the "negotiation of moral norms" and performance of moral identities (Shoaps, this volume: 111); analyzing how moral irony (using a particular set of modal particles) in Sakapultek is used to negatively evaluate the behaviors of imagined or hypothetical persons or situations while positioning speakers as morally upright and their addressees as being less so. Like Coupland and Coupland, Jaffe explores how institutional roles, practices, and positions of power enable particular speakers (in this case, teachers) to project and attribute stances of sociolinguistic ownership and legitimacy with respect to students' relationships with Corsican. Irvine's analysis shows the same process of stance attribution, but used to a contrasting end. In her analysis the letters of Mr. Taylor go through chains of reinscription and reentextualization by others in ways that strip him of his authorial (and thus moral and professional) legitimacy. These chapters also foreground the exercise of agency and power in stance attribution, which is simultaneously a form of control of others and control over one's own projected stance. In these various examples, we see the interplay between the agency connected to social and institutional position and the (sometimes separable) agency activated in social interaction.

In addition to examining the social consequences and implications of *linguistic* stancetaking, sociolinguistic approaches to stance look at the way that speakers draw upon *sociolinguistic* resources and repertoires to signal positionality. By *sociolinguistic resources* I mean forms of variation that have established social indexicalities. Below, I explore how a stance-based approach relates to a range of concepts and interpretive frameworks concerned with how speakers draw on both linguistic and sociolinguistic resources in practice to present the self, to stake claims to particular identities and positions, to do interpersonal work, and so forth.

Footing and Contextualization

Goffman's concept of *footing* and Gumperz's formulation of *contextualization cues* relate to the alignments speakers take up toward themselves and others by managing the production or the reception of an utterance. At a very basic level, stance can be seen as a form of *contextualization,* because stancetaking indicates how the speaker's position with respect to a particular utterance or bit of text is to be interpreted; contextualization cues are thus basic, culturally specific tools or resources for stance-taking. One way of thinking about stance, then, is as the inventory of footings taken in the course of communication: it is the "how" of the process of alignment (see Ribeiro 2006: 73–74).

From the vantage point of speech production, we can talk about degrees of *accommodation*, and their presumed social-psychological motivations. Sociolinguistic approaches to stance build on this notion in several ways. First, linguistic stance can be read as a more or less direct sign of a position, identity, or role with which an individual wishes to be associated. This line of analysis presumes alignment with conventional associations between linguistic form and expressive purpose, opinion, or identity. Using Goffman's terms, in such an analysis, author, principal, and animator are presumed to be congruent. Second, and perhaps more interesting, stance is the crucial operator for acts of *keying*, in which "a set of conventions by which a given activity (which is already meaningful in terms of a primary framework) is transformed into something patterned on this activity but seen by the participants to be something quite else" (Slembrouck 2004, paraphrasing Goffman 1974: 43–44). Keying redefines situations by introducing or laminating latent or potential frames and participant roles onto an interaction. Here, we see the connection with Bakhtin's notion of voice, and the inherently multivocal, dialogic nature of all utterances (1981: 353). A speaker may rekey a presumed authorial role as a "figure", a serious declaration as humorous, or a joke as serious. In all of these cases, what is shifting is speaker stance toward his or her words, the situation, or other social actors. Keying— or shifting stances and frames—signals the multiplicity and complexity of stances and identities: sometimes this very multiplicity can be the outcome or target of stance-taking (see discussion below). Stance is also implicated in *loading*, an extension of the notion of keying that refers to "the speaker's level of investment in the identity being negotiated" (Coupland 2007: 114). Although some conventional associations between "lighter" keys and lower identity loads (or greater potential role distance—

see discussion of performance below) can be made, Coupland makes the point that the stance of heavy or light investment in an identity cannot be read directly from key, but has to be interpreted in context (2007: 114).

Performative Approaches

The notion of sociolinguistic stance is a fundamentally performative one in the sense that a stance-based perspective views social identities as discursively constructed rather than fixed. Social identity can thus be seen as the cumulation of stances taken over time.

There are also more specific interconnections between stance, performance theory, and the sociolinguistics of performance. Let us begin with Bauman and Briggs, who write, "Performance puts the act of speaking on display—objectifies it, lifts to a degree from its interactional setting and opens it up to scrutiny by an audience" (1990: 73). Here they emphasize the marked, reflexive, artful nature of performance as well as the performer's accountability to an audience. In Bauman's more recent treatment of performance as reentextualization, he invokes "the dynamic tension between the ready-made, socially given element, that is, the persistent cultural entity that is available for recontextualization in performance, and the emergent element, the transformation of this element in the performance process" (Bauman 1996: 302). In short, every performance is recognized as the performer's "take" or stance on a particular speech genre, itself recognized as collective, cultural property. It is here that the audience is implicated and has an evaluative role to play; it is also here that we see connections between the esthetic and the social/moral orders.

The performance frame can also be indexed by particular acts of stancetaking (see also discussion of stylization below): linguistic and paralinguistic displays of stance can mark an utterance *as* performance, which implies a high degree of reflexivity with respect to form. The notion of *voice* is also implicated in a performance framework, as it is in discussions of footing, participation frameworks, and reentextualizations of speech through reporting, ironizing, and so forth. The degree to which speakers frame their utterances as performance and the degree to which their speech is *self-conscious* both have relevance for the interpretation of speaker alignment with the voice of an utterance. In general, higher levels of displayed orientations to performance can be seen as offering the greatest potential for displayed role distance (a possible stance).

With respect to the interpersonal dimensions of stance, studies of sociolinguistic style within a performative approach also provide a framework for understanding a range of orientations and motivations for the production of speech or writing. These include a focus on referee, recipient, and audience design (see Bell 1984, 2001, Schilling-Estes 2004, Coupland 2007), which focus on how speakers use and shift styles to align with various kinds of audiences (including copresent addressees, ratified and nonratified overhearers) as well as absent reference groups. This work emphasizes the point made above about the social-relational nature of individual expression, and provides some useful tools and categories for the understanding of the complex kinds of audience categories and roles to which speakers orient (copresent or not, ratified or not, etc.). Ethnographic, interactional, and discourse-analytic work also shows that stances taken in local interaction can presuppose or posit relationships between copresent and absent audiences (see Irvine 1996, Hall, Sarangi, and Slembrouck 1997). This points to the way that audiences—and "publics"—can be imagined and idealized in performance (see Gal and Woolard 2001, Jaffe 2000, 2007a). Stance is implied/presupposed in performance, and performances also coimplicate audience(s); thus stance is at work in the discursive positioning of performers to audiences and audiences to other audiences. In this volume, for example, Bucholtz's discussion of media entextualizations of "whassup" and "güey" shows how they presuppose and index particular kinds of audiences: those who are either "in the know" about the indexicalities of these expressions and/or those who can read the intertextual links between different media representations.

Dynamic/Reflexive Approaches to Context

Over the last 20 years, work in interactional sociolinguistics and linguistic anthropology has approached context as both a frame and a consequence of interaction (see Duranti and Goodwin's seminal 1986 volume); utterances are both "context-shaped" and "context-renewing" (C. Goodwin 2006: 443). To the extent that participant roles are a building block of context, this position implicates Goffman's notions of *footing* and *framing*, because frames are understood as inherently multiple and multilayered, and changes of footing are viewed as a "persistent feature of natural talk" (Goffman 1974, in Slembrouck 2004). Stances taken in interaction play a contextualizing role, creating a point of reference for subsequent utterances, which are both produced and interpreted in light of their relationship to prior talk. Acts of stance can thus be seen as one of the ways in which the multiplicity of contextual frames for talk get narrowed down or focused in interaction. Although this approach makes it clear that context cannot be seen as an independent variable that is detachable from specific interactions, it does not imply that all aspects of all contexts are fully negotiable by all participants. In this light, stance also has to be interpreted in light of the relative degree to which particular contexts shape or constrain individual action or expression. Put another way, conventional, socially and culturally embedded practices, roles, and expectations are the backdrop against which stancetaking occurs. For example, institutional contexts like schools heavily specify certain roles (student, teacher) and their interactional and linguistic prerogatives and patterns. Teachers and students may conform to or depart from these conventions (taking up diverse stances), but these conventions constitute a fundamental framework for the speech production and interpretation of those individual acts of positioning. A similar point can be made relative to the performance of gender, which, as Ehrlich points out, always takes place within a "rigid regulatory framework" that imposes "limits and constraints on speakers' agency in constructing [gender] identities" (2006: 139).

Indexicality: The Mediation of Sociolinguistic Variables and Social Identities

The role of stance in the indexical mediation of language practices and social identities is most clearly laid out in Ochs's 1993 analysis, in which she points out that linguistic variables conventionally assumed to have a direct link to gender actually have an indirect link, mediated by stance. That is, particular ways of talking are associated with kinds of stances, or subject positions. Certain stances or clusters of stances become associated with gender through practice conducted within gendered and hierarchical social formations. Thus using "mitigating" language to make requests or demands is not a direct index of femininity, but rather represents a kind of stance that is taken up (or imposed on) a variety of less powerful people in society, including, but not limited to, women. At the same time, political and ideological processes may "naturalize" some of these indexical relationships such that they are treated as having a direct, even iconic connection to social identities (a point made by Bucholtz, Kiesling, and others in this volume).

A sociolinguistic approach to stance is distinguished, then, by this specific focus on the *processes of indexicalization*. In doing so, it goes beyond traditional correlations between linguistic variables and social identities conceived as more or less fixed and unproblematic categories. That is, as an analytical framework, stance does not essentialize social categories, but rather, looks at the subject positions and relationships that can be enacted through forms of talk and then, as a second level of analysis, how these are statistically and/or stereotypically mapped on to named linguistic systems ("accent," "dialect," "language," "mixed codes") or less explicitly named discourse categories (register, genre, discourse) made up of clusters of features. The linguistic systems indexed by stance are all embedded in political, social, ideological, and cultural fields of action. All individual acts of stance are thus, by definition, *indirect indices* of these fields, and play a mediating role in processes of identification (Eckert and Wenger 2005: 584, Ochs 1996). This focus on indirect indexicality is also related to the interactional, emergent, and coconstructed nature of stance discussed above with reference to paired (or clustered) participant roles. That is, when interactional and social meaning is embedded in presuppositions of talk, interlocutors are implicated through the very process of interpretation. This active role can be a form of intimacy or complicity in which the speaker invokes shared membership or values (as we see in Kiesling's discussion of immigrant interviewees' orientations to an immigrant interviewer). It can also sharpen the sting of a critique, as Shoaps's analysis illustrates, by making the recipient complicit in the negative framing of his/her behavior (see also Basso 1976).

Stance, as a form of indirect indexicality also posits, presupposes, or proposes relationships that go beyond the social and interpersonal. So, for example, using a stigmatized or minority code in a formal register could be, simultaneously, an individual claim to specific social membership(s) and authority, an act of interpersonal positioning, and a political and ideological statement about the status and relationship of the codes in circulation (the language chosen and the language not chosen).

This leads us back to the cumulative effects of collective patterns of stance variation and the macrosociolinguistic implications of processes of indexicalization. Patterns of stances taken toward sociolinguistic norms or ideologies are part of this dynamic process, and become a new resource for the production and interpretation of speech. For example, in Dunn's analysis of Japanese honorific use, over 80% of speakers used humble forms in wedding speeches in conventionalized sections of the genre, showing conformity to and respect for normative uses of language to index conventional relationships associated with these events. However, when speakers stepped out of the formal speechmaking role, these humble forms were used half as often (2005). These differentiated patterns of practice within the genre represent a shift or extension of conventional indexicalities (deference) associated with humble speech, establishing the contrast between humble and not humble as a resource for the expression of shifts (or inherent multiplicity) in speakers' relationships of "self" to utterance. In short, patterns in the cumulative results of speaker stancetaking shape both what is understood to be indexed by particular linguistic forms or practices and, potentially, the language ideologies that underpin how people look at the connections between language forms and practices and the social world.

Style, Styling, and Stylization

There are a number of important connections between sociolinguistic approaches to style and stylization and the sociolinguistics of stance. Contemporary approaches to sociolinguistic style focus on the interaction between socially recognized speech styles and personal style. As Irvine points out, those socially recognized speech styles are part of systems of distinction in which "a style contrasts with other styles, and the social meaning signified by the style contrasts with other social meanings" (2001: 22). The study of style thus involves documenting co-occurring linguistic features found in a social or personal style as well as the broader social semiotic system that establishes salient comparisons and contrasts between various styles and their elements. The same is true, of course, for stance: individual stances are only meaningful in relation to other possible stances from which they can be differentiated.

The connection between the social and the personal is realized in acts of *styling* (or *stylization*, discussed below). Work on styling offers an account of how people use sociolinguistic variation in "identity projections." Much of this work explores how speakers position themselves with reference to the kinds of macrosocial identity categories (ethnicity, gender, class, and place) that have long been the stock of variationist sociolinguistics. The focus on individual agency and creativity in styling identities posits these categories as resources for, rather than determinants of, individual linguistic practices (see Coupland 2007: 76, 138, Johnstone 2007, Rickford and Eckert 2001: 5). Put another way, the macro categories themselves become stance objects; styling is by definition a form of stance-taking. Speaker stance in styling is operationalized through processes of selection (of sociolinguistic variants) and elements of performance that deploy a range of semiotic resources. That is, speakers do not necessarily enact a socially salient style wholesale: they select particular features, which they perform along a continuum of intensity (vowel quality, location, length, etc.) and frequency (of use of particular variables) (Bucholtz 1999, 2001, Eckert 2000, Mendoza-Denton 2008). As Johnstone points out in her analysis of stancetaking in performances of Pittsburgh speech, speakers also lay claims to greater or lesser direct, personal knowledge of and relationships to the dialect. In doing so, they situate themselves as more or less "authentic" and thus authoritative speakers and evaluators of the local dialect (2007: 50). Similarly, Jaffe and Walton found that in performances of Southern speech, speakers took up stances of greater or lesser distance or affiliation with that variety of American English (2000).

This suggests that at the same time as stancetaking indexes sociolinguistic style, stance is also a crucial, if not primary, resource for style. Both Kiesling and Bucholtz (this volume) argue that indexical connections between particular ways of speaking (styles) and kinds of persons (and thus with identities to which a speaker may align) are constructed through stance (see also Bucholtz and Hall 2005, Eckert 2000, Kiesling 2004, Johnstone 2007). This is partly because, as mentioned above, the work of identity projection in interaction is also always the work of interpersonal relationships. That is, linguistic variation used to position speakers toward "big" identity categories is often simultaneously used to take up personal stances with interpersonal consequences. These include stances marking degrees of personal competence, control, authority, expertise, compliance with institutional or social agendas, and so forth. The co-occurrence of this foundational stance work, enacted locally ("interior" in Kiesling's terms), using sociolinguistically salient variation thus builds styles.

At the same time, we can view sociolinguistic style as a resource for stance, in the contextually specific ways in which sociolinguistic variables can be mobilized to do relational work. This is illustrated several recent works, including Ervin-Tripp's (2001) study of Dick Gregory, an African-American civil rights era political activist and comedian, and Rampton's analysis of the use of "posh" versus Cockney accents by adolescents. Rampton shows how "posh" and "Cockney" are used to articulate stances toward the body-in-society, in which he writes that "a *relatively standard* accent is used to articulate an incompetent or uneasy relationship with the body and with feelings and emotion...an apparent regard for social decorum....A Cockney accent...is associated with bodily activity...feeling unconstrained by social manners" (2006: 342, italics in original). In Ervin-Tripp's analysis, we see that although Gregory sometimes uses the contrast between black and white speech styles in a conventional way, to index black versus white attitudes and perspectives, that contrast is also layered with multiple social indexicalities (sophisticated versus unsophisticated protesters, ignorant parents versus youth and sacred texts, etc.) and used in unexpected ways (black personas given white voices and vice versa). These examples illustrate the dynamic relationship between contextualized acts of stancetaking across time and conventional sociolinguistic indexicalities. That is, the mapping of Cockney and "posh" onto stances to body-in-society and of black and white styles onto attributed political stances in the personas voiced by Gregory are not just "given," ready-made exterior resources simply taken up by particular social actors: those social actors have agency in creating them. At the same time, they do not come from nowhere, and are consistent with broader, historical contrasts and stereotypes: about class, control, and physicality (in Rampton's example) and about race and political ideology (in Ervin-Tripp's). Thus, in these examples, we can see particular dimensions of circulating social and sociolinguistic resources being actualized through local acts of stancetaking, which in turn may create new indexicalities that become subsequent targets for further acts of stance. This point is also illustrated in Adkins's analysis of how, in a particular theater company, "stage Irish" is used by the director at moments in interaction in which she manages transitions between activity types (giving instructions and doing rehearsals) (2007). This local function is in fact a stance (that indexes expertise, authority), which, by being enacted through stage Irish over time, builds an indexical relationship between this language variety and those stances. It then becomes available to another (assistant) director for further stancetaking, who uses stage Irish in the main director's absence in order to signal and legitimate her claim to the authority of that position.

Another related point that is emphasized by both Kiesling's and Bucholtz's contributions to this volume is that stance is the dynamic operator that makes it possible for one set of indexicalities to be mobilized to do different (indexical) work in a different context. For example, when linguistic variants (like "dude") that index a kind of masculinity associated by "surfers" and "stoners" are taken up by people outside those categories to present themselves as having a laid-back, cool solidarity, it is those stances—not entire social category identities—that are being transported across speaker categories and domains of use. The same thing can be said about the phenomenon of "crossing" launched into the literature by Rampton and explored in subsequent work. When non-Asian teenagers use bits of Panjabi with teachers (Rampton 1995, 2005) or white male high school students adopt elements of African American speech styles (Bucholtz 1999), they selectively mobilize stances associated with those codes for immediate (and sometimes more enduring) social and interactional purposes. Bucholtz's contribution to this volume shows that this process of stance transfer (from "dude" to "güey") is not straightforward: the "old" and the "new" indexicalities exist in a certain tension, rendering them open to multiple and competing interpretations.

Crossing is of course relatively self-conscious speech, which brings us to the topic of *stylization* as a form of stancetaking that is deliberately and self-consciously performative, and which thus simultaneously draws attention to the agency of the performer in manipulating conventions and to the conventional associations between speech styles and identities and to the individual's stancetaking within those webs of associations. Eckert points to the constitutive role that stance and stylization play in the construction of social meaning and linguistic variation. In her analysis of iconic burned-out burnout girl speakers, it is the pairing of overtly stylized speech (such as emphatic uses of sociolinguistic variables) and other social displays of stance and style that "defines the meanings of the style that lead to the more general correlations between vocalic variables and social category affiliation" (2001: 125). We could argue that stylization in everyday talk and in its more overt occurrence in a variety of media genres makes stance its explicit object. Here, Coupland reminds us that stylization can "complicate the links between sociolinguistic practice and social meaning...[and]...also expose those links quite strikingly and make them available for critical reassessment" (2007: 171). These perspectives help us to understand the mixed reactions reported by Bucholtz (this volume) to advertisers' attempts to transfer the ironic, metapragmatic associations of "whassup" to the Spanish term "güey": the media frame lays the stance equivalence of the two terms open for public evaluation.

Examples of both the everyday and the stylized redeployment of stances across contexts and speakers highlight the significance of stances as both intimately linked to and situationally separable from styles and identities. In part, this is because of the multiple mappings of stances and other relevant categories. Describing Mendoza-Denton's work on young Latinas' styling, Eckert writes, "Class and gender...may be associated with stances such as toughness or intellectual superiority. A single linguistic feature, therefore, may be deployed in multiple styles and combined with others to create a style rich in social meaning" (Eckert 2005: 101–102). Similarly, in this volume, Bucholtz shows how the use of "güey" by adolescents can be deployed to take a boastful stance or to create a relationship of "cool solidarity" much like "dude" in Kiesling's work. The coupling/decoupling of stance, style, and identity is also related to the inherently reflexive and metalinguistic nature of stance. In this respect, even the mundane use of stance seems to have features of "high performance" (Coupland 2007: 146), including what Bauman and Briggs characterize as "decontextualizability" and accessibility for future reentextualizations (1990: 73).

Metasociolinguistic and Ideological Dimensions of Stance

As Bucholtz shows in this volume, stancetaking can be a window on individual interpretations of and positions toward metapragmatic stereotypes, including the identities and relationships conventionally associated with particular discourses, variables, or forms of talk. Stancetaking can also have as its object the underlying assumptions, processes, and motivations behind those sociolinguistic correlations. That is, speakers can use sociolinguistically salient forms in such a way as to call into question—or leave unchallenged—specific language hierarchies: convictions that particular variables are inherently more or less prestigious, intimate, authoritative, and so on. At an even more basic level, people can take up stances toward the assumed connections between language and identity, from the individual to the collective level. We might call this display of an attitude or position with respect to language hierarchies and ideologies a *metasociolinguistic* stance.

Such metasociolinguistic stances are enacted in a variety of ways. For example, speakers may align with "standard language ideology" (Lippi-Green 1997) through overt commentary. This is illustrated in Johnstone's chapter about Barbara Jordan, who, in her autobiographical accounts of her socialization as a public speaker, explicitly subscribes to the notion that there is one correct way to speak. She also engages in hypercorrection, which is an indirect form of the same kind of alignment (see also Bucholtz's 2001 analysis of "superstandard" English by self-styled 'nerd' high school students). Patterns of code choice can also be interpreted as stances in which language ideologies are simultaneously a resource and an object. Here, we can consider patterns of code choice among individuals who have a repertoire that includes both high and low status codes. When they choose to use the low status codes only in informal or unofficial contexts, they align with standard language ideology by conforming to models of functional differentiation of use based on status. Conversely, use of low status codes in a high-status, public, and institutional context represents a stance of disalignment with standard language ideology. In this volume, Jaffe explores the stance implications of teachers' uses of Corsican and French against a highly politicized language ideological backdrop.

Metasociolinguistic stance is also implicated in speakers' self-conscious displays of consistency or inconsistency in their uses of sociolinguistically salient linguistic forms or codes. For example, Johnstone shows how Barbara Jordan's deflection of questions about adapting language to audience or context resisted the ethos of persona such adaptations invoke, insisting instead on an ethos of self in which language is to be seen as the reflection of durable, stable elements of personal character rather than as a mere response to social contingencies. In doing so, Jordan subscribes to the ideology that language = self and that consistency of language = personal and moral consistency. This contrasts with the stance taken by Dick Gregory in his display of inconsistency in the use of African-American speech forms (in the analysis by Ervin-Tripp, above), which emphasized an ethos of a political ideology of self (and worth) that is separable from language. Both of these examples show that people can be construed as taking stances not only in particular utterances and interactions, but as constructing such stances across their public trajectories as speakers (see discussion below).

As the discussion of processes of indexicalization (above) suggests, metasociolinguistic stance can also be studied as a collective phenomenon, with a focus on patterns of collective positioning. That is, how often speakers do or do not align or comply with conventional sociolinguistic norms or indexicalities in their acts of stance plays a role in the reproduction (and potential change) of those norms and indexicalities.

Stance, Determinacy, and Indeterminacy

Processes of identification may be motivated by a desire to fix social categories and positions, because doing so can confer various forms of advantage/disadvantage on the stance taker (or on others). But identity work can also be oriented toward complex, multiple, and potentially ambiguous kinds of alignments and thus, toward the maintenance rather than the resolution of ambiguity and indeterminacy. That is, because it is often the case that multiple social and linguistic positions, identities, and stances are relevant or useful for particular social actors, they can have an interest in exploiting the fundamental indeterminacy or multivalency of stancetaking to maintain flexibility of self-presentation in potentially unpredictable or volatile social fields of reception and interpretation.

One use of indeterminacy is to defer moments of speaker commitment. Using linguistic variables that index multiple stances makes all of those stances potentially available to be claimed after the fact by the stance taker. Conversely, speakers can exploit indeterminacy to take up deniable stances, or in some way mitigate or mediate the extent to which they are held accountable for them. Some forms of stancetaking may also introduce uncertainty into interaction by drawing attention to the potential gap between linguistic form and intention or authorship. This is illustrated in Shoaps's analysis, in this volume, of the use of irony as a form of moral criticism: she points out that the role of principal (with primary accountability) for the moral positions taken through irony is not specifically attributable to the speaker. This gives the stance taken the value of a normative generalization: as emanating from the collectivity and its shared values (see also Scheibman 2007). Finally, there is the mediation afforded by the inherently multivocalic nature of stances that are actualized through other people's voices as they are reported (directly or indirectly), parodied, alluded to, recycled, repeated, ironized, and so forth. The robust literature on reported speech (see Besnier 1990: 426) shows how it can be strategically exploited by speakers who take up stances of simultaneous closeness to and distance from the stances in the speech they report. That is, by imposing a frame in which participant roles are destabilized, speakers can allude to multiple possible stances while fully committing to none. For example, the reporter of speech can position the self as "only" being an animator, while simultaneously exploiting the potential leakage between different speaker roles such that actually voicing words acquires a degree of authorship.

In other cases, speakers themselves are fundamentally conflicted, and stance multiplicity and indeterminacy expressively mediates that conflict. We see this in McIntosh's analysis of the narratives of white Kenyans whose identities *as whites* are constructed in contrast with "irrational" black African belief systems that nevertheless permeate their experiences and social practices as Kenyans. As a consequence, taking a position with respect to witchcraft and the occult causes existential conflict. In response to this, McIntosh's interviewees introduce multiple "I"s into their accounts, privileging the "I"s that can't believe while simultaneously speaking from the "I"s who have had persuasive encounters with the occult. In doing so, they give voice to multiple selves, but privilege those identities that they have been socialized into as whites.

Stance across Trajectories of Time, Space, and Texts

Stance is constructed across interpersonal encounters, but it is not limited to fleeting or temporary positionings. As Johnstone's chapter in the volume illustrates, we can also speak about durable personal stances (or stance styles) across longer time frames: in the case she analyzes, the stances taken by politician Barbara Jordan across her entire career. Johnstone argues that it is the cumulative patterning of Jordan's stance choices that constitute her unique stance signature, and thus her identity as a linguistic individual. In fact, part of this individuality (and through it, particular claims to authority) is a form of "metastance": the choice to adopt a consistent speaker stance across a range of different contexts in which people might reasonably expect some variation. One could argue that the discourse of elite tourism described by Jaworski and Thurlow in this volume also has as its target a durable individual and shared stance disposition, defined by multiple iterations (and consumption) of discourses of distinction.

Individual speakers' histories of usage and repertoires are thus critical resources for the interpretation of their stance choices in discrete speech events (Jaffe 2007b). This is because, as Du Bois points out, interpreting an act of stance requires knowledge of individual histories of stances both taken and not taken (2007: 147). This framework for choice can be constrained or shaped by social or linguistic conventions as the discussion of agency, above, indicates. But it is the individual stance repertoire (intraspeaker variation) that maps out patterned variation (frequencies, distributions) at the level of the speaker. These patterns of individual variation, compared and contrasted with patterns of collective variation, set the scene for the production and interpretation of specific stance events. Let me illustrate this with a concrete example: a French speaker of my acquaintance who, by her own account, defies normative patterns in her use of "vous" with many people with whom she has warm and friendly relations. This pattern of choice (itself a stance with a number of interesting implications) colors the stance potentials of her uses of "tu," which may carry a more intense affective stance of intimacy than the "tu"s of more normative speakers. Alternatively, although normative speakers' use of "tu" with acquaintances would simply be read as cordial, when she does the same thing it constitutes a departure from her preferred usage, and thus may be seen as a more significant act of social alignment with (or consideration for) interlocutors who desire a reciprocal "tu" usage with her.

Stances are also acquired, attributed, and accumulated through individuals' sequences of movement through participant roles. Jaffe's chapter on the Corsican classroom explores how teachers structure student stances and identities through the sequencing and scaffolding of student participation. Taken from this perspective, we can view movement itself as a crucial component of durable stance orientations in the individual, because the process itself establishes ideal sequences and paired stance relationships. From this perspective, different trajectories of apprenticeship arguably result in different stance outcomes, because they provide different social/ ideological warrants for expertise.

A focus on trajectories of stancetaking resonates with a more general attention to histories of practice: to the chains of signification in which individual utterances derive their meaning(s). This perspective aligns with Bakhtin's notion of *heteroglossia*, in which all utterances carry the traces of past utterances and the social and cultural contexts of talk and action in which they were embedded (1981: 276). It is also consistent with more recent attention to *intertextuality* and *interdiscursivity*. With respect to stance, this means that prior texts and discourses are both resources for stancetaking as well as inevitable frameworks for their interpretation and meaning. Moreover, stance is centrally implicated in the creation of intertextual and interdiscursive links. This is because practices of entextualization, reentextualizaton (Bauman and Briggs 1990, Urban 1996, Van Leeuwen 2008) and resemiotization (Iedema 2003) are not stance-neutral: they always inflect the reproduction as having a particular kind of link with prior texts and discourses and position the agent of reproduction in particular ways. We see this in this volume in Irvine's and Jaffe's chapters, in which acts of reinscription/copying create text trajectories that variously empower or disempower different social actors involved in these sequences.

Ideology and Power in Cultural Context

Issues of ideology and power, anchored in specific cultural and social contexts, are critical to a sociolinguistics of stance. The issue of power has already been alluded to in the discussion of institutional constraints on individual agency and of the role of stance in reproducing or challenging dominant language hierarchies or ideologies. In general, we can think of stance as a resource for individual action that can be productively studied within sociolinguistic traditions focusing on political economies and ideologies of language. That is, we can analyze the way that culturally and historically specific social, institutional, and political formations structure people's access (as individuals and as categories of persons) to particular linguistic stances (especially valued ones such as authority, legitimacy etc.) as well as shape the stances that are attributed to them. As Blommaert puts it succinctly, discourse is "both creative at a micro-level and constrained (determined) at higher levels" (2005: 125). In Irvine's chapter, Mr. Taylor's fragile social position means that he effectively has a legitimate stance to *lose;* his superiors, like the doctors in Coupland and Coupland's chapter, have stances to *give* and little threat of loss. The teachers in Jaffe's chapter, because of their institutional authority and paired, hierarchical relationships with students, also have stances to attribute. In Bucholtz's chapter, we discover that there are differing takes on the stance indexicalities of "güey" among adolescent users, teachers, and Spanish-speaking elders, and understand that issues of social and institutional power will influence which interpretations will prevail (and their consequences) in particular contexts. Thus the issue of individual agency that is central in scholarly assessments of access to linguistic capital is also central to the way in which stance is produced and interpreted.

To emphasize a point made above, cultural variability in this domain is also related to foundational ideologies of personhood and language ideological beliefs about the relationship of the "inner" life of the person and their "outer" or social, expressive behavior. As many authors have noted, although most Western cultural traditions take the distinction between the inner/personal and outer/social for granted (and often map the former onto notions of "true" or "essential" self), these distinctions are far less relevant in many other cultures (Besnier 1990, Duranti 1996, Stroud 1992). This has implications for the interpretation of stance: in cultures without the "inner/outer" dichotomy, all stances will be read as social or political rather than about some essential or private mental or emotional state. This would have the result of blocking, for example, certain kinds of individual stances, such as claims to have acted publicly in ways that conflict with "true" (hidden, interior) feelings or beliefs (see Shoaps, this volume).

Cultures also vary in their repertoires of spoken and written genres and discourses. One of the ways these repertoires inflect stancetaking is in the degree to which their components script personal participation and expression and thus define the nature and scope of individual agency. Genres of talk or writing that are heavily scripted/conventionalized and obligatory shape the variables that speakers deploy in stancetaking as well as the variables interlocutors attend to and the nature of their interpretation. To the extent that social actors are obligated to follow particular discursive scripts, following the required elements of those scripts cannot be read as a direct reflection of high personal alignment, affective stance (the individual's "true" feelings). This would be the case, for example, with certain politeness formulae. At the same time, the narrowing of space for individual maneuver can invest ever finer linguistic or sociolinguistic distinctions with significance for personal stance. We can extend the argument about obligation to a consideration of norms. To the extent that culturally specific genres establish some forms of linguistic usage as standard, normative or unmarked, they also define other variables (low frequency, nonnormative) as "marked" and thus as salient for the stancetaking and the interpretation of speaker intentionality (see Dunn 2005). To the extent that culturally specific genres, like performance, foreground and make issues of form explicit, they also provide a framework for the taking and interpretation of "metastances" (Harré and VanLangenhoeve's "accountive" positioning): the personal stances those speakers take up with respect to the social scripts and obligations, identities, and relationships they imply.

Wider cultural Discourses also have implications for stance in that they can serve as ready-made (ideological) scripts that can themselves be stance objects, activated by individual speakers/writers through the use of some subset of their elements (from phonological variables to specific phrases to chunks of discourse). Another cultural variable is the ideological load carried by particular discourses. In this respect, some discourses may be more "stance-saturated" than others: that is, they may be overtly recognized as sites for more or less obligatory positioning. In this volume, the topic of witchcraft among white Kenyans serves as just such a "stance prompt" for statements of belief (McIntosh); a similar claim is made for discourses on the body and aging in the United Kingdom and the United States (Coupland and Coupland) and for the issue of language choice and use on Corsica (Jaffe).

Stancetaking also plays a complex role with respect to the naturalization of social and linguistic ideologies and the social structures they legitimate. On the one hand, stancetaking plays a naturalizing role because it activates such ideologies indirectly. When ideologies are presupposed rather than articulated outright, they are represented as not being open to question or contestation, and the relationships between linguistic forms and social meanings may be perceived as direct (see Bucholtz, this volume, Irvine and Gal 2000). On the other hand, the performative dimension of some acts of stancetaking also puts on display the processes of indexicalization and iconization. This has the effect of "denaturalizing" the connections between linguistic and social forms by revealing those connections as situated, contingent, and socially created.

Plan of the Book

In chapter 2, Johnstone takes a discourse-analytic and rhetorical approach to the analysis of the speech and writing of Barbara Jordan, a prominent African-American politician, across different genres and contexts. This detailed analysis is coupled with interview, biographical, and historical research about the sociolinguistic and language-ideological contexts in which Jordan operated. Johnstone focuses on Jordan's repeated patterns of stancetaking, arguing that these patterns constitute a style associated with a particular individual. Jordan develops a durable stance that is rooted in a particular ideology about identity, character, and how they are/should be reflected in language that Johnstone calls an "ethos of self." This ethos of self is central to Jordan's political identity, in particular with respect to how she constructed a stance of moral authority that underpinned her rhetoric and was the cornerstone of her public career.

In chapter 3, Judith Irvine analyzes a nineteenth-century dispute between African missionaries documented in correspondence involving Nigerian missionaries, their local bishops, and church authorities in London. In this analysis, she shows how various social actors mediated—and took stances with respect to the "faultable" actions of one of the missionaries, Mr. Taylor. Like Johnstone's chapter, Mr. Taylor's moral authority is in question, but in this case, Taylor's agency in constructing his own stance is severely compromised. Irvine makes the important point that an over-emphasis on speaker intentionality and agency in stancetaking obscures the way that speakers can have thrust upon them stances that are not of their own choosing, and are shaped by the structures of power and ideology in which they operate.

The fourth chapter, by Janet McIntosh, examines the multiplicity of first-person indexicality in interview data with white Kenyans in which they make statements of belief about black African witchcraft. McIntosh shows that in response to existential vulnerability posed by belief in "irrational" belief systems, speakers express a set of fragmented and hierarchically ordered ontological stances: one associated with the "true" (and rational) self and another that is influenced by encounters with the occult. This analysis shows that complexity and inconsistency in speaker stance can reflect profound states of anomie in a context of rapid social and cultural change.

Shoaps's chapter (5) is based on ethnographic research on Sakapultek speakers, and also involves the taking and attribution of moral stances. Shoaps analyzes a category of utterances she labels "moral irony" used in indirect stancetaking that presupposes certain values as shared. In this chapter, as in McIntosh's and Irvine's, the analysis involves the fragmentability of participant roles. The Sakapultek speakers Shoaps describes exploit this fragmentability to invoke absent principals for evaluative actions, and to mitigate the potentially negative social consequences of more direct forms of negative evaluations of others.

In chapter 6, Jaffe explores how teachers' stancetaking and scaffolding of participant roles positions the two languages of a Corsican bilingual school with respect to authority and legitimacy and simultaneously attributes stances of authorship and linguistic competence to the students in the school. She shows how, in particular institutional contexts in which there are paired and hierarchical roles, stancetaking by individuals has stance-attributing entailments for others. Jaffe also emphasizes how the language ideological context "saturates" language choice with stance potential, and how acts of stance across trajectories of time contribute to processes of sociolinguistic indexicalization.

Bucholtz's chapter (7) examines the relationship between stance, style, and identity in the use of a single slang term, *güey*, often translated as "dude." Drawing on naturally occurring conversations among Mexican-immigrant adolescents and in contemporary media advertising texts, Bucholtz shows how the multiple stance indexicalities of this term are drawn on in interaction to do the work of alignment and to create a particular gendered style. She emphasizes that it is the work of stancetaking that creates indexical relationships between particular linguistic forms and social identities.

This argument is consistent with the position Kiesling takes in chapter 8 that stance is where the "baptismal essentializations" (Silverstein 2003) of indexicality associated with sociolinguistic variation occur. Kiesling illustrates this point with reference to three data sets: his earlier work on the use of ING in a fraternity, the use of "nonstandard" forms of Pittsburgh speech in a multiparty conversation among women professionals, and the use of elements of New Australian English by immigrants in interviews conducted in Sydney and Melbourne. In each case, he shows that stance is the best predictor and explanation of patterns of sociolinguistic variable use.

Chapter 9, by Jaworski and Thurlow, analyzes how an elitist stance is discursively constructed in a corpus of travel writing in two major British newspapers. They explore how these texts produce distinction (social difference) through a variety of textual stancetaking strategies. Jaworski and Thurlow show how these textual processes position both writers and readers as real or imagined consumers, and address the implications of these processes for the reproduction of dominant ideologies and social hierarchies.

In the final chapter, Coupland and Coupland examine the topic of body weight and health in two data sets: a corpus of policy texts and women's lifestyle magazines and a spoken corpus of geriatric doctor-patient interactions. Their analysis shows how authors and doctors, in taking up an authorial or discursive stance, attribute stances (moral and otherwise) to addressees or subjects of their discourse. It also highlights the connection between linguistic stancetaking and the production of a normative moral social order.

Conclusions

To return to the agenda laid out in the introduction to this chapter, a sociolinguistics of stance is concerned with two broad issues: the social processes and consequences of all forms of stancetaking and how sociolinguistic indexicalities are both resources for and targets of stance. Situated within the theoretical frameworks I have surveyed above, I would like to propose the following summary of the orientations that define the terrain occupied by a sociolinguistics of stance. A sociolinguistics of stance:

1. situates linguistic acts of stance within the sociocultural matrices that give stances their social meanings and frame the ways in which this particular kind of linguistic behavior is socially consequential;
2. explores how established sociolinguistic indexicalities serve as backdrop and resource for acts of stancetaking, as well as how stancetaking contributes to the production, reproduction, and potential change of indexical relationships between ways of speaking and speaker categories and hierarchies;
3. takes account of language ideologies as both resources for the production and interpretation of stance and as potential stance objects;
4. focuses on the reflexive, metapragmatic, and "metasociolinguistic" dimension of human communication, with a particular interest in the ways that speakers take up positions with respect to core sociolinguistic issues that shape their worlds, including the conventional associations between language and social categories, linguistic ideologies, and language hierarchies;
5. treats speaker stance as a crucial component of interactional processes and practices that have long been a focus of sociolinguistic study, including core concerns with issues of alignment/disalignment and the negotiation of power, as well as with the subtle ways in which speakers can exploit indeterminacy to take up multiple and/or ambiguous positions vis-à-vis copresent as well as absent social others;
6. incorporates stancetaking into analyses of identity as it is performed, socially and interactionally constituted /coconstructed across time and over encounters.

This list can be read as a reflection of what sociolinguistics has to offer the study of stance—in particular, what is gained by bringing sociolinguistic variables and categories into the picture as stance objects and resources for stancetaking. Sociolinguistic approaches clearly complement work on stance in a variety of other disciplinary traditions. At the same time, I would like to suggest that sociolinguistic explorations of stance can play a privileged role with respect to sociolinguistic theory, providing insight into processes of indexicalization as they occur over time and in particular social, cultural, political, and ideological contexts.

References

Adkins, Madeleine. 2007. Performance at rehearsal: The use of stage Irish in liminal moments. Paper presented at the American Anthropological Association Annual Meeting, Washington DC.

Austin, John. L. 1965. *How to do things with words*. Ed. John O. Urmson. New York: Oxford University Press.

Bakhtin, M. M. 1981. *The dialogic imagination*. ed. Michael Holquist and Caryl Emerson. Austin: University of Texas Press.

Basso, Keith. 1976. Wise words of the Western Apache: Metaphor and semantic theory. In *Meaning in anthropology*, ed. Keith H. Basso and Henry A. Selby, 93–121. Albuquerque: University of New Mexico Press.

Bauman, Richard. 1996. Transformations of the word in the production of Mexican festival drama. In *Natural histories of discourse*, ed. Michael Silverstein and Greg Urban, 301–329. Chicago: University of Chicago Press.

Bauman, Richard, and Charles Briggs. 1990. Poetics and performance as critical perspectives on language and social life. *Annual Review of Anthropology* 19: 59–88.

Bell, Allan. 1984. Language style as audience design. *Language in Society* 13: 145–204.

——. 2001. Back in style: Reworking audience design. In *Style and sociolinguistic variation,* ed. Penelope Eckert and John R. Rickford, 139–169. Cambridge: Cambridge University Press.

Berman, Ruth. 2004. Introduction: Developing discourse stance in different text types and languages. *Journal of Pragmatics* 37: 105–124.

Besnier, Niko. 1990. Language and affect. *Annual Review of Anthropology* 19: 419–451.

——. 1993. Reported speech and affect on Nukulaelae Atoll. In *Responsibility and evidence in oral discourse*, ed. Jane Hill and Judith Irvine, 161–181. Cambridge: Cambridge University Press.

Biber, Douglas, and Edward Finegan. 1989. Styles of stance in English: Lexical and grammatical marking of evidentiality and affect. *Text* 9(1): 93–124.

Blommaert, Jan. 2005. *Discourse*. Cambridge: Cambridge University Press.

Bourdieu, Pierre. 1981. *Language and symbolic Power*. Trans. Gino Raymond and Matthew Adamson. Cambridge: Harvard University Press.

Bucholtz, Mary. 1999. You da man: Narrating the racial other in the production of white masculinity. *Journal of Sociolinguistics* 3–4: 443–460.

——. 2001. The whiteness of nerds: Superstandard English and racial markedness. *Journal of Linguistic Anthropology* 11(1): 84–100.

Bucholtz, Mary, and Kira Hall. 2005. Identity and interaction: A sociocultural linguistic approach. *Discourse Studies* 7: 585–614.

Clift, Rebecca. 2006. Indexing stance: Reported speech as an interactional evidential. *Journal of Sociolinguistics* 10(5): 569–595.

Conrad, Susan, and Douglas Biber. 2000. Adverbial marking of stance in speech and writing. *Evaluation in Text: Authorial Stance and the Construction of Discourse,* ed. Susan Hunston and Geoff Thompson, 56–73. Oxford: Oxford University Press.

Coupland, Nikolas. 2007. *Style: Language variation and identity*. Cambridge: Cambridge University Press.

Du Bois, John. 2007. The stance triangle. In *Stancetaking in discourse*, ed. Robert Englebretson, 139–182. Amsterdam: John Benjamins.

Dunn, Cynthia Dickel. 2005. Japanese honorific use as indexical of the speaker's situational stance: Towards a new model. *Texas Linguistic Forum* 48: 83–92.

Duranti, Alessandro. 1996. *From grammar to politics*. Berkeley: University of California Press.

Duranti, Alessandro, and Charles Goodwin, eds. 1986. *Rethinking context*. Cambridge: Cambridge University Press.

Eckert, Penelope. 2000. *Linguistic variation as social practice*. Oxford: Blackwell.

——. 2001. Style and social meaning. In *Style and sociolinguistic variation*, ed. Penelope Eckert and John Rickford, 119–126. New York: Cambridge University Press.

——. 2005. Stylistic practice and the adolescent social order. In *Talking adolescence: Perspectives on communication in the teenage years*, ed. Angie Williams and Crispin Thurlow, 93–110. New York: Peter Lang.

Eckert, Penelope, and Étienne Wenger. 2005. What is the role of power in sociolinguistic variation? *Journal of Sociolinguistics* 9: 582–589.

Ehrlich, Susan. 2006. Trial discourse and judicial decision-making: Constraining the boundaries of gendered identities. In *Speaking out: The female voice in public contexts*, ed. Judith Baxter, 139–158. London: Palgrave Macmillan.

Englebretson, Robert. 2007. Stancetaking in discourse: An introduction. In *Stancetaking in discourse*, ed. Robert Englebretson, 1–26. Amsterdam: John Benjamins.

Ervin-Tripp, Susan. 2001. Variety, style shifting and ideology. In *Style and sociolinguistic variation*, ed. Penelope Eckert and John Rickford, 44–56. New York: Cambridge University Press.

Fairclough, Norman. 2003. *Analysing discourse: Textual analysis for social research*. London: Routledge.

Field, Margaret. 1997. The role of factive predicates in the indexicalization of stance: A discourse perspective. *Journal of Pragmatics* 27(6):799–814.

Fox, Barbara. 2001. Evidentiality: Authority, responsibility, and entitlement in English conversation. *Journal of Linguistic Anthropology* 11.2:167–192.

Gal, Susan, and Kathryn Woolard. 2001. Introduction. In *Languages and publics: The making of authority*, ed. Susan Gal and Kathryn Woolard, 1–12. Manchester, UK: St. Jerome's Press.

Gardner, Rod. 2002. *When listeners talk: Response tokens and listener stance*, Amsterdam: John Benjamins.

Goffman, Erving. 1974. *Frame Analysis*. New York: Harper and Row.

Goodwin, Charles. 1986. Audience diversity, participation and interpretation. *Text* 6: 283–316.

——. 2006. Retrospective and prospective orientation in the construction of argumentative moves. *Text and Talk* 26(4/5): 443–461.

——. 2007. Interactive footing. In *Reporting talk: Reported speech in interaction*, ed. Elizabeth Holt and Rebecca Clift, 16–46. Cambridge: Cambridge University Press.

Goodwin, Marjorie Harness. 1998. Games of stance: Conflict and footing in hopscotch. In *Kids talk: Strategic language use in later childhood*, ed. Carolyn Temple Adger and Susan Hoyle, 23–46. New York: Oxford University Press.

——. 2006. *The hidden life of girls: Games of stance, status and exclusion*. Malden, MA: Blackwell.

Hall, Christopher, Srikant Sarangi, and Stefaan Slembrouck. 1997. Silence and silenced voices: Interactional construction of audience in social work talk. In *Silence: Interdisciplinary perspectives*, ed. Adam Jaworski, 181–212. Berlin: Mouton de Gruyter.

Halliday, M. A. K. 1994. *An introduction to functional grammar,* 2nd ed. London: Edward Arnold.

Harré, Rom, and Luc VanLangenhoeve. 1991. Varieties of positioning. *Journal for the Theory of Social Behaviour* 21: 393–407.

Heritage, John, and Geoff Raymond. 2005. The terms of agreement: Indexing epistemic authority and subordination in talk-in-interaction. *Social Psychology Quarterly* 68: 15–38.

Hodge, Robert, and Gunther Kress. 1988. *Social semiotics*. Cambridge: Polity.

Iedema, Rick. 2003. Multimodality, resemioticization: Extending the analysis of discourse as a multisemiotic practice. *Visual Communication* 2: 29–57.

Irvine, Judith. 1996. Shadow conversations: The indeterminacy of participant roles. In *Natural histories of discourse*, ed. Michael Silverstein and Greg Urban, 131–159. Chicago: Chicago University Press.

———. 2001. Style as distinctiveness: The culture and ideology of linguistic differentiation. In *Style and sociolinguistic variation*, ed. Penelope Eckert and John Rickford, 21–43. Cambridge: Cambridge University Press.

Irvine, Judith T., and Susan Gal. 2000. Language ideology and linguistic differentiation. In *Regimes of language: Ideologies, polities, and identities*, ed. Paul V. Kroskrity, 35–84. Santa Fe, NM: School of American Research Press.

Jaffe, Alexandra. 2000. Comic performance and the articulation of hybrid identity. *Pragmatics* 10(1): 39–60.

———. 2007a. Codeswitching and stance: Issues in interpretation. *Journal of Language, Identity and Education* 6(1): 1–25.

———. 2007b. Corsican on the airwaves: Media discourse, practice and audience in a context of minority language shift and revitalization. In *Language in the media*, ed. Sally Johnson and Astrid Ensslin, 149–172. London: Continuum Press.

Jaffe, Alexandra, and Shana Walton. 2000. The voices people read: Orthography and the representation of nonstandard dialect. *Journal of Sociolinguistics* 4(4): 569–595.

Johnstone, Barbara. 2007. Linking identity and dialect through stancetaking. In *Stancetaking in discourse*, ed. Robert Englebretson, 49–68. Amsterdam: John Benjamins.

Kärkkäinen, Elise. 2007. The role of *I guess* in conversational stancetaking. In *Stancetaking in discourse*, ed. Robert Englebretson, 183–219. Amsterdam: John Benjamins.

Kiesanen, Tiina. 2007. Stancetaking as an interactional activity: Challenging the prior speaker. In *Stancetaking in discourse*, ed. Robert Englebretson, 253–282. Amsterdam: John Benjamins.

Kiesling, Scott. 2004. Dude. *American Speech* 79(3): 281–305.

Kockelman, Paul. 2004. Stance and subjectivity. *Journal of Linguistic Anthropology* 14(2): 127–150.

Labov, William, and Joshua Waletsky. 1967. Narrative analysis: Oral versions of personal experience. *Journal of Narrative and Life History* 7(1–4): 3–38.

Lippi-Green, Rosina. 1997. *English with an accent*. New York: Routledge.

Martin, J. R. 2000. Beyond exchange: APPRAISAL systems in English. In *Evaluation in text: Authorial stance and the construction of discourse*, ed. Susan Hunston and Geoff Thompson, 142–175. New York: Oxford University Press.

Matoesian, Gregory. 2005. Struck by speech revisited: Embodied stance in jurisdictional discourse. *Journal of Sociolinguistics* 9(2): 167–193.

Mendoza-Denton, Norma. 2008. *Homegirls: Language and cultural practice among Latina youth gangs*. New York: Wiley-Blackwell.

Modan, Gabriella. 2006. *Turf wars*. Malden, MA: Wiley-Blackwell.

Ochs, Elinor. 1993. Indexing gender. In *Rethinking context*, ed. Alessandro Duranti and Charles Goodwin, 335–358. Cambridge: Cambridge University Press.

———. 1996. Linguistic resources for socializing humanity. In *Rethinking linguistic relativity*, ed. John Gumperz and Stephen Levinson, 407–438. Cambridge: Cambridge University Press.

Rampton, Ben. 1995. *Crossing: Language and ethnicity among adolescents*. London: Longman.

———. 2006. *Language in late modernity*. Cambridge: Cambridge University Press.

Rauniomaa, Mirka. 2007. Stance markers in spoken Finnish: Minun mielestä and minusta in assessments. In *Stancetaking in discourse*, ed. Robert Englebretson, 221–252. Amsterdam: John Benjamins.

Ribeiro, Branca Telles. 2006. Footing, positioning, voice: Are we talking about the same things? In *Discourse and identity*, ed. Anna de Fina, Deborah Schiffrin, and Michael Bamberg, 48–82. Cambridge: Cambridge University Press.

Rickford, John, and Penelope Eckert. 2001. Introduction. In *Style and sociolinguistic variation*, ed. Penelope Eckert and John Rickford, 1–20. Cambridge: Cambridge University Press.

Schegloff, Emmanuel. 2001. Discourse as an interactional achievement III. In *The Handbook of discourse analysis*, ed. Deborah Schiffrin, Deborah Tannen, and Heidi Hamilton, 229–249. Malden, MA: Blackwell.

Scheibman, Joanne. 2007. Subjective and intersubjective uses of generalizations in English conversation. In *Stancetaking in discourse*, ed. Robert Englebretson, 111–138. Amsterdam: John Benjamins.

Schilling-Estes, Natalie. 2004. Constructing ethnicity in interaction. *Journal of Sociolinguistics* 8(2): 163–195.

Scollon, Ron. 1998. *Mediated discourse as social interaction: A study of news discourse*, Reading MA: Addison-Wesley.

Silverstein, Michael. 2003. Indexical order and the dialectics of social life. *Language and Communication* 23(3–4): 193–229.

Slembrouck, Stefan. 2004. What is meant by discourse analysis? Rev. June 5, 2006. http://bank.rug.ac.be/da/da.htm.

Stroud, Christopher. 1992. The problem of intention and meaning in codeswitching. *Text* 12(1): 127–155.

Stubbs, Michael. 1996. *Text and corpus analysis: Computer-assisted studies of language and culture*. Oxford: Blackwell.

Thompson, Geoff, and Susan Hunston. 2000. Evaluation: An introduction. In *Evaluation in text: Authorial stance and the construction of discourse*, ed. Susan Hunston and Geoff Thompson, 1–27. New York: Oxford University Press.

Urban, Greg. 1996. Entextualization, replication and power. In *Natural histories of discourse*, ed. Michael Silverstein and Greg Urban, 21–44. Chicago: Chicago University Press.

Van Leeuwen, Leo. 2008. *Discourse and practice: New tools for critical discourse analysis*. Oxford: Oxford University Press.

Verschueren, Jef. 1999. *Understanding pragmatics*. London: Arnold.

White, Peter. R. R. 2003. Beyond modality and hedging: A dialogic view of the language of intersubjective stance. *Text* 23 (2): 259–284.

Wu, Ruey-Jiuan. 2004. *Stance in talk: A conversation analysis of Mandarin final particles*. Amsterdam: John Benjamins.

2

Stance, Style, and the Linguistic Individual

Barbara Johnstone

Overview

Repeatable linguistic styles emerge out of stancetaking strategies that prove repeatedly relevant and useful for particular speakers in particular kinds of interactions. Previous research has explored how styles can come to be associated with interactional situations (e.g., Biber and Finegan 1989) or social identities (e.g., Ochs 1992, Eckert 2000). In some language-ideological contexts, styles associated with individuals can also become ethnographically and interactionally relevant. This chapter uses a discourse-analytic case study of one individual's talk and writing across genres, together with interview, biographical, and historical research about the sociolinguistic and language-ideological contexts, to illustrate how repeated patterns of stancetaking can come together as a style associated with a particular individual. The individual in question, a well-known twentieth-century U.S. political figure, was known for how she talked, which was sometimes referred to as "the Barbara Jordan style." As I will show, Jordan drew on discursive resources from the African-American church and from American traditions of legal and political debate and oratory, as mediated by particular people in her environment, to create a linguistic style that she adopted across discourse genres and across time. In keeping with one of the two the dominant Western ideologies about the role of identity in persuasion, this style was understood to index rhetorical credibility by constructing and calling attention to moral and epistemological authority stemming from consistent personal identity rather than changeable social identity.

I begin by sketching the models of stancetaking and style I draw on, summarizing corpus-linguistic, anthropological, and sociolinguistic research that shows how repeatable styles emerge in the course of repeated stancetaking choices. I then turn to my case study. After introducing Barbara Jordan, I claim that for reasons having to do with local beliefs about identity and discourse, Jordan's style needed, in her sociocultural environment, to be recognizably associated not just with one or more *social* identities, such as being female, black, an attorney, or a politician, but with a unique, consistent *personal* identity linked to a unique life history: with being Barbara Jordan. I provide four kinds of evidence for this claim:

1. Using historical evidence, I show that the classical rhetorical idea that persuasion is sometimes effected through the projection of individual personal identity into discourse continues to circulate in the American language-ideological context. I describe the rhetorical strategy associated with this idea, which, using a traditional rhetorical term, I call the *ethos of self:* the discursive enactment of epistemic and moral authority linked to a unique "lingual biography" (Johnstone 1999a).
2. Using biographical evidence, I show that the idea of the ethos of self as a valued rhetorical strategy was present in Jordan's particular sociolinguistic and language-ideological environment, and that some of the linguistic resources for enacting it may have been drawn from discursive registers that came together in Jordan's life history.
3. Using textual evidence, I show how "the Barbara Jordan style" emerges out of interactional and epistemic stancetaking moves that project personal epistemic and moral authority: informational, fairly noninteractive talk, full of markers of certainty, together with explicit references to Jordan's own life experience. I also suggest that, in this language-ideological context, cross-genre consistency itself works to project authority.
4. I turn more briefly to evidence about how Jordan's style is identified and understood by people who heard her speaking, suggesting that it is at least in part Jordan's use of the ethos of self that makes her seem so "powerful" to others.

My argument in this chapter is that focusing on ethos allows us to see that stancetaking has to do not only with indexing one's orientation to the propositional content of discourse, to one's interactional partners, or to conventional social identity categories, but also with indexing one's orientation to the nature of individual identity and its enactment in language. To see this, however, it is necessary to look beyond single, analytically isolated interactions, exploring in addition how individuals' stancetaking practices pattern over time and situation.

Theoretical Framework

What Is Stance?

Stance is generally understood to have to do with the methods, linguistic and other, by which interactants create and signal relationships with the propositions they utter and with the people they interact with. Early work (Biber and Finegan 1989) focused on evidentiality and affect, examining textual features that can signal the source of speakers' knowledge and their degree of certainty, as well as their attitudes about the propositions they utter. In more recent work taking a similar approach, Hunston and Thompson (2000) explore the linguistics of "evaluation." For them, "evaluation is the broad cover term for the expression of the speaker or writer's attitude or stance toward, viewpoint on, or feelings about the entities or propositions that he or she is talking about. That attitude may be related to certainty or obligation or desirability or any of a number of other sets of values" (5). According to Hunston and Thompson, evaluation has three functions (6–13): expressing the opinion of the speaker/writer vis-à-vis the propositions being expressed, manipulating the hearer/reader's attitude vis-à-vis these propositions (in part by constructing and maintaining relationships between speaker/writer and hearer/reader), and organizing the discourse, for example, by marking boundaries or highlighting significant parts. Because evaluating a proposition often involves comparing it to a norm, linguistic features associated with evaluation may include such things as comparative adjectives, negation, and adverbs of degree. The language of evaluation may also involve markers of subjectivity such as modals, sentence adverbs, and conjunctions and structures that report and attribute speech, as well as markers of value, such as lexical items that are evaluative and indications of whether goals are achieved (21–22).[1]

Because taking a particular attitude toward propositions—such as uncertainty—may index a particular social relationship or attribute—such as powerlessness—stancetaking inevitably has to do with both epistemic and interactional aspects of perspective-taking in discourse. Goffman's (1981) "footing" includes elements of both, though it highlights the interactional, as does Hunston and Thompson's second function of "evaluation" having to do with the ways in which interlocutors try to manipulate each other's attitudes vis-à-vis the propositions being expressed. Taking a more explicitly sociolinguistic approach, Ochs (1992) models how particular linguistic forms can index evidential stances such as certainty, interpersonal stances such as friendliness or intensity, or social actions such as apologizing. Du Bois (2007: 163) takes a similarly broad approach: "stance is a public act by a social actor, achieved dialogically through overt communicative means, of simultaneously evaluating objects, positioning subjects (the self and others), and aligning with other subjects, with respect to any salient dimension of the sociocultural field"; the "stance triangle" consists of two social actors and an object to which both are oriented. Because alignment or disalignment with another social actor could be accomplished through membership categorization moves, social identity claims and ascriptions also fall under the rubric of stancetaking. For Du Bois, "the stance act [is], perhaps, the smallest unit of social action" (173).

Stance and Style

Repeated sets and patterns of stancetaking moves can emerge as relatively stabilized repertoires, sometimes called "styles," associated with or situations or social identities (Bauman 2001). Styles are (at least to some extent) repeatable. That is to say that sets of stancetaking moves serving a common function are not always assembled *de novo* in each new situation. As they produce or interpret talk, people can often draw on already-made generalizations about the stance features that instantiate a particular style. Styles are often identifiable, by analysts and/or by participants; some have names. Styles associated with a particular set of contextual factors that confront a speaker with a particular set of rhetorical exigencies are sometimes called "registers" (Biber and Finegan 1994, Finegan and Biber 2001).[2] Sets of stancetaking choices associated with participant roles or subject positions are sometimes referred to under the rubric of "footing" (Goffman 1981) or "framing" (Tannen 1979, 1993). When people use terms like "dialect" or "variety" or more vernacular terms like "Pittsburghese" (Johnstone and Baumgardt 2004, Johnstone, Andrus, and Danielson 2006), they are sometimes referring to sets of stancetaking choices associated with places and/or associated social identities.

Biber and Finegan's (1989) pioneering work on stance and style identified statistical clusters of co-occurring stance markers and interpreted these clusters with relation to functional demands created by situation and participation structure. More recent work models *how* particular clusters of features come to serve particular functions. For Irvine (2001), styles emerge when particular patterns of differentiation become ideologically linked with local, ethnographically relevant social meanings. For example, in a particular sociocultural milieu, stance features that repeatedly proved useful in constructing linguistic deference might become indexically linked with femaleness (Ochs 1992). This happens because of the indexicality of all language use: forms that regularly occur in a certain context can come to call up that context.

Eckert's (1989, 2000) work in a Detroit high school links stancetaking to social identity via styles. For Eckert, adopting certain variants of vowels is one way adolescents take a stance vis-à-vis local life, just as is cruising in cars (or not), dressing in a particular way, or choosing among school activities. Such activities on all levels can become styles linked with social identities like "jock" or "burnout." Eckert's primary focus is on clusters of style choices that index stances with respect to social identity categories that are understood as already existing, while Kiesling (2004, 2005) focuses on "creative" rather than "presupposing" indexicality (Silverstein 1995[1976]: 204–205), asking how a particular style of stance comes to be associated with particular social identity in the first place. In a study of recent immigrants in Australia, Kiesling (2005 and this volume) shows that a particular set of morphophonological features that co-occur in the migrants' English work together to project a face-saving epistemic and interactional stance Kiesling calls "authoritative connection." This stance, Kiesling claims, is particularly likely to be relevant for members of subordinate groups. Because they work together as a stancetaking strategy, the features get used repeatedly together, and a repeatable style (locally called "wogspeak") emerges, ideologically linked with a repeatable social identity, that of the recent immigrant.

In much of this work, the object of study is language use across idealized groups of speakers. Whether the focus is primarily on language (e.g., Biber and Finegan, Hunston and Thompson), on social life (e.g., Goffman, Tannen, Ochs), or on the relationship between the two (e.g., Eckert, Kiesling), the styles that are described characterize registers, participant roles, or social identities. Here I redirect our attention to a locus of style that Western rhetoricians and literary critics have been exploring for centuries: the individual human being. My approach is sharply different from the understanding, in variationist sociolinguistics, of intra-speaker stylistic variation as resulting from differing levels of self-consciousness (Labov 1966, 2001), adaptation to real or imagined audience (Bell 1984, 2001), or other situational features. In certain language-ideological contexts, I claim, stylistic differentiation can be semiotically linked with particular speakers, such that individuals claim to recognize other individuals on the strength of their characteristic ways of using language, and some individuals' linguistic styles may come to be named and emulated.

Some of the material I use to illustrate this claim is drawn from earlier work about Barbara Jordan (Johnstone 1996, 128–155). I supplement it here with new observations about the discourse data assembled earlier, as well as new biographical and critical material about Jordan, of which a great deal has appeared since her death in 1996. The theoretical framework I have developed here is considerably refined from the 1996 version. The current chapter contributes to our understanding of stancetaking by providing a model of the interactional and ideological processes that can make the "linguistic individual" (Johnstone 1996, 2000) relevant ethnographically and interactionally (i.e., as a category to which participants orient, in terms of which to understand and evaluate each other in general and in particular interactions). In addition, it enhances our understanding of stancetaking by showing how stancetaking can work to construct and circulate language ideology. By means of patterns of stancetaking over time and situation, speakers index their understandings of how personhood and discourse are linked, positioning themselves with respect to ideologies of language that circulate in their particular historical and social contexts.

"The Barbara Jordan Style"

Who Was Barbara Jordan?

Barbara Jordan, born in 1936, grew up in Houston, Texas, where she attended all-black Texas Southern University. After graduating from law school in Boston, she returned to Houston and briefly practiced law there.[3] Then she went into politics. The first African-American woman elected to the Texas Senate and subsequently the first African-American woman from the South in the U.S. House of Representatives, Jordan rose to prominence through astute politics conducted in part via public oratory that audiences found inspiring. She first gained wide national attention as a result of her televised speech in 1972 as a member of the Judiciary Committee of the House of Representatives, which was deliberating whether President Richard Nixon should be impeached. In 1976 and again in 1992, Jordan gave keynote addresses at the Democratic Party's national convention. Her speeches are widely quoted. Until her death in 1996, she was frequently interviewed for print and broadcast, and after her retirement from politics she was a popular teacher at the University of Texas. She is seen as a model for African-Americans, for women, and for politicians, and as an authority on governmental ethics.

Ideologies of Identity and Language in the Western Rhetorical Tradition

I turn now to an exploration of how style can instantiate mainstream U.S. language ideology about the role of the individual in discourse. By "language ideology" I mean ideas about what language is and how it works, ideas which can be seen to vary from place to place and from time to time. Beliefs about how "language" and "reality" are related, beliefs about how communication works, and beliefs about linguistic correctness, goodness and badness, articulateness and inarticulateness are all aspects of language ideology, as are beliefs about the role of language in a person's identity, beliefs about how languages are learned, and beliefs about what the functions of language should be, who the authorities on language are, whether and how usage should be legislated, and so on (see Silverstein 1979, Joseph and Taylor 1990, Schieffelin, Woolard, and Kroskrity 1998).

In the classical Greco-Roman rhetorical tradition, the source of Barbara Jordan's training in legal and political debate and oratory, the speaker's "ethos" is seen as a fundamental tool in persuasion. As early students and teachers of oratory observed, a speaker's reputation or social position could enhance his (or her, though women could not speak in public in fifth-century B.C.E. Athens) credibility. Ethos, broadly defined, is the speaker's identity as it is constructed and/or deployed in discourse (Baumlin 1994, Cherry 1998). In the Western tradition of rhetoric, ethos is the name for one of the three *pisteis,* or basic modes of persuasive appeal. (The others are *logos*, or logical appeals to characteristics of the topic, and *pathos*, or appeals to characteristics of the audience.)

Barbara Jordan's style of stance instantiates one of the two primary ways this language-ideological tradition provides for imagining the relationship between identity and discourse, and, accordingly, for imagining how rhetorical ethos works.[4] From Platonic idealism comes the conception of ethos as the externalization of a good soul. The character a rhetor displays in discourse is understood as "central" rather than "social" (Baumlin, 1994); discourse is credible if the speaker is (and shows that he or she is) a person with preexisting moral and epistemic authority. Thus a credible rhetor is a "good man skilled in speaking," in Quintilian's well-known formulation. In this tradition, the speaker's character is understood as preexisting discourse rather than being constructed in it. This is an *ethos of self:* the projection of knowledge and moral authority derived from one's life history, a history that is necessarily unique because, even though individuals' social worlds may be shared in many ways, no two individuals' particular sets of experiences and memories are identical. The Platonic view of language as the reflection of a preexisting world and a preexisting self (as opposed to a being a tool for world and self-construction), along with the Platonic idea that truth and moral rightness become evident in introspection, underlies American "expressive individualism" (Bellah et al. 1985, Hansen 1990).

In Aristotle's pragmatic rhetoric, on the other hand, effective discourse means speaking in such a way as to seem credible, and personas can be adopted more or less like dramatic roles.[5] This could be called the *ethos of persona,* or the projection into discourse of changeable social identities adapted to audience and situation. In this view, credibility is linked not with indexing a perduring personal identity but rather with skill in adapting to the situation at hand. This way of imagining rhetorical and linguistic agency looks at identity and discourse from the perspective of culture rather than taking the phenomenological perspective of the individual, focusing on more or less stabilized sets of expectations about how individuals interact with other individuals in larger systems. In this view, knowledge and moral authority arise when certain social processes are followed successfully. An ethos of persona would be enacted via strategic inconsistency in style, performance of the ability to construct different identities to meet different rhetorical exigencies, and the indexing of this ability by means of metapragmatic (Silverstein 1993) indexes of flexibility (including nonlinguistic ones such as shifts in styles of dress or physical bearing).

Barbara Jordan's characteristic style of stance works to construct rhetorical ethos rooted not in Aristotelian persona but in Platonic self. In other words, her style draws on and helps to construct a world in which the source of morality and knowledge is not social agreement in the moment but lessons learned in the course of thoughtful reflection on one's necessarily idiosyncratic, unique personal biography. Assent, accordingly, is reached not through performances of (flexible) social identity and openness to epistemic and moral negotiation, but through performances of personal identity and epistemic and moral certainty. This requires stancetaking choices that project consistent personal identity rather than transient social identity. Among these are, as I will show below, noninteractivity, markers of moral and epistemic authority, and linguistic consistency across genres, as well as overt references to personal biography.

Linguistic and Language-Ideological Resources for Jordan's Style

In an interview conducted by Judith Mattson Bean, Delma McLeod-Porter, and me in February 1992, we asked Barbara Jordan to talk about the sources of her speech style.[6] She described several, which are corroborated in biographical accounts by others (Bryant 1977, Haskins 1977, Jordan and Hearon 1979, Crawford and Ragsdale 1992: 321–331, Rogers 1998). Jordan's linguistic and language-ideological environment in childhood exposed her to several different sets of ideas about language and multiple models for speech. At home, Jordan's mother encouraged careful, articulate speech ("My mother wanted us to use correct English, and she really never engaged in baby talk or black talk or whatever"). Jordan grew up attending a Baptist church where her father was a minister and her mother occupied public-speaking roles that were open to women ("The women would speak at their...missionary circles..., but women were not...encouraged to deliver any sermons...because that was anathema to the Black Missionary Baptist Church"). But although Jordan acknowledged the existence of gendered expectations for speech, she claimed not to have been expected to speak differently from boys herself.[7] Jordan's powerful baritone speaking voice might be linked in part to her resistance of gendered speaking roles. Jordan's tendency not to style-switch, her care in word choice, and her adherence to the norms of standard, writerly syntax, might all be traced to the standard language ideology (Milroy and Milroy 1985, Cameron 1995, Lippi-Green 1997: 53–62), rooted partly in the Platonic notion that correct language is language that reflects the world accurately, that underlay her mother's insistence on "correct English." The linguistic resources for doing this, as well as Jordan's choice of a profession that would require speaking in public, may also have been facilitated by her mother's model.

Research on African-American oratory and homiletics (Abrahams 1972, Pitts 1989, Wharry 2003) points to its roots in the "man of words" tradition of preaching and its interactive qualities in comparison with European-American preaching style. Although sociolinguistic research tends to highlight the generic qualities of preaching style, some African-Americans link its effectiveness with the ethos of self. In interviews with middle-class African-Americans (like Jordan), Speicher and McMahon (1992) found that for some, "the greatness of an [African-American] orator lies in each speaker's individual style and distinctiveness"; others pointed to "a combination of individual ability and black oral tradition" (393). Aspects of Jordan's style such as the response-like register-shifted codas we will encounter below, along with aspects of her delivery, might be traced to her minister father's oratorical model and that of other preachers she heard in her youth. Jordan spoke directly to this source of influence, although without claiming it for herself, in our conversation with her (I discuss the stylistic details of this part of the interview later on):

> You are going to find that there are any number of people who are public speakers who try to reflect what they have heard from their minister, and the black minister has a definable and totally, in my opinion, different style of oratory than anybody else in the country. And it is because of that role of the black minister, a role which I don't believe is paramount in any other race or group of people, but it is there for us, and it is that preaching that influences, I think, the way that a person who is black would deliver an address or a speech

However, as Jordan narrated her lingual autobiography in our interview with her, she repeatedly pointed to her high school and college experiences in competitive public speaking as the key influences on her understanding and practice of public speaking. Here, for example, she deflects a question about childhood and redirects it toward high school oratorical contests. She seems throughout the interview more inclined to account for her style with reference to the public sphere than to the private and with reference to formal, planned genres rather than casual talk. For her, the formation of a personal style is understood as something that happens in the process of learning to act as a credible, successful rhetor in public.

BARBARA JOHNSTONE: When you were growing up, were you encouraged to talk a lot, or was the rule that children should be seen and not heard?

BARBARA JORDAN: Well I did always talk a lot, but in junior and senior high school of course I was always participating in the various interscholastic leagues, [in] the declamation contests, and I was on the debate team at my high school, Phyllis Wheatley, and at TSU [Texas Southern University], and I think that those experiences of participating in the contests, because I always wanted to win the contests...is where I started to talk publicly.

Competitive public speaking, tracing its ideological lineage to the classical "good man speaking well," helped to shape Jordan's ethos of self. It may have provided fuel for the idea that speaking style can be learned and practiced, and it no doubt helped shape her delivery in many ways. Competitive debate and oratory is an element of the lingual biography of many U.S. politicians, but may have been especially impor- tant in Jordan's because of the presence of a particular extremely successful and influential university debate coach, Thomas F. Freeman.[8] Jordan spoke specifically about how Freeman encouraged "dramatic" delivery: "When I was a member of the debating team at Texas Southern, Thomas Freeman, who is still the debate coach at Texas Southern, used to really insist that we be dramatic in our presentation of mate- rial, because he was and is so dramatic in his presentation of material. And that was an influence which he put in place on everyone who came his way."

Freeman also encouraged Jordan to attend to the details of elocution, urging her to abandon a hypercorrect form (the use of /hw/ in a word which, for most speakers who use /hw/ at all, is not in the class of words that require it): "One thing that I recall Freeman saying to me is that I had a tendency to say 'hwe' [hwi] rather than 'we,' and that's the only thing that I remember that he ever corrected me on. He just made me repeat 'we, we' so that I never would dare say 'hwe' even right now."

Finally, Jordan talked about her legal training as a source of her style of speech. Law school, she said, taught her that she could "no longer orate and let that pass for reasoning" (Jordan and Hearon 1979: 93):

BARBARA JOHNSTONE: I think [in] the autobiographical book we read that you
    learned to speak differently in law school in the sense that you had to know
    what you were talking about more. I'm curious about that.
BARBARA JORDAN: Oh but I didn't learn to speak differently, I hope that's not
    in the autobiography because it's incorrect if it is. I did not learn to speak
    differently; I learned to think in law school, that was the difference. I stopped
    writing from the surface of my mind and decided to go inside and see if there
    was really something there, because it was important to get to the bottom of
    an idea and be able to make it hold up in legalese, in legal argument. That was
    important.

Among the ideas Jordan adduces here that may have shaped her style are the fol- lowing: reasoning precedes writing, more significant ideas are located deeper in the mind, and one should not talk without there being "anything there." Legal training, the need to "make it hold up in legalese, in legal argument" might have added to Jordan's rhetorical repertoire the idea that logos, the appeal to reason, should be valued along with ethos and the pathos of dramatic (but correct) delivery she learned in high school and college. Here is further evidence of the Platonic language ideol- ogy that underlies and is circulated by the ethos of self: language refers to things in the (already existing) world, so that thinking can be separated from writing or speak- ing, and speech that is "about" the world can be separated from, and is valorized over, speech that is not. In claiming that she did not learn to "speak differently" in law school and in correcting "legalese" to "legal argument," she voices the idea, also consistent with the ethos of self, that although the substance of her speech may have changed in the course of her life, her style has not.

This exploration of the sources of Jordan's ideas about public speech, and the resources for deploying and recycling them, underscores how linguistic ideologies, and the discursive resources for their construction and circulation, come together in different complex ways in the lingual biographies of different individuals. It also provides biographical evidence that the ideology associated with the ethos of self was specifically circulating in Jordan's sociolinguistic environment. I turn now to the textual evidence. Through a detailed examination of aspects of Jordan's speech related to stancetaking in particular, I show how they both instantiate and recycle the ideology about discourse and the individual associated with the ethos of self.

Style Emerging in Discourse: Authoritative Stance in the Jordan Corpus

To explore stance and style in Jordan's speech, I use a corpus of 11,967 words drawn from six transcripts that represent the range of Jordan's public speech on the unplanned–planned continuum, from unedited interview talk to highly planned, edited speeches. As a sample of unedited interview speech I use three excerpts from the interview quoted from above, totaling 2,237 words in all. One is from the beginning of the interview, one is from the middle (pages 9 and 10 of the 21-page transcript), and one is from the end. On the other end of the spectrum are published transcripts of Jordan's formal public oratory: excerpts from her House Judiciary Committee speech about the Nixon impeachment (Fernea and Duncan, 1977: 28–32; 1,415 words) and her Democratic Convention keynote speech of 1976 (Braden, 1977: 11–17; 1,804 words). These represent speech with a different purpose and audience (national TV in both cases). The settings were also less intimate, and Jordan had time in both cases to plan, edit, and revise what she was going to say. To check that the printed transcripts corresponded to what Jordan actually said, I audited both speeches on videotape. In the middle of the spontaneous-to-planned continuum, I examined three published interviews with Jordan, two conducted by journalists and one by a professor. One of these short interviews appeared in a collection of conversations with prominent people published at the time of the U.S. bicentennial (Murchland, 1987, 39–49; Jordan's speech totals 2,818 words), one was an interview in the newsweekly *Time* (Angelo, 1991; 1,725 words), and one was an interview conducted by Liz Carpenter, an old Texas friend, in the general-circulation feminist magazine *Ms.* (Carpenter, 1985; 1,868 words).

In Jordan's speech and writing, "the Barbara Jordan style" emerges out of repeated epistemic and interactional stancetaking choices calling attention to personal authority. These choices have to do with a relative lack of interactivity (Jordan does not invite interlocutors to coconstruct meaning) and an epistemic stance that projects certainty and identifies Jordan herself as the source of knowledge and evaluation. In public oratory as well as in face-to-face interview speech, Jordan spoke slowly, in a low, intense voice, articulating clearly and making it apparent that she was choosing words carefully. She projected moral and epistemological authority by drawing attention to her knowledgeability, thoughtfulness, intellect, and adherence to principle.

For example, in our conversational interview with Jordan, we asked her about regional differences in how political campaigns are conducted:

BARBARA JORDAN: Oh, I think, uh, it's not so much the style of campaigning, the issues are different. The issues of womanizing, to take one current one, are responded to differently, regionally, in my opinion. That you will find in the South more people, and this may be too much of a generalization but I am not sure, more people who place a greater store in marital fidelity than some other regions, now that may or may not be true but I get that sense, and the polls will indicate something like this if you will look at some national Gallup or Harris and how people have responded to the, uh, machinations the Clinton, uh, you may find some difference in how that is regarded. So the issues, the political issues, I think, may play out differently regionally, rather than campaign styles.

Jordan approached the response as a serious task, calling repeated attention to her thoughtfulness and thought processes, both via explicit markers of evidentiality like "I think," "in my opinion," and "I get that sense," and via careful hedging of claims: "this may be too much of a generalization," "that may or may not be true," and "you may find." Interestingly, her response is framed in moral rather than behavioral terms: asked to talk about regional differences in style, she talks about regional differences in values. Just as Jordan did when she insisted that she learned not "legalese" but legal reasoning and did not learn to "speak differently" in law school, she voices the idea here that political differences are differences in substance, not style. In claiming that the reason for regional differences in the uptake of political campaigns has to do with "values," she suggests either that other politicians are consistent in style the way she is or that their inconsistencies are inconsequential.

As has also been noted in other cultural settings (Rosaldo 1982, Briggs 1993, Duranti 1994), speakers whose appeal rests on being perceived as moral and intellectual authorities may encourage less overt negotiation of meaning with the audience than speakers who frame their ethical (i.e., ethos-based) appeal in more egalitarian terms.[9] Jordan constructs an authoritative stance by remaining detached from her audience, frequently making assertions of fact and infrequently attempting to create rapport. She sounds formal, precise, and careful rather than informal or relaxed the way a more audience-centered, rapport-building speaker might.

To operationalize these characteristics of Jordan's stance, I draw on Biber's (1988) work, identifying features in Jordan's talk associated with "informational production" (104–108; 128–135). These are features that clustered, in Biber's study, in official documents, academic prose, biography, press reportage, and other genres characterized by highly integrated, dense, precise representations of information. They include, for example, attributive adjectives, long words, and prepositional phrases, all of which are strategies for condensing information into relatively few words. Spontaneous speeches and interviews typically rank fairly low in the presence of these features; Jordan's discourse is exceptional in this regard. The following excerpt from our conversational interview illustrates some of these. As with all our interviewees, we asked Jordan to talk about the sources, as she saw them, of her identity and style. Material that will be discussed below is underlined.

```
 1   DELMA MCLEOD-PORTER:  Um, do you view yourself as a Southern
 2              speaker, or a Southern person, I mean is your identity sort of in some way
 3              tied up with being from the South? I, my own personal experience is that
 4              I really like being from the South, I find it to be uh something that I'm
 5              very proud of.
 6   BARBARA JORDAN:  Well I uh, uh I'm proud of the South too, I wasn't
 7              always but uh I grew to become uhh fond of the South and of course it's
 8              the race question that uh made the South a negative for me for so long,
 9              but when I was a member of Congress, uh the Southerners would y- sort
10              of get together, there was an affinity among the Southern contingent in the
11              United States House of Representatives, which you could not count on in
12              any other region of the country, and that was it, it was, there is even, I
13              think there is a Southern Caucus, there was not a Southern Caucus when I
14              was in Congress, but I think, I think there is one now. When when I was
15              there, uh, Texas was was sort of a a thing apart and we, at least we
16              considered ourselves a thing apart ((laughing)) and just a little bit
17              superior, eh to tell the truth of the matter. And that's a function of Texas
18              braggadocio, that's what that is.
19   MCLEOD-PORTER:  ((laughs))
20   JUDITH MATTSON BEAN:  I was going to ask you how you thought, is
21              Texas really Southern or is it outside of the South, just where does it
22              stand?
23              [[Jordan overlaps Bean several times with "no, that's" and "no"]]
24   JORDAN:  Lyndon Johnson said we are Southwest, and that, that's a, that's
25              good enough for me.
26   MCLEOD-PORTER:  Me too. I'll, I'll buy that. Um Barbara [[Johnstone]]
27              alluded to something earlier too that I'm curious about, and I noticed
28              that—I've, coached debate when I was at Kasimir [[High School]] too and
29              I had a lot of wonderful orators, [we went] all over the state=
30   JORDAN:                           [Um-hm,]                    =good.
31   MCLEOD-PORTER:  Um [[1.5 sec.]] do you think that um maybe—this isn't
32              uh n- not very uh articulated very clearly—do you think that black
33              speakers are more conscious of uh maybe the the value of performative
34              language?
35   JORDAN:  The uh what [[1.0]] black or- oratory is an important ingredient
36              of the black experience because preachers have been so paramount in
37              leadership roles in the black community throughout the country. You are
38              going to find that there are any number of people who are public speakers
39              who try to reflect what they have heard from their minister, and the black
40              minister has a definable and totally uh in my opinion different style of
               oratory than anybody else in the country. And it is because of that role of
```

the black minister, a role which I don't believe is *paramount* in any other
race or group of people, but it is that, it is there, it is there for us and it is
because of that preaching that uh influences I think the way that a person
who is black would deliver an an address or a speech.

A number of features of Jordan's style can be associated with density of information and care in encoding, which characterize relatively informational discourse.
Elevated lexical choices, drawn from a writerly register, project care in encoding:
a negative, an affinity, the Southern *contingent, braggadocio,* and adjectives like
definable and *paramount.* Like much Latinate vocabulary, these words tend to be
multisyllabic. Care in encoding is also projected through hypotactic, highly embedded syntax, often involving relative clauses: "people who are public speakers who
try to reflect what they have heard from their minister" "a person who is black".
This hypotactic style can be seen clearly in the final sentence; brackets indicate the
embeddings here:

And it is [because of that role of the black minister, a role [[which I don't believe
is paramount in any other race or group of people]] but it is that, it is there,
it is there for us] and it is [because of that preaching [[that uh influences [[[I
think]]] the way [[that a person [[[who is black]]] would deliver an an address or
a speech]]].

Jordan also calls attention to care in encoding via reformulations, stating a claim
once in a relatively casual register, and then restating it in a much more formal
way. In the previous excerpt, for example, Jorden overlays onto a first formulation,
"the Southerners would y- sort of get together" a legal-sounding second formulation: "There was an affinity among the Southern contingent in the United States
House of Representatives." For the politicians, "the Southern contingent" replaces
"the Southerners" with a more specific designation; the speakerly "would sort of
get together" is replaced by the more compressed and more informative "affinity
among," and the locus, unnamed in the first formulation, is designated in the second
by its full legal title, "the United States House of Representatives."
      A second pattern of overlay in Jordan's talk does the opposite, shifting from a
relatively dense, carefully encoded formulation to a less formal one. In both edited and
unedited modes, Jordan's uses of demonstrative pronouns (*these, that,* and so on) are
striking. Like other deictic elements, demonstrative pronouns are often said to characterize talk whose interpretation requires immediate context, like face-to-face conversation, rather than more context-free, noninvolved talk. Particularly notable are the
demonstrative pronouns in short style-shifted codas Jordan appends again and again to
long, carefully worded sentences. There are two examples in excerpt (2) above, one in
line 16, "*that*'s what *that* is," and one in lines 21–22, "*that*'s good enough for me." The
following two examples are from Jordan's 1976 Democratic convention speech:

We believe that the people are the source of all governmental power; that the authority of the people is to be extended, not restricted. This can be accomplished only by

providing each citizen with every opportunity to participate in the management of the government. *They must have that.*

We have a positive vision of the future founded on the belief that the gap between the promise and reality of America can one day be finally closed. *We believe that.*

Like the call-and-response patterns they bring to mind, the overlays in these examples project moral certainty; it is as if a second, responsive voice supplements the carefully encoded first formulation with a spontaneous assertion of its truth. They also have the effect of drawing the listener into the moral universe Jordan is depicting, both via their relatively casual style and via the use of *we*.

Jordan often uses *be* as a main verb. Because, in general, *be* is often used in situations in which there would be a more informative alternative, this would appear to be inconsistent with the projection of informativity. However, Jordan's main-verb use of *be* has to do with another fact about this verb: copular *be* is useful in stating universal, eternal truths. Excerpt (6) provides several examples in a paragraph from the *Time* magazine interview:

> *It is not right; it is not correct;* it should not occur. These things may not be illegal, but *it is so important for a public servant to sort out what is legal from what is ethical.* I tell appointees, "You must not engage in any fine-line drawing." Ed Meese as Attorney General did that many times. *It is not enough for the Attorney General to say, "I have not violated the law."*

Here, even more overtly than in previous extracts, Jordan presents herself as the moral authority, providing no other justification for her claims than her beliefs: "It is not right; it should not occur."

The displays of certainty that permeate Jordan's epistemic stancetaking ground her stance in personal principle and experience. She accomplishes this via stancetaking strategies that point to her cognitive and emotional states. In relatively edited as well as relatively spontaneous discourse, Jordan also expresses epistemic certainty via verbs and adverbials such as *know* and *of course*, predictive modals such as *will* and *would*, and "private verbs" (Biber 1988: 105) such as *believe* and *feel,* with first-person subjects. The interview excerpt above includes several examples: *I think* (twice), *I get the sense*, and three uses of *will.*

Even Jordan's displays of hedged uncertainty ("this may be too much of a generalization"; "that may or may not be true") help suggest that her authority comes from her own knowledge and moral principle. Jordan iconically performs measured, deliberate, thought processes, enacting her care in thinking in her care in speaking. Her hedges serve to suggest that she does not make groundless assertions. Showing that she is not always willing to make unmitigated truth claims serves as support when she does make emphatic and absolute assertions (as when she uses the totalizing *be*)—evidence that, as pointed out above, the functions of stancetaking moves need to be seen in the context of styles, and in the context of an individual's repertoire of stancetaking patterns.

Jordan's tendency to base claims on her own authority is also clear in this excerpt from the *Time* magazine interview. Asked "But don't most people think, cynically, that politics is a crooked business?" Jordan answered:

> I am very disheartened by the public perception of politicians not having the public welfare at heart because *I absolutely believe* politics is an honorable profession. I wish more people would see politicians as public servants, because that's what they are.

Asked, implicitly, to defend politicians, Jordan refers not to statistics, anecdote, or logical or quasi-logical proof, but to her own moral and epistemic certainty: "I absolutely believe politics is an honorable profession"; "[Public servants] is what [politicians] are."

In addition to calling attention to to her own belief and certainty, Jordan sometimes called attention to the personal history that she claims gave rise to this authoritative stance, linking authoritativeness directly with personal experience. Her two best known public speeches both begin this way. In both, Jordan begins by adducing the racist history of the United States, not in the abstract but as connected to her own personal history. In her 1972 speech in the House Judiciary Committee, Jordan said this:

> "We the people"—it is a very eloquent beginning. But when the Constitution of the United States was completed on the 17th of September in 1787, *I was not included in that "We, the people." I felt for many years that somehow George Washington and Alexander Hamilton just left me out by mistake.* But through the process of amendments, interpretation and court decision, *I have finally been included in "We, the people."*

Jordan's framing of her discussion of the U.S. Constitution in first-person terms is especially striking given the historical context. Jordan was not alive in 1787, so the *I* in "I was not included" must be read as a synecdochic reference to African-Americans. The same is true of the *I* in "I have finally been included in 'We, the people,'" because, although enforcement of their civil rights has always been inconsistent, African-Americans became U.S. citizens long before Jordan's birth.

Jordan similarly framed U.S. history as a history of personal exclusion in her 1976 keynote address to the Democratic National Convention. Here, the evidentiary link between this personal history and Jordan's epistemic authority is made explicit: "my presence here is one additional bit of evidence that the American Dream need not forever be deferred."

> One hundred and forty-four years ago, members of the Democratic Party first met in convention to select a presidential candidate. Since that time, Democrats have continued to convene once every four years and draft a party platform and nominate a presidential candidate. And our meeting this week is a continuation of that tradition.
>
> But there is something different about tonight. There is something special about tonight. What is different? What is special? *I, Barbara Jordan, am a keynote speaker.*

> *A lot of years have passed since 1832, and during that time it would have been most unusual for any national political party to ask that a Barbara Jordan deliver a keynote address . . . but tonight here I am. And I feel that notwithstanding the past that my presence here is one additional bit of evidence that the American Dream need not forever be deferred.*

Rather than saying, as she could have, that during most of the time since 1832 it would have been unusual for "an African-American" to be invited to speak to a political party, she says "a Barbara Jordan," linguistically appropriating African-American experience as her own; instead of "tonight, here is an African-American" she says, "tonight here I am." The experience of personal exclusion and subsequent inclusion leads into a characteristic use of a private verb with a first-person subject: "I feel."

A third example can be found in the following excerpt from Jordan's keynote address to the 1992 Democratic National Convention. Speaking of the "trickle-down" economics associated with Ronald Reagan and his vice president, George H. W. Bush, the then current Republican presidential candidate, Jordan made reference to her own upbringing in the Fifth Ward in Houston, where she attended public schools:

> I certainly do not mean the thinly disguised racism and elitism of some kind of trickle-down economics. I mean an economy where *a young black woman* or man *from the Fifth Ward in Houston* or South-Central Los Angeles, or a young person in the colonias of the lower Rio Grande Valley *can attend public schools and learn the skills that will enable her* or him *to prosper. We must* have an economy that does not force the migrant worker's child to miss school in order to earn less than the minimum wage just so the family can have one meal a day.

Into a list of references to hypothetical youths from inner city Los Angeles or the industrial slums along the Mexican border, Jordan inserts references to her own history that would have been unmistakable to many listeners in 1992. She explicitly links this personalized account with an epistemic claim: "*We must* have an economy that. . . ." Jordan's own life experience is proffered as the source of her moral certainty.

Consistency across discourse genres is another way in which Jordan enacted an ethos of self.[10] That she made relatively little concession to circumstance in linguistic style, as also in dress and carriage and in the political positions she publicly espoused was taken as a sign of moral constancy. She was aware of this and claimed repeatedly in our interview not to accommodate her speech to the styles or expectations of audiences:

DELMA MCLEOD-PORTER: Well, whenever you're preparing a speech and you
    know that you're speaking to an audience predominantly of men as opposed to
    an audience predominantly of women, do you make adjustments to meet the
    needs of that particular, those particular groups?
JORDAN: ((laughing)) I don't. I really don't.

She then talked about a recent address to a group of women, claiming to make minimal adjustments: "after I do the rest of the stuff that I want to say here I better throw in . . . a good quote that may be appropriate for the occasion, that sort of thing." McLeod-Porter probed again:

McLEOD-PORTER: Interesting. Then you're not conscious of any kinds of
    adaptations that speakers make when they're addressing different audiences?
JORDAN: I'm not. I am not.

If she was aware that other politicians altered their styles for strategic reasons (and she no doubt was), Jordan acted throughout the interview as if she was not. We saw this above in her answer to our interview question about regional styles in politics, and it is evident here as well. It is possible to read this as an effort not to dignify a more relativistic understanding of the world than hers with her notice, much less her response. A moral absolutist, Jordan would have felt that someone engaging in strategic style-shifting, rather than relying on careful representations of the truth, uncovered by means of systematic inquiry, represented the kind of disreputable rhetoric to which the term "rhetoric" typically applies in public discourse. It is, of course, consistent with her Platonic understanding of the individual as consistent self rather than mutable persona.

Jordan did not write out even her most formal speeches, relying instead on minimal notes. This is evidence of the value she placed on extemporaneous oral articulateness, an attitude linked to the preaching tradition of the Baptist church, to her high school and college debate training, and to her training as a lawyer. She claimed to value not just the ability to think of something to say in any situation, but the ability to think of the one right thing to say and to phrase it correctly and precisely, choosing the word that would reflect most accurately the world she understood as existing outside of and prior to discourse. By choosing to speak extemporaneously rather than read from a script, and by choosing to speak on preplanned occasions the same way she did on unplanned ones, Jordan projected authoritative thoughtfulness. Thus her choice of medium (speaking rather than writing) is connected, just as her more micro-level choices are, to the ethos of self.[11]

To summarize, the personal epistemic and moral authoritativeness that reflects and constructs the ethos of self is enacted Jordan's discourse in several ways, on several levels: via sentence-level features associated with precision, care, informativity, and certainty; via consistency in their deployment across discourse practices and speech situations; via explicit references to personal experience and its connection to knowledge and belief; and via even more global choices about what sorts of things to do with language and in what media to do this text building.

Evidence from Reception

Audiences noticed Jordan's consistent, authoritative style and commented on it, often linking it with personal identity. Biographies of Jordan invariably mention her "characteristic oratorical style and delivery" (Crawford and Ragsdale 1992: 322), sometimes explicitly calling it the "Barbara Jordan style." Commentators allude indirectly to its authoritativeness in several ways. Often noted is the "power" of Jordan's oratory. In a more direct allusion to Jordan's projection of personal authority, political humorist Molly Ivins commented repeatedly that Jordan "sounded like the Lord God Almighty" (Ivins 1996a:17, see also Ivins 1993). Commentators also frequently spoke of Jordan's "dignity" and "confidence." In a *New York Times Magazine* essay after Jordan's death in 1996, Ivins wrote that "[Jordan's] personal dignity was so substantial even admirers hesitated to approach her" (Ivins 1996a: 17); elsewhere, Ivins spoke of Jordan's "strikingly magisterial" presence (Ivins 1996b). The editorial obituary for Jordan in the *New York Times* spoke explicitly of how her style drew on her personal history: "Combining remarkable oratorical skills with the powerful symbolism of her own personal story, she strove always to rally Americans around the ideals expressed in the Constitution" (*New York Times* 1996).

Discussion

To summarize, this chapter has built on recent research about how repeated stance-taking moves can come together as a repeatable, locally noticeable style by exploring a case in which a style of stance comes to index not a social identity but a personal identity, a particular lingual biography. I showed how Barbara Jordan's style of stance, often referred to as "the Barbara Jordan style," instantiated a set of ideas about individuals and discourse that underlies one strain of American political discourse. This style was shaped by multiple influences in this woman's sociolinguistic environment, associated with circulating language ideologies mediated through the influence of particular people and situations in her life history. Key among these are the Platonic view of the self as "central," socially shaped but essentially unique, and the view that correct speech is speech which mirrors truths about the preexisting world.

I referred to the rhetorical enactment of this ideology as the ethos of self, defining this as the discursive display of consistent personal identity, rooted in a speaker's unique personal biography, as contrasted with the flexible ethos of persona that makes strategic use of flexibility of social identity. For Barbara Jordan, rhetorical appeals based on the ethos of self could deflect issues that might otherwise separate and disadvantage her, issues such as race, region, and gender. When asked to talk about strategy and style, she deflected the talk to truth and correctness. She used language that pointed to and reinforced her personal identity as a thoughtful, consistent, authoritative person, more a stateswoman than a politician, and that pointed to and reinforced the idea that careful speech is accurate speech, not speech that is tactically designed for the situation at hand. Jordan's style of stance positioned her outside the world in which people have to act differently at different times to appeal to different audiences or to changing situations. Paradoxically, Jordan's rhetorical ethos was rooted in a non-rhetorical view of identity and discourse. Her ethos also aligned her against an alternative way of imagining the rhetorical and linguistic individual and the flexible, inconsistent style of stance that enacts the ethos of persona. For Jordan, this meant not acknowledging that either she herself or anyone else made strategic stylistic adaptations to situation. At the risk of straining others' credulity (she was, after all, a master politician), Jordan avoided a risky ideological dilemma: accusing others of pandering or "flip-flopping," a common tactic in U.S. political discourse, amounts to acknowledging that strategic adaptation of persona, style, or ideology is possible, even effective, and this can be seen as buying into the relativistic worldview Jordan saw as fundamentally opposed to her own.

More generally, I have suggested that stancetaking can involve not just orientation to interactants, propositional content, or conventional identity categories but orientation to the nature of identity and its enactment and use in language. In using a consistent style of stance across time and situation, Barbara Jordan was not so much aligning herself with or against styles or associated social identities as positioning herself outside of the need for such alignments and disalignments. This is not to say that elements of conventional, locally circulating styles cannot be seen in Jordan's discourse. I have described influences such as the tradition of African-American preaching, the tradition of elocution and debate, and the tradition of legal argumentation, and I have shown that all were in fact present in Jordan's environment and that all arguably shaped her oratorical style. She undeniably sounded somewhat like other African-American preachers and orators such as Martin Luther King, Jr.; she sounded like a lawyer; she sounded like a debater. But, as I hope to have shown, Jordan's ethos did not work simply by aligning her with these (and other) identities. It worked because it indexed a consistent, unchanging self anchored in a morally and epistemologically absolutist world.

I have also suggested that the concept of ethos, borrowed from classical Western rhetoric, is a useful analytical tool. Ethos, the individual-in-discourse, is the platform on which ideologies of identity come together with ideologies of language. As I have suggested here (and shown comparatively in Johnstone 1996: 128–155), different ideologies of identity are enacted in discourse via different modes of ethos. A speaker for whom identity is fundamentally social, a matter of situated strategic alignments and disalignments with circulating identity categories, could be expected to adopt different styles in different situations, perhaps even to highlight her adaptability. A speaker for whom identity is fundamentally personal, the result of personal experiences made coherent in a narrative different from anyone else's, could be expected to adopt a more consistent style. And because both ideologies of identity have circulated on the Western scene for centuries, associated with differing understandings of language and discourse, it is not surprising to find that both the ethos of persona and the ethos of self are available to contemporary Americans, or that the difference itself can function as a political tool.

Methodologically, this chapter points to the need to explore how stancetaking works across time, situation, genre, audience, and interlocutors. It was only by hearing her speak repeatedly that audiences came to see Jordan's oral style as consistent, and only by attending both to more spontaneous speech and to carefully preplanned, even written-down speech does her consistency across genres become visible. In other words, for analysts as for participants, the possibility that consistency or inconsistency is an element of a style of stance is visible only over time and situation. This means that studies of stancetaking based on a single interaction or even a set of similar ones may miss an important aspect of how stance can work to link an individual with a style of stance.

Acknowledgments

This chapter has been a number of years in the making. I am grateful to the people who have helped me with it. Robin Shoaps, Paul Kockelman, Scott Kiesling, audiences at the American Anthropological Association and Texas A&M University, and an anonymous reviewer made comments on an earlier version that helped me turn it into this one. Alexandra Jaffe and another anonymous reviewer have given me invaluable suggestions for revising this version. Andreea Ritivoi and Michael Witmore helped me with ethos and with autopoetics (which unfortunately didn't make it into the final draft) in our occasional reading group, and David Herman provided help by e-mail. I am grateful to my cointerviewers Judith Mattson Bean and Delma McLeod-Porter and, especially, to Barbara Jordan, to whose memory I dedicate this chapter.

Notes

Note on transcription: Excerpts from the Barbara Jordan interview that are quoted to make substantive points, but not analyzed, are presented as quotes conventionally are. These excerpts have been edited for readability. In contrast, the extracts that serve as illustrations in the text analysis section of the paper come from transcripts made according to the following conventions. The transcription represents all the words spoken that could be identified and located. Unidentifiable words are in empty single parentheses. I also represent audible paralinguistic material like laughter in double parentheses, as well as simultaneous talk, with left-aligned square brackets, and latching, with =. Double square brackets enclose editorial clarification. Otherwise, readability is a higher priority than realism.

1. In his analysis of personal experience narrative, William Labov (Labov and Waletzky 1997 [1967], Labov 1972) uses the term "evaluation" for the features of a narrative whose function is to underscore the extraordinary quality of the represented events and hence the conversational value of the telling. The "evaluative" features Hunston and Thompson describe can all serve Labov's more specific "evaluative" function, because narrative evaluation is a matter of stancetaking.

2. Agha (2003) uses the term "register" in a broader way, to refer to any set of linguistic forms that comes to seem fixed and associated with stable social meaning through ideological/discursive processes of "enregisterment." For Biber and Finegan, situational "registers" and regional/social "dialects" or "varieties" are taxonomically distinct.

3. My primary sources on Jordan's biography are Jordan and Hearon 1979, Crawford and Ragsdale 1992: 321–331, and Rogers 1998; see also Bryant 1977, Haskins 1977. I have also made use of the Barbara Jordan archive at Texas Southern University in Houston, TX. A useful source is the online Biographical Directory of the United States Congress: http://bioguide.congress.gov/scripts/bibdisplay.pl?index=J000266.

4. The discussion that follows represents Platonic and Aristotelian ethos as they have conventionally been understood. An overview like this runs the risk of "propounding the reductive and tired disjunction between Plato and Aristotle, and dividing subsequent rhetorical traditions derived from each of them" (Swearingen 1994: 116). A longer exposition of the idea of ethos in scholarly discourse in rhetorical studies would be considerably more nuanced. Debate continues about what ethos meant to classical rhetoricians, and there is ongoing discussion about how the concept can be applied across the range of discursive practices with which rhetoricians concern themselves today (Baumlin and Baumlin 1994). Postmodernist rhetorical theorists draw on the Aristotelian conception of ethos, but point to the ways in which

the character projected into discourse is determined by social positioning and language rather than a matter of choice.

5. Robin Shoaps (personal communication) points out a similar dualism in anthropological classification systems for conceptualizations of personhood across cultures, oppositions such as *egocentric* versus *sociocentric,* or *individualistic* versus *relational.* (See, for example, Mauss 1985 [1938].) This convergence may have to do with the fact that Western social theory has its roots in the same Western intellectual tradition that gives rise to rhetoric.

6. Current scholarly discourse in sociolinguistics, linguistic anthropology, and cultural studies has moved to accounting for human behavior with reference to personhood rather than selfhood, describing individuals in terms of roles and adaptations to situation (e.g., Rosaldo 1984) and replacing the idea of *self-expression* with that of *self-fashioning* (e.g., Greenblatt 1980). Speakers' ability to shift styles and identities in response to audience or situation, constructing responsive, changing identities in the interactional moment, has been the focus of an enormous amount of recent sociolinguistic and anthropological scholarship, much of which draws on Goffman's (1959) important observations about "the presentation of self."

7. On the larger project of which this interview was part, see Johnstone 1995, 1999b, Johnstone and Bean 1997.

8. Like other public American women in a larger study of self-reports about identity (Johnstone 1995), Jordan acknowledged gendered social expectations and gender discrimination but denied that they applied to her. In connection with gendered and/or sexualized aspects of Jordan's sense of self, it should be noted that Jordan's lifelong companion was a woman, and it has been claimed that she was a lesbian (see, for example, http://lesbianlife.about.com/cs/woc/p/barbarajordan.htm and http://www.planetout.com/news/history/archive/11081999.html). Lesbianism was not a social identity Jordan ever claimed publicly (if she self-identified as a lesbian, she never came out about it), and it was probably not an identity from which Jordan consciously drew stylistic resources in public life. Nonetheless, some members of her audiences may have heard elements of her style as indices of a lesbian identity.

9. Thomas F. Freeman, Distinguished Professor of Forensics at Texas Southern University, jointed the faculty in 1949 and founded its debate team that year. The team has had many successes; a month after our conversation with Jordan, the TSU team won the International Forensic Association tournament in London to great acclaim in the Houston press. Among Freeman's former students are many leaders in the Texas and national African-American communities.

10. Because, as Du Bois (2007) points out, stancetaking involves the mutual orientation of two (or more) social actors, it is always interactive: speakers position themselves, with respect to attitude or affiliation, relative to other speakers. The interactivity of stancetaking is particularly evident in conversational data, in which the ways in which interlocutors' uptake shapes each other's contributions are often obvious. But although interactivity in this sense is a sine qua non of any discourse—intersubjectivity is always being negotiated—the degree to which speakers shape each other's utterances in real time varies. Some genres are more interactive than others, and some conversations are more interactive than others. This is the level of "interactivity" I am interested in here.

11. See Johnstone 1996: 135–156 for an analysis of the cross-genre consistency of Jordan's style compared to that of another African-American woman.

References

Abrahams, Roger D. 1972. The training of the man of words in talking sweet. *Language in Society* 1: 15–29.

Agha, Asif. 2003. The social life of a cultural value. *Language and Communication* 23: 231–273.

Angelo, Bonnie. 1991, June 3. An ethical guru monitors morality. *Time,* pp. 9–10.

Bauman, Richard. 2001. The ethnography of genre in a Mexican market: Form, function, variation. In *Style and sociolinguistic variation,* ed. Penelope Eckert and John R. Rickford, 57–77. Cambridge: Cambridge University Press.

Baumlin, James S. 1994. Introduction: Positioning ethos in historical and contemporary theory. In *Ethos: New essays in rhetorical and critical theory,* ed. James S. Baumlin and Tita French Baumlin, xi–xxvii. Dallas, TX: Southern Methodist University Press.

Baumlin, James S., and Tita French Baumlin, eds. 1994. Ethos: New essays in rhetorical and critical theory. Dallas, TX: Southern Methodist University Press.

Bell, Allan. 1984. Language style as audience design. *Language in Society* 13: 145–204.

———. 2001. Back in style: Reworking audience design. In *Style and sociolinguistic variation,* ed. Penelope Eckert and John R. Rickford, 139–169. Cambridge: Cambridge University Press.

Bellah, Robert N., et al. 1985. *Habits of the heart: Individualism and commitment in American life.* Berkeley: University of California Press.

Biber, Douglas. 1988. *Variation across speech and writing.* Cambridge: Cambridge University Press.

Biber, Douglas, and Edward Finegan. 1989. Styles of stance in English: Lexical and grammatical marking of evidentiality and affect. *Text* 9: 93–124.

———. 1994. An analytical framework for register studies. In *Dimensions of register variation,* ed. Douglas Biber and Edward Finegan, 31–56. Cambridge: Cambridge University Press.

Braden, Waldo W. 1977. *Representative American speeches 1976–1977.* New York: H. W. Wilson Company.

Briggs, Charles. 1993. Generic versus metapragmatic dimensions of Warao narratives: Who regiments performance. In *Reflexive language,* ed. John. A. Lucy, 179–212. Cambridge: Cambridge University Press.

Bryant, Ira Babington. 1977. *Barbara Charline Jordan: From the ghetto to the capital.* Houston: D. Armstrong.

Cameron, Deborah. 1995. *Verbal hygiene.* London: Routledge.

Carpenter, Liz. 1985, April. On my mind: Barbara Jordan talks about ethics, optimism, and hard choices in government. *Ms.,* pp. 75–76, 112.

Cherry, Roger D. 1998. Ethos versus persona: Self-representation in written discourse. *Written Composition* 15: 384–410.

Crawford, Ann Fears, and Crystal Sasse Ragsdale. 1992. *Women in Texas: Their lives; their experiences; their accomplishments,* 2nd ed. Austin, TX: State House Press.

Du Bois, John W. 2007. The stance triangle. In *Stancetaking in discourse: Subjectivity, evaluation, interaction,* ed. Robert Englebretson, 139–182. Amsterdam: John Benjamins.

Duranti, Alessandro. 1994. *From grammar to politics: Linguistic anthropology in a Western Samoan village.* Berkeley: University of California Press.

Eckert, Penelope. 1989. *Jocks and burnouts: Social categories and identity in high school.* New York: Teachers College Press.

———. 2000. *Linguistic variation as social practice.* Oxford: Blackwell.

Fernea, Elizabeth W., and Marilyn P. Duncan. 1977. *Texas women in politics.* Austin, TX: Foundation for Women's Resources.

Finegan, Edward, and Douglas Biber. 2001. Register variation and social dialect variation: The register axiom. In *Style and sociolinguistic variation,* ed. Penelope Eckert and John R. Rickford, 235–267. Cambridge: Cambridge University Press.

Goffman, Erving. 1959. *The presentation of self in everyday life.* Garden City, NY: Doubleday Anchor Books.

———. 1981. Footing. In his *Forms of talk,* 124–159. Philadelphia: University of Pennsylvania Press.

Greenblatt, Stephen Jay. 1980. *Renaissance self-fashioning: From More to Shakespeare.* Chicago: University of Chicago Press.

Hansen, Olaf. 1990. *Aesthetic individualism and practical intellect: American allegory in Emerson, Thoreau, Adams, and James.* Princeton, NJ: Princeton University Press.

Haskins, James. 1977. *Barbara Jordan.* New York: Dial.

Hunston, Susan, and Geoff Thompson, eds. 2000. *Evaluation in text: Authorial stance and the construction of discourse.* New York: Oxford University Press.

Irvine, Judith T. 2001. "Style" as distinctiveness: The culture and ideology of linguistic differentiation. In *Style and sociolinguistic variation*, ed. Penelope Eckert and John R. Rickford, 21–43. Cambridge: Cambridge University Press.

Ivins, Molly. 1993, August 25. If the Lord comes callin', ask for some ID. *Bryan–College Station Eagle*, p. A6.

———. 1996a, December 29. She sounded like God. *New York Times Magazine*, p. 17.

———. 1996b, January 19. Creating justice in law. *Bryan-College Station Eagle*, p. A11.

Johnstone, Barbara. 1995. Sociolinguistic resources, individual identities and the public speech styles of Texas women. *Journal of Linguistic Anthropology* 5: 1–20.

———. 1996. *The linguistic individual: Self-expression in language and linguistics.* New York: Oxford University Press.

———. 1999a. Lingual biography and linguistic variation. *Language Sciences* 21: 313–21.

———. 1999b. Uses of Southern speech by contemporary Texas women. *Journal of Sociolinguistics* 3: 505–522.

———. 2000. The individual voice in language. *Annual Review of Anthropology* 29: 405–424.

Johnstone, Barbara, Jennifer Andrus, and Andrew E. Danielson. 2006. Mobility, indexicality, and the enregisterment of "Pittsburghese." *Journal of English Linguistics* 34: 77–104

Johnstone, Barbara, and Dan Baumgardt. 2004. "Pittsburghese" online: Vernacular norming in conversation. *American Speech* 79: 115–145.

Johnstone, Barbara, and Judith Mattson Bean. 1997. Self-expression and linguistic variation. *Language in Society* 26: 221–246.

Jordan, Barbara, and Shirley Hearon. 1979. *Barbara Jordan: A self-portrait.* New York: Doubleday.

Joseph, John E., and Talbot J. Taylor, eds. 1990. *Ideologies of language.* New York: Routledge.

Kiesling, Scott F. 2004. Dude. *American Speech* 79: 281–305.

———. 2005. Variation, stance, and style: Word-final *-er*, high rising tone, and ethnicity in Australian English. *English World Wide* 26: 1–44.

Labov, William. 1966. *The social stratification of English in New York.* Washington, DC: Center for Applied Linguistics.

———. 1972. The transformation of experience in narrative syntax. In his *Language in the inner city*, 354–396. Philadelphia: University of Pennsylvania Press.

———. 2001. The anatomy of style shifting. In *Style and sociolinguistic variation*, ed. Penelope Eckert and John R. Rickford, 85–108. Cambridge: Cambridge University Press.

Labov, William, and Joshua Waletzky. 1997 [1967]. Narrative analysis: Oral versions of personal experience. *Journal of Narrative and Life History* 7: 3–38.

Lippi-Green, Rosina. 1997. *English with an accent: Language, ideology and discrimination in the United States.* London: Routledge.

Mauss, Marcel. 1985 [1938]. A category of the human mind: the notion of person, the notion of self. In *The category of the person: Anthropology, philosophy, history*, ed. Michael Carrithers, Steven Collins, and Steven Lukes, 1–25. Cambridge, UK: Cambridge University Press.

Milroy, James, and Lesley Milroy. 1985. *Authority in language: Investigating language prescription and standardization.* London: Routledge and Kegan Paul.

Murchland, Bernard. 1987. *Voices in America: Bicentennial conversations*. Ann Arbor, MI: Prakken Publications.

New York Times. 1996, January 19. Barbara Jordan's ideals.

Ochs, Elinor. 1992. Indexing gender. In *Rethinking context: Language as an interactive phenomenon*, ed. Alessandro Duranti and Charles Goodwin, 335–358. New York: Cambridge University Press.

Pitts, Walter. 1989. West African poetics in the black preaching style. *American Speech* 64: 137–149.

Rogers, Mary Beth. 1998. *Barbara Jordan: American hero*. New York: Bantam Books.

Rosaldo, Michelle Z. 1982. The way we do things with words: Ilongot speech acts and speech act theory in philosophy. *Language in Society* 11: 203–237.

———. 1984. Toward an anthropology of self and feeling. In *Culture theory: Essays on mind, self, and emotion,* ed. Robert A. Shweder and Robert A. Levine, 137–157: Cambridge University Press.

Schieffelin, Bambi B., Kathryn A. Woolard, and Paul V. Kroskrity. 1998. *Language ideologies: Practice and theory*. New York: Oxford University Press.

Silverstein, Michael. 1979. Language structure and linguistic ideology. In *The elements: A parasession on linguistic units and levels*, ed. Paul R. Clyne, William F. Hanks, and Carol L. Hofbauer, 193–247. Chicago: Chicago Linguistics Society.

———. 1993. Metapragmatic discourse and metapragmatic function. In *Reflexive language*, ed. John A. Lucy, 33–58. Cambridge: Cambridge University Press.

———. 1995 [1976]. Shifters, linguistic categories, and cultural description. In *Language, culture, and society: A book of readings*, ed. Ben G. Blount, 187–221. Prospect Heights, IL: Waveland Press.

Speicher, Barbara L., and Seane M. McMahon. 1992. Some African-American perspectives on black English vernacular. *Language in Society* 21: 383–407.

Swearingen, C. Jan. 1994. Ethos: Imitation, impersonation, and voice. In *Ethos: New essays in rhetorical and critical theory*, ed. James. S. Baumlin and Tita French Baumlin, 115–148. Dallas, TX: Southern Methodist University Press.

Tannen, Deborah. 1979. What's in a frame? Surface evidence for underlying expectations. In *New directions in discourse processing*, ed. Roy Freedle, 137–181. Norwood, NJ: Ablex.

———, ed. 1993. *Framing in discourse*. New York: Oxford University Press.

Wharry, Cheryl. 2003. Amen and hallelujah preaching: Discourse functions in African American sermons. *Language in Society* 32: 203–225.

3

Stance in a Colonial Encounter:
How Mr. Taylor Lost His Footing

Judith T. Irvine

In one of his last papers ("Radio Talk," 1981), Erving Goffman reflected on two themes that will be useful for this chapter. One is the notion of *faultables:* elements in an individual's linguistic performance that either the speaker or the listener can find fault with, or can find reasons to try to repair or to counter. As Goffman remarks about these trouble spots, a faultable *"can be almost anything"*; a faultable does not have to be "error in any obvious sense but any bit of speech behavior to which the speaker or listener applies a remedy," or places in doubt (1981: 224; italics added).[1] The second theme concerns *audience.* The radio announcer's audience is distant, heterogeneous, and partly unpredictable. As Goffman comments, "The announcer has little specific control over who joins his audience, and often little knowledge of who has elected to do so" (1981: 242). Put together, these themes suggest that "it is true of any communication system that trouble enters from different points, these points located at different levels or layers in the organizational structure of the undertaking" (ibid.: 242).

My aim in this chapter is to bring these themes to bear upon the analytical concept of "stance," which I take to be useful, yet also a little perilous for the unwary. This concept is perhaps better thought of as a family of concepts, because it finds genealogies in several academic traditions. What seems to be in common to all of them is that "stance" concerns the speaker or author's evaluation and assessment, either of some object of discourse or of an interlocutor. Some commonly discussed types of stance would include epistemic stance, which concerns the truth-value of a proposition and the speaker's degree of commitment to it—at issue, for example, in a sentence such as "The moon *might* be made of green cheese but I doubt it." Another type is affective stance—the speaker's feelings about a proposition, an utterance, or a text—an attitude, that is, toward some bit of discourse, illustrated in a sentence such as "It's disgusting to think that the moon might be made of some nasty old bit of green cheese." A third type of stance concerns a speaker's self-positioning in relation to an interlocutor, or some social dimension of an interaction and its personnel, as might be found in an utterance such as "Who are *you* to tell *me* what the moon is made of? And call me 'sir' when you speak to me." These three types are not exhaustive of the ways "stance" has been discussed in the scholarly literature.

Recently, as the introduction to this volume notes, "stance" has emerged as a theme of research in sociolinguistics, in which it focuses the analysis on the speaker's point of view and evaluation of utterances, objects, and interlocutors. In particular, the emphasis is on stance*taking*, as a social act performed in speaking and located within an interaction, whose course it influences. For example, Jack Du Bois (2007), an important contributor to this theoretical project, considers what the stancetaker is responding to, and to whom the response is directed. He locates stancetaking and its linguistic realization in the developmental history of the discourse in which it occurs, and ultimately within a sociocultural field that provides evaluative frameworks and relevant social identifications.

To me, the utility of the concept lies in its emphasis on point of view and action, and in the fact that it potentially brings together several types and scales of analysis, from the grammatical through the interactional and on to the cultural and sociological. The issues brought together under this rubric (stance) are not really novel. Our understanding of speech as social action has for decades relied on discussions of "footing"—a position within a set of participant roles in an act of speaking—as well as on discussions of social positioning on a larger scale, thus indexing social groups or even broad categories of participation in social life. By now there is an enormous body of scholarship on the relations between linguistic forms and social formations, such as class or ethnicity, and the ideological regimes that underwrite these relations. What a concept of "stance" contributes is an emphasis on point of view and action, which is sometimes attended to but often neglected in this other scholarship. Just as important is the potential of the concept of stance to bring types and scales of analysis together, to produce analyses that are at once detailed and far-reaching. This is one of the present chapter's main goals.

If there is a pitfall, however, a place for "stance" to stumble, it lies in the possibility that the enthusiastic analyst may attribute too much explanatory power to individual agency in conversational interaction. So agent-centered a concept, emphasizing an individual speaker's knowledge, intentions and attitudes explicitly expressed in talk, risks producing a form of methodological individualism, such that the speaker's role in constructing social and linguistic outcomes is taken to be the only, or at least the most crucial, focus of analysis and locus of explanation. But just as a "faultable" may be noticed by someone other than its producer, and a train of consequences—perhaps even dire ones—may ensue, so, too, we must notice the importance of coconstructions, unintended messages, revisionist interpretations, and complex mediations. This is scarcely a new point, but it must not be lost from view.[2] The footings, ideological positions, and social group memberships that inform "stance" are not simple or obvious assignments. They are emergent in the sense that they depend on performances and some degree of coconstruction, by persons who take stances of their own; and they all involve elements and frameworks that are culturally embedded and historically contingent. These processes involve social relations on more than one analytical scale. Within an interaction, speakers attribute stances to others, and so may project and even shape the positioning of their interlocutors (interpellating them, in effect). On a wider scale of social relations, subject positions (as discussions of "interpellation" suggest)[3] are embedded in institutions and can be called into play by historical, cultural, and ideological forces that reach beyond the moment of interaction.

The particular case presented in this chapter draws on material in the archives of the Church Missionary Society (CMS), from their nineteenth-century missions in West Africa.[4] What can a nineteenth-century archive tell us about a concept of stance in sociolinguistics, or vice versa? Principally, it gives us a chance to situate linguistic detail in a long train of consequences and in a global context. Moreover, it also offers a chance to explore complex embeddings and layerings of stances—and, in the particular case at hand, to consider the ways stances might be unintentional. Stances might even reside, sometimes, in aspects of a communication other than the explicit assertions and referential functions of language that have been so much the focus of research on "stance."

In this archival material I will consider a complexly "faultable" linguistic behavior—at least, a faultfinding—in which it is difficult even to see the agent behind all the coconstruction of the trouble and its historical contingencies. Just as in radio talk, the consequences of the trouble hinge upon the distance, cultural heterogeneity, and unpredictability of mediations and audiences. The case in point comes from nineteenth-century missions in what is now Nigeria. It concerns a violent dispute among missionaries, a dispute that erupted into physical violence and occasioned a flurry of correspondence among the missionaries themselves, their bishop (based elsewhere in West Africa), and the church authorities in London. At issue are participants' analyses of what went wrong, and how to interpret the statements of one of the main parties to the dispute, one John Christian Taylor. Although the immediate trouble was the violence, it was on Taylor's statements that the faultfinding concentrated.

The documentation in the archive is not ideal from a sociolinguistic point of view because the events of violence, and whatever talk occurred in them, are evidenced only indirectly, in participants' reports. But I focus on the characteristics of the reports themselves, and take advantage of the historical depth-of-field that allows us to see the various parties, their political and moral positions, and their cultural assumptions, in a very broad context. What we shall see is the complexity of mediations and audiences that intervene between Mr. Taylor's statements, their interpretations, and their outcomes.

So, to the case. The scene is the Church Missionary Society's mission at Onitsha in what is now eastern Nigeria (see map in figure 3.1); the time is mid-October 1868. Onitsha, an independent town in Igbo territory some 140 miles up the Niger River, is at this time relatively isolated from European contact, visited only by occasional merchant ships coming upriver to trade.[5] Colonial conquest of the region has not yet taken place and is not yet expected. The missionaries are upset and nervous because of recent Onitshan attacks against the local Christian converts and against mission buildings, some of which were burned down—and there is a rumor that the king of Onitsha plans to expel the missionaries or even have them killed. Although that rumor has been put to rest for the moment, the missionaries have begun to suspect one another of plotting with the king in order to expel their rivals and have the mission to themselves. Then, on the evening of October 19, someone brings a fugitive slave woman to the mission compound. Two missionaries quarrel over what to do with her, and the quarrel turns violent. Other missionaries and their wives rush in, until some four men and four women are involved in the struggle.

Fugitive slaves presented African missionaries in this period with a dilemma. On the one hand, religious ethics and British public opinion demanded that missionaries do everything possible to help slaves and stop the slave trade. On the other hand, missionary presence in Onitsha, as in many other African polities, was tolerated only on condition that missionaries not interfere actively with local politics and law, including local Africans' right to own and trade in slaves. Missionaries might (and did) preach against slavery, but they were not to remove slaves from African owners. In Onitsha Mission on October 19, what would have been a difficult decision at any time—what to do with the fugitive—was made worse by the tensions and rumors of the previous few weeks. Some of the missionaries worried that the woman's arrival might be part of a plot to get them to violate the terms of their residence in Onitsha and give the King an excuse to expel them. Or expel some of them. Was there a plot, and were any of the mission personnel themselves complicit? Suspicion, and tempers, ran high.

Table 3.1 lists the cast of characters in our little drama. These are the persons mentioned in the correspondence. First are those—mostly the mission personnel and their wives—who were present at the Central Station of the Onitsha Mission on the evening of October 19, 1868. Some of these people normally occupied satellite stations within the Onitsha Mission orbit, but they were staying at the Central Station on the evening in question. Second are people located within walking distance of

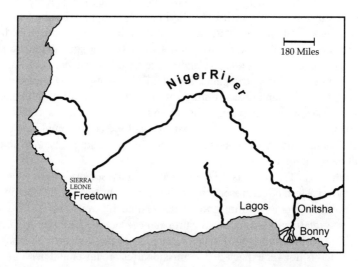

FIGURE 3.1 Map of West Africa, showing places referred to in the text.

TABLE 3.1 Dramatis Personae in the "Onitsha Affair"

1. Present at Onitsha Mission (Central Station), October 19, 1868

   John Christian TAYLOR, missionary pastor at Onitsha (Central Station)
   Sophia TAYLOR, his wife
   Obadiah E. COLE, missionary schoolmaster at Onitsha
   Edward G. PHILLIPS, catechist at Onitsha (Obori Station)
   Mrs. PHILLIPS, his wife
   W. G. ROMAINE, catechist and bricklayer, later pastor
   Mrs. ROMAINE, his wife
   Francis LANGLEY, Scripture reader
   Isaac Thomas GEORGE, mission industrial agent and carpenter; qualified to preach
   Mrs. GEORGE, his wife
   Fugitive slave woman
   Man bringing the fugitive slave to the mission

2. Elsewhere in Onitsha

   Thomas LEWIS, general agent of the West Africa Company, on board the *Bazley* (docked at Onitsha)
   "Late governor's brother," probably in charge of the trading station
   King (Obi) AKUZUA, king of Onitsha
   King's messenger

3. Farther afield

   Samuel A. CROWTHER, Bishop of the Niger, based at Lagos
   Crowther's clerk(s)
   Henry VENN, secretary, Church Missionary Society (London; member of the CMS Parent Committee)
   Other CMS Committee members and clerks

the mission station: the King of Onitsha, who resided elsewhere in the town, and Mr. Lewis, the British commercial agent whose ship, the *Bazley*, had sailed up the Niger to Onitsha and was anchored nearby. Third are more distant personnel of the Church of England and the Church Missionary Society, to whom correspondence passed.

The precise, blow-by-blow order of events is confused, because the participants' accounts do not exactly agree. In brief, but perhaps not quite in this order: The fugitive slave woman is brought to the mission compound. Mr. Phillips takes her to his room, where he gives her some food. Mr. Taylor finds her there, with Mr. Phillips and Mr. Cole. Confronting Phillips and Cole, Taylor removes the woman and takes her to his own rooms. A struggle ensues among the three men, and others rush in to join the fray. In the struggle, clothing is ripped and pulled off. Mr. Taylor picks up a revolver and points it at Mr. Cole. Several people—Mr. Phillips, Mrs. Romaine, Mrs. George, and perhaps others—pull Taylor back, but Mrs. Taylor grabs a bottle of iodine and breaks it on Mr. Cole's head. Mrs. Phillips climbs in through the window. She bites Mr. Taylor on the trigger finger (and perhaps elsewhere). One of the women manages to twist the revolver out of Taylor's hand, while Mr. Cole, escaping from Taylor, runs out to get his double-barrel shotgun. Eventually, Mr. and Mrs. Taylor manage to get away, running (separately) to the river, where they take refuge on board the *Bazley*, the merchant ship that happens to be in port. The next morning, deputations go back and forth between the Agent of the West Africa Company from the ship (Mr. Lewis), the king of Onitsha, and the mission personnel—and letters begin to circulate, some among the missionaries and some addressed to the bishop in Lagos. Taylor, who is officially head of the mission, tells the others to pack their bags and leave, and asks the bishop to expel them. Meanwhile, the other missionaries want the bishop to expel the Taylors. But the letters take weeks to reach the bishop, who is unwilling to take such drastic action without the approval of the church authorities in London. Finally, the CMS secretary in London, acting on the bishop's recommendation, expels the Taylors, who leave Onitsha in October of the following year, 1869. Table 3.2 outlines the correspondence contained in the CMS archive.

Why pick on Taylor, the head of the mission, a man who had been 12 years in Onitsha and in whom the bishop and other authorities had invested much training and effort? Taylor, who had been charged with working on translations of the Bible into Igbo, and continuing the missionaries' linguistic efforts on the language? This was a serious matter. The bishop, writing to the London authorities, argued that Taylor should be removed from Onitsha and from mission work because he had fallen into bad habits. Taylor, the bishop claimed, had become habitually drunk and irritable, and the skirmish of October 19 was Taylor's fault for being drunk.

Now, I'm not interested here in what actually happened on October 19 (much as it appeals to the dime-novel reader in me), nor in whether the bishop's assessment of Taylor was correct. Instead, the point is to look at what the bishop presented in evi-

TABLE 3.2 Onitsha Mission Correspondence Concerning the Events of October 1868

October 3–4, 1868: Taylor to Crowther, three letters, alleging the existence of a conspiracy to kill him (suppressed by Crowther until after the Oct. 19 incident)

October 7: Samuel Crowther Jr. to Crowther, describing conflicts at Onitsha a few days earlier

October 19: Langley to Crowther, requesting to send his family away from Onitsha, but remain there himself

October 20:
Cole to Crowther, concerning the incident of Oct. 19
Phillips to Crowther, concerning the same incident
Romaine to Crowther, concerning the same incident
Taylor to Lewis, requesting removal of Phillips and Cole
Lewis to Taylor, expressing willingness to give passage to Phillips and Cole
Taylor to Cole: Pack your bags
Cole to Taylor: Not unless the Bishop orders me to
Taylor to Cole: You're replaceable
Taylor to Phillips: Pack your bags
Phillips to Taylor: Not unless the Bishop orders me to

October 21: Taylor to Crowther, concerning the incident of Oct. 19

November 27: Crowther to Venn (of the CMS Parent Committee in London), requesting him to withdraw Taylor from Onitsha and give permission to ordain Langley and Romaine. A description of the events of October 19 is enclosed, along with copies of the letters listed above.

May 23, 1869: Venn to Crowther, agreeing to pay Taylor's passage to Sierra Leone, and to ordain Langley and Romaine

May 24, 1869: Venn to Taylor, telling him he needs a rest

Source: CMS Archive, Niger Mission, A3/ 04(a).

dence: copies of Taylor's letters to him (e.g., figure 3.2), letters whose language, the bishop argued, betrayed drunkenness. Notice incidentally that it could not have been Taylor's handwriting or anything about the letters as physical objects that should have served in evidence, because the bishop did not forward the originals, only copies made by a clerk. Moreover, the crucial letter from Taylor to the bishop on October

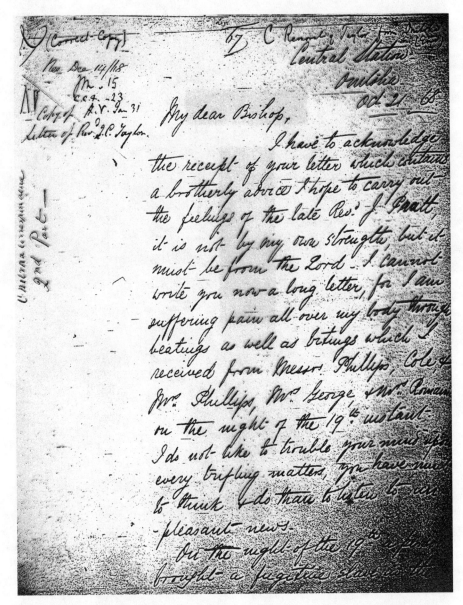

FIGURE 3.2 First page of missionary J. C. Taylor's letter to Bishop Crowther, October 21, 1868; copy produced by Crowther's clerk. CMS archive, Niger Mission, C A3/04 (a).

21 was not actually in Taylor's handwriting to begin with. As the letter indicates, he dictated it to his wife because his hand was too painful—from being bitten and squeezed in the fight—to hold the pen.

Figures 3.2 and 3.3 show the beginning of the copy of Taylor's letter, as it exists in the CMS archive.[6] On the letter, several different handwritings can be seen: the

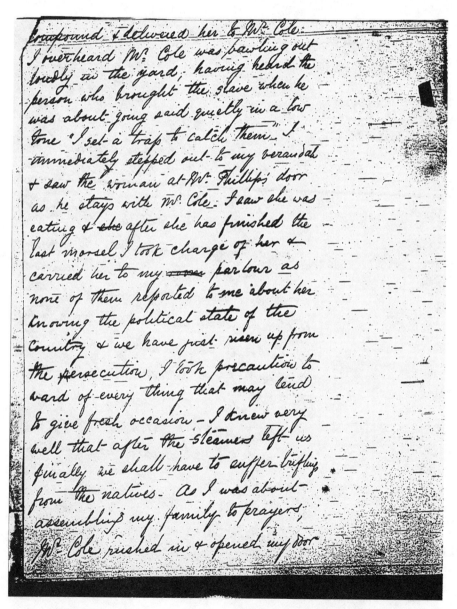

FIGURE 3.3 Second page of J. C. Taylor's letter to Crowther, October 21, 1868; copy produced by Crowther's clerk. CMS archive, Niger Mission, C A3/04 (a).

bishop's clerk, who copied Taylor's letter; the bishop himself, who wrote "(Correct Copy)" and "by C" at the top of the page; the CMS clerk in London, who wrote "Rec. Dec 14/68" on the upper left; and three members of the CMS leadership, including Henry Venn [H.V.], with the dates on which they read the file. Venn's hand also appears in the comments, "Copy of Letter of Rev'd J. C. Taylor" and "Removal of Taylor from Onitsha (End)." (The side inscription, "Onitsha correspondence 2nd Part __" is in a clerk's hand, but it is not clear which clerk.)

It was the disfluency and loquacity of Taylor's letters that was cited as evidence of his drunk and disorderly condition. As the bishop wrote in his report to London (Crowther to Venn, November 27, 1868):

> ...I have heard here as well as at Onitsha, that he [Taylor] is getting into the habit of indulging in ardent spirits, which upset him at times. I myself did suspect him [when the bishop visited Onitsha a few weeks earlier] to have been a little overpowered twice by the influence of ardent spirits, through his *unusual loquacity*, though it did not amount to actual drunkenness.... When he went on board these ships at night in October last, and wrote me such *disconnected notes, breathing hostile feelings* against all the mission agents,... his last desperate acts [are] very much suspected to be excited by the same influence, when he took up his revolver against Mr. Cole. This habit, combined with a haughty and irritable disposition, must disqualify him for his spiritual duties among the heathens.... You will perceive that I did not send you copies of Mr. Taylor's [earlier] letters to me [sent about two weeks before the Oct. 19 incident], because they appeared to me *so unconnected, written with excited mind* and in other respects *very personal*... but other more serious circumstances have since transpired between Mr. Taylor and Mr. Cole, that I am obliged to send you now the whole correspondence from Onitsha for your information and decision. [italics added]

The phrases I have italicized—"loquacity," "disconnected notes," "unconnected, written with excited mind," and "very personal"—are faultable aspects of Taylor's letters to which the bishop directed London's attention.[7]

Let us look at Taylor's "disconnected notes" themselves. His letter of October 21 follows; I have transcribed it from the microfilm and italicized some of the expressions that might be considered faultable on grounds of grammatical disfluency, although there are other expressions that are candidates for "faultability" as well. The letter (Taylor to Crowther, October 21, 1868) reads as follows:

Central Station
Onitsha
Oct 21 68

My dear Bishop,

I have to acknowledge the receipt of your letter which contains a brotherly advice I hope to carry out the feelings of the late Rev'd J. Pratt, it is not by my own strength, but it must be from the Lord—I cannot write you now a long letter, for I am suffering pain all over my body through beatings as well as bitings which I received from Messrs. Phillips, Cole, & Mrs. Phillips, Mrs. George, & Mrs. Romaine on the night of the 19th instant; I do not like to trouble your mind upon every trifling matters, you have *much to think & do than* to listen to unpleasant news.

On the night of the 19th a person brought a fugitive slave in the compound & delivered her to Mr. Cole. I *overheard Mr. Cole was bawling* out loudly in the yard, having heard the person who brought the slave *when he was about going said* quietly in a low tone "I set a trap to catch them". I immediately stepped out to my verandah & saw the woman at Mr. Phillips' door as he stays with Mr. Cole. I saw she was eating & ~~she~~ after she has finished the last morsel I took charge of her & carried her to my ~~room~~ parlour as none of them reported to me about her Knowing the political state of the country & we have just risen up from the persecution, I took precaution *to ward of* every thing that may tend to give fresh occasion—I knew very well that after the steamers left us finally we shall have to suffer triflings from the natives. As I was about assembling my family to prayers, Mr. Cole rushed in & opened my door to carry away the woman—I refused. Then came in Mr. Phillips & the women I have named, my revolver was on the table as we are troubled with leopards. I held it in hand & told them to walk out of my parlour, then Mr. Cole jumped upon me at once, & Mr. Phillips pretending to take Mr. Cole away *whilst his wife biting me & the beatings* I have received from them—Mrs. Taylor who is still ill, tried her best to take Mr. C. away but five of them upon me, I delivered the revolver, & *told to kill me* at once—Mrs. T saw how I was roughly handled by them, flung a bottle at them, which made them to scatter. Mr. Cole went & brought his double barrel & rushed again the second time into my parlour determined to shoot at me—then the second row took place—Mrs ran off to call for help &c. fortunately she met with the king's messenger by the way *as she going down* to Mr. Lewis—However, I found the slave under the mango trees & I took her to the town & delivered her up to the late Governor's brother.[8] Having been bitten fearfully I went on board, & I do not know how to render my thanks to Mr. *Lewis when I was fainting to give me* a glass of port wine & water—He did all in his power by way of medicine to alleviate the pains I was labouring under. Moreover he called his smith to break off the ring I wore on my finger which was compressed by their teeth &c &c.

On the 20th Mr. Lewis kindly walked up to the compound to see if he could make things good. The king after *hearing the conducts of these gentlemen*, sent down a force to protect me & said he cannot allow these men to remain in his country any longer "it is a disgrace to fight a king in his house next will be his own"—Mr. Lewis first demanded the revolver that he should take possession of &c——He will tell you the insults he had received from them. Knowing what will follow, as the chiefs determined that they must quit the country, I wrote to each of them as you will see the whole correspondence &c. I am not able to sit up long & my arm is paining me—I begged Sophia to copy out the letters—I am sorry to state that I do not know *whether I will put up the roof of the Church & finished it* this year—The Sawyers one of them is employed by Capt Croft—Be assured of this my dear brother, I will do my best as far as my strength goes, I am unable to send you the general expenditure, as *the whole concern is mixed up when the persecution took place.* I send you the account of *the issues* &c.

I remain,

Yrs sincerely
(Signed) *J. C. Taylor*

P.S. I am sorry to say that the king had sent a deputation of the elders this morning to fine Messrs Phillips & Cole. I am trying to oppose them and to convince them that I will suspend the matter till next year when you come up.

(Signed) J. C. Taylor

Now, consider Taylor's "disconnected notes" as communicative acts whose footing, point of view, and indexical relationship to broad social categories is in question. In other words, what are the various ingredients of his stance? His letter is faultable; but how, why, and in whose eyes?

One must bear in mind that the spelling and punctuation, particularly the dashes, cannot be considered Taylor's own. The copyist, who was in any case working from Sophia Taylor's version, evidently worked in haste—see for example, in figures 3.1 and 3.2, how his hand moves ahead when crossing *t*'s—and there are many signs that look like dashes but might have been intended as periods. There are other places where a period seems to be missing, and many places where it is difficult to distinguish between a punctuation mark and a spot on the paper. Yet, the dashes and other oddities of punctuation contribute a great deal to an effect of excitement and disconnection.

Obviously, however, punctuation problems are not the only disfluencies in the letter. Other problems conspicuous in the text are its grammatical departures from normative nineteenth-century English style. Grammatical disfluencies might be the result of drunkenness, as the bishop would have it, but they can be interpreted in other ways, too. Disfluencies can result from emotional distress, for example, or from difficulties in reconciling internal conflicts (aspects of the self; see Hill 1995), shifts of footing (alignment of participant roles) in mid-utterance, hypercorrections, hesitations and interruptions, conventional disfluency (see, e.g., Irvine 1990 on the "disfluent" performances of high nobles, in a Wolof tradition), creative disfluency for special effect (consider Rimbaud's *Je est un autre*,[9] whose violation of subject-verb person agreement suggests alienation), and so on. Of course, a stretch of discourse may itself contain clues that narrow down the choice among interpretations, but not always and not incontrovertibly. As Goffman (1976) pointed out, there always remains the possibility that a subsequent utterance will reframe the previous one and forever alter what it "counts as." Stances are situated in discourse histories and embedded in cultural frameworks that suggest what interpretations make sense.

In the case of Taylor's letters, one possible interpretation is emotional distress. He certainly expresses this and it is not an unreasonable explanation, given his account of events and the extremely tense situation in which the missionaries found themselves. (Recall that they were under threat from the Onitshans; Taylor's house had burned down, probably in an Onitshan attack.) He also claims to be in grave physical pain, especially in the arm and hands. Another possibility, however, is that Taylor lacked perfect competence in written English and was therefore likely to make mistakes when writing a letter in haste, without time to polish the grammar. Here I have to mention an important fact: Taylor, despite his name, was not British but a mission-educated African, as indeed were all the people involved in the scuffle of October 19. Taylor was born in the colony of liberated African slaves in Freetown, Sierra Leone, to parents who considered themselves "Ibo." Educated in the mission schools, he was recruited for missionary service in "Iboland," as the missionaries called that part of eastern Nigeria, because of his ethnic background. English was not his first language; instead, the variety of "Ibo" spoken in Freetown was. (That turned out not to be quite what was spoken in Onitsha, incidentally—a fact that contributed a good deal to Taylor's troubles there.)

Taylor's letter to the bishop shows some spelling mistakes, some non-English constructions, some expressions that look as if a word is missing, a couple of self-corrections, and some run-on sentences. However, there are similar kinds of problems in grammar, spelling, and punctuation, in the letters written by the other mission personnel. Here is the beginning of one of them, the account by Mr. Cole addressed to the bishop (Cole to Crowther, October 20, 1868). Because Cole's letter is quite long I have transcribed only part of it. Again, I have italicized some of its disfluencies:

Central Station

Onitsha

Oct. 20 1868

Right Rev. & dear Bishop,

Sir,

I am extremely sorry to acquaint you of a dreadful quarrel, between the Rev. J. C. Taylor & myself on the evening of the 19th instant which would have proved fatal, had not the good providence of God ordered it otherwise. *I went down the landing place* about ½ past two, to furnish myself with necessaries for the year as hitherto, and returned with Mr. Phillips about 7 ½ o'clock.

No sooner we got into the compound than we met a man belonging to Umudei,[10] *held a woman's hand calling* for "Obi Aje". He being left down the wharf together with Mr. George, made me inquire the man's wish of Aje. He said this is now two of their weeks = 8 days, since the woman was missing, and as he *was going to a fishing,* he begged that the woman be *kept for few minutes* till her master comes. I inquired of the man how soon the owner will come; he replied "<u>tata</u>," equal to just now. I then told *one of Mr. George's boy* to take special care with her till the right owners come.

She spoke in the Igara tongue, not being acquainted with the Onitsha language, that she was hungry. Mr. E. G. Phillips who is acquainted with that language took her into his room, being formerly mine, & gave her something to eat. No sooner the woman sat to eat, Mr. Taylor entered into Mr. Phillips' room took away the plate of rice from her and dragged her out of the house, then to the gate. Mr. Phillips called me from my dinner to see the proceedings of Mr. Taylor, with the woman delivered me *for few minutes' protection,* and if she should be dragged away, the responsibility will be on my head—I immediately *left my dinner came out,* met Mr. Taylor ~~upon~~ *and* the poor woman, and asked him most respectfully to leave her, as she was delivered directly to my care. Saying to him in these words "Please sir, dont; *she is just found by her owner and begged* that we detain her till her right master comes. He absolutely refused leaving her stating that this compound is his, & can do whatever he likes. "Yes sir, yours as well as mine." "I do not care, but I must have this woman out;" whilst dragging her forward I was now trying to hold her backward. Mrs. Taylor seeing this came out in height of temper seized on me at once, & tore my clothes, leaving me in perfect nudity. The only word I told her after this, was, "Mrs. I cannot touch you, the woman being got that is all I want." I left them to go into my room for covering, then Mr. Taylor came out of his with a new revolver of 5 rounds, choked me with one hand ~~point~~ *pointing* with the other, the revolver right to my breast; I was guiding the mouth from me at the same time, when Mrs. Romaine sang murder; (her room being opposite to ours) "Mr. Phillips you sit here & Mr. Taylor committing murder upon that young man", this stirred Mr. & Mrs. Phillips, Mrs. George

&c to come in & deprived Mr. Taylor of the revolver—*He still keep* his hold on me, & while I was making every effort to get rid of him,. Then Mrs. Taylor came with a full bottle of iodine, and *break it* on my head. This being done, the cry from every quarter *was that I am killed.* Fear now took hold of both, they left the house right into the Bazley....

Cole's disfluencies include some kinds of grammatical errors that are similar to Taylor's, and a few, such as problems with indefinite articles that do not occur in Taylor's writing. More important, perhaps, the punctuation—at least, what *appears* to be punctuation—is a little different: fewer dashes, and more periods and commas. It is not clear to me whether the two letters were copied by different clerks, or whether the same clerk copied Cole's letter at a different time and with less haste, much less whether the originals were different. Although both Taylor's letter and Cole's letter exhibit what are probably signs of agitation, the bishop cites Taylor's letters as evidence of drunkenness, not Cole's.

Consider now the stance of these letters in terms of the organization of participant roles in the communication. At one level, there is the letter writer (Taylor or Cole) and the addressee (the bishop)—although here, too, we may want to distinguish between the letter-event participants and the narrated-event participants, especially because the narrated events include reported speech. But the letters are embedded in a more complex communication chain, involving copyists and forwarding. Recall that the bishop, addressee of both letters, had them copied and forwarded the copies to London. Recall, too, that with oddities of punctuation, spelling, word omissions, and crossings-out, one cannot really distinguish between what is in the original letter and what, instead, is an effect of the copying, because (for example) a hastily copied period can look like a dash.[11] The question, then, is this: where is Taylor, and what is his stance in his letter? Although we can identify a subject position, Taylor as originator of the communication and signatory of the original, the "presentation" of Taylor in and through the letter is not just his own construction. Instead, it is coconstructed by several parties, including Sophia Taylor, the copyist(s), the bishop (and bishop's commentary), and a set of distant addressees whom Taylor may or may not have anticipated as ultimate recipients.

Now consider another level of analysis: how these performances are mapped onto social categories and characteristics—in particular, the attribution to Taylor of drunkenness, bad habits, and unsuitability for mission work, an attribution not made about Cole or the other participants in the Onitsha affair. Whether the bishop was right or wrong about Taylor is not really the point. If he was right, he must have relied on evidence other than the letter presented here. Although one could examine other letters from Taylor that I have not transcribed here, they would present the same kinds of problems. In fact, I think it is a mistake to try, as I did when I first came upon this correspondence, to look for something in the letter—in the trace of Taylor's linguistic acts—that would provide evidence of drunkenness, and thereby lead the bishop to fault him in this particular way.

How then to understand the particular allegations? It is useful to consider the bishop's position, as presented in his letters to London and as developed in his relations with Taylor and Onitsha over the years. Though a fervent supporter of the "African church," that is, a church organization in Africa staffed by Africans, Bishop

Crowther had a long history of difficulties with the Onitsha operation, and some with Taylor in particular. Over the years since the Onitsha mission's establishment under Taylor's direction in 1857, there were many troubles with the local authorities. Moreover, Taylor's linguistic work on Igbo had not gone well. Other CMS missionaries, including Crowther himself, had previously worked on Igbo language back in Freetown, and Taylor was supposed to continue this study in "Iboland," extending the vocabulary and grammatical analysis and producing Igbo translations of biblical and liturgical texts. Perhaps Taylor lacked the requisite linguistic talent, or perhaps as a second-generation "Ibo" born in the Freetown Creole community he was actually only a semispeaker. Certainly Onitsha "Ibo" differed, then and now, quite substantially from the variety ("Isoama Ibo") that had been identified in Freetown. Whatever the reasons may have been, Taylor's analyses and translations did not conform to CMS expectations. In 1867, the year before our drama, the CMS had sent him to England to work on his translations with John Frederick Schön, one of the missionary linguists who had earlier contributed to the Igbo linguistic work in Freetown, but the two men could not agree. I mention the disagreements over the Igbo translations because Bishop Crowther did so in his correspondence with London about the October 19 incident (Crowther to Venn, November 27, 1868):[12]

> I am very slow to believe evil reports, especially when such reports are against any missionary, be he native or European.... But since [Taylor's] return from Sierra Leone last year, it appears his mind has become alienated from Onitsha.... It also appears that he has been in the habit of exercising an air of authority over [the other mission agents at the station] which they considered unbrotherly. *Mr. Taylor cannot bear to be crossed in what he considers his right view of things: the matter of the rejected translations is an instance—I could not get him to yield.* [italics added]

So the decision about Taylor, along with the declaration about his character and unsuitability for mission work, emerged from a long history of interactions, not just from the particular letters of October 1868. Notice, incidentally, that Taylor's letter of October 21 does not offer incontrovertible evidence of arrogance any more than evidence of drunkenness. Looking back at the letter, we can see several expressions in which he takes an explicit stance asserting competence and authority: "I took charge of her," "I took precaution," "I knew very well," "knowing what will follow." Because Taylor was the head of the mission, running its central station, as well as the longest-serving missionary in the group, he might be expected to take charge at a difficult moment. Had there not been other problems, this stance could have gone unremarked—and in fact, it is not what the bishop calls special attention to in Taylor's letter, unlike the drunkenness supposedly evidenced in its "disconnected notes."

Consider now Crowther's own stances when he discusses Taylor's character and actions. His just-quoted November 27 letter to London continues:

> I have been advised by Europeans, and by Natives, competent to give opinion; and I have received messages from the Converts at Onitsha, begging me to get Mr. Taylor removed back to S. Leone for a time, till his present highly irritable temper and feelings cool down.... I fully concur in recommending to the Parent Committee this change.

Although the bishop may have received some communications that he did not forward to London, no messages or advice from third parties about Taylor's drunkenness are included in the archive, other than those offered by the other mission agents (Cole, Romaine, and Phillips). Did he receive any? What is the basis of his characterization of Taylor? If we look at the epistemic stances Crowther takes in his text, we see him carefully distinguishing between hearsay knowledge about Taylor and knowledge based on his own experience. The bishop avoids fully committing himself to the truth of many of the negative assessments of Taylor reported in the letter: thus, "*I am very slow to believe* evil reports," "*it appears* his mind has become alienated," "*it also appears* he has been in the habit of exercising an air of authority," "*I have been advised*," "*I have heard* that he is getting into the habit of indulging in ardent spirits," and so on. On the other hand, where the linguistic analyses are concerned he is explicitly committed to the truth of his assertion: "*Mr. Taylor cannot bear to be crossed...the matter of the rejected texts is an instance.*" Crowther's own linguistic analyses and translations were already famous in missionary circles; here as in other linguistic debates he does not hesitate to assert his own point of view. On the claims about Taylor's arrogance and drunkenness, Crowther takes a different stance, avoiding personally vouching for the truth of the claims.

For both kinds of claims, however, there is also another factor: the testimony of European witnesses. On Taylor's alleged intransigence on linguistic issues, it was the European missionary Schön whose opinion on Igbo language and on Taylor was to be trusted, not only Crowther's own. On Taylor's alleged drunkenness on October 19, when Crowther mentions that he must cite not only "native" but also European advice, he represents his allegation as relying on European testimony. That is, Crowther accepts—or represents himself as accepting—that Taylor may have been drunk, because there were European witnesses on board the *Bazley* who thought he was (Crowther to Venn, November 27, 1868): "Passengers and men in board the 'Thomas Bazley' and the 'Myrtle' asserted that he was not sober, when he went on board these ships at night in October last." Before the events of October 19–21, Bishop Crowther had received troubled letters from Taylor and the other Onitsha personnel, but he had refrained from forwarding them or any accusation deriving from them. After October 19, however, when Captain Lewis and other Europeans had become involved, the bishop acceded to their assessment (that Taylor had been drinking). Or so he represents his decisions.

Why drunkenness, as an attribution? When Taylor boarded the *Bazley* there may have been some alcohol fumes (but remember the bottle of iodine, which might have contributed them). Or perhaps Taylor accepted the proffered cordial with unseemly eagerness. I do not reject the possibility that Taylor had indeed been drinking. But in order to understand why the accusation was so prominent and so grave we must consider the stereotypes that were current during this period about Western-educated Africans, and about Africans in general. The idea that Africans could be educated to a level that would make them suitable missionaries to other Africans, rather than mere converts, members of a European missionary's congregation, was a notion much contested at the time. To some Europeans, Africans were not educable at all; to other Europeans, they were only barely educable, and always liable to relapse into some form of carnal sensuality or indolence. There were also European writers who saw Western-educated Africans as especially problematic—an anomaly (neither fish nor fowl), lacking genuine principles of good conduct, either traditional or British, and apt to assume unwarranted "airs," claiming the status of whites and lording it over other Africans as if they were not all equally black.

The Church Missionary Society, however, had been founded on the principle that Africans and other non-Western, non-Christian peoples could be converted and educated. And the Niger Mission (which included Onitsha), like many other Christian institutions and proselytizing activities in West Africa, relied on African missionaries because, in this period, Europeans seldom survived long enough to sustain the effort. West Africa was famous as "the white man's grave," an apt assessment before the development of reliable treatments for malaria and yellow fever later in the nineteenth century. Nevertheless, African missionaries always walked a thin line. They were always vulnerable to accusations, either that they were arrogant (uppity, so to speak) or that they had slipped "back" into venality, carnality, and disorder. Specifically, the most common accusations were of drunkenness, or having an affair with a local woman, or collaborating in the slave trade they were supposed to be trying to combat. Therefore, in attributing drunkenness to Taylor, rightly or wrongly, the bishop mapped a familiar stereotype onto him—a stereotype that derived from European racist ideologies.

Moreover, Taylor and his "unbrotherly" attitude also fit another stereotype that was beginning to emerge at the time: the image of the Igbo as quarrelsome, excessively individualistic, and generally troublesome. There were several sources for this stereotype of Igbo as an identity category, including the problem of lumping together a population very diverse in linguistic and cultural forms under a single "Ibo" rubric, but that is a story of its own. For present purposes, the point is that Taylor's linguistic failures, and especially his disagreements with linguistic authorities, could be attributed to the troublesomeness of Igbos, of whom Taylor was one. The disorder revealed in the October 19 scuffle, and in Taylor's letters, could be interpreted as consistent with his quarrels over linguistic analysis and with the Igbos' annoying unwillingness to unite with other Igbos in language or in polity. As Bishop Crowther later wrote (1874), "Like disunion in their government, the dialects of the Ibos...are multifarious; how to arrive at the leading one has been to us a puzzle for years." And more specifically about the Onitsha mission personnel, all of whom were "Ibos" from Freetown (Crowther 1875):

> I wish there were among them a spirit of brotherly love; but instead of which, there is a spirit of jealousy and ambition, of pride and contempt; every one watching to find fault with a fellow labourer....This state of feelings, I must confess in justice to the Agents of other tribes in other stations in the mission, does not exist among them except among those of the *Ibo tribe* at Onitsha and Bonny. I have had more difficulties to contend with them, than with all the other stations put together. [italics original]

For the bishop, it would have been important to find a way to remove Taylor without impugning all missionized Africans. Drunkenness could be considered just an individual failing, even if a common one, and Igbo troublesomeness could be taken as limited to members of that ethnic category. Not only was Bishop Crowther, as bishop of the Niger, invested in the success of African missions run by Africans—he was one himself, a mission-educated African and the CMS's poster boy for the success of their enterprise. Clearly, Crowther walked the same tightrope himself. Although he was never seriously accused of anything venal, eventually he, too, was brought down. In the early 1880s he was removed from his position as bishop on charges of incompetence, charges that later generations of historians judge trumped up. He had become too old, his British detractors claimed, to manage the finances and complex affairs of the missions under his authority. By that time, medical advances had enabled Europeans to occupy West Africa in greater numbers. As more Europeans moved in and as they extended their military domination of the region, Africans who held positions of responsibility were demoted, especially if those positions might put them in authority over whites.

In short, missionized Africans in positions of authority in this period were highly vulnerable to attack, on grounds of performing in some inappropriate manner. The attribution of fault, though supposedly supported by evidence, was overdetermined by a global context of increasing European power and increasingly powerful racial ideologies. In these circumstances, it is the observers of the performance who make the attribution, who find a way to map the stereotype onto the performance no matter what.

Where is our concept of "stance" in this case of "faultables" and their audiences? It has been useful to consider this material on several analytical scales: (1) the linguistic and graphemic features of texts, particularly those suggesting epistemic stances and internal states; (2) the participant role structure of communicative acts, bearing in mind that such acts can be embedded in others, and in complex histories of transmission; (3) broader social categories such as ethnicity and race, and the characteristics associated with those categories from the perspective of dominant outsiders. Although authors (or speakers) align themselves with positions and identifications they want their audience to attribute to them (such as innocent victim of biting and beating), their intentions, I hope to have shown, are in cases like this one only a small part of the story. There are several reasons. Linguistic behaviors that are crucial to an audience's impression may be unintentional, such as some forms of disfluency. Moreover, speakers (or authors) may not be able to predict all the audiences their performance may have, or the interpretations those audiences make, especially where there are many mediations and where audiences are distant and heterogeneous. As Goffman (1976) pointed out years ago, the audience or responder's interpretation, mapped onto a performance, can dictate what the performance "counts as."

What of ourselves, now an audience for the statements by Taylor, Cole, and Crowther? What does it all count as, for us? When presenting this material orally, I have usually waited until late in the presentation to reveal the information that our missionary *dramatis personae* were black Africans. The effect is noticeable. Amiable laughter at the tale of the "Onitsha affair" suddenly dies down. Although of course I may just have ceased to relate the tale in an entertaining way, I suspect the effect has more to do with the contemporary audience's stance toward the kinds of people and actions represented in the story. Among many academics today, there is a strong assumption that missionaries in Africa must have been Europeans or white Americans, and that as colonialists or proto-colonialists they offer easy targets for ridicule. (*We* would not break iodine bottles on one another's heads.) For similar reasons, most of us do not laugh at black Africans who were made the objects of colonial domination. We do not want to align ourselves with the colonizers, many of whom were apt to ridicule the people over whom they had power. Sharing in this sentiment—this hope not to be aligned with the tellers of racist jokes—I have felt conflicted about how to present the story. We who analyze stances also, necessarily, have them.

To conclude, let us return to the analytical role of a concept of stance. The concept is useful in calling attention to how communicative acts are formulated and how they are positioned in an interactional structure of participation, as well as in broader social structures. It calls attention, too, to how these positions rely on linguistic conventions for their enactment, and it helps remind us how ideologized the processes are by which linguistic performances and social identity attributions are mapped onto one another. However, when we draw on a concept of "stance" we must not suppose that an individual can just go ahead and take one, end of story. That is, we must not overemphasize a speaker's intentions, agency, and perspective to the neglect of unintentional signals, incompetent performances, and coconstructions by other parties to a complex situation. We say a person takes a stance, but they—and we ourselves—may also find themselves in one, willy-nilly. A stance can be given or accorded, rather than taken. Sometimes, as in the present case, the specifics of a speaker's linguistic acts scarcely matter, even when they are cited in evidence. An analysis must make room for those mappings—retroactively imputed stances, other parties' positionings, the complexity of mediations, and the unanticipated audiences who find fault and impose consequences—if we are to begin to account for what happened to John Christian Taylor.

Notes

1. The original reads, "can be *almost* anything."
2. In fact, Du Bois (2007) alludes to "other-positioning"—how a speaker assigns stances to others—and Kockelman (2004) includes a notion of "second-order" stances, but although these ideas are directly relevant to the point at issue, the discussions are yet to be developed, as far as I know. Meanwhile, there is much other literature on positioning, including how people manage to position others (e.g., Harré and Van Langenhove 1991, 1999 on "performative positioning," Goffman 1976, and many other works), but these works do not draw on a linguistic or sociolinguistic concept of "stance."
3. See Althusser (1994 [1970]).
4. More precisely, it comes from the microfilms made of the CMS archives some decades ago. The microfilms appear to be a complete record of the archives, but without delving thoroughly in the actual boxes of papers on deposit with the CMS it is not possible to be certain that nothing relevant was omitted.
5. "Igbo" is a modern spelling for what most English-language texts of the nineteenth and twentieth centuries up to the time of Nigerian independence usually wrote as "Ibo." In languages of the region, the central consonant is a double-articulation (near-simultaneous velar and bilabial stop), heard and articulated by Europeans of the time as "b." In this chapter I use "Igbo" when writing in my own voice, but "Ibo" when quoting a text that spells it that way.
6. The images in figures 3.1 and 3.2 are reproduced from the microfilm of the CMS archive, not from the original documents.
7. The packet of correspondence that was sent to London in late November 1868 includes more than one statement written by the bishop himself. One is his cover letter, addressed to Venn and dated November 27. There is also a sort of postscript, apparently part of the same letter; I have

excerpted from both of these in producing the text quoted at this point. A third item is the bishop's own summary of the October events at Onitsha. I quote from this third item later in the chapter.

8. It is not clear to me who this person was, or what official Taylor means by "Governor." Onitsha in 1868 had no British official with that title. At that time, the British maintained a small trading station at the harbor in Onitsha, so the man to whom Taylor says he delivered the fugitive was probably the person in charge of the station.

9. The Rimbaud quote is discussed in Benveniste 1971: 199.

10. *Umudei* is a ward (neighborhood, where residents are kin) within Onitsha.

11. The effects attributable to the copying process are complicated. Clerks worked under varying conditions, and the bishop had more than one clerk in his employ. It looks to me as if two clerks may have worked on Taylor's letter, because the handwriting seems to change after the third page.

12. This excerpt, and the next, from Crowther's correspondence come from the same packet as the letter quoted earlier in the chapter. As I mentioned, however, there is more than one statement by Crowther in the packet. This passage comes from the bishop's summary of events.

References

Unpublished Sources

Church Missionary Society (London), Archives relating to Africa, 1803–1923. Niger Mission, Crowther letters and journals, CMS C A3/ 04(a). (Church Missionary Society Archives relating to Africa, Mauritius, Madagascar, and Palestine, 1799–1923, records on microfilm, Center for Research Libraries, Chicago.)

Crowther, Samuel Ajayi. 1874. A charge delivered at Onitsha on the banks of the Niger on the 13th October, 1874. CMS C A3/ 04(a). (Records on microfilm, as above.)

Crowther, Samuel Ajayi. 1875. Annual Report [of Niger Mission], 1875. CMS C A3/ 04(b). (Records on microfilm, as above.)

Published Sources

Althusser, Louis. [1970] 1994. Ideology and ideological state apparatuses (Notes toward an investigation). In *Mapping Ideology*, ed. Slavoj Žižek, 100–140. London: Verso. First published 1970 in *La Pensée;* this translation from *Essays on Ideology*, London: Verso, 1984.

Benveniste, Emile [1946] 1971. Relationships of person in the verb. In *Problems in General Linguistics*, 195–204. Trans. Mary Elizabeth Meek. Coral Gables: University of Miami Press. First published 1946, *Bulletin de la société de linguistique de Paris* 43: 1–12.

Du Bois, John W. 2007. The stance triangle. In *Stancetaking in Discourse*, ed. Robert Englebretson, 139–182. Amsterdam and Philadelphia: John Benjamins.

Goffman, Erving. 1976. Replies and responses. *Language in Society* 5: 257–313.

———. 1981. Radio talk: A study of the ways of our errors. In *Forms of Talk*, 197–327. Philadelphia: University of Pennsylvania Press.

Harré, Rom, and Luk Van Langenhove. 1991. Varieties of positioning. *Journal for the Theory of Social Behaviour* 21(4): 393–407.

———. 1999. *Positioning Theory: Moral Contexts of Intentional Action*. Malden, MA: Blackwell.

Hill, Jane H. 1995. The voices of Don Gabriel. In *The Dialogic Emergence of Culture*, ed. Dennis Tedlock and Bruce Mannheim, 97–147. Urbana: University of Illinois Press.

Irvine, Judith T. 1990. Registering affect. In *Language and the Politics of Emotion*, ed. Catherine Lutz and Lila Abu-Lughod, 126–161. Cambridge: Cambridge University Press.

Kockelman, Paul. 2004. Stance and subjectivity. *Journal of Linguistic Anthropology* 14: 127–150.

4

Stance and Distance

Social Boundaries, Self-Lamination, and Metalinguistic Anxiety in White Kenyan Narratives about the African Occult

Janet McIntosh

Introduction: The Inconsistency of Persons and the Privileging of Stances

Clifford Geertz famously characterized the quintessential Western model of the person as a "bounded, unique, more or less integrated motivational and cognitive universe, a dynamic center of awareness, emotion, judgment and action organized into a distinctive whole and set contrastively against other such wholes and against its social and natural background" (1983: 59).[1] Of course, the essentialist impulse to perceive persons as "more or less integrated" and "organized into a...whole" is an idiosyncratic notion, one that Geertz and others have described as "a rather peculiar idea within the context of the world cultures" (ibid.; see also Markus and Kitayama 1991; Shweder and Bourne 1991).[2] Peculiar or not, an ideology of organized and consistent personhood motivates the nonverbal and verbal performance of this delicate fiction, and in the verbal domain, self-narration provides one proscenium upon which speakers may attempt to order themselves. Indeed, scholars of language in Western contexts have noted how often narratives of personal experience attempt to achieve what Ezzy terms "the coherence of the self-concept" (1998: 243; see also Linde 1993). Similarly, in their discussion of literary, historical, and conversational narratives in the West, Ochs and Capps describe the appeal of—and general bias toward—representing events (and, often, by implication, persons) as if they are linear, seamless, and integrated, providing a kind of internal unity and "a sense of psychological closure" (2001: 5).

But what happens to narratives of personal experience when the self's sense of consistency, coherence, and closure is threatened? In this chapter I focus upon the narratives of former colonial settlers in Kenya and their descendants, a population that, for reasons not only cultural but also highly political, prizes the notion of a rational, level-headed, and coherent self that has remained "integrated and whole" by virtue of its relative immunity to influence by what they consider the "superstitions" of the African cultural surround. Yet this postcolonial group suffers from a dilemma, for their mystical experiences with indigenous spirits, "witchcraft," shamanistic powers, and the like frequently run against the grain of their ideologies of what they ought to "believe" (and I use "belief" here in the unmarked Western sense of subscription to a proposition's truth, with the proviso that my informants sometimes do not use the term in precisely that way, a matter I shall clarify as I go).[3] After a lifetime of exposure to local ideas, many whites in Kenya evince a complex fragmentation of the self between stances of apparent belief and of avowed disbelief vis-à-vis the African occult—a seeming paradox that is readily apparent in many of their personal narratives.[4] To be sure, the disruption of coherent stances within narrative is hardly unique to this population; Ochs and Capps, in fact, frame it as a ubiquitous tension: "when conversationalists informally recount incidents, they . . . are pulled between the proclivity to cast what happened in terms of comforting schemata and the proclivity to air doubts and alternatives in an effort to regain the authenticity of the experience" (2001: 6).

But in the case of the white Kenyan narratives I describe, the conflict between "comforting schemata" and their "alternatives" is no minor matter; rather, it is the forum for a struggle between the self-ascribed rational and distinct identity of a white managerial class and the unsettling notion that the boundary between whites and black Africans might be dissolving, and with it, white entitlement to socioeconomic superiority. Speakers, then, may concede the existence of mysterious powers, but they are ideologically motivated to abhor this very concession as a threat to their self-image.

This struggle plays itself out through the minutiae of linguistic stances. In several of the narrative excerpts below, for example, we see an array of ontological stances—many of them ambiguous or in tension—concerning whether or not the powers of the African occult exist. Some of these stances, furthermore, seem to be more ideologically motivated and strategically deployed than others. Speakers may adopt conflictual ontological stances, but their ideological proclivities motivate them to privilege some of these stances over others as closer to who they *want* to be, in a kind of performative effort to fashion a level-headed and socially acceptable self out of the contradictions. In some of the narratives I describe, stancetaking and metapragmatic commentaries upon stances are shaped by a folk understanding of a nested hierarchy of selves, in which socialization by one's natal cultural group is meant to establish a kind of "core" self that is ideologically and morally appropriate, whereas further socialization by the African social surround may inspire ontological stances that are framed as secondary, pernicious, undesirable, and otherwise in uneasy competition with the core self. And, as will be seen, ideology shapes not only the stances adopted toward the African occult, but also stances taken toward speakers' own belief—and even toward the *language* of belief itself. Stancetaking, then, performs the speaker's identity in relation to the African Other by way of that speaker's relationships toward ontology, values, language, and even toward the several different selves they invoke in personal narrative.

In this analysis of stance, I examine several different linguistic strategies white Kenyans use as they confront their experiences with and attitudes toward African metaphysics and attempt to carve out a position of ideological comfort relative to them. One such strategy involves using tropes and indices of "distance," including using certain kinds of belief (and disbelief) statements, to perform a general stance of aversion toward the African occult, as well as—more subtly—toward the speaker's own apparent belief that the African occult exists. A second strategy speaks to what might be called "self-lamination" (see Hill 1995: 116). As Goffman (1974) and others (Crapanzano 1996; Hill 1995; Urban 1989: 29) have pointed out, the "I" of discourse does not merely index the immediate speaker; it can refer also to a "kaleidoscopic" series of selves, to use Hill's term, each located in a somewhat different world (e.g., past, future, hypothetical, reported), each with a different stance. White Kenyans' discussions of the African occult are laminated with many different versions of "I," but they also tend to engage in the prioritization of some "I"s—and, hence, of some stances—as more representative than others of the kind of personhood they wish to inhabit. Although these maneuvers do not entirely resolve the dilemma at stake, they are born of an attempt to achieve some level of ideological equilibrium in the face of an existential threat.

I also suggest that white narratives about indigenous forces are sometimes infused by a kind of metalinguistic anxiety in which speakers deploy stances to establish a relationship not only with African metaphysics but also with utterances about African metaphysics. Ideologically incorrect beliefs are entertained but often not directly stated. Instead, direct professions of belief vis-à-vis the African occult are danced around, choked upon, fearfully alluded to, yet scrupulously avoided, as if their very utterance were a deeply problematic betrayal of who the speaker most hopes to be. Near the end of this chapter I contend that my subjects' metalinguistic stances are partially conditioned not only by anxiety about the clash between "superstition" and the nominally rational white persona, but also by a more complex kind of folk anxiety in which certain entextualized utterances (and their proscribed alternatives) have taken on a mystical, virtually talismanic kind of power. Belief statements, in other words, are sometimes treated by my informants as generative of a state of metaphysical vulnerability that can lay the person open to Other spiritual forces by reifying and engaging the actuality and perhaps the sociality of the powers spoken of. The stances these speakers adopt toward language sometimes have particularly high stakes, fashioning not only the self but the world beyond the self as well.

At the same time, however, white Kenyan stances toward the African occult frequently invoke issues that are in tension without neatly resolving them. Stancetaking may raise contradictions, but—like other modalities of communicative indeterminacy, such as ritual and metaphor—it does not always require a final declaration or resolution on the part of the stancetaker.

White Kenyans Today

My analysis draws on the accounts of whites born in Kenya, mostly of British descent, who are now living in coastal areas such as Mombasa, Kilifi, and Malindi. Most whites in this area are retired colonial settlers or officers and their descendants, some of them third- or fourth-generation Kenyan. Their ancestors arrived in the upcountry highlands from Europe to make a living as farmers, missionaries, administrators, entrepreneurs, and overseers of various sorts, but many families moved east to the sunny beaches of the coast when they retired or lost their lands at independence. Those in the younger generation often work in the tourism industry, managing hotels, safari companies, or deep-sea fishing boats. Some have become entrepreneurs in small or large businesses; others work in managerial positions for NGOs, development agencies, or national organizations such as the Kenya Wildlife Service. And all of them must contend with the now tenuous status of white power and authority in the postcolony.

It is by now a truism among scholars of colonialism that "the colonial experience shaped what it meant to be... 'European' as much as the other way around" (Cooper and Stoler 1997: vii).[5] To give but one example of this dynamic, colonials often perceived their own identity as precisely antithetical to the qualities they thought they perceived in the colonized Other. In the postcolonial era, too, whites who remain in Kenya distinguish themselves from those whom they call "Africans," though a significant number have devoted portions of their lives and careers to efforts to better the lot of the country's most disadvantaged people. Still, even whites would agree that by and large they remain a financially privileged group in this now-independent nation. Kenya's majority, of course, has long protested this racial hierarchy; indeed, the era of independence and the expulsion of many whites from land in the highlands were predicated on an ethnonationalist discourse that coded whites as interlopers, a discourse that continues to threaten white advantages. Most whites no longer draw freely upon overt racism or state sanctions to rationalize their privileges, yet many white Kenyans share a quiet but enduring conviction that those of European descent, whether by nature or by nurture, simply manage the country's natural resources and institutions better than most Africans, largely by dint of a rational and pragmatic kind of personhood that is supposedly distinguished from "African mentalities."[6]

The catch, though, is that most white Kenyans have lived in Africa long enough to be influenced by the cultural surround of the African Other—and it is religious or metaphysical influence that particularly concerns me here. Even in the colonial era, indigenous metaphysics held a kind of disturbing appeal and fascination (Weiner 2003; Pels 1998). In the postcolonial era, whites interact with witchcraft, spirits, and local ritual practitioners perhaps more than ever, but in ways they still find deeply discomfiting. Such intensified contact with Africans creates a tension between whites' apparent susceptibility to African lifeways and their simultaneous need to express a kind of immunity to them. It is perhaps for this reason that I found such rich narratives on the part of whites as they strove to articulate the boundaries of their identity and to determine what kind of people they actually are.

The whites I spoke to have been in contact with many Kenyan ethnic groups, but most have had especially prolonged exposure to the coastal Mijikenda, a cluster of nine culturally related groups, the largest being the Giriama. Most whites on the coast learn about indigenous religious beliefs and practices through contact with their Giriama domestic staff.[7] Giriama and other coastal groups are famous among whites for their prominent use of indigenous ritual specialists, their experiences of spirit possession, and their anxiety about bewitchment. Although there are many indigenous distinctions between positive and negative occult forces, European colonials, Christian emissaries, and (to some extent) representatives of the postcolonial state have tended to regard nearly all indigenous forces and rituals as pagan and primitive, and to gloss most of them under the negative English terms "black magic" or "witchcraft." Yet the extent of white exposure to and involvement with the African occult is impressive (McIntosh 2006). Even the oldest former settlers, those most reluctant to associate themselves with local magic, admit that mysterious bewitchments in their community have planted a seed of fear in them. And a surprising number of whites, most of them middle-aged and younger, have themselves enlisted the assistance of *waganga*, indigenous ritual practitioners, to mediate their power struggles with their Giriama staff or even with other whites.

Of course, such sentiments and practices run against the grain of white Kenyans' own religious upbringing. Settlers and officers of English descent were typically brought up under the Church of England and attended Anglican grade school; those of other faiths such as Catholics, Quakers, and Lutherans were often able to find other like-minded Europeans with whom to worship and study. In the postcolonial era, regular church attendance is no longer a part of life for many white Kenyans, and although most describe themselves as "Christian," quite a few indicate their reluctance to attach their faith to a particular denomination. Several of my subjects profess affinity for other systems of thought, including Buddhism and Scientology. Some young people frame their religiosity in spiritual rather than institutional terms, saying they see God in the natural beauty of the Kenyan landscape and wildlife, and require no church to feel worshipful. But for all, whether Christian or not, mainstream white ideologies valorize a kind of level-headed empiricism when considering the causality of everyday occurrences and activities. To believe that curses, minor spirits, ancestors, or rituals can affect one's fate is to indulge in native-like "superstition" that is part of a culture of wasted energy and paranoia that is inconsistent with Christian salvation and that currently valorized path to progress: development. After all, Western ideologies of rationality hinge upon mental states that include well-regulated, empirically justified, and internally consistent beliefs (Luhrmann 1989; Gellner 1974), purged of the quirks and suspicions associated with primitivity (although, in a familiar paradox, belief in the Abrahamic God has historically been considered within the bounds of rationality). Furthermore, indigenous religiosity threatens not only Western notions of rationality but also Western models of power, for it locates potency in mystical agents that elude control by economic, state, and other bureaucratic forces whites have historically overseen. Both white personhood and white power, then, are thrown into question by the African occult.

The discussions of the occult I analyze here are selected from about two dozen recorded interviews with male and female white Kenyans ranging in age from 21 to 83. As noted, those middle-aged and younger are most likely to have actively sought the help of African ritual specialists; whites aged 50 and above have had more limited contact with such experts, though they still have many secondhand tales to tell about, for instance, mysterious happenings amongst their staff or their white friends. Younger people also participate more than their elders in a globally circulating discourse of cultural tolerance, but this hardly extinguishes their fear of and ambivalence toward African metaphysics. Indeed, all generations evinced a general discomfort with overt, positive pronouncements of belief that might align them with the African occult.

Before I turn to white narratives, it is worth a word about my own position in this social context, and its potential influence on the interview data I collected. I was known to a number of my informants before I began this project because I had previously spent many months on the coast studying ethnoreligious and linguistic relationships between Giriama and Swahili. At the time I occasionally socialized with white Kenyans but, as a white American graduate student with an unusual depth of interest in native cultures, I was considered something of an oddity. When I returned, the white Kenyan population was surprised to find that I was focusing on them. Many were receptive and indulgent, and I owe them a debt of gratitude. I am also mindful that their complex and shifting stances I document below were at least sometimes infused by their assumptions about who I was and what I might want or need to hear. It seems likely, for instance, that my informants expected that we shared an understanding about the value of rational personhood, effective management, and other features associated with the Western world. At the same time, as an anthropologist and an American I may have represented a strain of transnational liberal humanism that has largely repudiated the legacy of colonialism, thereby provoking some measure of defensiveness on their part. Although I cannot reconstruct precisely how their stances were shaped by their assumptions about me, there can be no doubt that these narratives were not only elicited by me, but performances textured by my presence.

Idioms of Distance and Metalinguistic Aversions

As I have indicated, many whites, particularly those in the younger generations, find themselves in the paradoxical position of trafficking in local concepts while trying to sustain a strategic distance from them. Each of their conversations with me afforded them an opportunity to performatively deal with this threat to their self. In this section, I focus upon two ideologically motivated strategies of stance that recurred in the narratives I collected. The first strategy involves indexical phrases wielded to establish a kind of virtual "distance" between whites and the African occult, as well as their apparent belief that the African occult exists. The second strategy involves adopting metalinguistic stances that achieve a distance from overt statements of belief vis-à-vis the African occult.

Both strategies are exemplified in a conversation I had in the summer of 2004 with Richard, a fourth-generation white Kenyan in his mid-30s who works as a safari guide. Richard told me of a time when he lived and worked amidst Giriama and found himself having a series of uncanny experiences, culminating in his being pinned to his bed one night by an invisible presence. On the same night, Richard tells me, his Giriama servant Katana had a nearly identical experience in his own bed in the downstairs quarters. At Richard's own request, Katana consulted a *mganga*, a Giriama diviner-healer, for an explanation and remedy for these terrifying events. The *mganga* explained that the events were caused by an evil spirit who would quit the house when his current tenant left. "And what did you make of it all?" I asked Richard.[8]

1   RICHARD: I don't know I mean don't ask ME. It's just one of those things. I mean I
2   really can't sort of go on find explanation for these things but I am
3   definitely (.5) will say that I am slight—yeah I've been exposed to these
4   things so I ca—I have to admit that I am slightly (.) I do I (.5) from a
5   distance (1) feel (.5) [we both start to chuckle, perhaps at the awkward
6   disfluency of his speech] hh hh thhhat there's something there.
7   JANET: Why is it that...you phrased it that way?
8   RICHARD: Um...'cause I don't really want to be—I don't want to delve into it. Yeah?
9   I do believe from a DISTANCE there's something there.

Although my question ("And what did you make of it all?") invites a subjective report of his interpretation of these events at the time of their happening, Richard's initial response—"Don't ask ME!" (line 1)—subtly presupposes that I have asked him for an objective evaluation, perhaps of the empirical causes of these events. It also positions him as someone unwilling and/or unable to comment on such matters, as if to suggest that he is not the sort of person who ponders, cares, or knows much about them. Richard goes on to use a stock demurral that deflects any precise ontological commitments: "It's just one of those things" (line 1). Although he initially appears to have to deflected my question, he eventually states, haltingly, that that "there's something there" (line 6)—an admission he arrives at after a disfluency (lines 3–5) begotten not of linguistic carelessness, but rather of exquisite care. It seems imperative that even as he arrives at this ontological concession, he must distance himself from any straightforward or enthusiastic statement of belief. Notice, for instance, that although Richard appears on the brink of an emphatic articulation of his stance in lines 2–3 with "I am definitely," he draws himself up short with a pause, and then mitigates his claim: "will say that I am slight—." Slightly afraid? Slightly "superstitious"? One can only guess what he was on the brink of saying. At this point Richard steps back to contextualize, even justify, his aborted admission, scrutinizing himself almost abashedly as a kind of figure whose imperfect psychology stems from his past experiences: "Yeah I've been exposed to these things, so I...have to admit that I am slightly" (lines 3–4). Once again, he hesitates, groping for a stance that will preserve his preferred identity. He concludes the matter with the following statement: "I (.5) from a distance (1) feel (.5) hh hh thhhat there's something there" (lines 4–6). Notice that Richard inserts a linguistic gap, in the form of pauses and the indexical phrase "from a distance," between the first person pronoun and the verb of feeling, thus creating a discursive distance from his own admission that iconically mirrors the metaphysical and social gap he would prefer between himself and the occult. In his next utterance, Richard uses the term "belief" for the first time to indicate his ontological stance toward the occult, but again separates himself from his own profession: "I do believe from a DISTANCE there's something there" (line 9). On the one hand, it is his ontological position; on the other hand, he paradoxically suggests, he does not wish to identify with it. The coherent person of Geertz's formulation is not obviously to be found in the thick of such ambivalence, although the performative effort to sustain it is.

Richard's aversions resonate with themes I heard many times as I explored contemporary white narratives about indigenous mysticism. Many white Kenyan formulations posit a kind of social and metaphysical buffer zone between the speaker and African mystical ontologies. Again and again, my white informants told me that locals such as Giriama are "steeped" or "mired" in witchcraft, implying an almost physical permeation of their selves by these beliefs and practices, whereas whites stand at a remove from them. "I don't delve into these things," as several whites (including Richard, line 8) put it, despite the fact that several of the same people reported having used, at one time or another, the assistance of *waganga* to heal mysterious illnesses, to divine the future, or to guard against witchery. Evidently, belief that the occult exists is profoundly discomfiting, and although one might experience the occult as an ontological fact, one must not adopt an attitude or value of embracing it. An elderly retiree, Letty, articulates the tension felt by many of her peers, and in so doing, exemplifies the way some white Kenyans hold "belief" at a distance:

1   [H]onestly there is something in us:: that half BELIEVES or WANTS to
2   believe but we know we SHOULDN'T believe in this sort of
3   thing...because that's the way we're brought up that you're not
4   SUPPOSED to believe in things like that.

Letty opens by framing what comes next as a kind of confession: "honestly" (line 1). Then, before lingering on the final consonant of the word "us::" (line 1) as if searching carefully for her next words, Letty uses the phrase "something in us" (line 1), thus indexing some strange, semi-agentive "thing" within white people. In Letty's phrasing, it is almost as if white Kenyans are inhabited by some alternative locus of intentionality, something that does not map onto the identity they wish to inhabit, almost like a possessing spirit. We can infer from line 3, furthermore, that Letty appears to locate the source of desirable and perhaps enduring personal identity in familial socialization—how one is "brought up"—whereas the secondary socialization provided by the African surround apparently provides pernicious, alien messages that destabilize the desirable, core self established by upbringing. Still, this secondary self, this "something in us," adopts only a stance of "half believ[ing] or want[ing] to believe" (lines 1–2). The belief held by the Africanized alter agent within "us" is thus only indirect, partial, or inchoate, blocked by the superego-like core self's sense of what one "ought" to believe.

Letty's and Richard's words raise the question of why the word "belief" arises so frequently in white Kenyan narratives. After all, the term obviously inspires discomfort when used in relation to the African occult, and in my discussions with informants, I was careful to almost never invoke it unless or until it had been brought up by my interlocutors. But as Crapanzano (1996: 108) reminds us, "An utterance situates itself pragmatically with respect to prevailing discursive conventions, succumbing slavishly, for example, to them...assuming an ironic or parodic distance, a disengagement from them, or more radically, transgressing them iconoclastically."[9]

Among white Kenyans, the prevailing "discursive convention" in discussions about metaphysics, religion, and ontology was to answer the question of what they do or don't "believe," whether or not such a pronouncement had been overtly elicited by me. This is perhaps not surprising given that personhood in Western cultural contexts is often defined according to (supposedly) stable interior states, and that "beliefs" tend to be treated as definitive and relatively perduring elements of the person. When the topic of religion arises, then, it seems to be read as a "stance prompt," evoking, if not requiring, the articulation of one's personal beliefs. Often, I found, such enunciations took the form of entextualized utterances; repeatable, routinized phrases that may pretend to be indifferent to context, and that may be treated (whether explicitly or, as in this case, tacitly) as emblematic of group identity (cf. Silverstein and Urban 1996). In the midst of their narratives, then, several of my informants leapt from the details of specific anecdotes to general assertions about what they do or don't believe. Such stock articulations embody Western assumptions about the person and about belief as a perduring state; as such, they make up part of what Ochs and Capps term the "comforting schemata" so frequently invoked in autobiographical narratives in the face of the contradictions of experience (2001: 6). Yet entextualized professions of disbelief vis-à-vis the African occult are particularly striking when the same speaker, elsewhere in the same conversation, engages in a vexed, sometimes anguished, and typically indirect admittance of some kind of engagement with the occult phenomena being renounced or denied.

Take, for instance, my first discussion with Stephen, a middle-aged businessman living in the town of Kilifi. In our first conversation, we spoke initially about his upbringing in Kenya, his distaste for what he considered the racist mentality of many whites, and his relationship with a Kikuyu woman. After about half an hour of talk, I broached the topic of Stephen's knowledge of *uganga* (indigenous beliefs and practices). His response is telling:

```
1    JANET:   So one thing I want to know is since you've lived on the coast for so long
2             what do you know about uganga? There's a huge amount. I know a fair
3             amount although it's much bigger than I can=
4    STEPHEN: =I don't believe in it. But these people have been brought up with
5             magangarism [sic] right from the word go and it's rather like being
6             brought up on mother's milk or goat's milk you know. And maganga the
7             works of maganga is to gain money and they'll always point their finger
8             at someone else who's getting more money than they are [unintelligible]
9             sort of thing.
```

Stephen interrupts my query about his knowledge of *uganga* (and my brief, awkward meditation on how expansive this field of knowledge is) with a stock, entextualized profession of disbelief: "I don't believe in it" (line 4). His next statements naturalize *uganga* ("*maganga*rism") to those who have "been brought up with [it]" (line 4), again invoking the notion that socialization within one's natal or home group has primacy in establishing predictable religious stances. Stephen goes on to imply that *waganga* practitioners are avaricious and petty, and perhaps that their practice is more about commerce than about genuine or sincere contact with the supernatural. Yet, by the end of that same conversation, Stephen divulges that he regularly visits a Giriama diviner "up in the hills," taking her counsel so seriously that on two separate occasions he used her insights to determine which of his Giriama servants had bewitched or otherwise betrayed him and, armed with this information, fired the offending party. What Stephen's initial announcement of disbelief may embody, then, is the performance of an ideologically correct stance of social orientation away from the African Other, even in the face of an ideologically incorrect ontological stance (not to mention social practice).

This is an opportune moment to note that my informants' use of the term "belief" is sometimes—though by no means always—inflected by a distinction between the phrases "belief that" and "belief in." Robbins has summarized some historical differences between these phrases in Christian theological understanding, contending that "belief that" has tended to imply a mental assent to an ontological proposition at the same time that (by contrast with "know that") it implies the possibility of epistemic doubt toward that proposition, whereas "belief in" implies trust, commitment to act a certain way toward the object of belief, and a kind of "conviction" or "certainty" about what one is saying or doing in the name of that belief (2007: 14). Following Smith (1998), Robbins also suggests that over time, Christian discourse has tended to converge on "belief that," with its attendant focus on ontology and implications of uncertainty, as the unmarked meaning of the term "belief." In the context of my informants' discourse, however, "belief" and "belief in" have varying and sometimes ambiguous connotations, sometimes carving out primarily ontological stances, sometimes alluding more to trust in and social allegiance to the object of belief, and sometimes both. And although it does indeed seem that a common understanding of the term "belief" focuses upon the mental subscription to an ontological proposition, it also seems that in some narratives—in spite of the etymological history discussed by Robbins—to profess "belief" is *not* necessarily to index one's uncertainty, which is precisely why the metapragmatics surrounding the uses of "belief" we see here (as in Richard's narrative above and others' below) sometimes require *marking* ambivalence or uncertainty where it obtains. Furthermore, as will be seen, "belief in" is sometimes weighted more toward the ontological than toward the social or moral. That said, Stephen's above announcement that he doesn't "believe in" *uganga* (line 4) may indeed articulate a stance of social and moral alignment away from the occult rather than an ontological stance, given that he so obviously gives the occult ontological credence by using the powers of ritual specialists. Important, though, is to note Stephen's aversion to making *any* kind of affirmative belief statement about the African occult (whether "believing in" or "believing that")—a theme to which I return below.

Other interlocutors who invoke their "beliefs" move ambiguously between belief as ontological or social stance (or both), but always register their desire to distance themselves from beliefs concerning the occult. Consider, for instance, my conversation with Frederick, the 40-something manager of a wildlife park on the Kenya coast. Frederick regaled me with tales of mystical happenings and deaths by witchcraft, and after listening to these I attempted to probe his stance toward indigenous ontology:

```
 1   JANET:  It sounds like you're willing to grant there's some potential for
 2          supernatural power—
 3   FREDERICK:  Well amongst (.)
 4   JANET:  Amongst themselves
 5   FREDERICK:  Because they believe in it…the local people themselves I mean amongst
 6          the Giriamas and some of the upcountry people really believe very
 7          strongly and some of them actually could pass. (3) And if they are
 8          bewitched they're BEWITCHED and that's it. You can't do anything
 9          about it. So they REALLY believe in them. (2) I believe that—in it on a
10          fact for THEM.
11   JANET:  You believe in it how?
12   FREDERICK:  For THEM. Yeah…I believe that they amongst themselves believe it. But
13          I don't believe—or (3) I wouldn't get myself involved in anything of their
14          spirits and such because actually I think I have may be my OWN stronger
15          power.
```

Frederick's statement that "I believe…in it…for THEM" (lines 9–10) is ambiguous. At first, it poses as a relativist expression of tolerance of local beliefs, or perhaps—based on his own gloss ("I believe that they amongst themselves believe it," line 12)—the even more benign and incontestable assertion that locals believe that such things exist and/or that locals trust in and are committed to such things. Like Stephen, furthermore, Frederick goes on to offer a stock, entextualized profession of disbelief—"I don't believe" (line 13)—that, it should now be clear, articulates an ideologically correct stance (whether ontological, social, or both) toward the African occult. Yet Frederick goes on to carve out a stance of social aversion that presupposes the occult's supernatural potency, saying, "I wouldn't get myself involved" because "I have maybe my OWN stronger power" (lines 13–15; later, when I ask for clarification about this "stronger power," Frederick adds, "It's a Christian thing"). Furthermore, through his use of the pivotal word "or" (line 13) between his profession of disbelief and his statement of social aversion, we are left suspecting that the former stance of disbelief was at least partly ontological, and hence in tension with what he goes on to say ("or," after all, implies a contradiction between what came before and what comes after). Like Richard and Stephen, then, Frederick appears at some level to presume that the forces at stake exist, but he finds it difficult to concede or confess this in the form of a direct belief statement, and it is evidently important to him that he underscore a social stance of distance from the occult. Looked at in hindsight, lines such as "I believe…in it…for THEM" are a kind of linguistic sleight of hand. Perhaps Frederick means that he does not trust in or align himself with occult forces and hence, although he apparently thinks they are real, they can't affect him; if so, this phrase also has some parallels to Richard's metaphors of "distance." Whereas Richard indicates that he wishes to hold himself at a remove from his ontological concessions to the occult, Frederick displaces value-laden "belief in" the occult onto African Others.

The Many Stances of "I"

As we have seen, some white Kenyans adopt multiple, contradictory attitudes toward the African occult. Sometimes these are played out through narrative "self-laminations," in which speakers render themselves as complex beings who cannot be analytically seen in terms of "mere elaboration around a single 'essential' core of the self" (Hill 1995: 111). Nevertheless, many white Kenyans find this plurality discomfiting, particularly when it threatens the ideal model of level-headed and consistent personhood. If white Kenyans can't create cohesion per se in their narratives, they can still strive for a modicum of ideological comfort, establishing some kind of order within their own contradictions by carving out a kind of "preferred stance" in their self-lamination. In this section I expand on this process using the concept of "participant roles," a theoretical tool offered us by Goffman to help us delineate the stances (or "footing," to use Goffman's term) that speakers may adopt toward the world, their interlocutors, their utterance, and their own selves.

The concept of participant roles emerged from Goffman's observation that communication is rarely reducible to a simple dyadic exchange between a unitary "speaker" and a solitary "hearer," for interlocutors can be decomposed into more complex participant roles. At issue in the present analysis is the speaker, who according to Goffman can be broken down into several roles, including "animator," "author," "principal," and "figure." The animator is the party who produces the message in physical form—through speech, writing, or other means. The author is the one who composes the message by selecting and arranging the sentiments expressed. The principal is the person "whose position is established by the words that are spoken, someone whose beliefs have been told, someone who is committed to what the words say" (Goffman 1981: 144). And the figure is the persona projected into the audience's imagination by the utterance. Often, the roles of animator, author, and principal are assumed to cluster in the speaker (Hanks 1990: 153)—yet often, speakers' stances are more complex and divided than this. Furthermore, the speaker him- or herself may serve as a figure in his or her own narration, which means that the "phantom imagined others" described by Ezzy (1998: 246) whose perspectives we use as we narratively attempt to make sense of our lives can include versions of the self. Finally, in this analysis I am inspired by Irvine's (1996) complication of Goffman's framework, particularly her suggestion that we not restrict ourselves to a set of prelabeled participant roles, but rather identify role parameters as they emerge idiosyncratically from context.

Among white Kenyans, narratives about the supernatural often involve the laminating of several, contradictory selves, and correspondingly contradictory footings toward the African occult, yet some of these selves and footings are more discursively privileged than others. This privileging is not as simple as the distinction between the "narrating self" (or the "me-here-now") versus the "narrated self" (the "I-there-then") that some scholars of narrative have drawn upon (see, for instance, Koven 2002), for many of these "I"s appear to reference the (virtual) present, but target different components or aspects of the self, each with different stances—as Letty's discussion of the fragmented believer implies may be possible.

Take, for example, the discourse of Agnes, a second-generation white Kenyan in her early 70s, who tells me over tea and biscuits that she prefers to keep a distance from the personal lives of her Giriama servants. She urges them not to bring their family members onto her compound because "I don't want a village in my back yard," a locution that encapsulates her discomfort with being too closely associated with the African surround. Yet when I turn the conversation to indigenous religion and how much she knows about it, Agnes has quite a few anecdotes to relate—of mysterious deaths by witchcraft, of uncannily accurate prophesies, and of the *mganga* her own servants called in to put a halt to the petty thefts from her husband's office. "What do you think of all these practices?" I ask.

1	AGNES: It might be all hocus-pocus or it might indeed work. And it obviously—
2	although I personally don't believe in it there are those who do. And for
3	those who do it is obviously a potent weapon or a potent cure. Whichever
4	way it's going to be.
5	JANET: .... What do you mean when you say "I don't believe it"? Do you mean I
6	think it's impossible that any sort of supernatural something could be
7	going on? Or what do you=
8	AGNES: =no no no no. I I I grant that [she clears her throat] supernatural things do
9	happen. But [she enunciates each word distinctly] I personally cannot
10	believe IN the supernatural.

In this complex formulation, Agnes begins with an ambivalent statement: "It might be all hocus-pocus, or it might indeed work" (line 1), then seems to swing the pendulum back and forth, first disavowing "belief in" the forces we are discussing, "I personally don't believe in it" (line 2), then "granting" the existence of "supernatural things" (line 8). Finally, Agnes achieves her wished-for distance from these supernatural things with the forceful clarification: "But I personally cannot believe IN the supernatural" (lines 9–10). Although the earlier "I" of "I grant that" (line 8) offers a nod to African ontologies, and although Agnes is clearly in some fashion a principal of this utterance, this is not an "I" in which she invests her identity; indeed, her throat-clearing mid statement appears to signal a kind of discomfort with the admission. The verb "grant," too, evokes a kind of objective, evaluatory stance; a concession to facts that have (we soon learn) nothing to do with her. In line 9, Agnes shifts footing. With the word "But," her conspicuous diction, and the emphatically indexical "I personally cannot believe IN the supernatural," Agnes seems ostentatiously to perform a different kind of principalship. Agnes becomes not just a disinterested principal observing "mere fact," but an identified principal of a statement that embodies her most preferred stance (and self). Indeed, by marking her refusal to "believe in" the supernatural as a "personal" stance, she implies a contrast between subjectively held value and objective ontology. Finally, it is worth noting the parallels to Richard's locutions: through her emphatically indexical "believe IN," Agnes situates her preferred persona at a quasi-spatial distance from indigenous supernatural powers. Although African locals, she implies, are located "in" or inextricably from these modes of thought, Agnes keeps a kind of virtual distance from the very ontology she has just "granted." And notice that, like her peers, although she concedes the existence of occult ontology, she does not offer any kind of positive belief statement in the African occult.

A profusion of first person stances can also be seen in the narrative of a white Kenyan in her late 30s named Priscilla. Priscilla runs a farm on the coast and admits here her ambivalence toward the matter of indigenous witchcraft:

1   I prefer not to say that I believe or I do not believe. I remain a bit uhm (3)
2   I'm quite scared of it. I'm quite scared. I—(1) So it means that I probably
3   do believe in it … I presume that magic uh power d—— it does exist and
4   uhm:: (1) it's not a joke let's put it that way. I do respect it but I:: (.) I'm
5   quite (.) yeah (.) it's something I don't want to …

As her words fade away, Priscilla is reduced to mere gesticulation: she points her finger-tips to the ceiling and makes blocking motions with her hands as if to fend off an invis-ible adversary or create a boundary between her and the forces she finds so frightening.

Yet the boundary itself is thrown into question by her language; indeed, this stretch of talk, much like Richard's (lines 2–6), is telling for its false starts and awkward pauses, and for its exemplification of what Hill calls the "kaleidoscope of…selves…distributed in fragments" across Priscilla's narrative (1995: 139). Priscilla's disfluencies mark the challenging task of conceding the potency of mystical African powers while avoiding a direct commitment to a first-person belief statement. The pronoun "I" is endlessly scrutinized and turned over as Priscilla creates several embedded and displaced versions of the self, seeking a comfortable resting place for her identity. Priscilla opens by expressing a metalinguistic preference for avoiding belief statements (line 1): "I prefer not to say that I believe or I do not believe." Notice that in, "I prefer not to say," Priscilla's "I" indexes the metalinguistic preference of the immediate animator and principal in the (virtual) present, while with her next phrase, "that I believe or I do not believe" (line 1), Priscilla's "I" embeds herself as a hypothetical animator and principal, and thereby distances herself from commitment to a belief statement. In her next utterance, "I remain a bit uhm (3)" (line 1), Priscilla hedges; the "I" in conjunction with the verb "remain" denotes a figure suspended in an indecisive state. After admitting her fear—"I'm quite scared of it. I'm quite scared" (line 2)—Priscilla comes close to professing belief with the next statement, "I prob-ably do believe in it" (lines 2–3), yet the "I" seems not so much to index the speaker in the immediate present as it does a figure that Priscilla is holding at arm's length and scrutinizing, as if to guess its state of mind. (Interestingly, her use of "believe in" evidently marks out a mental stance toward ontology rather than an articulation of social values; it is clear, after all, that she does not trust in or commit herself to the African occult, and her next statement continues in an explicitly ontological vein.) She goes on, more definitely aligning the "I" in her narrative with her immediate state: "I presume that magic uh power d—it does exist and uhm:: (1)" (lines 3–4). Yet Priscilla here uses "presume" instead of "believe"—a term that implies an assump-tion rather than a conviction, thus mitigating her principalship (rather in the same way that Agnes's word "grant" implies an objective concession rather than a subjective commitment). And no sooner has she uttered this than she begins to falter over her phrasing, perhaps out of unease that she has come so close to a straightforward first-person belief statement. In her next utterance, Priscilla safeguards the "I" by removing it altogether: "it's not a joke" (line 4), then indicates what might be a degree of relief at the compromise she has struck, through the metalinguistic statement "let's put it that way" (line 4). She goes on: "I do respect it but I::—I'm quite (.) yeah (.) it's something I don't want to…" (lines 4–5). Indicating that she "respects" these powers, Priscilla again offers a nod to the existence—and perhaps the intimidating qualities—of these occult forces, but again she loses linguistic conviction, saying only that she "doesn't want to"—to what? To take part in these magic powers? To believe that they exist? To trust in or commit herself to them? To admit any kind of belief about them? Perhaps all of these are almost equivalent, because in this cultural group, admitting that one believes something exists seems tantamount to opening the mind to it and simultaneously, inviting participation in it—a theme to which I return below. Still struggling to explain herself, Priscilla soon recovers her voice, and achieves clarity about one thing: "We Westerners are a—*pretending* to be rational. Rationalize everything."

Talismanic Stances

To explore more fully the metalinguistic aversions I have described so far, I return to Stephen, the businessman who early in our first conversation told me point blank, "I don't believe in *uganga*," but who went on to describe his extensive use of local diviners for assistance. After offering details about his encounters with witchcraft and diviners, Stephen cycles back to a striking contention he made early in our conversation—one that I heard from other informants as well: namely, that "witchcraft will only get you if you believe in it." (Although Stephen's formulation uses the phrase "believe in," I heard other variations on this claim that drew on "believe that" or simply "believe," suggesting the possibility that both social and ontological senses of belief are at stake.) Here is how Stephen explains the idea:

1	JANET: What [do] you mean it's only if you believe in it?
2	STEPHEN: If you're not with God…I believe that if you're if you're not a great
3	believer in God and you trust and you have your whole heart with Jesus
4	that if anybody does anything bad to you it'll go against you. Let me give
5	you let me give you uh my experience. A lot of the people in this town
6	who own security companies are African people. And an African (.) if he
7	sees somebody else who's got the same business as him doing better than
8	he is will immediately run to a *mganga*. To get medicine to go against
9	them to push their business down. And that's happened. To ME. And sure
10	enough I've lost a little bit of business but not to the extent of having—of
11	being forced to close down. Nearly did once. And I strongly believe that is
12	because I'm not brought up to believe in *mganga*rism. That I [enunciates
13	each word for emphasis] DO REALLY BELIEVE IN GOD AND I
14	REALLY DO PRAY WITH JESUS. I honestly believe that Jesus has
15	more strength than the witchcraft…
16	JANET: So here it's like you're NOT talking about well if you believe it then
17	you'll make yourself sick mind over matter (.) you're talking about if you

18		believe in witchcraft
19	STEPHEN:	=as opposed to GOD=
20	JANET:	=as OPPOSED to God you're sort of making yourself vulnerable to the
21		forces that are= out there
22	STEPHEN:	=yes you are that's right. There are—they have forces. That's—I've seen
23		it (.) I've seen it with my own eyes.

In this excerpt, Stephen explains that African business owners use witchcraft to disadvantage their competitors. He has been the target of such efforts, he says, and has "lost a little bit of business" as a result (line 10), narrowly escaping having to shut down his business altogether (line 11). He chalks his financial survival up to his "belief in" God and Jesus—and here again he appears to inflect the phrase "belief in" with connotations of trust, commitment, and social alignment, established through a social upbringing that overwhelms the destabilizing potential of subsequent social-ization, including exposure to witchcraft ideas. Some of my other informants, too, suggested that the wrong kind of belief can in itself make a person fall prey to witch-craft. Take, for instance, the vignette of an elderly white Kenyan named Lucy, who told me of a friend of hers (another white Kenyan) who fired a domestic servant and promptly developed strange spots on her body, dying almost immediately. She was, explained Lucy with mingled wonder and horror,

> A very sophisticated woman! Not a—you know—whatever! And she just believed it was witchcraft! And she died!...Who'd done it? [It was] one her servants who she'd got rid of....She came to see me seven days before she died. And she was all right!

Lucy's tale is ambiguously interpretable as a claim about real supernatural powers or as a claim about psychosomatic illness (e.g., through belief, one convinces oneself that one has been "cursed," and one's health falters as a result of the stress). In Stephen's narrative, however, it is harder to imagine how the chain of events linking bewitchment to loss of business could be chalked up to "mind over matter"; indeed in lines 16–18, I confirm that Stephen is not talking about psychosomatic effects. Instead, Stephen claims the reason his business was spared has to do with the fact that "I'm not brought up to believe in *mganga*rism...I DO REALLY BELIEVE IN GOD AND I REALLY DO PRAY WITH JESUS" (lines 12–14)—a faith that somehow protects the believer from the deleterious effects of witchcraft. In other words, for Stephen this "belief in" is partly but not merely a matter of moral precepts and social alignment, for it has a kind of ontological power to fend off witchcraft from the believing self. It is thus vital to Stephen that he verbally *perform* his Christian beliefs in demonstrative fashion; he is not merely a Christian; he "DOES REALLY"—and, for further emphasis—"REALLY DOES" believe in Christianity, an alignment that in Stephen's formulation gives the Christian forces extra ontological strength to trump indigenous occult ones in protecting his well-being. The importance of performing desirable stances of belief is further evident when Stephen emphasizes his belief in his disbelief: "I strongly believe [my business remained afloat] because I'm not brought up to believe in *mganga*rism" (lines 11–12). Meanwhile, despite Stephen's concessions to occult ontology ("they have forces...I've seen it with my own eyes," lines 22–23), he frames these as but a reasonable response to empirical evidence, yet like so many other white Kenyans, he declines to offer a single positive statement of belief (of any kind) in the African occult.

Evidently, belief and talk about belief, in Stephen's formulations and that of other white Kenyans I spoke to, have supernatural properties of their own. Belief and belief statements are not simply about subscribing to the truth of a proposition and/or professing trust and allegiance, but also, in their ideologically incorrect forms, generative of a state of vulnerability that can lay the person open to Other ontological forces. But how does one hold at bay such an elusive entity as belief? Although I don't wish to go as far as Needham (1974), who more or less denies there is a mental state that corresponds to the standard Western definition of belief, I acknowledge that such a mental state may often be more inchoate than many Western folk definitions of belief as enduring and context-independent imply. Particularly in situations of ambivalence or doubt, then, verbal performance comes to the fore as definitive of one's ontological and social beliefs—and as I have indicated, stance is a crucial forum for such performance. For this reason, statements of belief take on the same kind of talismanic potential sometimes imputed to private mental states, whereby to verbally admit to giving these powers ontological credence, and/or to trusting in and committing oneself to them, is to come into proximity with them and lay oneself open to them. One might even detect shades of that conflation that early-twentieth-century theorists of language liked to impute to so-called primitives; namely, the "superstition" that there is a direct, even causal or identical, relationship between words and the things to which they refer. Belief statements about the African occult must therefore be held at bay, even if an ontological concession to the occult is present.

One wonders, in fact, whether the publicness of talk raises the stakes of belief statements still higher than the stakes of private belief, in part because talk invokes a social landscape of spiritual, mystical interlocutors. As Irvine has noted, "an utterance is situated not only in the dialogic relation immediately given in grammatical person forms, but in many such relations, overt, covert, and implicit" (1996: 146). Perhaps occult forces are tacitly framed as covert, invisible bystanders in conversations about belief, leading to a special kind of metalinguistic anxiety in which what's at stake is not merely the performance of the self for human interlocutors, but for watchful occult powers that may be seeking an opening. Such conversations thus may reify the sociality of the spirits and witches, as well as—indirectly—that of the Africans who wield them, and in the process reify a host of various obligations, forms of reciprocity, and so forth, toward the African occult, toward Africans, or both, all of which white Kenyans are at risk of violating. Arguably, then, anxiety about belief is partly about acknowledging and reifying African grievances, as well as the possibility of occult vengeance. (Certainly I heard no shortage of tales from whites about disgruntled servants and other Africans casting curses and spells upon their white employers; see, for instance, Lucy's vignette above.) If this conjecture has any merit, it helps to explain white Kenyans' patterned avoidance of direct, first-person affirmations of belief vis-à-vis the African occult.

In the stances they adopt here, white Kenyans reveal their anxiety about cultural assimilation and their conspicuously bourgeois preoccupation with control over their own unwieldy minds. Yet the cognitive mastery that just might legitimate their privileges in Africa appears to be more a matter of performance than it is a psychological actuality, and even the performances I have analyzed above are frequently ambiguous and contradictory. Stancetaking may not always clarify for white Kenyans where they stand, but it nevertheless expresses some of the realities and contradictions of what it means to be a white African today. Although white Kenyans in the postcolonial era still align their values and their preferred identities away from stances marked as "African," their ontological stances appear to have been influenced by a sociocultural field that, after many decades of contact, overlaps with those of black Kenyans, creating a disjuncture between the ontological and social stances that comprise personhood, and resulting in multiple subjectivites in the process. In whites' efforts to repair the situation and protect themselves from occult harm, a further paradox arises, as they traffic in stances—such as entextualized professions of disbelief, and tacit proscriptions of positive belief statements about the occult—that might themselves be deemed "superstitious" by an unsympathetic onlooker.

Acknowledgments

Special thanks to Alexandra Jaffe, Alaina Lemon, Michael Silverstein, and Robin Shoaps for exceptionally useful comments on an earlier version of this work. Thanks are also due to the magnificently helpful members of the Cambridge Writer's Circle who offered feedback on this project: Elizabeth Ferry, Chris Walley, Ann-Marie Leshkowich, Heather Paxson, and Ajantha Subramanian.

Notes

1. Although the terms "person" and "self" have somewhat different connotations in some contexts, for purposes of this essay I will use them interchangeably.

2. The notion of the behavioral consistency of the person is one that social psychologists (among other scholars) have challenged on empirical grounds (see, for instance, Ross and Nisbett 1991).

3. As for my use of "ideology," for purposes of this paper I adhere to Comaroff and Comaroff's (1991: 23–24) definition of the concept as an "articulated system of meanings" that is generally self conscious, explicit, and "the expression and ultimately the possession of a particular social group."

4. I use the phrase "belief vis-à-vis the African occult" because in some cases the phrase my informants invoke is "believe in," whereas in others it is "believe that" or simply "believe," distinctions that are sometimes, though not always, meaningful in my informants' discourse. Because the distinction is sometimes meaningful, it would be misleading to use one of these phrases or terms to stand in for the others.

5. Indeed, among settlers in Africa, the colonial experience generated the push-pull of desire and repugnance toward the Other (cf. Cooper and Stoler 1997; Baucom 1999: 7; Gikandi 1996: 48) while furnishing the Kurtzean prospect of "going native"—a prospect that challenged European essentialisms by hinting that European personhood might just be a fragile fiction of modernity. The residue of these dilemmas continue to echo among white Kenyans, even as they have lost most of their authority to be in Kenya at all, and find themselves increasingly influenced by ideas and practices from the African surround.

6. Performing certain kinds of personhood was a longstanding colonial concern as well—see, for instance, Stoler's (2002) documentation of the colonial obsession in Indonesia

with asserting superiority not through race or color alone, but additionally through particular dispositions and sentimental patterns.

7. A few whites I spoke to have had sufficient contact with Muslim Swahili to know something of their occult practices as well, but Giriama and other Mijikenda beliefs and practices have had more of an impact on whites overall, in large part because most domestic servants to whites on the coast are of Mijikenda background.

8. The names and other identifying details of all informants have been altered. All quotations in this paper are transcribed from audio recordings. I indicate paralinguistic cues using the following transcription conventions:

Capital letters indicate the speaker's emphasis, typically through volume and pitch.

Numbers in parentheses, such as (3), denote the number of seconds of a pause.

An equals sign [=] indicates the "latching" or overlapping of one speaker onto another's speech.

Sequential colons [::] indicate a prolonged sound.

A period indicates a falling tone at the end of a tone group.

A period within parentheses [(.)] indicates a micropause, typically less than one second.

A question mark indicates a rising tone at the end of the tone group.

An em-dash [—] indicates a broken off word, false start, or self correction.

An ellipsis [. . .] indicates the removal of some portion of talk from the transcript.

9. For a related discussion of "culturally given plots" in narrative, see Ezzy (1998: 247–248).

References

Baucom, Ian. 1999. *Out of place: Englishness, empire, and the locations of identity.* Princeton, NJ: Princeton University Press.

Comaroff, John, and Jean Comaroff. 1991. *Of revelation and revolution: Christianity, colonialism, and consciousness in South Africa,* Vol. 1. Chicago: University of Chicago Press.

Cooper, Frederick, and Ann Laura Stoler. 1997. *Tensions of empire: Colonial cultures in a bourgeois world.* Berkeley: University of California Press.

Crapanzano, Vincent. 1996. "Self"-centering narratives. In *Natural histories of discourse*, ed. Michael Silverstein and Greg Urban, 106–127. Chicago: University of Chicago Press.

Ezzy, Douglas. 1998. Theorizing narrative identity: Symbolic interactionism and hermeneutics. *Sociological Quarterly* 39(2): 239–252.

Geertz, Clifford. 1983. From the native's point of view: On the nature of anthropological understanding. In his *Local knowledge: Further essays in interpretive anthropology,* 55–70. New York: Basic Books.

Gellner, Ernest. 1974. *Legitimations of belief.* Cambridge: Cambridge University Press.

Gikandi, Simon. 1996. *Maps of Englishness: Writing identity in the culture of colonialism.* New York: Columbia University Press.

Goffman, Erving. 1974. *Frame analysis.* Cambridge MA: Harvard University Press.

——. 1981. Footing. In his *Forms of talk,* 124–159. Philadelphia: University of Pennsylvania Press.

Hanks, William F. 1990. *Referential practice: Language and lived space among the Maya.* Chicago: University of Chicago Press.

Hill, Jane. 1995. The voices of Don Gabriel: Responsibility and self in a modern Mexicano narrative. In *The dialogic emergence of culture*, ed. Dennis Tedlock and Bruce Mannheim, 97–147. Urbana: University of Illinois Press.

Irvine, Judith. 1996. Shadow conversations: The indeterminacy of participant roles. In *Natural histories of discourse,* ed. Michael Silverstein and Greg Urban, 131–159. Chicago: University of Chicago Press.

Koven, Michele. 2002. An analysis of speaker role inhabitance in narratives of personal experience. *Journal of Pragmatics* 34: 167–217.

Linde, Charlotte. 1993. *Stories: The creation of coherence*. New York: Oxford University Press.

Luhrmann, Tanya M. 1989. Persuasions of the witch's craft: Ritual magic and witchcraft in present-day England. Oxford: Blackwell.

Markus, Hazel, and Shinobu Kitayama. 1991. Culture and the self: Implications for cognition, emotion, and motivation. *Psychological Review* 98: 224–253.

McIntosh, Janet. 2006. "Going bush": Black magic, white ambivalence, and boundaries of belief in post-colonial Kenya. *Journal of Religion in Africa* 36(3–4): 254–295.

Needham, Rodney. 1974. Belief, language, and experience. *American Anthropologist* 76: 861–866.

Ochs, Elinor, and Lisa Capps. 2001. *Living narrative: Creating lives in everyday storytelling.* Cambridge, MA: Harvard University Press.

Pels, Peter. 1998. The magic of Africa: Reflections on a Western commonplace. *African Studies Review,* 41(3): 193–209.

Robbins, Joel. 2007. Continuity thinking and the problem of Christian culture: Belief, time, and the anthropology of Christianity. *Current Anthropology,* 48(1): 5–38.

Ross, Lee, and Richard E. Nisbett. 1991. *The person and the situation: Perspectives of social psychology*. Philadelphia: Temple University Press.

Shweder, Richard, and Edward Bourne. 1991. Does the concept of the person vary cross culturally? In *Thinking through cultures*, ed. Richard Shweder, 113–155. Cambridge, MA: Harvard University Press.

Silverstein, Michael, and Greg Urban, eds. 1996. *Natural histories of discourse*. Chicago: Chicago University Press.

Smith, Wilfred Cantwell. 1998. *Believing: An historical perspective*. Oxford: One World.

Stoler, Ann Laura. 2002. *Carnal knowledge and imperial power: Race and the intimate in colonial rule*. Berkeley: University of California Press.

Urban, Greg. 1989. The "I" of Discourse in Shokleng. In *Semiotics, self, and society*, ed. Benjamin Lee and Greg Urban, 27–51. Berlin: Mouton de Gruyter.

——. 1996. Entextualization, replication and power. In *Natural histories of discourse*, ed. Michael Silverstein and Greg Urban, 21–44. Chicago: Chicago University Press.

Weiner, Margaret J. 2003. Hidden forces: Colonialism and the politics of magic in the Netherlands Indies. In *Magic and modernity: Interfaces of revelation and concealment*, ed. Birgit Meyer and Peter Pels, 129–158. Stanford University Press.

5

Moral Irony and Moral Personhood in Sakapultek Discourse and Culture

Robin Shoaps

In this chapter I aim to demonstrate the necessity of ethnographic research for the study of resources for indirect stancetaking and how they are deployed in naturally occurring speech situations through an account of a family of modal constructions in Sakapultek, a Mayan language spoken in highland Guatemala.[1] The constructions in question share many characteristics with constructions that have been analyzed as ironic in English, and I dub them "moral irony," due both to their similarities to irony in other languages and to their primary interactional function. Moral irony constructions, always morphologically marked, translate most closely to "as if p" in English; however, in Sakapultek p is best understood not as an imagined utterance but rather a stance. For example, in Sakapultek people might say "as if being a witch doesn't matter" when they mean to warn their addressee that her activities might arouse suspicion in the village that she is studying witchcraft or hiring a witch.[2] Thus they bear a surface resemblance to ironic constructions in English, although their morphologically marked modal nature makes more explicit some of the indexical properties that characterize irony generally.

Using ethnographically situated discourse data from a range of naturally occurring Sakapultek speech events—from casual conversation to ritual advice—I outline and present an analysis of the morphosyntactic and semiotic characteristics of Sakapultek moral irony in order to demonstrate how it provides a vital resource in Sakapultek for indirect stancetaking and what this reveals about Sakapultek moral personhood.[3] I analyze moral irony as a stancetaking strategy that acts to indirectly index "shared community values" as it criticizes stances of unspecified social actors. In indexing, rather than predicating on or directly stating, "shared values," moral irony (like all irony) requires interlocutors to collude in evaluation by the fact that they retrieve—or coconstruct—what these values might be. It is the interpretive work required for processing indirect stancetaking that contributes to its social power vis-à-vis direct assessments. Indirect stances invoke an authority—of "shared cultural values"—that lies beyond a speaker and an addressee (as opposed to direct stances, for which the speaker is primarily held accountable). Furthermore, moral irony expressions do not only indirectly presuppose moral norms; due to their indexical value they also entail them, and thus are resources not only for the reproduction of moral norms, but for their generation and contestation as well. In contradistinction to direct stancetaking strategies, for which a speaker is held responsible, the complicity of the interlocutor in determining the meaning of moral irony (and other indirect stancetaking strategies) is what allows for these forms to be used to challenge moral norms without recourse to personal authority. By locating moral authority "in tradition" (even if this "tradition" is only being presupposed as shared), speakers can challenge norms without necessarily having the elevated social status or power that are required as "backing" for reformulating moral norms propositionally.

My semiotic functional analysis draws upon Goffman's (1981) model of production formats to argue that Sakapultek moral irony is semiotically much more complex than most treatments of irony and sarcasm in English would lead us to believe, and that ironic meaning is not best analyzed in terms of a hearer's retrieval of speaker intentions. In other words, through such stancetaking resources as those discussed in this paper, I argue that social actors not only evaluate other actors and events (thereby negotiating the moral code), but also position themselves as moral authorities (see Johnstone and Coupland and Coupland this volume). In doing so, they can be said to be negotiating moral personhood, an ethnographically situated concept that encompasses morally evaluated notions or models about the relationship between the individual and the social order, as well as conventional subject positionings.

The concept of personhood originated with Mauss's classic 1938 discussion of the person as an object of anthropological inquiry—a historically and culturally situated category (see also Taylor 1989). As Agha explains, models or "ontologies" of personhood are "schemes...grounded in cultural frameworks of person-reckoning having a particular history" (2007: 241). I also draw from Watanabe's (1992) coinage of "moral personhood" in his work among the Mam in Guatemala, as this collocation highlights how models of personhood always implicitly characterize "moral" concepts, such as agency, authority, and responsibility along axes of evaluation.

Approaches to Irony and the Interpretation of Indirection

Irony has received much attention in pragmatics largely because of its indirect nature.[4] It is considered indirect in that there is said to be a mismatch between utterance and "meaning" (a distinction captured in Grice's 1989 definition of nonnatural and natural meaning). This purported mismatch has been of great interest for cognitive reasons—and has led to many studies that have probed how hearers are able to discern and interpret the unspoken aspect of ironic messages (e.g., Brown 1995, 2002; Giora 1995, 2003). According to traditional linguistic approaches to irony, the indirect nature of irony is accounted for by asserting that ironic utterances "mean" the opposite of what they say. For example, Searle (1991: 536) writes "the most natural way to interpret it is as meaning the opposite of its literal form" (cited in Clift 1999: 524). Similarly Brown (1995) analyzes Tzeltal Mayan irony as "NOT *p*," where *p* is the proposition that is uttered. This approach to irony as oppositional is also represented in Haiman's more refined assessment of the linguistic (or, more appropriately, semiotic) function of sarcasm and irony: "Whatever our social or psychological purposes in being sarcastic, *from a purely linguistic or grammatical point of view*, we are doing two things at once: we are communicating an ostensible message to our listeners but at the same time we are framing this message with a commentary or *metamessage that says something like 'I don't mean this: in fact, I mean the exact opposite'* " (Haiman 1998: 12, emphasis added).

Although researchers have increasingly suggested defining irony in ways that go beyond arguing that ironic utterances simply mean the opposite of what is propositionally stated as *p*, most of these redefinitions do not arise from examination of the social significance—or discourse functions—of irony in naturally occurring interaction. Of the existing literature on irony, the work of Rebecca Clift is the most similar to the approach that I will develop here. In a 1999 paper, Clift draws from a corpus of naturally occurring British English talk to propose a novel analysis of irony and critically appraise the prior linguistic literature on the topic. The primary aspect of Clift's approach that I will draw upon and adapt (in addition to methodological similarities between our studies in that both consider naturally occurring talk) is her deployment of Erving Goffman's (1981) notion of participant roles, most notably the distinction between speaker as animator (person who animates the message), author (person who composes message), or principal (the person responsible for the stance expressed in the message). In Clift's account, and the present analysis, irony indicates, much like reported speech, that the speaker role is divided. More precisely, in my analysis, the ironist is merely the animator of the ironic expression and has the option of distancing themselves from principalship or authorship. I will demonstrate that, unlike the case that Clift makes for British English irony, which hinges the fact that irony projects an alter *author* (who may be irretrievable) in the division of speaker roles that it entails, authorship is not salient to Sakapultek moral irony. Rather it is the irretrievability of the alter *principal* that is at the crux of its social power in moral discourse.

Before moving to the description and analysis of Sakapultek irony, it is useful to review the relationship between irony and personhood that has been proposed in the literature, which will allow us to focus more closely on what issues are at stake for ethnographic description in analyzing irony.

Irony, Divided Selves, and Personhood

Among treatments of irony, John Haiman's *Talk Is Cheap: Sarcasm, Alienation, and the Evolution of Language* has offered the most elaborate and sophisticated argument linking irony to models of personhood. Haiman illustrates, mainly through mass-mediated English examples, the many ways that irony can be cued, observing that there does not appear to be a grammatical construction (in any language) that serves only to indicate irony. Although the focus of the book is on sarcasm, which is defined as "overt irony intentionally used by the speaker as a form of verbal aggression" toward either the addressee, a clichéd phrase, or nonpresent speaker (1998: 20), many of his claims this subcategory of irony apply to less aggressive forms of irony and other seemingly dissimilar forms of indirection, and all stem from, and give expression to, what we might call a model of personhood:

> What is common to sententiousness, affectation, sarcasm, ritual language, and politeness, and what distinguishes them from metaphor, is the idea of the speaker as a divided self: more specifically the speaker's self-conscious alienation from the actual referential content of his or her message... What is common to all these genres, *including self-conscious plain speaking*, is a marked degree of speaker's *detachment from* (which is the same thing as "awareness of") the social role which he or she is performing, as well as from the message which he or she is ostensibly delivering. (Haiman 1998: 10, emphasis in original)

This alienation from the self, he argues, consists in people "repressing" their "private spontaneous genuine selves and play[ing] instead a public role" or roles (Haiman 1998: 62; 1989). Thus, underlying his discussion of irony is a model of personhood: beginning with the idea that individuals can have (or feel themselves to have) divided or alienated selves.

Haiman's book is extremely suggestive; however, his definitions of sarcasm and linguistic indirection (versus irony and "plain speaking," respectively) share a core weakness with that of most philosophers of language and psycholinguists who have addressed irony, in that their definitions of irony all hinge upon the notion of sincerity. The notion of sincerity is itself related to Western notions of personhood that construe meaning as deriving from speakers' inner states. This model of personhood is intricately linked to an ideology of communication that presumes and ideal speaking subject for whom speaker roles are all aligned (see Shoaps 2002 on the role of speaker role alignment in "earnest" prayer among North American Pentecostals). In contrast, this study examines irony and personhood in a society in which such assumptions do not hold. In a study of Samoan theories of meaning, Duranti could just as aptly be describing Sakapultek lingua-culture when he writes, "Samoans typically see talk and interpretation as activities for the assignment of responsibility rather than as exercises in reading 'other minds,'" (Duranti 1992: 24).

Irony as Indirect Stancetaking in Maya Discourse

In contrast to the functions that Clift attributes to irony—wherein it is argued to be a resource for humor, softening criticism, and for aggression—Sakapultek irony is not used humorously. Nor does it imply an "alienated," "hip," or divided sense of self as Haiman argues. My Sakapultek consultants said that irony was "gentler" than some

other ways of expressing criticism; however, they pointed out that it is used in reasonable, appropriate moral instruction. Furthermore, authorship of particular words
(*p* in the "not *p*" formulation) is not at all at stake in Sakapultek because irony does
not play upon clichéd phrasings or words so much as on negatively evaluating alter
principals who are responsible for unformulated stances. Little cultural importance
is placed originality in speech.

Part of the claim that I will make about Sakapultek irony is that it is a resource
for indirect evaluative stancetaking, which itself serves "moral" purposes.[5] In analyzing my corpus of transcribed recordings of Sakapultek conversations I was struck by
the fact that aside from relatively "low stakes" sorts of evaluations (such as positive
comments upon things rather than negative comments about the social landscape
and human behavior) in Sakapultek discourse, "direct" evaluative stancetaking pack-
aged as propositional assessments (e.g., *he's a jerk*) is relatively rare and tends to
be restricted to conversation among coresident kin and other intimates. Similarly,
stances prefaced by first-person verbs of speech or cognition are also restricted in
usage. The pragmatic and formal relationship between these direct forms and moral
irony is illustrated by the fact that my consultants were able to provide "direct" ways
of putting ironic utterances—in the form of directives and, less commonly, assessments—however, notably these direct versions of ironic utterances were not the
"opposite" of what was said in the ironic frame.

Both the lack of frequency of "high-stakes" propositional assessments and
complement-taking predicates of cognition and desire make sense when viewed
within the context of Maya sociality. Maya interaction has been widely noted for
its "indirect" nature (see Brody 1991: 89 for a compilation of Mayanists' observations on the value of indirection) and in Sakapultek, first-person complement-taking
predicates of desire and cognition, as well as evaluatively weighted lexical items
(e.g., *lazy, liar, whore*), are seldom found in gossip, scolding, advice, or any of the
other moral discourse genres in which we would expect to find evaluative stancetaking.[6] Indeed, I was drawn to investigate moral irony by way of responding to the
following question: If assessments and locutive forms, which explicitly name a particular stancetaking action and/or are marked for first-person semantic experienc-
ers or agents, are not commonly preferred resources for moral stancetaking, what
are the stancetaking resources used among communities that value indirectness in
expression?

Brown (1990, 1995, 2002) and Brody (1991) have explored the discursive manifestations of the importance that the linguistic ideologies of two different Maya
groups, the Tzeltal and Tojolab'al, place on indirection (see Brenneis 1986 and
Brody 1991 for a breakdown of criteria for categorizing varieties of indirection).
They each examine talk among women, the social category in both groups that is
held to the strictest standards of avoiding conflict or public emotional expression.
Conversational norms in Sakapultek closely resemble what they describe; indirection—for instance, through strategic use of ambiguity—is a favored strategy both in
verbal art and everyday talk. And similar to what they describe among the Tzeltal and
Tojolab'al Maya, Sakapultek women are particularly constrained with respect to the
degree of negative evaluation or contention that is considered appropriate to express
in public contexts.

The emphasis these Maya groups place on indirect expression suggests a particular idealized model of moral personhood—or conception of how the individual fits within a moral landscape. In Sacapulas one model of moral personhood (which is now being contested by Protestantism and changes in political economy) locates moral authority in adherence to tradition (Shoaps 2004). An individual's moral worth is evaluated by how well he or she fulfills his or her social and familial role as a parent, first son, daughter, and so on (see also Watanabe 1992 for an insightful exposition of a similar model of moral personhood among a Mam community). In the ontology of Sakapultek moral personhood, one does not "create" one's own social niche or destiny so much as do an admirable job at meeting or exceeding preexisting expectations for one's age, ethnicity, gender, and relationships with kin. Despite the fact that, in practice, new social roles are being negotiated as more women go to school and get jobs outside the home, and as men shift from subsistence farming to other income-generating strategies, in rural Sakapultek communities the core set of recognized age-graded, gendered, and family-defined social roles and expectations is still fairly fixed. Most important, social roles and expectations are still considered to exist outside of—rather than be defined by—particular individuals. Even as people adopt newer roles and sets of expectations, such as successful student, professional woman, and so on, there is tension around, and an effort to (at least publicly) meet or satisfy expectations of what are felt to be the more "traditional" roles as well, particularly those based upon gender and age. Furthermore, one's authority to rebuke others, draw from, or contest what are taken to be traditional community values is indexed by indirect rather than direct strategies. I argue that moral authority, felt to derive from adherence to tradition, is asserted linguistically through indirect means of stancetaking such as moral irony because they allow "traditional" values to be indexed without being directly stated (Shoaps 2004b). In contrast, "I"-prefaced assessments, or directives (the glosses Sakapulteks most frequently supply for expressions involving moral irony), index a subjective or egocentric basis for authority in which the speaker asserts that his or her own opinions are sufficient basis for taking negative evaluative stances.

The changing moral landscape of contemporary Sacapulas prompts us to approach these briefly sketched ethnographic findings about Sakapultek moral personhood by questioning how moral values are perpetuated and enacted in practice and how new values are negotiated in real- time interaction. With these questions and observations in mind, the following sections will turn to how the Sakapultek model of personhood is embodied in interaction through moral irony and how its semiotic properties make it uniquely suited for indirect evaluative stancetaking of the sort that indexes "traditional" grounds of moral authority.

Conflict as a Site for Evaluative Stancetaking

In this section I aim to draw attention to the significance of moral irony as an indirect evaluative resource within the Sakapultek communicative ecology by offering an extended example that is contextualized with respect to the social and cultural context and a set of particular, morally fraught events. In upcoming sections, I will supplement this example with briefer extracts illustrating moral irony types and functions. Furthermore, my analysis of the semiotic function of moral irony in this example demonstrates that irony does not mean the opposite of what is said.

A prime location to look for strategies of moral stancetaking, even among communities that value indirection, is discussion of conflict (Brown 1995), in which the teller's stance toward events and people is inherently implicated—putting into high relief the fact that in discourse no narrative choices are entirely morally neutral (Voloshinov 1986). In rural Sacapulas most disputes are dealt with by mediated discussions (described below) instead of courts or, preferably, to the parties involved, behind the scenes through avoidance, gossip, or even witchcraft. Thus, direct confrontation is difficult to capture on tape or to witness for those not involved in the dispute. The following excerpt from a conversational narrative is an example of the sort of behind-the-scenes gossip that typically follows a face-to-face conflict. This excerpt is informative because it not only contains a representation of conflict but it also reveals firsthand displays of emotional distress and moral evaluation on the part of the teller. Spontaneous (as opposed to researcher-elicited) first-person narrative representations or retellings of events are also interesting because, in the case of a verbal conflict, presumably the narrator recounts only the most damning and unfair actions or accusations of her aggressor, implicitly offering an interpretation of what happened and evaluating the aggressor with respect to locally salient moral norms (while positioning the narrator as blameless). When such retellings are questioned or challenged in conversation, there is evidence that the represented confrontation departs from familiar, presupposed cultural ideals or "stories."

In cases in which conflict is overt and mediated, the aggrieved party contacts the *q'atb'al tziij, ajkaltanh,* or (in local Spanish) *alcalde indígena,* a civic official who serves the community and ideally accompanies the aggrieved and any witnesses to the home of the accused.[7] Every large village or cluster of small hamlets has an appointed q'atb'al tziij, who is chosen not based upon any personal or moral characteristics, but rather to serve an obligatory *patan,* or term that all adult men who reside in the community must perform for one or two years.[8] Typically, when intervening in disputes, the q'atb'al tziij does not overtly take sides and ideally facilitates a resolution between the parties and ensures that conflict does not escalate into threats, violence, or witchcraft.

The segment below is excerpted from a recorded conversation about a q'atb'al tziij-mediated confrontation and captures an interaction in which the woman narrating the encounter is clearly morally and emotionally invested, as evidenced by her uncharacteristically public display of affect. This conversation represents the most explicit and judgmental Sakapultek "gossip" that my consultants were able to record or I was able to witness during nearly 18 months of fieldwork. As suggested above, Sakapulteks, when judging others, seldom label them or evaluate them lexically. Rather, a conversational focus is on responsibility and the social effects of actions— in this case, a neighbor is characterized as "wanting" conflict or acting in a way that demonstrates he seeks to bring about problems.

The scene is the home of my hosts, Marta and Tono, in Praxin, a pseudonym for an ethnic Sakapultek hamlet with a population of approximately 270, early one weekday morning in November 2001.[9] As we finished breakfast we heard a shrill wailing coming from the road uphill from the house. Tono went to the window and saw Yanaanh, a 50-something neighbor woman, outside, crying loudly and heading down the path to our house. "She's drunk," he informed us, grimacing at the prospect of having to deal with a nuisance (the inebriated have the annoying habit of begging money to buy more alcohol and of trying to convince others to drink with them).[10] Incidentally, drunkenness is the first explanation for Yanaanh's behavior that most Sakpulteks would offer, as displays of anger or grief are rare and primarily occur when people are. Note that this bit of evaluative stancetaking (labeling another person as intoxicated and implying, because of gender and the fact that it was during a weekday morning—women are not supposed to drink outside of ritual occasions—a moral lapse) took place in a family home among intimates—the local context most conducive to candid evaluation—and regarding a topic that most Sakapulteks consider to be a clear cut physical state.

Tono stood in the kitchen doorway and shouted to Yanaanh to take a seat on a bench in the outdoor patio while he finished his breakfast. Martanh went out and brought her a cup of coffee (a Sakapultek token of hospitality) and came back reporting that Yanaanh did not smell drunk or look disheveled. Sensing an exciting recording opportunity, I hurried to my room to ready my recording equipment.[11] Yanaanh, it seemed, had been wronged by another neighbor and had come over to complain and try to enlist Tono and Martanh as allies. A year earlier, Yanaanh's son "robbed" the baby Jesus figurine from the Christmas nativity scene of a neighbor—a local custom known as *robo del niño,* "theft of the child," or *entrega del niño,* "delivery of the child," that creates a bond of fictive kinship between the family of the "thief" and that of the figurine's owner. After the figurine is stolen, the thief's family sends a *k'amal b'eey,* or ritual speaker, to the owner's home to announce responsibility for the theft and arrange a date for its return. The figurine, decked out in new clothes and adorned with flowers, is usually returned 6 to 12 months later as part of a ceremony that involves a marriage-like procession of guests from the home of the thief to that of the owner. At the ceremony, two k'amal b'eeys act as intermediaries representing both families and perform a formulaic dialogue that creates a kinship bond between them and their guests. The thief pays for the expenses of the festivity, which include food and drink, live marimba music, new clothing, and a special basket for the baby Jesus.

Because Yanaanh's son lived and worked in Guatemala City at the time, she and her daughter-in-law were in charge of arrangements for the party that was to leave from her house. All initial negotiations and preparations had gone well, including setting the date for the festive return of the baby Jesus. Then, suddenly, a week before the party (to which Yanaanh had already invited about 50 guests, Marta, Tono, and myself included), the owner of the Jesus sent the village's q'atb'al tziij over to Yanaanh's house to request the immediate return of the baby, in effect treating this ritual theft as a real one. All plans for new ties of *compadrazgo,* or ritual coparenthood, were off, as was the ceremony. Part of Yanaanh's purpose in visiting was to assert that she would still have a party on that day, which happened to be her husband's birthday.[12] She also wanted to enlist Tono, the leader of the local Catholic *conjunto,* or music group, to perform for the first part of the party.[13] What follows is an excerpt from Yanaanh's (Y) telling of the event to Marta (M) and Tono (who does not speak in this segment). Yanaanh begins by quoting the official (glossing conventions appear at the end of the chapter):

(2) Conversational moral irony as third-person evaluation [SSAK 68][14]

1   Y: *para qué tantas problemas kicha' kaan*[15]
            Para   qué   tantas   problemas   ki- 0- cha'   kaan
            L2.For L2.what L2.so.many L2.problems Inc- 3Abs- say remain
            "why all the problems?" he says

2   *nikomalanh cha'*
            ni-   komalanh   0- 0-   cha'
            1Erg- co-mother   Cmp- 3Abs- say
            "my comadre" he said

3   M: →   *xa' t ch'o'oj t riij*
            xa'   + t   ch'o'oj   + t riij
            just + NF   problems   NF over.it
            as if it's just for problems

4   Y: →   <u>*xa'* ch'o'oj <u>t</u> riij k'anh Marta- Martanh</u>
            xa'   ch' o' oj   + t   riij   k'anh Marta- Martanh
            just   problems   + NF   over.it   DM   Marta- Martanh
            just about problems then Marta—Martanh

5   →   <u>*ni xa'* ch'o'oj riij Marta xaak'aam ol nee' laa'</u>
            Nɪ   xa'   ch'o'oj   riij   Marta x- aa- 0- k'aam ol   nee'   laa'
            Emph just problems over.it Marta Cmp- Mvt- 3Abs- Psv.bring here baby Dist
            as if only to cause problems Marta that the baby was brought

6   *# porque*
            # L2.because
            # because

7   *pa utziil pa utziil ka'al kaan laa'*
            Pa   utziil   pa   utziil   k- 0- al   kaan   laa'
            Loc well Loc well   Inc- 3Abs- enter remain Dist
            in a good manner, in a good manner it stayed there

8   *por qué kirk'am ul alkaltanh laa'*
            Por   qué   k- 0- r- k'am   ul   alkaltanh laa'
            L2.for L2.what Inc- 3Abs- 3Erg- bring hither alcalde   Dist
            why did he bring that official?

9   M: *ch'o'oj kikaaj l e'era'*
            ch'o'oj   k- 0- k- aaj   l_e'era'
            problems Inc- 3Abs- 3pErg- want 3p.PRO
            they want [to make] problems

10   Y: *pues ch'o'oj kikaaj*
            pues   ch'o'oj   k- 0- k-   aaj
            L2.well problems Inc- 3Abs- 3pErg- want
            yeah so they want problems

      ((SEVERAL MINUTES LATER))

11   Y: *pero ee ra en xinal kaan sin nada*
            pero   ee   ra_en   x- in- al   kaan   sin   nada
            L2.but Foc 1Pro Cmp- 1Abs-stay remain L2.without L2.nothing
            but then I'm left without anything

12   *por qué q'atb'al tziij kitaaq ul*
          Por   qué   q'atb'al_tziij   k- 0- taaq   ul
          L2.for L2.what municipal.official Inc- 3Abs- Psv.send hither
          why was the official sent for?

13   *pro qué ra' peetek*
          Por   qué   ra'   0- 0- peet- ek
          L2.for L2.what 3Por Cmp- 3Abs- come- IF
          why did he [the q'atb'al tziij] come?

14   *k'oo t moodo pee l ara' #*
          0-   k'oo +t   moodo 0- 0- pee   l_ara' #
          3Abs- exist +Neg way   Cmp- 3Abs- come 3Pro #
          there is no way he [the neighbor] could come #?

15   *<# achenh taj #>*
          achenh taj
          man   Neg
          <# he's not a man #>

16   *k'oo t moodo pee l ara' ch wichanh*
          0- k'oo + t   moodo 0- 0- pee   l_ara' ch w- ichanh
          3Abs- exist +Neg way   Cmp- 3Abs- come 3Pro to 1Erg- house
          there's no way he could come to my house himself?

17   *o achenh peetek*
          o achenh 0- 0- peet- ek
          or man   Cmp- 3Abs- come- IF
          or did a man come?

In line 1 Yanaanh juxtaposes the official's conciliatory *por qué tantas problemas,* "why all the problems," with a quotation of how the complaining neighbor had purportedly addressed Yanaanh as *nikomalanh,* "my comadre," a respect term referring to a relationship between them that the "robbing" and return of the Christ child would have created.[16] In doing so Yanaanh subtly sets up the neighbor's hypocrisy, a theme that is emphasized in lines 3–10. Community norms are indexed and mobilized to condemn the neighbor as Marta and Yanaanh collaboratively construct a moral evaluation of his hypocritical actions. In this case, the hypocrisy is due to his involving local authorities in—and thereby escalating or even, as Marta and Yanaanh imply, *creating*—a dispute, while allegedly blaming the resulting discordance on Yanaanh (who, in her account, was only trying to initiate a fictive kin relationship with him). In Yanaanh's telling, the neighbor (through the intermediary) couched this in the very "respect" language associated with the fictive kin relationship that his actions called off.

The linguistic resource for evaluative stancetaking that occurs in lines 3–5, and that sets the interpretive frame for the remaining lines (which involve explicit propositional evaluation in lines 9–10), is what I have termed "moral irony." Moral irony is a morphologically cued metalinguistic construction that makes strategic use of ambiguity, much like the Tzeltal irony described by Brown (1990, 1995). In addition to occurring in conversation, such as this highly evaluative (by local standards) example of talk about nonpresent third persons, moral irony occurs in other, addressee-focused

Sakapultek moral discourse genres, most notably *yajanek* "scolding"/"judgmental talk"/"gossip" and *pixab'* "wedding counsel."[17]

Morphosyntactic Properties and Types of Moral Irony Constructions

Moral irony is the only type of verbal irony that exists in Sakapultek, and it is morphologically marked by some combination of the nonfactual and modal elements t(aj), ni, and xa'. This is significant because unlike English and other languages more familiar to investigators of irony, at the time of my fieldwork Sakapultek did not have purely prosodically or sequentially cued irony. In Sakapultek, as we saw in the example above, an ironic frame is created exclusively by the moral irony morphological construction (were this frame not invoked by moral irony, lines 16–17 could only be interpreted as factual, not rhetorical, questions). The obligatory presence of morphological marking indicates that recognition of speakers' intentions is less likely to play a role in interpretation than in English irony. A closer investigation of the morphosyntactic properties of these constructions is instructive, as it suggests that the moral irony construction has a semiotic and evaluative precision apparently not found in prosodically cued ironic expression.

Modal Particles: Sakapultek Metapragmatic Resources for Cueing Moral Irony

Moral irony constructions are composed of a combination of evaluative and/or negatively evaluative counterfactual modal elements and may also contain an irrealis marker, or what I refer to as a nonfactual marker. Because the discourse-pragmatic functions of modal markers have not been well documented in Mayan languages (aside from a treatment of Q'eqchi' in Kockelman 2002), I will consider each particle that participates in moral irony constructions.[18] I use the term "construction" deliberately, as the meaning of the individual constitutive parts do not predictably indicate the meaning of the whole (Goldberg 1995). Table 5.1 presents the apparently related Sakapultek evaluative modals xa' and xaq, with examples of their use in nonmorally ironic discourse (examples of their role in moral irony are given in Table 5.3). In other languages similar morphemes have been called "focus" or "focal" particles (König 1991), and in the case of Sakapultek, when the construction flanks a constituent that constituent is "focused" in the sense that it falls under its scope. But their function is much more complex than providing discourse emphasis, as we will see in a later section. Modal particles xa' and xaq appear to be different stages of grammaticization of the same source, the scalar quantifier xaq, which seems to have undergone phonological reduction and semantic bleaching or expansion of possible syntactic and discursive contexts and moved from indicating measure to indicating negative evaluation of stances or actions (an example of subjectification in grammaticization, confirming Traugott's 1995 predictions). The semantic and syntactic properties and discursive functions are illustrated with clauses excerpted from naturally occurring Sakapultek discourse (when followed by recording number in brackets) or elicited forms based on conversations I witnessed but did not record and were approved by multiple native speakers. Evaluative modal particles are underlined in the examples, for ease of reference.[19]

TABLE 5.1 Sakapultek Evaluative Modal Particles

Form	Gloss	Syntactic Characteristics	Discourse Functions
xa' ~xu'*	Scalar quantifier 'just' 'only'	• precedes the constituent over which it has scope • occurs with NPs, VPs, and adjectives: *xu' saqa'n* 'only a little' (for food or amount of activity, etc.) • interacts with *waa* 'if' and nonfactive *+t* to form counterfactual conditional construction: *waa t xa' k'oo nipwaq kinloq'anh* 'if only I had money I would buy it'	• indexes that something has fallen short of expectation • negatively evaluates stance or action: *ee l ara' xu' yajanla'* 'she just goes around scolding'
xaq	'just'	• cannot replace *xa'* in most scalar contexts • more restricted in occurrence than *xa'* • combined with *+t(i)* in a counterfactual conditional construction: *xaq t ya' kirtij carro laa' qatoq'aaj a'n p richaq lix* 'if only that car took water [not gas] we would go up there and put the pressure on' [SSAK 02:B16:95]	• negatively evaluates action: *ee k'oo jojoon b'a laa' que xaq tal vez kikimal tziij* 'there are some that maybe just collect gossip' [SSAK32:B6:281]

*The occurrence of xa' versus xu' seems sensitive both to the vowel in the first syllable of the word immediately following it, as well as to dialectal variation and even individual preference (not all individuals observe vowel harmony in using it).

Table 5.2 contrasts the two pragmatically rich particles that I analyze as marking irrealis or nonfactual mood. The choice of "irrealis" as a descriptive label does not imply a grammaticized, or obligatorily marked realis/irrealis distinction, and is merely intended as a recognition that both these forms invoke meanings or cast utterances in the notional domain of modality or hypothetically (cf., Bybee 1998; Mithun 1995). There is some ambiguity in the analysis of how many distinct form-meaning pairings there are; negative taj and its contractions may be distinct from, or polysemous with, the nonfactual clitics. My focus in Table 5.2, however, is not on resolving this ambiguity but on the participation of taj in moral irony constructions.

Lastly, note that many of the elements in Table 5.1 and Table 5.2 can have other, nonironic, functions as well. These include negation, as mentioned above, as well as forming several counterfactual conditional protasis markers, for example, xaq t and waa t xa' "if it were the case that."

Moral Irony Construction Types

Having presented the distinct morphological elements that participate in moral irony, and their use in other construction types, I will now briefly present the variety of

TABLE 5.2 Sakapultek Irrealis Mode Markers

Form	Syntactic Characteristics	Discourse Functions
+t ~ +ti ~ ta ~ taj		Negative/non-factual marker
Nonfactual marker	Follows the constituent over which it has scope as a negative:	• Triggers nonfactual rather than negative reading when combined with other modal particles and conditional marker *waa*:
	. xinwil t b'eek l ara'	
	'I didn't see him leave'	*wee t peetek...*
		'if he had come . . .'
		[SSAK02B17:51]
Ni	Precedes and has scope over questions:	• Emphatic question marker/nonobligatory polar question marker
Emphatic or negative evaluation marker of counterfactual scenarios	*. ni k'oo kiitijanh?*	• Emphasizes nonfactual mood and negative evaluation
	'do you (pl) get anything to eat?'	
	Combines with other particles to form *ti ni (ra')*, an emphatic counterfactual adverbial that follows verbs:	
	kaaxim ti ni ra' aapwaq tza'm l aawuq ee kaaxim jun aawalk'aal 'you can't even tie your money up in your skirt, how are you going to control your child?' [SSAK15.5:3]	
	l ara' ka'pan ti ni jun Ríos *Montt p Congreso cha'*	
	'It's said Ríos Montt [politician] doesn't even show up at Congress' [SSAK22:97]	

morphosyntactic combinations of these particles that I analyze as morally ironic constructions. The following list of construction types presents the variety of recurrent combinations of these particles that I have encountered in my corpus. Each receives an "ironic" reading and is illustrated with an excerpt from naturally occurring talk; the English gloss is free but gives a sense of the "flavor" of moral irony that a more literal gloss might not convey (see Shoaps 2007 for full interlinear gloss of all examples). It should be noted that many of the following constructions also function in forming the protases of counterfactual conditionals and thus are not necessarily always "ironic," whereas all instances of irony that I have encountered in Sakapultek are triggered by a combination of these morphosyntactic frames. Aside from containing the nonfactual +ti/+t and/either or both of the particles ni and xa' or xaq, these constructions also have in common the fact that they are translated similarly by Sakapulteks into the regional Spanish as acaso que, which is best captured by ironic uses of "as if..." or "like" in colloquial English. In addition, what unites these constructions morphologically is the fact that they each involve a combination of a negatively evaluative modal marker (from Table 5.1) with an irrealis mode marker (from Table 5.2). Each construction type is illustrated with a short example taken from naturally occurring talk, and not coincidentally, many examples come from recordings of pixab', the ritual counsel brides and grooms are given by their kin the night before a wedding.

TABLE 5.3 Moral Irony Construction Types

Example	Gloss
I. *(ni) xa' t* ADJ *taj*	
Ex. from wedding advice—uncle to bride [SSAK 04:26]	
ni xa' t junam <u>taj</u> ajk'oo pa qachanh	**"as if it isn't the same** as us being in our own house"
II. *(ni) xa' t* VERB *taj*	
Ex. from wedding advice—father to bride [SSAK 06:8]	
→ *<u>ni xa' t</u> katnijit <u>taj</u>*	**"Is it that I just** offered you [in marriage]?
mayiij aapensar entonces	you thought it through"
III. *(ni) xa't [rimaal chanh]*	
Ex. from wedding advice—aunt to bride [SSAK 04:50]	
→ *<u>xa't</u> rimaal chanh k'oo t chek aawajaaw*	**"as if** because you don't have a
kaaya' rik'ex l aachonh	father anymore
→ *ii <u>n xa' t</u> rimaal chanh ya b'antajek ya estuvo*	you can put your mother to shame and **as if** he's over and done with"
IV. *xa' t [EMPHASIS] taj*	
Ex. from wedding advice—elderly aunt to groom [SSAK 39 B6:371]	
cha'nem kixwa'laj saqa'n	"get up (2pl.) a little early
→ *<u>xa' t</u> ee <u>t</u> l aachonh kiwa'ljek*	**as if your mother's the one** going to wake up first
ni ee t chek kiiwilkiij le'era'	as you're waiting until they [your parents] get up"
V. *xaq t* NP/VP	
A. Ex. of nominal modification from wedding advice—great aunt to bride [SSAK 06:18]	
<u>xaq t</u> k'ulb'ek pa q'atb'al tziij	**"as if it were just** marrying in the courthouse"
B. Ex. of predicate modification from wedding advice—aunt to groom [SSAK 48.1:5]	
→ *<u>xaq t</u> sencilla cosa kib'aanek*	**"as if it were just** a simple thing that
pwaq kraaj	happens it costs money"

The frequent occurrence of moral irony in pixab' is not surprising because pixab' is the prototypical and most ritualized positive moral discourse genre among traditionalist Sakapulteks (Shoaps 2004b.). With the exception of the example in II, all of these tokens were uttered by women, although moral irony is not considered by Sakapulteks to belong to a women's speech register or to be associated with gender.

The examples illustrate that the particles can occur in several combinations and either form a discontinuous syntactic frame that flanks a constituent (I, II, and IV), or combine to form a unit that precedes and has scope over an entire clause (as in III and V).

Morphosyntactically, some of the moral irony constructions, particularly V, resemble conditionals. This is due to the fact that, as mentioned above, xaq t also marks the protasis of a counterfactual conditional construction. However, the xaq t that occurs in counterfactual conditionals differs both syntactically and syntactically from its use in moral irony. Formally, the difference between this counterfactual conditional construction and moral irony is that moral irony lacks an apodosis or consequence conjunct: in moral irony a consequence of the counterfactual condition is never stated.[20] Semantically there is no allusion to or emphasis on actions that would be possible if (counterfactual) conditions were met.

Having presented a formal description of Sakapultek moral irony, I will now address its meaning and functions in discourse more carefully.

An Analysis of the Semiotic and Social Functions of Sakapultek Moral Irony

In this section I will build upon the grammatical analysis in order to present a semiotic analysis of irony and address the question of whether or not "sincerity" or "mental states" of the speaker need to be invoked in order to account for it. Investigation of the semiotic projections of irony, particularly with respect to the notions of stance and Goffman's participant roles, makes it apparent that moral irony constructions are at once modal, ironic, and moral, while bringing into relief the similarities and differences between Sakapultek moral irony and morphologically unmarked irony common in many other languages. Sakapultek irony—indeed, as Haiman (1989, 1998) has claimed about all varieties of irony—is "modal." I will argue that irony's modal nature stems from semiotic processes that alter the production format of utterances. In my view, linguistic constructions that fall into the notional domain of modality are indeed metalinguistic (as others have recognized), though not in the ways that have been described in the literature. Sakapultek moral irony constructions are metalinguistic in that they create alternative frames, or in Kockelman's formulation, they differentiate Commitment Events from Signaling or Speaking Events (Kockelman 2005; see also Jakobson 1971). In the analysis I present here I probe the implications of shifts in footing between the Speaking Event and Commitment Event further. Modal utterances create a footing in which the speaker distinguishes whether she is a "committed" animator *and* principal of the Speaking Event, versus merely the animator of a stance belonging to an alter principal in an alternative Commitment Event (the latter semiotic process I view as true of nondeclarative modal utterances).

The following segment, taken from ritual wedding advice given to a young prospective bride, offers an illustration of how moral irony combines elements of shifts in footing with the entailment of a separation between Speaking and Commitment Event in a particular way. In pixab', prospective brides and grooms each receive counsel from their kin the night before the wedding. The kin, depending on age and gender, take turns individually giving their "advice" to the young person. In the idealized case, brides move into grooms' households upon marriage, thus much advice centers on how to adjust to new kin and living arrangements. In this example, the counselor, the bride's aunt, has just spoken about the importance of behaving well in the household of her in-laws and not making her family members ashamed. After saying, in the lines preceding the excerpt, maaya' k'ix aawajaaw "don't make your father ashamed," she qualifies this, as the girl's father is deceased:

(3) Excerpt from ritual wedding counsel from aunt to future bride [SSAK 04:T50]

1   *xa' t rimaal chanh k'oo t chek aawajaaw*
     xa' +t   rimaal _chanh 0- k'oo   +t   chek aaw- ajaaw
     only +NF because   3Abs- exist +Neg again 2Erg-father
     as if because you don't have a father anymore
2   *kaaya' rik'ex l aachonh*
     k- 0- aa- ya'   ri- k'ex   l   aa- chonh
     Inc- 3Abs- 2Erg- give 3Erg- shame the 2Erg- mother
     you [can] put your mother in shame
3   → *ii n xa' t rumaal chanh ya b'antajek ya estuvo*
     ii   n   xa'   +t   rimaal_chanh ya   0- b'an- taj- ek   ya estuvo
     and Irr only +NF because L2.already 3Abs-do- CmpPsv- IF already L2.was
     and as if he's over and done with

In traditionalist Sakapultek belief, one's actions have repercussions not only on living kin but also on deceased relatives and ancestors. In this example the bride's aunt uses moral irony to index an imagined stance of some other principal who endorses the erroneous idea that because the girl's father is dead he is "over and done with," and that she is not held in the same way to standards of respectability. In doing so the aunt has indexed some other possible scenario or commitment event, in which there is a principal committed to the stance that responsibilities to one's parents end with their deaths. Furthermore, the moral irony construction goes beyond other related types of Sakapultek modal constructions (such as counterfactual conditionals) by negatively evaluating these stances or actions. In order to do this, it presupposes a shared understanding of norms or truths that the projected principal's stance or actions have violated. The mechanism by which moral norms can be presupposed in Sakapultek moral irony is one dimension that differentiates it from other types of calibrations of footing, such as Bakhtinian voicing and the evaluative uses of reported speech that I have addressed in my previous work (Bakhtin 1981; Shoaps 1999). In those examples, the culturally specific indexical values of particular linguistic features (such as a lisp as an emblem of effeteness) are presupposed as being shared; however, unlike moral irony constructions, there is nothing about reported speech construction or formal framing itself that negatively evaluates these features (rather, the "quoted" feature itself indexes a stereotyped way of being or persona). In fact, without the projection of a purported alter author of the animated speech, it is impossible to indexically link the (reported) expressions to social stereotypes or personalities (as the "quoted" speech is meant to reflect on the personality or social identity of the author). In contrast, moral irony offers negative evaluation of projected stances of an alter principal (not words of an alter author) and thereby mobilizes indexicality to presuppose cultural values and moral norms. Thus in our example from wedding advice, above, the information that is presupposed as shared is that family ties extend beyond the grave and an adult child's immoral behavior still has consequences for deceased parents. This semiotic projection is represented in figure 5.1.

This analysis illustrates that irony has subcategories that have not been attested in the existing literature. Although Haiman (1989, 1998) has treated mor-phosyntactic distinctions between types of irony, attention has not been paid to semiotic differences between ironic constructions. The Sakapultek data suggest that ironic expressions may be categorized based on the target of the irony and the nature of the evaluative work that they do: whether stances of alter principals versus imagined words of alter authors (or both) are negatively evaluated. The Anglo-American examples offered by Clift (1999) and Haiman (1998) differ from Sakapultek irony along such semiotic axes. In many of Haiman's examples, irony is a resource for implicitly (negatively) evaluating clichéd expressions or animat-ing a principal-author responsible for clichés. In contrast, in the Sakapultek data the negative evaluation is of an imagined stance—not the actual (imagined) words of—an indexed imagined principal or author. And although it is not impossible to imagine English equivalents of Sakapultek moral irony constructions, the con-verse does not hold: Sakapultek irony never hinges on authorship or resembles the examples Haiman and Clift cite. However, I argue that all varieties of irony rely heavily upon a separation of speaker roles, negation, and shared common ground.[21] For example, in both the English examples Clift and Haiman analyze, as well as the Sakapultek examples, in order to "get" the irony one must be familiar with shared presuppositions about the way the world is and the organization of interaction. For example, Clift claims that in irony the "evaluations thus make reference to such [shared] norms and standards, which the ironic utterance throws into focus by invoking them—and, often, by apparently contravening them. So it is only by reference to the generally held norm—say that rain is bad and sunshine is good—that *it's a beautiful day* is ironic in a context where it is evident that it is pouring with rain" (Clift 1999: 538). However, due to the centrality of the principal and the lack of importance of the author, in moral irony the norms are not norms about speech that is invoked in order to indirectly critique the appropriateness of particular types of utterances to context, but rather about the appropriateness of particular *stances* with respect to a realm of the "ought" and "should," which is the very definition of the moral domain. Attesting to the relationship between irony and moral evaluation is the fact that during my fieldwork it was only after I had a picture of local idealized moral norms and conventional evaluations—not just pragmatics—that I was able to "get" or process moral irony, although I felt its sting in rebukes far earlier.

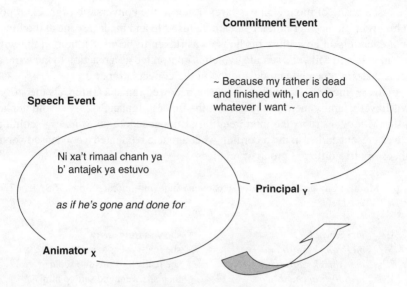

FIGURE 5.1 Modal and moral work accomplished by Sakapultek irony.

Moral Irony as a Resource in Negotiating Moral Personhood: Contesting Tradition

The Sakapultek excerpts discussed thus far illustrate the presupposing side of the coin of indexical meaning.[22] Yanaanh's statement "as if it is just to make trouble that the baby was brought" presupposes detailed knowledge of the ritual theft of baby Jesus figurines. Specifically, she presupposes as shared the knowledge that such "thefts" are performed in order to create fictive kinship between families and bring them together. Likewise, in (3) the bride's aunt presupposes as shared the cultural ideal that a person's kin ties remain important even after death.

   Let us now turn to a more complex use of moral irony in order to see another dimension of its semiotic function: entailment. In the next segment, excerpted from a recording of food preparation and dinner table conversation, moral irony invokes *as presupposed* values that do not in fact match idealized Sakapultek moral norms. This demonstrates that moral irony constructions are a powerful resource for indirectly negotiating and challenging moral norms.

   The following conversation is between an extended family about the recent suicide of a young man named Mikyel, who is unrelated to the conversationalists. Earlier in the conversation it was established Mikyel had been married to a woman who left him and took their small child to Guatemala City. One conversationalist, 65-year-old Ignacia, the matriarch of the assembled household, went to the funeral and says that she heard from Mikyel's mother that Mikyel went to Guatemala City several times to bring his wife back. His mother apparently disapproved and told

Ignacia (as a report of what she told Mikyel) that his attempts at reconciliation were just a waste of money on bus fares. Later in the conversation Ignacia reports that his sister blamed her brother's death on his wife and made a scene at the funeral by commenting on how filthy his house was (taken to be a reflection on the wife). The bad wife and Mikyel's suicide, which is interpreted as a reaction to the wife, are themes that are repeated and developed in the conversation.

In the segment that we will look at, the widowed Ignacia (I) repeats the story of how Mikyel's family members reacted at the funeral. Ignacia's 23-year-old nephew, Martin (M) coconstructs the interpretation of the anecdote (as *yajanek* "scolding") and was present earlier in the recording when Ignacia recounted a condensed version of this story to a different group of relatives.

(4) Moral irony as a means of creatively indexing moral norms [SSAK 47 B12:149–51]

1	I:	*mer riiwaal*	she was truly angry
2	M:	*mer yajnek xaarb'ana'*	she really went to scold
3		*mer yajnek xaarb'una'*	she really was there to scold
4	I:	*te' xaarb'aj chanh*	then she went and said to him
5		*chee xaab'ananh* Mikyel	"what did you do Mikyel?
6		*ni k'oo p wa' aasentid*	don't you have any sense?
7		*ke' wa' xaab'ananh*	you did this [killed yourself]
8		*xaaya' kaan l aachonh*	you left your mother"
9		*kicha' chanh*	she said to him
10		*xaaya' kaan l aachonh*	"you left your mother"
11		_ni xa'- xa' jun li ixaq k'oo p muund_	"as if there is only one woman in the world

((several IUs omitted about how there are many women in the world))

12	I:	*waa xa' utztaj l ixaq*	if the woman just isn't good
13		*waa utztaj l aawixaqiil*	if your wife isn't good
14		_ni k'oo t mood xaajiyiij jun chek aaweenh_	there isn't any way you could have found another?
15		*weeno xaajiyiij jun chek*	fine, you found another one
16		*waa t ee ra en in achenh*	if I were a man
17		*ki- ki-*	
18		*waa utztaj li winaq*	if the person isn't good
19		*aj p richanh*	have her go back home
20		*kaank'ama' jun chek*	I'm going off to get another"
21		*kicha' chanh*	she told him.

In line 1 Ignacia says that Patricia, one of Mikyel's relatives (her exact relationship is not made clear in the conversation) who went to the funeral, was "very angry," *meer riiwaal*. Lines 5–20 are direct reported speech of what Ignacia reportedly heard Patricia angrily say to the corpse. Focusing on line 10, we see the action that will be evaluated and that prompts a (reported) indirect commentary challenging local moral norms. In line 11, after accusing the corpse of leaving his mother (sons are expected to care for their parents in their old age, and horizontal and vertical kin of parents have the right to remind children of this fact), the transposed Patricia uses moral irony to suggest that a man's wife is not the only woman to whom he has responsibility. In 12–14, Patricia's (alleged) remarks project a distinction between the (narrated) speech event and commitment event, the nature of which is specified by conditional constructions in 12 and 13, a world in which it is "true" (i.e., a principal endorses the stance) that Mikyel's wife was a bad wife. In 14, she is presented as using moral irony, in the form of a rhetorical question, to invoke and dismiss the stance that there is only one woman for each man. She continues to elaborate this commitment event in 16, using a counterfactual construction to place herself as a principal and to explicitly articulate (as direct reported speech) what she would do, or the stance she would endorse if she had been in Mikyel's position.

In this extended example, moral irony—aided by related modal constructions such as counterfactual and hypothetical conditionals—presupposes as shared the notion that a man's duty to his mother comes before that to his wife, and secondly, by rejecting its converse, that wives are expendable. This assertion about kin relationships and marriage differs markedly from the "party line" of idealized Sakapultek moral values that are evidenced in pixab' for example, in which young men are told (by their female and male relatives) that marriage is a lifetime commitment and that a married man can only seek another wife if he becomes a widower and wherein men are told that their wives are now their "mothers." My consultants noted the fact that in this excerpt Patricia utilizes moral irony to challenge "traditional" beliefs about marriage, in which it was held that it is shameful to separate for any reason (causing much suffering to women in the past). In Ignacia's representation of the funeral encounter, Patricia uses the appearance of presupposition offered by the moral irony construction in order to indirectly assert a different value as a shared one.

Moral irony is a powerful linguistic resource for implicitly ordering the social world because it allows for just this type of resistance. The ability to account for change, resistance and challenges to normative behaviors and normative stances can be seen as a prerequisite for any overall theorizing of relating "subjectivity," language and morality (see Kulick and Schieffelin 2004). We can easily imagine explicit evaluative stancetaking that openly challenges moral norms, but for others to take heed of the new "prescriptions," the person doing the challenging usually has to have a great measure of status and power, and do the challenging in a cultural context that allows direct evaluative stancetaking. How can moral norms be challenged and evaluated *without* access to positional privilege or recourse to confrontational, direct evaluation? In the Sakapultek context moral irony is one solution to this dilemma.

Furthermore, moral irony and indirect stancetaking generally, due to the amount of inference and work interlocutor must do, make interlocutors complicit in the speaker's evaluation and thus provide powerful tools for negotiation of moral norms (see Scheibman 2007 on the moral work performed by generalizations in English, which also distance speakers from their evaluative stances). Some of the power of irony as a resource lies in its being "simultaneously assertion and denial: a way of mentioning the unmentionable" (Clift 1999: 544). The interpretation of Sakapultek moral irony requires that interlocutors participate in presupposing as shared particular norms and stances.

This evaluative potency accounts for why moral irony occurs most commonly in scolding, gossip, and pixab'—all of them socially "risky" contexts in which interlocutors morally evaluate other social actors and primary sites of tension in Sacapulas (witness the confrontation Yanaanh describes). One formal difference between the social repercussions of moral irony in two different moral discourse genres—what Sakapulteks call scolding and wedding advice—is that in the latter the principal could be taken to be the addressee. For example, in (3), when the bride's aunt says "as if your father is over and done with," she leaves open the possibility that the bride herself is the principal or (Im)moral Other who is responsible for the rejected stance. If someone who is not socially entitled to "scold" an interlocutor uses moral irony that suggests the identity of the principal could potentially be the addressee (i.e., any use of moral irony outside of what North Americans would call "gossip"), the speaker is subject to being accused of scolding, a culturally circumscribed activity.

We can summarize the relationship between the modal and moral work accomplished by Sakapultek moral irony in terms of the distinct linguistic elements that participate in the construction. For example, with reference to (3):

Summary of Social and Semiotic Functions

- Irrealis particle ni and nonfactual clitic +t indicate the proposition is nonfactual
- xa' negatively evaluates the proposition—positions it as counter to expectations and norms
- Moral norms that are violated by the proposition are presupposed as shared knowledge; for example, in (3) these may include:

  - one has a responsibility to be behave well even if parents aren't around (or because one's father isn't around, one cannot stop avoiding behavior that brings shame to the family)
  - one is responsible that one's actions do not bring shame to living and dead relatives

  - Interpretively, the interlocutor is invited to "connect the dots"—by supplying what the presupposed norms are and matching them to how they are violated by the principal's action or stance.

In sum, in all discourse environments moral irony involves the interlocutor in evaluation. It is thus an available resource for intersubjective evaluation, making it an effective tool for reproducing or subtly challenging social norms as well as implicitly rebuking the behavior of others. As Clift observes, "even understanding the irony—for which one must share enough of the ironist's assumptions in the first place—effectively makes the addressee complicit in the attack" (1999: 545).

Conclusion

In this chapter I have argued that the constructions that I have called "moral irony" are at once modal, ironic, and moral. In my analysis, moral irony is "modal" not only because the construction makes use of modal particles, but because, semiotically, it projects a realm of possible stances and actions and a possible division between the speaker or animator and principal or agent who takes responsibility for or is committed to the hypothetical stance or action. It is "ironic" in the sense that it indicates that the Goffmanian principal who is committed to the possible stance is distinct from the animator who, in the moment of speaking, rejects the stance or action. Moral irony is "moral" because it negatively evaluates the possible stance by presupposing as shared (and perhaps merely entailing) a set of norms that are violated by it. Because the norms subscribed to and the intended identity of the principal are implicit or presupposed, the interlocutor is actively engaged in coconstructing the evaluative stance. This is evidence that stancetaking needs to be considered not as the direct transmission of a speaker's private interior states, but rather as a public, interactive process (Engelbretson 2007). Furthermore, moral irony allows speakers to indirectly propose (by presupposing as shared) moral norms—in effect, to indirectly negotiate moral values and concepts in real time. In sum, in Sakapultek, moral irony is an important evaluative stancetaking strategy that positions speech event participants with respect to imagined principals whose stances and actions are characterized as violating moral norms.

On a larger scale, the example of Sakapultek moral irony suggests a specific relationship between culturally variable models of personhood or "subjectivity" and particular linguistic resources. In contrast to much of the writing about irony in Anglo-American contexts, the interpretation of Sakapultek irony is not considered by Sakapulteks to hinge upon intuiting speaker's intentions any more than other sorts of language use. In introducing the importance of the Goffmanian principal to the discussion of stance, differences between a Western folk model of meaning and subjective expression and Sakapultek stancetaking practices come into sharp focus. More important than sincerity in determining the meaning of ironic utterances is the ability to intuit what are presupposed (therefore indexed) as moral norms: precisely the "unsaid" portion of moral irony. In other words, accounting for irony, not only in the Sakapultek case, but in general, hinges not on intention but on indexicality. And our analyses must ask what moral values and cultural concepts (including, in the Western case, concepts of "real meanings," "hollow words," and "intentions") are indexed by ironic forms. Thus, the empirical study of the interconnection between ideologies of communication, models of personhood, and axes of moral evaluation—ethnography—is crucial in understanding the social functions of stance markers.

In closing, by illustrating how irony is inescapably moral and suggesting that analyses that focus primarily on defining it as "meaning the opposite of saying" fail to capture its complexity as a social resource, I hope to inspire future research on manifestations of linguistic subjectivity and stancetaking to include a deeper consideration of ethnographically situated talk and how cultural concepts—rather than intentions—are indexed by linguistic resources.

Acknowledgments

Ethnographic research for this study was facilitated and supported by a predoctoral research grant from the Wenner-Gren Foundation (#6602), a social science/humanities small grant, and a graduate dissertation fellowship, both of the latter awarded by the University of California, Santa Barbara. It is based on over 18 months of linguistic and participant-observation fieldwork in a rural Sakapultek-speaking hamlet, "Praxkin." I will be eternally indebted to my Sakapultek family, friends, neighbors, and teachers for generously sharing so much of their lives with me and for their aid in recording, transcribing, and explaining Sakapultek discourse. In particular, Griselda Flores Vasquez and Maria Dionicio Lopez generously aided me with the transcription and double-checked my analysis of the particular data herein.

Portions of this chapter have appeared as Shoaps 2007. I am grateful to the editors of *Pragmatics* for permission to reprint them here. Furthermore, I would like to express my gratitude to Misty Jaffe for her comments and useful suggestions in revising it for this venue. Of course, all errors and shortcomings that still remain are my own.

Notes

Sakapultek Glossing Conventions

1	first-person singular
2	second-person singular
3	third-person singular
1p	first-person plural
2p	second-person plural
3p	third-person plural
Abs	absolutive
AP	antipassive
Cmp	completive
CmPsv	completive passive
Dat	dative
Dem	demonstrative
Dist	distal deictic
DM	discourse marker
Emph	emphatic
Erg	ergative
Foc	focus
FS	false start
HRSY	hearsay
IF	intransitive phrase final
Inc	incomplete
Iter	iterative
L2	Spanish codeswitching
Loc	locative
Mvt	movement
Neg	negative
NF	nonfactual
Psv	passive
Pro	pronominal form
Prox	proximal deictic
TA	transitive active
TF	transitive phrase final
TM	transitive movement suffix
V:	morphologically lengthened vowel

1. Sakapultek is a K'iche' branch Mayan language spoken by approximately 5,000–7,000 people. With the exception of a small group of Sakapulteks living in Guatemala City, Sakapultek is primarily spoken in the municipality of Sacapulas, in the Department of Quiché. Sakapultek is mildly agglutinative and displays morphological—and some syntactic—ergativity. For a descriptive grammar of Sakapultek see Du Bois 1981.

2. One of my Sakapultek hosts did, in fact, say this to me, as an implicit directive not to continue to visit our neighbor, a traditional calendar priest, quite so frequently.

3. I emphasize "naturally occurring" in order to highlight that the data that I analyze come from indigenous speech events and are not the response to elicitation or informal interviews with the researcher.

4. See Shoaps 2007 for a more thorough discussion of the literature on irony.

5. The "direct" stancetaking resources that Sakapultek moral irony stands in contrast to include assessments and first-person marked verbs of speaking and cognition (such as *kimb'aj* "I say [she lied]," which is rather like *I think* in English, *nigaan* "I'd like [the police to arrest him," *kwaaj* "I want [her to go away]," etc.). An investigation of these forms would require another study.

6. This observation is based on the analysis of a corpus of over 30 hours of recordings of naturally occurring Sakapultek talk, representing a range of speech genres and social categories of participants.

7. Offices such as *alcalde indígena* are known as *cargos*, part of a widespread form of civil-religious organization introduced to Latin America by Spanish colonial authorities. On the cargo system among Mesoamerican communities, see Cancian (1965) and Chance and Taylor (1985).

8. In Sacapulas the other responsibilities of this post include delivering mail and messages from the town center to the villages and attending regular meetings with other *alcaldes indígenas*. The concerns raised in these meetings are reported to the elected *alcalde* of the municipality of Sacapulas. This institution is apparently much less beholden to municipal center authority than in the past, when, according to my older consultants, mayors used to require that the *alcaldes indígenas* obtain rural Sakapultek men and children as occasional unpaid servants, field hands, and porters for the wealthy *ladinos* or non-Indians in the town center.

9. No real names have been used, and identifying details have been changed.

10. Note that "she's drunk" is a direct evaluation; however, it is a highly conventional form of framing behavior and demeanor, mitigating somewhat the responsibility of both the drunk (the inebriated are not considered responsible for their actions and are condemned only if their drinking impinges upon family responsibilities) and the person who makes such an evaluation. It is not considered judgmental to assess someone as intoxicated (unless the implication is that the drinking is inappropriate to the context); rather, such assessments are regarded as reasonable descriptions of physical states of affairs.

11. A note on recording methods: in order to minimize the effect of participants' awareness of being recorded on conversation, I sometimes began recordings surreptitiously and notified participants (all of whom had given me earlier "blanket consent" to record them) just afterward that they had been recorded and asked for their permission to keep the recording to help me understand the Sakapultek language and culture. Participants were assured that I would change their names in transcripts and that I would not play the recordings for (or show the transcripts to) other Sakapulteks with the exception of those who were present in the original event or their immediate family members. I also promised to obscure identifiable characteristics of recorded participants in all published work, although people were much more concerned that the recordings be protected from the scrutiny of other Sakapulteks than they were about strange gringos and academics.

12. After the segment excerpted below she indicated that she would get her revenge by having the best party of the year, to which this neighbor would not be invited: "Let him hear the marimba all night as he sits alone in his house."

13. Incidentally, by hiring the Catholic *conjunto*, who play hymns at religious gatherings in people's homes, Yanaanh positions herself as pious and perhaps not initially interested in the *robo del niño* in order to have an excuse for a party (but rather for the kinship bonds it would have created).

14. Transcription conventions reflect those proposed by Du Bois et al. (1993): each line represents an intonation unit. Indented lines are part of the intonation unit that precedes them. The symbol # represents an unintelligible syllable, whereas speech bracketed by <# #> is a "best guess" of difficult to decipher talk. For clarity, in the gloss, I have bracketed clearly identifiable direct reported speech in quotation marks and have inserted question marks where questions are cued by prosody or morphological marking.

15. The Sakapultek orthography is based on the standard orthography for Guatemalan Mayan languages documented in Kaufman (1976): I write long vowels as double vowels, ch for a voiceless palato-alveolar affricate, tz for a voiceless alveolar affricate, j for a voiceless velar fricative, x for a voiceless palato-alveolar central laminal fricative, nh for a velar nasal, apostrophe for glottal stop and apostrophe following a consonant for glottalized or ejective consonants. I have followed Du Bois (1981) in the designation of word boundaries, particularly in the convention of separating definite articles and nonfactual clitics from the words to which they affix.

16. I went over this recording with both Marta and Tono, who agreed that line 2 is doubly embedded reported speech. They said that in such situations it is usual for the intermediary to use direct reported speech to represent the claimant's complaints as accurately as possible, lest he appear to be taking sides. Note also that Marta and Tono said that this particular q'atb'al tziij most likely spoke with Yanaanh in Spanish, as he does not prefer to speak Sakapultek publicly. Because Sakapulteks view reported speech to be a veridical accounting of the exact words (and exact code) used in a prior speech event, we can safely infer that the Spanish in line 1 is close to the official's "own" phrasing, whereas the Sakapultek, framed by a completive verb of speaking, in line 2, represents what the official reported the neighbor as saying.

17. Readers interested in the complex Sakapultek concept of *yajanek* are referred to Shoaps 2004b.

18. Following recent convention, I use the morphologically imprecise term "particles" here deliberately: the term is a convenient way of referring both to semantically empty, phonologically simple (unstressed, monosyllabic) "function" words or operators, such as xaq, as well as to clitics.

19. Refer to Shoaps (2007: 326–331) for the full interlinear gloss of these and all unparsed examples that follow.

20. Shoaps (2004a) provides an analysis of hypothetical and counterfactual conditionals in Sakapultek and their role in moral reasoning.

21. See Giora (1995) for a useful discussion of the relationship between irony and negation.

22. See Silverstein ([1976] 1995) on indexical forms as simultaneously presupposing and entailing meanings.

References

Agha, Asif. 2007. *Language and social relations*. Cambridge: Cambridge University Press.

Bakhtin, Mikhail. 1981. *The dialogic imagination*. Caryl Emerson and Michael Holquist, trans., Michael Holquist, ed. Austin, TX: University of Texas Press.

Brenneis, Donald. 1986. Shared territory: Audience, indirection and meaning. *Text* 6: 339–347.

Brody, Jill. 1991. Indirection in the negotiation of self in everyday Tojolab'al women's conversation. *Journal of Linguistic Anthropology* 1(1):78–97.

Brown, Penelope. 1990. Gender, politeness and confrontation in Tenejapa. *Discourse Processes* 13:121–141.

———. 1995. Politeness strategies and the attribution of intentions: the case of Tzeltal irony. In *Social intelligence and interaction: Expressions and implications of the social bias in human intelligence*, ed. Esther Goody, 153–174. Cambridge: Cambridge University Press.

———. 2002. Everyone has to lie in Tzeltal. In *Talking to adults: The contribution of multiparty discourse to language acquisition,* ed. Shoshana Blum-Kulka and Catherine Snow, 241–275. Mahwah, NJ: Lawrence Erlbaum.

Bybee, Joan. 1998. Irrealis as a grammatical category. *Anthropological Linguistics* 40(2): 257–271.

Cancian, Frank. 1965. *Economics and prestige in a Maya community: The religious cargo system in Zinacantán.* Palo Alto, CA: Stanford University Press.

Chance, John, and William Taylor. 1985. *Cofradias* and *cargos*: An historical perspective on the Mesoamerican civil-religious hierarchy. *American Ethnologist* 12(1): 1–26.

Clift, Rebecca. 1999. Irony in conversation. *Language in Society* 28: 523–553.

Du Bois, John. 1981. *The Sacapultec language.* Ph.D. diss., University of California, Berkeley. ProQuest accession number AAT 8211912.

Du Bois, John, Stephan Schuetze-Coburn, Susanna Cumming, and Danae Paolino. 1993. Outline of discourse transcription. In *Talking data: Transcription and coding in discourse research,* ed. Jane Edwards and Martin Lampert, 45–90. Hillsdale, NJ: Lawrence Erlbaum Associates.

Duranti, Alessandro. 1992. Intentions, self and responsibility. In *Responsibility and evidence in oral discourse*, ed. Jane Hill and Judith Irvine, 24–47. Cambridge: Cambridge University Press.

Engelbretson, Robert, ed. 2007. *Stancetaking in discourse: Subjectivity, evaluation, interaction.* Amsterdam: John Benjamins.

Giora, Rachel. 1995. On irony and negation. *Discourse Processes* 19: 239–264.

———. 2003. *On our mind: Salience, context, and figurative language.* New York: Oxford University Press.

Goffman, Erving. 1981. *Forms of talk.* Philadelphia: University of Pennsylvania Press.

Goldberg, Adele. 1995. *Constructions: A construction grammar approach to argument structure.* Chicago: University of Chicago Press.

Grice, Paul. 1989. Meaning revisited. In his *Studies in the way of words,* 283–303. Cambridge, MA: Harvard University Press.

Haiman, John. 1989. Alienation in grammar. *Studies in Language* 13: 129–70.

———. 1998. *Talk is cheap: Sarcasm, alienation, and the evolution of language.* New York: Oxford University Press.

Jakobson, Roman. 1971. Shifters, verbal categories, and the Russian verb. In *On language: Roman Jakobson*, ed. Linda Waugh and Monique Monville-Burston, 386–392. Cambridge, MA: Harvard University Press.

Kaufman, Terrence. 1976. *Proyecto de alfabetos y ortografias para escribir las lenguas mayanses.* Guatemala: Proyecto Lingüístico Francisco Marroquín.

Kockelman, Paul. 2002. *Subjectivity as stance under neoliberal governance: Language and labor, mind and measure, among the Q'eqchi'-Maya.* Ph.D. diss., University of Chicago. ProQuest accession number AAT 3060226.

———. 2005. Stance and subjectivity. *Journal of Linguistic Anthropology* 14(2): 127–150.

König, Ekkehard. 1991. *The meaning of focus particles: A comparative perspective.* London: Routledge.

Kulick, Don, and Bambi Schieffelin. 2004. Language socialization. In *A companion to linguistic anthropology*, ed. Alessandro Duranti, 349–368. Malden, MA: Blackwell.

Mauss, Marcel. 1985 [1938]. A category of the human mind: The notion of person, the notion of self. In *The category of the person: Anthropology, philosophy, history*, ed. Michael Carrithers, Steven Collins, and Steven Lukes, 1–25. Cambridge: Cambridge University Press.

Mithun, Marianne. 1995. On the relativity of irreality. In *Modality in grammar and discourse*, ed. Joan Bybee and Suzanne Fleischman, 367–388. Amsterdam: John Benjamins.

Scheibman, Joanne. 2007. Subjective and intersubjective uses of generalizations in English conversations. In *Stancetaking in discourse: Subjectivity, evaluation, interaction*, ed. Robert Engelbretson, 111–137. Amsterdam: John Benjamins.

Searle, John. 1991. Metaphor. In *Pragmatics: A reader,* ed. Steven Davis, 519–539. New York: Oxford University Press.

Shoaps, Robin. 1999. The many voices of Rush Limbaugh: The use of transposition in constructing a rhetoric of common sense. *Text* 19(3): 399–437.

——. 2002. "Pray earnestly": The textual construction of personal involvement in Pentecostal prayer and song. *Journal of Linguistic Anthropology* 12(1): 34–71.

——. 2004a. Conditionals and moral reasoning in Sakapultek discourse. Paper presented at the joint meeting of the Society for the Study of Indigenous Languages of the Americas and the Linguistic Society of America, January 9, 2004, Boston, MA.

——. 2004b. *Morality in grammar and discourse: Evaluative stancetaking and the negotiation of moral personhood in Sakapultek Mayan wedding counsels.* Ph.D. diss., University of California, Santa Barbara. ProQuest accession number AAT 3145760.

——. 2007. "Moral irony": Modal particles, moral persons and indirect stancetaking in Sakapultek discourse. *Pragmatics* 17(2): 297–235.

Silverstein, Michael. 1995 [1976]. Shifters, linguistic categories, and cultural description. In *Language, culture, and society: A book of readings*, ed. Ben G. Blount, 187–221. Prospect Heights, IL: Waveland Press.

Taylor, Charles. 1989. *Sources of the self: The making of modern identity*. Cambridge, MA: Harvard University Press.

Traugott, Elizabeth. 1995. Subjectification in grammaticalisation. In *Subjectivity and subjectivisation: linguistic perspectives*, ed. Dieter Stein and Susan Wright, 31–54. Cambridge: Cambridge University Press.

Voloshinov, V. N. 1986. *Marxism and the Philosophy of Language*. Ladislav Matcjka and I. R. Titunik, trans. Cambridge, MA: Harvard University Press.

Watanabe, John. 1992. *Mayan saints and souls in a changing world*. Austin: University of Texas Press.

6

Stance in a Corsican School

Institutional and Ideological Orders and the Production of Bilingual Subjects

Alexandra Jaffe

In monolingual contexts, speakers take stances by using a variety of linguistic forms, some of which are sociolinguistically salient. In bilingual contexts, speakers have an added stance resource: language choice. The significance of language choice is, of course, related to the specifics of the sociolinguistic context, including the political economy in which the two languages circulate as well as ideologies about language and its relationship to individual and collective identity. This chapter explores teachers' stancetaking in one such context: a bilingual Corsican school. Language choice in these bilingual schools is heavily saturated with stance significance for several reasons. First, a history of minority language shift and three decades of linguistic activism has made the contrast between the status and functions of Corsican and French culturally and politically salient in almost all domains of use. This is nowhere more dramatic than in bilingual schools, where the use of Corsican is very explicitly linked with an ideological agenda to redress the power imbalance between Corsican and French and promote and legitimate the minority language. The very same sociolinguistic history has also reinforced general ideologies linking language with collective identity and the specific value of Corsican as the quintessential marker of Corsicanness.

Against this backdrop, this chapter focuses on the way that teachers' acts of sociolinguistic stance position the two languages within the classroom, propose ideal models of bilingual practice and identity, and *attribute* stances to their students. These projected stances position students with varying levels of Corsican language competence as authoritative or legitimate speakers/authors of the minority language. The stances that teachers take are sociolinguistic because they involve both the taking of social positions *through* language choices that are already loaded with sociolinguistic meaning as well as the taking of positions on the status and relationship between the two languages and on the salience of language choice for identity and cultural membership (what I have called a "metasociolinguistic" stance in the introduction to this volume). I investigate the stances teachers take and attribute by looking at classroom interactions over time as well as in specific instances, focusing on how language choice is mapped onto the enactment of particular social roles, statuses, relationships, and identities. The argument is that patterned choices in the use of Corsican and French to do particular kinds of discursive, pedagogical, interactional, and literacy work constitute a set of related language ideological stances: toward the status and value of the two languages, and toward the relationships between those codes and identity categories—in this case, being Corsican and being bilingual.

This argument is premised on a reading of the stance potentials built into the institutional order in which classroom practice is embedded. First, the institutional order defines both teacher and student roles and participation structures. Because they are role models and agents of evaluation, all teachers' language choices are marked as acts of stance: when they choose a language, they assert its appropriateness—or preferential status—for school use in general as well as for specific school practices. In this sense, the authority of the teachers' social stances is transferred to Corsican and French: that is, teacher talk establishes stance indexicalities between the languages they use and the status and functions associated with their teaching roles. Second, teachers exercise a great deal of control over the distribution of the two languages across different categories of social and pedagogical activities. These patterns of distribution create indexical associations between each of the two languages and different categories of practice that also carry particular social meanings (from the status of particular kinds of literacies to the identity load of certain kinds of representations and performances). Teacher language choices also position the two languages with respect to each other; as such, they are metasociolinguistic stances on the nature of the relationship between French and Corsican. Teacher stances thus set the scene, within the classroom context, for future acts of stance by students using the variable of language choice. Finally, it is the institutional context that defines the paired and hierarchical teacher : student relationship that makes it possible for teachers to scaffold or project student stance. The teachers' simultaneous positioning of self, languages and students is thus both shaped by and contributes to dynamic processes of indexicalization (between language and social meaning) in this context of minority language revitalization.

Within this framework, I explore the following aspects of teacher practice as acts of stance: (1) language choice and the distribution of languages across different social, discursive, and pedagogical activities and functions; (2) the structuring and attribution of participant roles to self and students over time; and (3) performative displays in both oral and written modes. Teacher stance across these three domains of practice responds to two dynamic tensions at play in the construction of a contemporary Corsican bilingual identity. The first has to do with the dual goals of the bilingual school agenda: differentiating Corsican and French as cultural resources and lending them equivalent authority and legitimacy. The second has to do with individual versus collective models of bilingual competence. In the former, individual speakers are evaluated in each language with reference to a monolingual norm; in the latter, bilingual competence is viewed as distributed across the collectivity and across both languages.

Research Context and Corsican Bilingual Schooling: History, Background, and Agenda

The data analyzed below was gathered in an ethnographic study of a Corsican bilingual school conducted in 2000, four years after changes in French educational policy sanctioned the equal use of use of Corsican and French as media of instruction in public schools. This was a milestone for the Corsican language movement, which had struggled since the mid-1970s to make the school—once an agent of language shift—into an agent of Corsican language revitalization. By 1996, most schoolchildren were French-dominant, and this was no exception in the Riventosa village school that I studied, where only 4 of the 27 children had learned Corsican as their first language and another 3 to 4 students came from households in which it was spoken often. Like most Corsican children, the rest of the students in the school were exposed to Corsican quite regularly in the society outside the school, but it was almost exclusively in school that they practiced the language.

Because of its small size, the school was divided into two multiage classrooms, one for the 3- to 6-year-olds and one for the 7- to 11-year-olds, each taught by a single teacher with some assistance from teacher aides. Both of the teachers used both Corsican and French as the medium of instruction for all subjects (with the exception of French lessons for the older children, which were taught exclusively in French), and used the two languages for all social, pedagogical, and classroom management functions. Although both teachers sustained long stretches of monolingual Corsican or French practice, they also routinely switched between the two languages in the course of a given interaction. Both teachers were strong advocates of cooperative pedagogies, and placed a great premium on fostering student collaboration in shared learning projects. This is important background for the analysis of how teachers structured participation and responded to and evaluated student utterances. As the discussion of literacy practices below will illustrate, collaboration and cooperation were both part of the school ethos and a core didactic framework.

Elsewhere (Jaffe 2003, 2005, 2007b) I have written about the challenges faced by schools that are agents of language revitalization in contexts like this one, in which few of the children speak the minority language. Chief among these challenges is coordinating the work of language teaching and the work of linguistic identification. In classic models of language and identity that have their origins in nineteenth-century nationalist ideologies, language and identity are viewed as fused at both the individual and the collective levels. Language shift, however, disturbs this presumed essential link. Bilingual schools on Corsica are thus concerned with restoring that connection by transmitting linguistic competence in Corsican and creating the conditions in which children can acquire or strengthen a privileged affective cultural connection with the language. The second major goal of these schools is to raise the status of Corsican with respect to French and counteract the negative effects of linguistic stigma on the motivations of the Corsican general population to transmit or learn the language.

We can see that the bilingual school agenda has a fundamental concern with creating and managing relationships, dispositions, and stances of students with respect to Corsican and French. Teachers in bilingual schools are oriented both toward positioning the individual learner vis-à-vis Corsican as a language of identity, and with positioning Corsican as a language of equal legitimacy and distinct cultural value vis-à-vis French. First, they attempt to create the conditions in which children will be able to take up stances as "legitimate" and "authentic" speakers of Corsican in order for them to be recognized within a traditionally defined sociolinguistic economy. At the same time, these schools are inevitable agents of change in the sociolinguistic landscape, because they are the source of new forms of language practice and linguistic capital. Some schools, including the Riventosa one, are also fairly self-consciously oriented toward language ideological change, specifically with respect to how legitimate and authentic speakers are defined, and move toward models of bilingualism and social identification that validate multiple levels and types of Corsican language competence as well as the mixed language practices found in and out of school. The work of stance in this agenda is less direct, and involves the pairing or association of stances and participant roles that are validated within the institutional agenda with the mixed language practices and varied competencies in question.

Institutional Frameworks and Simultaneous Levels of Teacher Stance

In this section, I elaborate on the proposition introduced briefly in the introduction to this chapter—that teacher stance is simultaneously individual, interactional, and ideological—and trace the institutional origins and implications of these connections in the Corsican bilingual educational context.

Individual Stance and Ideological Implications

Teachers, like all other occupants of heavily specified social roles and positions, take up personal stances with respect to the normative expectations associated with those roles, enacting them in ways that signal greater or lesser alignment with those norms. Two salient features of the teacher role are *authority* and *legitimacy*. When teachers in the bilingual school display a stance of high alignment with these features through the medium of Corsican or French, they transfer authority and legitimacy to those languages. They also display an indexical relationship between Corsican and/ or French language use and authoritative/legitimate stance to their students. Displays of similar stance alignments with authority and legitimacy through both languages position those languages as having equivalent status; conversely, displays of different stance orientations to authority and legitimacy differentiate the languages. Because teachers are role models, the stances that they display and project with respect to the languages of the curriculum are held up as ideal ones, as well as components of imagined future adult identities.

Teachers also display (ideal) stances toward Corsican and French through affective displays of appreciation or enjoyment of the two codes as well as through the use of the codes for affective purposes, such as expressing approval or disapproval. The former are relatively directly associated with evaluation. The latter kinds of affective stance propose indexical relationships between particular codes and emotion and are indirectly evaluative. That is, to the extent that emotions and feelings are viewed as components of deep, essential identity, affective stances taken through the two languages can position them as more or less fundamental (or valued) to identity.

Finally, the teaching role is centrally concerned with knowledge construction and, thus, with epistemic stance. Again, teachers display their own personal and professional stances vis-à-vis the foundations, presuppositions, acquisition and validity of knowledge in the classroom through Corsican and French. In doing so, they link those languages (in potentially equivalent or differentiated ways) to the process of learning, which has a clear evaluative dimension in the school context. To the extent that different pedagogical practices are ranked with respect to their role in the development of valued learning processes or outcomes, those rankings can also be transferred to the languages of the classroom.

These teacher stances can be interpreted in discrete moments of interaction, but must also be traced across longer time trajectories in order to capture the patterns of stancetaking toward and through the medium of the two languages of the classroom. These patterns in turn are a crucial backdrop for the interpretation of stances in any particular moment. Finally, it is over time that teachers display durable identity orientations (Johnstone, this volume) and ideological positions about the relationship of language to identity. In the Corsican sociolinguistic context, these more durable stance orientations can be taken as modeling appropriate ways of identifying through language(s) and being bilingual.

Interactional Stance: Institutional Particularities and Ideological Implications

Stance can be considered an interactional accomplishment in a number of ways. First of all, stances are constructed across turns (Clift 2006; Kiesanen 2007) and the stances taken by individual speakers both invite others to take a stance (Kärkkäinen 2007: 212) and structure the stance possibilities for speakers in following turns (Rauniomaa 2007). As both Rauniomaa (2007) and C. Goodwin (2006) point out, in addition to being prospective, acts of stance are also retrospective and attributive, responding to and/or framing other speakers' prior stancetaking. It is thus possible for people to "take" stances that are not recognized by their conversational partners or to be attributed stances (or compelled to respond to a set of stance possibilities) that they did not choose. In short, stances are subject to social ratification, which takes place through interaction and is influenced by the interplay of agency and power that different interactants bring to bear.

Teacher-student interaction is obviously a very specific kind of talk, in which teacher and student roles and statuses affect stancetaking and its consequences. One of the most salient features of classroom talk is the high degree of control exercised by teachers over the structure of participation, the assignment of participant roles, the distribution of turns at talk, and the evaluation of student contributions. Insofar as they scaffold and assign participant roles, teachers thus shape the stances available to the children; in their evaluative role, they also heavily influence the student stances that "stick" socially.

Second, because of the teachers' roles in the education and socialization of children, teacher stances by definition are oriented toward an interactional outcome: student uptake and alignment. That is, positive alignment with teacher stance can be viewed as the preferred (perhaps even demanded) student response. This preference structure confers special ideological status on the teacher's stance even if students disalign with it. It is in this respect that we can see teacher stancetaking as an act of incorporation of students into sociolinguistic stances that are "naturalized" along with the ideologies that underpin them.

Finally, because teachers and students occupy paired and hierarchically ordered participant roles, teachers' stances *entail* student ones. If teachers position themselves as audiences, children are positioned as performers; if teachers attenuate their displays of authority, children are attributed a stance of greater autonomy, and so forth. In other words, teachers' acts of personal stance activate paired roles, treat students as holding particular positions, and thereby attribute stance to them.

These acts of student stance attribution and ratification have implications for those students' processes of linguistic and cultural identification. They add an experiential dimension to the teachers' modeling of ideal ways to be bilingual: students are incorporated (by being "treated as" particular kinds of speakers and social actors) into idealized frameworks for language and cultural identity.

In the following two sections, I explore how the teachers in this school took up metalinguistic stances with respect to Corsican and French through the explicit, evaluative stances they displayed toward linguistic form and esthetics, through acts of alignment with the authority associated with the teacher role (in particular, evaluation and assessment) enacted through the two languages, and through the social and affective work they did in interaction. The following section focuses on how these acts of stance position Corsican and French as equivalent in status and legitimacy; the one after it describes how the two languages are differentiated. This is followed by a more detailed analysis of how trajectories of texts and participant roles over time scaffold and attribute stances of legitimate authorship in Corsican to students and propose a model of collective linguistic competence and identity. The final section examines some of these same processes at work at the level of discourse structure, with a focus on discursive cohesion across languages, and provides some brief examples of student uptake of the indexical relations between linguistic stance (in particular language choice) and social roles and categories.

Performing Equivalence

It should be stated at the outset that the status and legitimacy of French was taken for granted in this school (and in most, if not all, French schools). Even when not explicitly stated, it can be assumed that all legitimate functions and practices described below for Corsican were also done in equal measure in French.

One of the ways in which equivalence was performed was through the curriculum. Teachers in this school made a self-conscious effort to use Corsican and French equally in the enactment of their role as teachers and legitimate speakers and for all pedagogical practices with high academic legitimacy and status. They were sensitive to the way that the minority language could be undervalued if it was relegated to "light" or "soft" subjects or activities, and made certain to use Corsican to teach all subjects, spending considerable time developing teaching materials in science and math, which both carried high status and were often viewed as "difficult" to teach in the minority language. They also used Corsican to engage with complex subject matter and ideas and for higher order pedagogical practices such as explanation and elaboration. This was reflected in into their framework for assessment, in which they maintained equivalent conceptual and content-area expectations for children's performance in the lessons and activities regardless of the language used as the medium of instruction.

The teachers also displayed similar personal relationships to the two languages through the expression of identical levels of esthetic appreciation of Corsican and French as codes. This was expressed overt expressions of linguistic appreciation for a rare, particularly apt or semantically nuanced piece of language. "Ghjè una bella parolla" ("That's a beautiful word"), the teacher of the older children might say when a child used an uncommon Corsican vocabulary word. Likewise, a felicitous turn of phrase in French might be repeated appreciatively by her out loud and designated "une belle tournure" ("a nice turn of phrase").

These kinds of stances were also displayed indirectly through patterns of teacher practice and their attendant evaluative orientations. In the older children's class, in which there was a good deal of collective composition of texts in both French and Corsican, the teacher exhibited very similar standards and orientations toward criteria of good style, precision, poetic qualities, creativity, and so on in her comments and editorial interventions in the texts being edited. She also set the bar quite high, often prompting students to replace "adequate" but not exceptional language in their drafts with language she considered superior. This positioned both languages as equally appreciable, equally subject to the same kinds of standards of esthetic judgment. At the same time, the work of appreciation in these kinds of activities—particularly the scaffolding of student authorship—projected high stylistic competence onto all members of the classroom. In its strongest form, it had the potential to position students as legitimate authors (see discussion below with respect to Corsican). But even if and when children were not positioned as full authors, the teacher's involvement of the students in discussions of the esthetic and communicative value of different stylistic choices attributed a stance of connoisseurship to those students. That is, she treated them as being able to recognize "le bon usage" (or "good language"): itself a sign of distinction (Bourdieu 2007; see also Jaworski and Thurlow, this volume).

In the French context, the notion of *le bon usage* is particularly tightly connected with a linguistic legitimacy and authority: it evokes a single authoritative standard against which all written and oral use can be compared. Le bon usage is clearly about orthographic, phonetic, and grammatical correctness, but it is also the discursive and imaginary nexus for the link between individual linguistic practice, French as an authoritative code, culture, education, and citizenship. Speaking well is how you show your respect for the French language and, by extension, for the very idea of France. This is reflected in an oft-cited quotation from Raymond Barre, former prime minister, who said, "La première des valeurs fondamentales de notre civilisation est le bon usage de notre langue. Il y a, parmi les jeunes, dans la pratique loyale du français, une vertu morale et civique" ("The foremost of the fundamental values of our civilization is the correct usage of our language. Among our youth, there is a moral and civic virtue in the loyal practice of French") (quoted in Cohen 2000).

This language ideological backdrop helps us to understand the salience, for the status of Corsican, of the teacher displaying equivalent stances vis-à-vis good usage in Corsican and French. It also provides support for a stance-based interpretation of acts of inscription (handwriting and copying) and recitation. These elements of the "scriptural economy" are concerned uniquely with form rather than propositional content; both involve the disciplining of the body in interaction with text and, as de Certeau puts it, reflect how society "makes the body tell the code" (1984: 138). Thus we can view inscription and recitation as sites for the display of stances of respect for the form and authority of language in general, as well as of specific languages—in this case, French and Corsican. This connection was made quite explicit in the Riventosa teachers' own displays of beautiful penmanship and animated recitation of texts no matter what the language of the text, as well as in how they evaluated the neatness of children's written work and the quality of their oral presentations. For example, "substandard" handwriting in the notebook of one of the older children earned the marginal comment by the teacher, "Surtout, ne t'appliques pas" ("Above all, don't apply yourself"). Children were expected to apply themselves by writing neatly in, and showing respect for, both languages. They were also rewarded for "animating" written texts in both Corsican and French with feeling and a high regard for performance (Jaffe 2005).

These examples illustrate how stance enactment and stance attribution are linked within language-ideological and institutional frameworks. They also show how teachers' stances created structures of stance preference in the classroom. Students could take up personal stances of resistance to those frameworks; they could disalign with teachers' stances, write and recite with no attention to form, and display disrespect for language and the school agenda. But even in exercising this agency, students could not disrupt the underlying indexical connection between modes of inscription and recitation as indicators of linguistic and social stances and ideologies. In this respect, we can see how the structuring of stance potentials and of stance preference works in the establishment and reproduction of language ideological orders.

Another way in which teachers performed equivalence between the two languages was by using them interchangeably for the work of social evaluation, including positive and negative assessments of behavior, effort, cooperation in class, and so forth. The tenor of these assessments was often highly charged from an affective perspective, because of the almost familial relationships that developed in a small school in which students had the same teacher for three years in a row. In this respect, teachers displayed Corsican and French as equally powerful reflections of personal feelings.

Stance and Differentiation

In this section, I discuss those patterns of teacher stance orientations toward Corsican and French that differentiated the two languages. We can see the work of equivalence, described above, as establishing Corsican's academic parity, and the practices described below as adding additional value to that language. Against the backdrop of equivalence/parity, adding value involves preferential use of Corsican. I also document some subtle but important differences in the nature of individual evaluation of student performance in the two languages that also position the two languages (and children's relationships to them) in different ways. It is again important to situate the notion of preference for Corsican against the backdrop of the incontrovertible status and power of French in the society outside the school and in the institution of the school itself. I would argue that none of the practices I describe as showing preference for Corsican undermine the status of French; rather, given the status of Corsican, they should be viewed as only partially tipping the balance of power toward an equilibrium.

First, preference was expressed in frequency of use. Although the curriculum prescribed a 50–50 split between Corsican and French, both teachers used Corsican for more than 50% of class time. In the younger children's class, Corsican was used dramatically more often than French: so much so that some parents told me (inaccurately) that the teacher "spoke only in Corsican." Children in this school could thus observe that their teachers spoke Corsican more often than French in school, but they could also assess their teachers' language use with reference to sociolinguistic patterns outside school. It was clear that their teachers used Corsican far more than teachers in many other (nonbilingual) schools, and more often than most of their parents and grandparents. This could certainly be interpreted as reflections of a personal stance of preference for Corsican and as evidence of positive valuation of Corsican as a school language. In fact, almost all the children told me in interviews that their teachers' preferred language was Corsican. The teachers' choice to use Corsican more often than French was also, of course, a pedagogical stance: using it among children who were more proficient and willing speakers of French displayed Corsican as a target of instruction.

Preference was also reflected in a number of statistically infrequent yet routine instances in which teachers deliberately flouted sociolinguistic norms of accommodation to the language preferences and competencies of their interlocutors. These practices contrasted quite sharply with the teachers' frequent use of French among themselves and with parents and other visitors, their expressed respect for others' language choices and their demonstrated willingness to accommodate linguistically. Despite—or perhaps even because of—their low statistical frequency and contrast with habitual practice, I consider the examples below highly sociolinguistically salient and thus important indicators of teacher stance.

First, there were notes home to parents. Many were bilingual, but in some cases— particularly in the younger children's class—they were monolingual Corsican. On one occasion that I witnessed, a four-year-old gave voice to the obvious implications of this practice, complaining that if they wrote a class note about an upcoming field trip in Corsican, his mother would not be able to read it. In fact, many parents were not proficient readers of that language, and I observed a group of mothers in the corridor one morning poring over a snack roster, ostentatiously "deciphering" the names of the food items (written in Corsican) they were supposed to provide for the following week. Arguably, none of the content of these notes was really inaccessible to the parents, but both they and the children recognized them as acts that prioritized the political and the symbolic over communicative efficiency and social accommodation. The notes proposed a hierarchy of linguistic stances and projected them on the parents. The preferred stance involved recognition of Corsican as a language one *should* know, and the display of effort to understand it. Second, in the younger children's class, the teacher also routinely addressed the nursery aide in Corsican, even though this woman was not a Corsican speaker and never exhibited any desire to use the language. In many cases, the Corsican content of the teacher's utterances was relatively transparent and/or consisted of routine instructions that the aide understood; in other cases, her level of comprehension was not crystal clear. However, the key issue for the implications of the teacher's practice with her was not the aide's actual level of comprehension but the fact that the teacher positioned her, as she positioned the parents, in exactly the same way as she positioned her students: as recipients of a beneficial instructional discourse in the "target" language. In other words, the teacher imposed a stance framework (with a clear language preference hierarchy) on another adult, which was a significant act of nonaccommodation in the service of the symbolic legitimation of Corsican.

Corsican also had a clear preferential status for activities and practices involved in the representation of the school to the outside world, including letters of invitation and thanks to visitors and hosts of field trips, end-of-year school performances, posters and reports displayed for parents and families at open houses, songs and poems composed and performed for a variety of audiences (including, in the year of my research, songs recorded on a semiprofessional CD made and distributed across the island), and "staged" performances of everyday activities for a documentary video project (Jaffe 2007a). Almost all of the teachers' contributions to weekly cooperative meetings, the mainstay of the school's organizational structure and pedagogical philosophy, were also in Corsican. Thus Corsican was associated with core practices that defined the core identity of the school, and by extension the core identity of the teacher and the students.

Moreover, despite their general tolerance for children's use of French to make good-faith contributions to class discussion, the teachers imposed Corsican on the children for the following three requests: asking if they could blow their noses, asking to be excused to go to the toilet, and asking if they could go to collect balls that had been kicked outside the playground fence. These ritualized and highly coercive verbal routines punctuated every school day, and displayed Corsican both as a target of instruction and as the preferred language of the school. They also aligned Corsican with an authoritarian stance, with the act of coercion itself. The act of imposing Corsican also indirectly represented it as a language of both lesser power and lower preference for students, who were represented as unwilling to choose it on their own.

Corsican was also sometimes positioned as preferred with respect to epistemic frameworks. In an analysis of a French literacy lesson for five- and six-year-olds, I show that patterns of teacher codeswitching lent Corsican a preferred status as the language of significant learning (explanations, questions, expansions, clarifications) and positioned French as an "object language" (Jaffe 2007a). This pattern did not hold for all of this teacher's French lessons, because she routinely used French as a language of learning. But the roles for the two languages were never reversed: she never used French to teach about Corsican, and Corsican was never given a subordinate epistemic role. I observed a related pattern of practice during the English classes that I taught for several months to the older children. Their teacher used Corsican, not French, as the mediating language to translate, explain, or comment on the linguistic content of my lessons. This positioned Corsican as a privileged language of learning, and also positioned it as "given" and "known" in contrast to the newness and obscurity of English.

Finally, despite the fact that teachers promoted the same evaluative and esthetic standards of Corsican and French usage, they distinguished the two languages in one important way in the evaluative process. In their French oral and written work, children often did individual work and were evaluated individually; in Corsican, almost all composition was collective and children were seldom graded on an individual basis, something I explore in some detail below.

To summarize, teachers' practices, observed over time and across multiple academic and social functions and activities, displayed a set of stance orientations toward Corsican and French that, in the institutional context, positioned Corsican as a language of equal authority and legitimacy as French, and as a language of added value for identity. Stance emerges as a crucial resource for these acts of positioning: it is the preferential stance hierarchy mobilized by teachers as role models engaged in evaluative activities that confers particular kinds of value and status on the two languages of the classroom. Sociolinguistic stance is also a target of instruction: teacher practices offer children a set of stance possibilities that can be understood as preferred dispositions toward language learning and toward Corsican itself. The following section explores this theme in some greater detail, looking closely at how teachers structure and attribute stances of authority and authorship to children through the scaffolding of participation structures over time.

Stance and Trajectories: Texts and Participant Roles

The analysis in this section is informed by work on social action as it occurs within *networks* and across *trajectories* (Latour 1999; Lemke 2005; Wortham 2005). A key premise of this approach is that schools are sites of networked practice that simultaneously produce knowledge, social, and linguistic identities. In the case of Corsican bilingual schools, what Corsican is and what it means for identity is inseparable from *how* the language is learned and used in school, and, in particular, the stances displayed, projected to, and made available to children. More durable social and linguistic identities, in this model, result from the accumulation of inhabited stances across social and temporal trajectories (see Wortham 2005). This analysis focuses on both *individual* trajectories (of students and teachers) as well as *collective* trajectories constituted in a several-month sequence of literacy activities surrounding processes of entextualization and reentextualization of a particular text. In a previous analysis of this text, I show how linguistic competence was "imagined" or projected onto the children through specific discursive processes in interaction (Jaffe 2003). Here, I pull back from the interaction proper to situate the trajectory of the text in question across several months in the school year, mapping closely both how the text moves across languages, modes, and genres and how children move across different participant roles and stances in relation to this text. Tables 6.1 and 6.2 summarize this movement.

The first column of both tables is a chronological account of processes of entextualization and reentextualization. In the early spring of the school year, the teacher brought in a French-language book of folktales from around the world, and read out loud a tale from India titled "The Tiger, the Brahman and the Jackal." This introduced the story as having a prior life as a text in another place and time. The fact that it was clearly a translation positioned the text as mobile across language and cultures, and provided a warrant for the fourth step in the chronology: the adaptation of the French version into Corsican. We see this movement reflected in the second column, labeled "language." The term "adaptation" was a deliberate choice of the teacher's, who emphasized that the goal was not to do a literal translation. She guided the children in the transposition of the setting and characters to the Corsican context (in which the tiger became a bear, the Brahman became a monk, and the jackal became a fox). Although they were expected to follow the basic plot outline, the teacher encouraged the children to let the logic of the Corsican context shape the dialog and specific elements of the narrative they crafted. The frame of "adaptation" placed several propositions/positions about literacy on the table. First, it presumed intertextual continuity, but not equivalence; second, it pointed to the way that processes of inscription and reinscription "make" or change their objects; and finally, it foregrounded the agency of the adaptor, giving her a stronger authorial role (a point to which I will return in the discussion of table 6.2).

The remaining steps of the sequence show the Corsican narrative undergoing a transformation of genre as it is rewritten as a script in step 8. We can also see, in column 3 of table 6.1, that the text moves through both oral and written modes, within and across specific classroom episodes, and ends up being embodied (kinesic mode) in an end-of-year performance. In both step 4 (adaptation) and step 8 (scripting), composition was done first orally. Stretches of narrative or bits of dialog were proposed by individual children and evaluated orally by the teacher and the whole group before they were written on the board. The text on the board was then subject to further evaluation and modification by the group. Once finalized, segments of text went through a chain of inscription. Although I have represented this as two discrete steps for the narrative and the script, both of those texts were composed over several class periods, and so there were several cycles of composition and inscription per product. The inscription process began when the children (and often the teacher) copied texts from the board into their notebooks by hand. Sometimes, one of these text exemplars (what I'm referring to as a "clean copy" on the table) was xeroxed and distributed in step 5; on other occasions, it was word-processed, printed, and copied for the same purpose.

These reinscriptions did not change the propositional content or even the linguistic form of the text. They did, however, have implications with respect to the stances and participant roles offered to the children. As de Certeau (1984) points out, every act of inscription is a form of appropriation and ownership. I would argue that the elements of time and repetition intensify this effect: the successive acts of inscription involved in the creation of each chapter or segment of this text reenacted

TABLE 6.1 Trajectory of a Text

Text Chronology	Language	Oral versus Written*	Other Semiotic Modes	Individual versus Collective	Novice-Expert Stance: *Teacher*	Novice-Expert Stance: *Children*
1 Indian folktale	?	O, poss. W		C (unknown)	n/a	n/a
2 French translation of Indian folktale	Fr	W → W		I	n/a	n/a
3 Translation read out loud by teacher	Fr	W → O		I	E	n/a
4 Adaptation into Corsican	C	**O → W**		C	E+	N→E
5 Chains of inscription: Blackboard → notebooks → word processing or "clean copy" → xeroxing	C	**W → W**		C	E	E
6 Completed segments of Corsican adaption read out loud by teacher	C	W → O		I	E	n/a
7 Completed segments read out loud by children	C	W → O		I	E	N→E
8 Corsican adaptation made into a script	C	W → O → W		C	E+	N→E
8a Chains of inscription						
9 Script "read back"	C	W → O		I	E	N→E
10 Memorized (increasingly) script rehearsed by children	C	**O**	kinesic	C/I	E	N→E
11 Play performed at end of school year	C	**O**	kinesic	C/I	n/a	E

*Bold represents the dominant mode in the interaction.

and thus amplified the children's links to, and ownership of, it. Steps 9–11 progressively shift the emphasis and work to the oral mode: the script goes from being a text that is read to one that is memorized and finally performed.

There are several implications of the text's trajectory across modes. Perhaps the most obvious is that it couples, rather than decouples, the oral and the literate. The

TABLE 6.2 Trajectories of Participation

Text Chronology	Children's Participation in Text Production			Teacher's Participation in Text Production			Other Participant Roles: Performer; Audience, Evaluator, Scribe*			
	Motive	Transmission	Form	Motive	Transmission	Form	**Perf.**	**Aud.**	**Eval.**	**Scr.**
1 Indian folktale	–	–	–	–	–	–				
2 French translation of Indian folktale	–	–	–	–	+	–		Fr		
3 Translation read out loud by teacher	–	–	–	–	+	–	T	S		
4 Adaptation into Corsican	–	+	+	–	+	–			T s	
5 Chains of inscription	n/a	n/a	+	n/a	n/a	+				T S
6 Completed segments of Corsican adaption read out loud by teacher	+	–	+	+	+	+	T	S		
7 Completed segments read out loud by children	+	+	+	–	–	+	S	T	T	
8 Corsican adaptation made into a script through collective oral-to-writing process	+	+	+	+	–/+	+	T	T (PF)	T s	
8a Chains of inscription	+	+	+	+	+	+				T S
9 Script "read back"	+	+	–	+	–/+	–	T S	T S (PF)		
10 Script rehearsed by children	+	+	–	–	–	–	S	T S (PF)	T s	
11 Play performed at end of school year	+	+	+	–	–	–	S	PF T		

*T = teacher; S = student; PF = parents and friends; Fr = French general public.

text is a product of both; they are experienced as complementary and interlinked. This has some special relevance in the teaching of a language that, until recently, did not have a written or an academic tradition. We can view the intertwining of the oral and the written in school practice as a form of mediation between two different models of legitimacy and value for the Corsican language: the academic/literate/formal one that is tied to the institution of the school and the colloquial/oral one that authenticates mother-tongue speakers of the language. It is no accident that in the final step (11) it is oral mastery that is put on stage for public consumption: oral competence is the barometer that the public will use to evaluate the outcomes of bilingual education (see Jaffe 2007b).

The fifth column in table 6.1 reflects the texts' trajectory through both individual and collective forms of action. If we subject this data to the same argument used in the discussion of modes, we can point to the way that the individual and the collective are imbricated over time. On the road to mastery (leading to skilled individual performance of roles), the work of composition and evaluation is always done collectively. Children's individual contributions and readings are always on behalf of the collectivity: they are neither framed nor evaluated as measures of individual competence. Once folded into the collective project, individual authorship is effaced: the product is referred to as something that "we wrote." This means, crucially, that children with lower levels of Corsican competence who contribute less (sometimes even nothing) to the composition process are attributed coauthorship. This is not just a conceit: it is a stance on what counts as "knowing Corsican." The attribution of authorship frames Corsican language competence as distributed *across* the class, as constituted by joint engagement in a network of practice.

The lengthy period of composition, the recycling through oral and written modes, and the multiple opportunities for copying and repeating often-heard material also provided children with an extensive period of apprenticeship before they were placed in a position of being individually accountable for their words. This is reflected in the last column of table 6.1, where we see the children's shift from novice to expert stances vis-à-vis the language of the text. This emphasizes that the *way* that the children learned how to use Corsican in writing and in speech was a projection of the meaning of the language in the society at large as a form of *shared*, cultural heritage. In the practices described here, children experienced Corsican first and predominantly through relatively stress-free collective practice and then were given the opportunity to activate an individual relationship with the language through performance. This local pedagogical sequence is conditioned by the personal linguistic trajectories experienced by school-aged children in a context of language shift: that is, few of those children experience individual linguistic competence in Corsican *before* they activate it in the service of a collective endeavor. The trajectory of the text, then, parallels personal (and generational) linguistic trajectories. This kind of trajectory also mitigates linguistic insecurities about that language competence in the minority language, insecurities that have repercussions for identity to the extent that being "authentically" Corsican is viewed as "knowing" the language.

We can also see, in this example, the concrete ways in which *trajectory* and *network* intersect. Through their shared and evolving forms of engagement over time with a text that moves through genres, languages, and modes, students build membership in a local network. The collective nature of action and engagement in that network actively defines the nature of that network: what it means to belong to a community of Corsican speakers. The elements of movement and time that are central to trajectories connect local (to the school) and contemporary experiences of community through Corsican with societal and historical ones. Because of the contemporary sociolinguistic context, in which there is generational rupture with respect to speaking Corsican, forging this connection is part of the work that schools do: it is not something that can be taken for granted.

Table 6.2 allows us to explore in greater detail the way that stances of linguistic expertise and ownership accrue to the children through the 11-step process by focusing on shifting configurations of participant roles over time. This analysis is grounded in Goffman's seminal decomposition of the speaker role into discrete functions: *author, animator,* and *principle* (1974: 517; 1981: 226). Since that time, scholars like Levinson (1988) have elaborated on this typology of participant roles and functions, showing how they can be fragmented and distributed across different persons. Irvine has extended the theoretical reach of these concepts by focusing our attention on the *processes* of fragmentation themselves, and on the relationship between a given communicative act and other acts—past, future, hypothetical, and so on—that make up the multiple and intersecting frames within which a particular utterance takes place (1996: 134–135).

What this perspective postulates is that we cannot base our analyses on the notion of a unified speaker, who is at once the author (person responsible for the creation of a message), the principle (person responsible for its content/position), and the animator (person responsible for its transmission). That is not to say to say that these roles are never unified in a single speaker, but that they are not necessarily so. As a consequence, our analytical focus must be drawn to the way that "participation structures are constructed, imagined and socially distributed" (Irvine 1996: 136). Table 6.2 schematizes how this works in the unfolding literacy event. The first six columns apply Levinson's (1988) feature classes to track underlying shifts in the participant roles occupied by the students and the teacher in relation to text *production*. The plusses and minuses reflect (a) the extent to which an individual is responsible for the text or utterance's *motive*, which indicates authorship/ownership such that the text or utterance can be attributed to that person; (b) responsibility for the text/utterance's *transmission*—who does the actual speaking or writing; and (c) responsibility for the linguistic *form* of the utterance or text. The table shows that the children progressively take up stances of responsibility for all three dimensions of participation in the production, transformation, and performance of the text. In doing so, they move toward a unified speaker stance of full authorship/ownership over the text and language (Corsican) being used. Conversely, we see a progressive reduction in the teacher's displayed responsibility in all three dimensions, culminating, in the final step, with the children being credited with motive, transmission, and form as the teacher joins family and friends as a member of the audience. The final columns in table 6.2 show shifts in other participant roles: performer, evaluator, audience, and scribe. The role of *performer* is in fact a variation on *transmission*, and indicates oral productions in which there is a heightened attention to delivery.

It is a mode of animating a text in which the speaker orients toward role enactment and an accountability to local (or generic) audiences and their esthetic standards. In general, we can see the children progressively taking over the performer role and the teacher progressively dropping back after scaffolding those performances through modeling in steps 3, 6, and 9. Here, we see another way in which classroom process orients to the priority given to oral fluency in Corsican by the wider Corsican speaking public: children are given the opportunity to craft a legitimate social voice in Corsican.

The shifts in the teacher's stances index the coconstructed and interactional nature of stancetaking, as well as how it is institutionally grounded. First of all, the teacher exploits the pairing of participant roles by taking up a stance as an audience. In doing so, she attributes a stance of author/performer to the children. Second, within the institutionally defined and hierarchically ordered role pair of teacher-student, she calibrates her own stance with an attention to the implications of the power differential for the attribution of authorship. Specifically, the teacher downgrades her own agency in the process of text production and stage performance because, due to her institutional status and power, she cannot be construed as an equal partner in a jointly authored text. Thus the teacher stance downgrade with respect to authorship constitutes a student stance upgrade.

To summarize, the analysis so far shows that intertextual links between Corsican-language speech events and texts as they are reworked and transformed over time allows students with varying levels of competence to develop a shared repertoire of linguistic practice. This deliberate element of the Corsican part of the bilingual curriculum is thus a calculated tool for identity work in which the network's shared use of linguistic resources gains precedence as an identity resource over individual competencies. The process the children went through also emphasized process itself: in this case, processes of entextualization and reentextualization as fundamental components of linguistic authorship, ownership, and belonging. That is, the children experienced increasing ownership of the text (and by extension, Corsican) through work on that text: they were active agents in the appropriation of a Corsican-speaking identity. This is a nonessentializing view of identity that validates learning language (rather than just having language) as a legitimate form of cultural identification and has obvious utility in a context like the Corsican one in which few Corsicans "own" the language of cultural heritage.

Discursive Cohesion across Languages: Creating a Bilingual Stance

One of the side effects of the analysis of how Corsican and French are differenti-ated as well as adequated through classroom practices is a heavy emphasis on code boundaries. This emphasis is not unwarranted, because bilingual schools inevitably invite comparison between the roles, functions, and values of the two languages. But it is by no means the whole picture, and there were other aspects of bilingual practice in this school that shifted the focus away from language boundaries, empha-sizing instead how discursive coherence and the achievement of communication and learning could be integrated across both languages. Teachers' active construction of this coherence can be viewed as the projection of a preferred bilingual stance: a model of how to be in two languages.

The analysis below focuses on two processes that have been studied extensively in monolingual contexts—how conversational coherence and interactional alignment are discursively established across speakers and turns (Ribeiro 1993; Schegloff 1990, 2001; Schiffrin 1985, 1993, 2001; Tannen and Wallat 1993)—and examines their occurrence across languages. In their seminal work on cohesion in English, Halliday and Hasan outline four major categories of cohesive relations: those established through conjunction, reference, lexical cohesion, and substitution (1976: 324), all of which involve some form of deixis or coreference. In the analysis of the transcript below, I focus on the following selection of lexicogrammatical forms of cohesion that fall under Halliday and Hasan's categories, adding a final category that relates to discursive coherence at the level of the utterance:

1. Substitution and reference: the use of indexicals in one language (pro-nouns, demonstratives, articles, comparatives, ellipsis, repetition) that point backward to persons, names, topics, characters, places, times, or utterances in the other language;
2. Lexical cohesion: relationships of semantic similarity—terms introduced in one language referred to through semantically related terms in the other language including synonyms;
3. Conjunction: relationships of conjunction, causality, contrast, and so on that are established between utterances or themes (either by apposition or through conjunctions, etc.) across the two languages;
4. Parallelism, "resonance" (Du Bois 2007), format tying (C. Goodwin 1990; M. H. Goodwin 2006), and repetition (Tannen 1990) across languages, sometimes involving lexical cohesion, above.

There are two crucial connections between the functioning of discursive coher-ence and the establishment of social stances, identities, and social relationships. First, the accomplishment of coherence is a joint activity in which all speakers depend on, and thus index, their interlocutors' linguistic and communicative competencies. For example, cross-linguistic cohesion (as in 3, above) assumes interlocutors who are able to understand both parts of themes or utterances that are brought into relation in some way, as well as the different languages in which they were uttered. Second, as Scollon (1998: 71) points out, the frame of relationship (the interpersonal) is hierarchically superior to the frame of topic, such that breakdown in relationship often entails break-down in conversational cohesion, as shown in work by Erickson and Shultz (1982). This relationship of entailment creates an indexical connection between the successful conduct of interpersonal work and the successful conduct of conversation such that cohesion at the discourse level can come to represent social cohesion at the group level. Finally, as Martin points out, textual and linguistic cohesion is motivated by "the social context a text simultaneously realizes and construes" (2001: 47). Textual coherence, in his view, is built up through the interaction of linguistic practice and social context and serves to "naturalize a reading position for reader/listeners"

(2001: 35). We can argue, therefore, that textual coherence presupposes and indexes a social order. In the analysis below, my claim is thus that coherence created across Corsican and French utterances both assumes and performatively attributes bilingual competence to the students in the classroom and that the practice of bilingual coherence itself indexes an ideal model of a cohesive bilingual society that privileges communicative engagement and cooperation over individual language choices.

The following transcript begins as the teacher (T) takes leave of one group of children to work with three 5- and 6-year-olds who have been filling out a worksheet on a text that they had begun earlier in the week.

TRANSCRIPT 1: Task and Topic Articulated across Languages

1	T	emu da lascià qui Andria, Morgane	We are going to leave A, M, and
2		è Michela travaglià in u scornu;	M to work in the corner;
3		emu da travaglià inseme, emu da	we are going to work together,
4		**fà** un picculu <u>travagliu</u>	we're going to **do** a little <u>work</u>
5	Child	Marylène	Marylene
6	T	Andria, Michela, è Morgane qui ci	Andria, Michela, è Morgane
7		hè un <u>travagliu</u>, chì ghjè?	here's some <u>work</u>, what is it?
8	Child	*C'est :::: de **faire** ça.*	*It's:::: to **do** that.*
9	T	Chì ci vole à **fà**? Ah, de ***faire çà,***	What do we have to **do**? Oh, to
10		ùn sò micca ciò ch'ellu vole *dì*	***do that.*** I don't know what that
11		***faire ça!***	means to ***do that!***
12	Child	*Le <u>chat</u> va MANGER <u>**la souris**</u>.*	*The <u>cat</u> will EAT <u>**the mouse**</u>.*
13	T	**U topu** hà da CHJAPPÀ…	**The mouse** is going to GET…
14	Child	A ghja…u to…	The ca…the mou…
15	T	**U tupichjulu** o **u topu.** Chì ghjè,	**The little mouse** or **the mouse**.
16		chì hà da CHJAPPÀ chì?	Who is going to GET whom?
17	Child	U <u>ghja</u>—u <u>ghjattu</u>, *le <u>chat</u>.*	The <u>ca</u>—the <u>cat</u>, *the <u>ca</u>t*
18	T	U <u>ghjattu</u>. U <u>misgiu</u>, <u>misgettu</u>.	The <u>cat</u>. The <u>cat</u>, <u>the kitty</u>.
19	Child	U <u>misgiu</u>.	The <u>cat</u>.
20	Andria	*Je suis <u>parti de là</u>.*	*I <u>started from there</u>.*
21	T	*Eh ben alors non,*	*Uh, well, no I don't think so, no,*
22		*heh heh heh.*	*heh heh heh.*
23		Ghjè **u topu** chì corre o ghjè u	Is it **the mouse** was running or is
24		misgiu?	it the cat?
25	Child	Misgiu.	Cat.
27	T	*Bon,* allora <u>d'induve si parte?</u>	*Good,* so <u>where do we start from</u>?
27	Morg	*Moi <u>je suis parti de là</u>.*	*Me, <u>I started from there</u>.*
28	Andria	Si <u>parte di quì</u>.	We <u>start from here</u>.
29	T	Un' hè micca <u>ciò</u> chè tù ai dettu	That isn't <u>what</u> you said
30		nanzu.*	before.*

Key: normal typeface = Corsican; italics = French. Text format for themes: **do**; <u>work</u>; <u>the cat</u>; **the mouse**; EAT; <u>start</u> + <u>location</u>. * Index of prior utterance.

A visual scan of this transcript shows that conversational themes (each theme represented with a unique, shared typeface) carry across both speakers and languages. A theme introduced in one language is sometimes picked up in the other through direct translation; alternatively, it may be referenced with pronouns, synonyms, or other indexical forms, creating cross-linguistic cohesion. This can be viewed as a joint accomplishment, as well as a proficiency displayed by the children. But there is no doubt that the teacher plays a central role in this activity because of her greater control over Corsican. In this respect, her high and visible level of engagement in the work of cross-linguistic cohesion represents this kind of bilingual practice as a model of social interaction, cooperative communication, and expert, adult practice.

In lines 3 and 4, the teacher topicalizes in Corsican the work that the children are about to do, followed by a direct question to them in line 7 ("what is it?"). In line 8, one of the children responds to the question by saying in French, "it's::: to do that." The elongation of "it's" introduces an element of play and displays a prospective awareness that the answer to follow is less than optimal. In line 8, the teacher recycles her original question in Corsican in a slightly more elaborate form ("What do we need to do?") and provides the anticipated nonratification of the child's answer. In this exchange, then, both teacher's and students' orientations to evaluation are displayed and played out across both languages.

In line 9, the teacher repeats the child's use of the French phrase "do that" in its original language and claims in Corsican that she "doesn't know what it means." This utterance is both not literally true and a seeming breach of the principle of cooperative cross-language communication that is otherwise held up as an ideal. The conversational maxim of relevance thus allows us (and the students) to interpret the statement in reference to some other salient frame of reference. This, I would argue, is established in the interactional sequence in lines 1–11, in which the teacher orients the children toward *increasing specificity* of reference as a linguistic target. This implicit in the format of her original question, which provides a relatively general topicalized theme ("work") and is clearly a "known-answer" question type. Posing it is therefore a fairly obvious request for students to elaborate on "work" and display more specific knowledge than the teacher has already provided in her question. It is this evaluative criterion that motivates both the student's anticipatory downgrading of her answer on line 8 and the teacher's recycling of the question on line 9. Both of these utterances, then, warrant an interpretation of the teacher's revoicing of "do that" in its original language as primarily oriented toward emphasizing and negatively evaluating its low specificity.

The focus of the teacher's comment on the vagueness of "do that" is interesting in two ways. First, it indexes the referential link between the child's utterance in French (through the use of "it's") to the topic and question the teacher had introduced in Corsican. It thus creates and presumes cross-linguistic cohesion. Second, it shows how, in bilingual interactions, sociolinguistic stance is implicated in speakers' framing of the nature of their alignment with the speech that they report. In this particular case, the stance framework is established, first, by the contrast between the teacher's direct quotation of the child in French and her use of Corsican for the negative evaluation of the adequacy of the child's response. The fact that the teacher uses only French in the direct quotation of the child's words in this stretch of discourse also gives Corsican preferential status as the reflection of the teacher's own voice and as the language through which she exercises her authority to pass judgment. Another important backdrop to the stance framework in this specific interaction is the patterning of this teacher's evaluations of children's French-language responses to questions she asked them in Corsican. These responses were almost always ratified if evaluated by the teacher as being on topic; moreover, that ratification was almost always accomplished through the teacher's revoicing and expansion of the content of the child's utterance in Corsican (see discussion below of "cat" and "mouse" in this segment). In other words, the preference structure established both over time and in particular instances of discourse linked positive evaluation with the teacher's incorporation of a child's utterance into her preferred language and negative evaluation with lack of incorporation. Stance (toward the two codes) is thus mobilized as a resource for further acts of stance (evaluation) whose object is communicative cooperation.

In line 12, another child offers a brief characterization of a plot element in the story they are all reading, saying in French that the cat is going eat the mouse. The teacher's next utterance (line 13) takes up and recasts the child's proposition in Corsican, switching the mouse from the object to the agent position, and reformulating the verb "to eat" as "to get/grab," but retaining a parallel format "the X is going to _____ the Y," which she deploys again on line 16. At the level of form, then, the teacher tightly coordinates her (Corsican) talk and the students' (French and then Corsican) talk. As in the previous exchange, the focus of the teacher's commentary is not on the language the child used to respond, but on its content: in this case, as it relates to the issue of characters' agency. Again, the teacher's talk both presupposes and builds on the propositional content of the child's utterance in French and presumes (and thus attributes) student knowledge of Corsican. In the following lines, the teacher introduces several Corsican synonyms for the words "mouse" and "cat"; one of these ("misgiu") is taken up by children in lines 19 and 25.

In line 20, Andria makes a claim in French about where he had begun to read in the text, pointing to a physical spot on a page. The teacher's dispute of his claim on the following line is also in French. It is, however, keyed as a milder form of disalignment than her repetition of "do that": first, by her voice quality and use of laughter and second, by the fact that she presents herself as author, principle, and animator of the French she uses. In line 23, she reformulates, now in Corsican, the line of questioning (about which character was doing the running) she had been following before Andria's claim and receives an answer in Corsican from another child. The teacher's switch to Corsican, her resumption of a prior topic, and her recycling of a question all serve as nonratifications of Andria's contribution. However, this proves to be temporary: in line 27, she takes up the theme of Andria's original statement in French by formulating it as a question in Corsican. This elicits another student response in French and a new answer from Andria, who points to another spot in the book, and claims in Corsican to have started reading there. To this, the teacher replies in Corsican, "That isn't what you said before," with the demonstrative pronoun 'that' indexing his previous utterance in French.

What is of particular interest here is that even though Andria has produced a correct answer in the preferred language, he is held accountable for his prior contributions in French. The teacher's utterance in line 27 shows that she also holds *herself* accountable for assessing his contributions in both languages, and frames her previous nonratification of Andria as content motivated rather than language motivated. This structure of accountability and evaluation itself works to integrate the two languages. It also prioritizes good faith engagement in learning and cooperative communication and interaction as they are demonstrated in either or across both languages of the curriculum. The teacher's use of alignment/disalignment with the language of the child's utterance as a form of evaluation also demonstrates that good faith can be operationalized and made visible through speakers' engagement in creating cross-linguistic discursive cohesion. We could say, therefore, that these kinds of teacher-student interactions establish an indexical link between doing cross-linguistic cohesion and taking up a stance as a cooperative member of a bilingual community.

Children's Stance Uptake

One of the goals of the bilingual school was student uptake of and alignment with teachers' stances toward Corsican, including orientations of respect, appreciation, and identification. Some of these orientations can be studied only in the long term as they emerge across children's life trajectories. But there is some evidence of uptake and alignment in student practices and commentary. I have already mentioned students' displayed uptake of teacher preference for Corsican in response to explicit questioning. Many of these students also attributed greater Corsican language competence to their teachers (which was not accurate) and identified most of their classmates' strongest or first language as their preferred one. These judgments are *not* stance-sensitive, because they identify language choices as direct reflections of language competencies rather than as expressions of speaker position. However, there were two students who were not first-language speakers of Corsican who self-identified and were identified by their peers as preferring that language. This showed an awareness that individuals could display, through extraordinary patterns of practice, a personal stance toward different languages in their repertoire and environment. It also suggests that stance awareness may be part of the developmental process (see Kiesling this volume) and be exhibited to varying degrees among children.

Children also differentiated between Corsican and French in displays of affective stance, using Corsican as a tool of conflict mitigation through alignment. For example, in one cooperative meeting, there had been a fairly long discussion about the appropriateness of tongue pulling following an incident in which one of the four-year-olds stuck his tongue out at another child. Most of the children's contributions to this discussion (including the offending child's) were in French; the teacher spoke Corsican. Eventually, a distinction was made based on motive and key: sticking out your tongue to be funny was not as bad as sticking it out to be mean. The teacher then turned to the original tongue puller and asked him directly in Corsican if he had done it to annoy his classmate or to "act the clown." "To act the clown," he asserted emphatically, and in Corsican. The use of Corsican in this utterance is both set off from his prior use of French and coincides significantly with an effort to please the teacher, fend off a negative evaluation, and present himself in the best possible light. On several occasions that I witnessed, the children also collectively increased their use of Corsican after having been scolded as a group by their teacher for not working hard or responsibly enough. Here, we can see an orientation to teacher stance (alignment with positive and/or preferential status of Corsican) as well as with the indexical relationship that school practices established between Corsican and group identity.

Children also spontaneously enacted the preferred status of Corsican as a display of a bilingual group identity during the filming of a TV documentary on bilingual education in their school. When the camera crew recorded one of their weekly cooperative meetings the children, without being directed to by the producer or teacher, used Corsican for the majority of their utterances. This was in stark contrast to their habitual greater use of French than Corsican in these meetings (Jaffe 2007a). When left to their own devices, the children also treated Corsican as the default choice for correspondence sent outside the school, modified only if they thought the recipient could not read the language.

Corsican was also used by the children to occupy specific interactional stances in ways that showed their uptake of indexicalities proposed by teacher practice. For example, over a period of several weeks, a group of four-year-olds repeatedly played with the form of the question "Can I blow my nose?" (one of the ritualized utterances in which Corsican was imposed), using an "incorrect" form, each time corrected by the teacher. After the first of these teacher corrections, the children displayed through their intonation, facial expression, and voice quality that they knew the "right" structure but were deliberately and playfully choosing not to use it. This manipulation of linguistic form in Corsican to resist (albeit in a very lighthearted way) teacher authority by introducing a humorous key for a type of interaction that the teacher defined as serious was an indirect index of their uptake of the pairing of Corsican with an authoritarian stance and, perhaps, of their understanding of formal proficiency in Corsican as a source of personal authority. Children also, although infrequently, used Corsican to take up authoritative stances with respect to one another. This was dramatically illustrated in one notable recording that I made of a five-year-old attempting (unsuccessfully) to impose himself as the teacher through the use of Corsican while playing at school before the official start of the school day (Jaffe, forthcoming).

Conclusions

In conclusion, I would like to outline how this analysis engages with some of the major orientations of a sociolinguistics of stance that I have proposed in the introduction to this volume. First, I have emphasized the importance of situating the analysis of stancetaking in the classroom within several crucial social and cultural matrices. Teacher stance—and its implications—in the Corsican bilingual classroom has to be interpreted with respect to (a) the institutional context and how it constitutes roles, statutes, and participant structures; (b) the contemporary sociolinguistic context: in particular, patterns of language choice and use outside the classroom; and (c) a wider cultural context and a specific institutional context (the bilingual school) as it has been shaped by a history of language shift and language revitalization. These three sociocultural conditions constitute shared points of reference for the production and interpretation of individual acts of stance: they delimit the range of possible stances and establish conventional sociolinguistic indexicalities linking particular linguistic choices, social stances, and social identities. The institutional framework, and the teachers' evaluative and modeling role within it, ascribes ideal status to their language choices and practices as well as giving them the interactional power to attribute stances to their students. The sociocultural context also loads their uses of Corsican with symbolic and political significance, lending Corsican value as a language of identity and making comparison and contrast with French salient with respect to Corsican's legitimacy and authority.

The analysis of teacher stance is also framed against a language-ideological backdrop as it informs issues of language hierarchy (and thus, the salience of parity with French) as well as how people construe the relationship between language and identity at both the individual and collective levels. Acts of stancetaking draw on established sociolinguistic indexicalities and language ideologies as resources and, in this respect, contribute to their reproduction. In the practices I have described, teachers reproduce indexical relationships between authorship, evaluation, and authoritative stance, as well as the connection between linguistic authority and linguistic and cultural authenticity and ownership. At the same time, stances displayed and attributed in the classroom create new indexical pairings. The data I have presented show that teachers also rework the positions of both the Corsican language and of children as novice speakers and writers by using Corsican as the medium through which they do authoritative pedagogical and social work, and by creating the conditions in which children can have a simultaneous experience of Corsican linguistic proficiency/ownership and cultural membership.

At the ideological level, these practices index and thus reproduce dominant or conventional ideologies about the relationship of language and identity. This can be seen in the way that stance is mobilized to both differentiate Corsican from French as a privileged language of identity and position it as equal to French in authority. These two elements of the bilingual school agenda are responses to historical language hierarchies and a diglossic relationship between Corsican and French. In taking on the work of identification through Corsican, the school is positioned as a surrogate for social processes and linguistic practices that are no longer in place in the society, and thus evokes an idealized past in which linguistic and cultural identity were direct and congruent.

However, teachers' acts of stance also break with dominant language ideologies. First, they enact a model of bilingualism that does not propose an ideal of two perfectly balanced monolingualisms as the only legitimate basis for a bilingual identity. The participation structures they set up and managed over time made it possible for students with multiple levels and kinds of Corsican competence to be counted as legitimate participants and, by extension, as legitimate speakers and authors. This involved a shift in the locus of the experience, display, and evaluation of Corsican competence from the individual to the collectivity, and defined that collectivity as a linguistically heterogeneous one. In general, these practices challenged the dominant one-language–one-culture principle, as did the teachers' displays of positive orientations toward codeswitching, and their use of discursive practices that downplayed the salience of code boundaries. In fact, bilingual identity emerges in these practices not so much as a narrowly defined set of language practices, but as a *stance* of positive engagement in social and communicative practice involving more than one language. Overall, the analysis reflects the reflexive, metapragmatic, and "metasociolinguistic" nature of stancetaking in the classroom: that is, the conventional associations between language and social categories, linguistic ideologies, and language hierarchies are themselves "stance objects."

Finally, the analysis has taken stance as a crucial component of interactional processes and practices as they occur over time and across different activities, with a particular focus on issues of alignment/disalignment and the negotiation of power. In focusing on how durable personal stances are built, accumulated, and coconstructed across social and temporal trajectories, it points to the role of stance as a building block in processes of identification. These processes are at the heart of the agenda of Corsican bilingual education, and it for this reason that stance in this school context has important sociolinguistic consequences.

References

Bourdieu, Pierre. 2007. *Distinction: A social critique of the judgment of taste*. Trans. Richard Nice. Cambridge, MA: Harvard University Press.

Clift, Rebecca. 2006. Indexing stance: Reported speech as an interactional evidential. *Journal of Sociolinguistics* 10(5): 569–595.

Cohen, Paul. 2000. Of linguistic Jacobinism and cultural balkanization: Contemporary French linguistic politics in historical context." *French Politics, Culture and Society* 18(2): 21–48.

de Certeau, Michel. 1984. *The practice of everyday life*. Berkeley: University of California Press.

Du Bois, John. 2007. The stance triangle. In *Stancetaking in discourse*, ed. Robert Englebretson, 139–182. Amsterdam: John Benjamins.

Erickson, Fred, and Jeffrey Schultz. 1982. *The counselor as gatekeeper: Social interaction in interviews*. New York: Academic Press.

Goffman, Erving. 1974. *Frame Analysis*, New York: Harper and Row.

——. 1981. *Forms of Talk*, Philadelphia, PA: University of Pennsylvania Press.

Goodwin, Charles. 1990. Interstitial argument. In *Conflict talk*, ed. Allan Grimshaw, 85–117. Cambridge: Cambridge University Press.

——. 2006. Retrospective and prospective orientation in the construction of argumentative moves. *Text and Talk* 26(4/5): 443–461.

Goodwin, Marjorie Harness. 2006. *The hidden life of girls: Games of stance, status, and exclusion*. Malden, MA: Blackwell.

Halliday, M. A. K., and Ruqaiya Hasan. 1976. *Cohesion in English*. New York: Longman.

Irvine, Judith. 1996. Shadow conversations: The indeterminacy of participant roles. In *Natural histories of discourse,* ed. Greg Urban and Michael Silverstein, 131–159. Chicago: University of Chicago Press.

Jaffe, Alexandra. 2003. "Imagined competence": Classroom evaluation, collective identity and linguistic authenticity in a Corsican bilingual classroom. In *Linguistic anthropology of education,* ed. Stanton Wortham and Betsy Rymes, 151–184. Westport CT: Praeger.

———. 2005. Collaborative literacy practices in French and Corsican: The ideological underpinnings of a bilingual education. *CLIC* (Crossroads of Language, Interaction and Culture) 6: 3–28.

———. 2007a. Corsican on the airwaves: Media discourse, practice and audience in a context of minority language shift and revitalization. In *Language in the media,* ed. Sally Johnson and Astrid Ensslin, 149–172. London: Continuum Press.

———. 2007b. Discourses of endangerment: Contexts and consequences of essentializing discourses. In *Discourses of endangerment: Interests and ideology in the defense of languages,* ed. Alexandre Duchene and Monica Heller, 57–75. London: Continuum.

———. Forthcoming. The production and reproduction of language ideologies in practice. In *The new sociolinguistics reader*, ed. Nikolas Coupland and Adam Jaworski, New York: Palgrave.

Kärkkäinen, Elise. 2007. The role of *I guess* in conversational stancetaking. In *Stancetaking in discourse*, ed. Robert Englebretson, 183–219. Amsterdam: John Benjamins.

Kiesanen, Tiina. 2007. Stancetaking as an interactional activity: Challenging the prior speaker. In *Stancetaking in discourse*, ed. Robert Englebretson, 253–282. Amsterdam: John Benjamins.

Latour, Bruno. 1999. *Pandora's hope: Essays on the reality of science studies*. Trans. Catherine Porter. Cambridge, MA: Harvard University Press.

Lemke, Jay. 2005. Multimedia genres and traversals. *Folia Linguistica* 39(1–2): 45–56.

Levinson, Stephen. 1988. Putting linguistics on a proper footing: Explorations in Goffman's concepts of participation. In *Erving Goffman: An interdisciplinary appreciation*, ed. Paul Drew and Anthony Wooton, 161–227. Oxford: Polity Press.

Martin, J. R. 2001. Cohesion and texture. In *The handbook of discourse analysis*, ed. Deborah Schiffrin, Deborah Tannen, and Heidi Hamilton, 34–53. Malden, MA: Blackwell.

Rauniomaa, Mirka. 2007. Stance markers in spoken Finnish: Minun mielestä and minusta in assessments. In *Stancetaking in discourse,* ed. Robert Englebretson, 221–252. Amsterdam: John Benjamins.

Ribeiro, Branca Telles. 1993. Framing in psychotic discourse. In *Framing in discourse,* ed. Deborah Tannen, 77–112. New York: Oxford University Press.

Schegloff, Emmanuel. 1990. On the organization of sequences as a source of "coherence" in talk-in-interaction. In *Conversational organization and its development,* ed. Bruce Dorval, 51–77. Norwood, NJ: Ablex.

———. 2001. Discourse as an interactional achievement III. In *The handbook of discourse analysis*, ed. Deborah Schiffrin, Deborah Tannen, and Heidi Hamilton, 229–249. Malden, MA: Blackwell.

Schiffrin, Deborah. 1985. Conversational coherence: The role of "well." *Language* 61: 640–667.

———. 1993. "Speaking for another" in sociolinguistic interviews: Alignments, identities, frames. In *Framing in discourse*, ed. Deborah Tannen, 231–261. New York: Oxford University Press.

———. 2001. Discourse markers. In *The handbook of discourse analysis*, eds. Deborah Schiffrin, Deborah Tannen, and Heidi Hamilton, 54–75. Malden, MA: Blackwell.

Scollon, Ron. 1998. *Mediated discourse as social interaction*. New York: Longman.

Tannen, Deborah. 1990. Ordinary conversation and literary discourse: Coherence and the poetics of repetition. *Annals of the New York Academy of Sciences* 583(1): 15–30.

Tannen, Deborah, and Cynthia Wallat. 1993. Interactive frames and knowledge schemas in interaction: Examples from a medical examination/interview. In *Framing in discourse*, ed. Deborah Tannen, 57–76. New York: Oxford University Press.

Wortham, Stanton. 2005. Socialization beyond the speech event. *Journal of Linguistic Anthropology* 15(1): 95–112.

7

From Stance to Style

Gender, Interaction, and Indexicality in Mexican Immigrant Youth Slang

Mary Bucholtz

Introduction: Indexicality and Identity in Sociolinguistics

The sociolinguistic study of identity has increasingly become the study of style. Traditionally, style has been understood within sociolinguistics as a unidimensional continuum between vernacular and standard that varies based on the degree of speaker self-monitoring in a given speech context (e.g., Labov 1972). However, recent theories offer a much richer view of style as a multimodal and multidimensional cluster of linguistic and other semiotic practices for the display of identities in interaction (e.g., Coupland 2007; Eckert and Rickford 2001; Mendoza-Denton 2002). This perspective also proposes a correspondingly more sophisticated theory of identity. Rather than assigning sociolinguistic meaning in a correlational fashion via a direct mapping between linguistic forms and social categories, as in earlier approaches to sociolinguistic variation, current theorists draw either implicitly or explicitly on the concept of indexicality, or contextually bound meaning (Silverstein 1976, 1985, 2003), in their understanding of stylistic practice (cf. Eckert 2000, 2003, 2008). In an indexical theory of style, the social meaning of linguistic forms is most fundamentally a matter not of social categories such as gender, ethnicity, age, or region but rather of subtler and more fleeting interactional moves through which speakers take stances, create alignments, and construct personas. Such an approach therefore demands that sociolinguists pay close attention not only to the patterning of linguistic variants but also their distribution and function in the performance of social actions within unfolding discourse. At the same time, styles are the product of ideology, insofar as they are posited by speakers (as well as by analysts) as more or less clearly defined and socially specifiable collections of coinciding symbolic forms bound to particular social groups via metapragmatic stereotypes (Agha 2007). Contemporary sociolinguistic research on indexical stancetaking in interaction (e.g., Chun 2007; Coupland 2001; Johnstone 2007; Kiesling 2005; Mendoza-Denton 2008; Schilling-Estes 2004) illustrates the complex, real-time process whereby linguistic forms associated in the first instance with interactional stancetaking may come to be ideologically tied to larger social categories, as well as how linguistic forms that have become linked to particular categories may variously exploit or set aside such associations as speakers deploy these forms for their own interactional purposes.

This chapter seeks to contribute to this emergent body of scholarship by demonstrating how the relationship between stance, style, and identity is formed both from the bottom up, as it unfolds in local interaction, and from the top down, through the workings of broader cultural ideologies (cf. Bucholtz and Hall 2005). I examine this bidirectional process as it is constructed via the use of a single slang term popular among many Mexican and Mexican American youth, *güey* ([gwej], often lenited to [wej]). Although this term is frequently translated as 'dude', I argue, building on Kiesling's (2004) recent work on *dude*, that although these terms index similar stances they often participate in rather different styles of youthful masculinity. In my analysis, I draw on interactional data as well as media representations to argue that the semiotic multivalence of *güey* allows it to operate (often simultaneously) as a marker both of interactional alignment and of a particular gendered style among Mexican American youth.

The Indexicality of Stance and Gender Style

The most extensive theoretical articulation of how indexical processes construct identity within interaction is found in the work of Elinor Ochs (1990, 1992, 1993, 1996). Although Ochs situates her discussion primarily in relation to the study of language socialization, her research on the role of indexicality in the social construction of gender has been particularly influential within identity studies. She notes that a fundamental challenge for researchers concerned with identifying gendered language use is that "*few features of language directly and exclusively index gender*" (1992: 340; original emphasis). Rejecting a correlational view of the connection between language and gender, she argues that only a semiotic perspective rooted in indexicality can account for the complexity of this relationship:

> Knowledge of how language relates to gender is not a catalogue of correlations between particular linguistic forms and sex of speakers, referents, addressees, and the like. Rather, such knowledge entails tacit understanding of (1) how particular linguistic forms can be used to perform particular pragmatic work (such as conveying stance and social action) and (2) norms, preferences, and expectations regarding the distribution of this work *vis-à-vis* particular social identities of speakers, referents, and addressees. To discuss the relation of language to gender in these terms is far more revealing than simply identifying features as directly marking men's or women's speech. (1992: 342)

Ochs proposes that the indexical relationship between language and social meaning should be seen as involving two levels. At the level of direct indexicality, linguistic forms most immediately index interactional stances—that is, subjective orientations to ongoing talk, including affective, evaluative, and epistemic stances (cf. Du Bois 2007). At the level of indirect indexicality, these same linguistic forms become associated with particular social types believed to take such stances. It is at the indirect indexical level that ideology comes most centrally into play, for it is here that stances acquire more enduring semiotic associations. Over time, the mapping between linguistic form and social meaning comes to be ideologically perceived as direct, and the connections to interactional stance may undergo erasure or be back-grounded (cf. Irvine and Gal 2000). For example, a mitigated interactional stance may be ideologically associated with women, and hence linguistic forms used to take such stances may come to be seen as inherently "feminine." The indexical perspective therefore suggests that gender is not the explanation for a speaker's use of a particular linguistic form, but rather the indirect effect of using such language, a reversal of causality that underlies current social-constructionist thinking about language and gender. However, where many social-constructionist theories assume that semiotic resources such as language directly index gender, an indexical theory of gender posits an intermediate step that recognizes the multifunctionality of linguistic forms and hence is less deterministic.[1]

Moreover, linguistic forms that may come to be ideologically linked to broader social meanings via indirect indexicality are generally associated not with broad social categories like women but rather with more specific sorts of social types and personas, such as child-oriented, middle-class mothers (Ochs 1992) or rebellious, "burnout" teenage girls (Eckert 2000), through the process of creating metapragmatic stereotypes. That is, indirectly indexical linguistic forms are markers of highly differentiated styles of identity that operate within a semiotic system in relation to other locally available—and often competing or contrasting—styles. A single feature, then, is typically insufficient to index a style; rather, styles comprise clusters of co-occurring semiotic elements, including both linguistic and nonlinguistic resources (Ochs 1990; Eckert 2003). As I show in my analysis of *güey*, this term gains part of its indexical meaning from the other symbolic practices in which its users engage while taking stances and building styles of identity.

Stance, Style, and Gender in Slang

Within language and gender research, slang has been a topic of interest since the early days of the field. On the one hand, researchers have investigated whether sexist asymmetries exist in slang terms referring to each gender (e.g., Braun and Kitzinger 2001; Cameron 1992; de Klerk 1992; James 1998; Sutton 1995). On the other hand, a rather smaller body of work has documented the frequency and strength of slang and other taboo terms used by speakers of each gender (e.g., de Klerk 1990, 1997; Hughes 1992; Risch 1987). Such studies rely primarily on surveys and other elicited data in order to compare the slang repertoires of female and male speakers, an approach that assumes that self-reports accurately capture actual language use. This assumption is questionable, however, in an ideologically fraught area of language such as slang. Moreover, although the focus in such research on cross-gender comparison importantly allows scholars to identify gender differences and especially asymmetries, this approach also obscures the possibility that slang terms ideologically associated with one gender or the other may in fact be shared in practice. More recent work on gender and slang demonstrates the important mediating roles of ideology (e.g., L. Miller 2004) and interaction (e.g., Stenström 2003) in constructing the gendered meaning of slang. Such research suggests that the social meaning of slang cannot be read off directly from its semantics or the demographic distribution of its use. Rather, slang, like all linguistic resources, gains its semiotic value only within the sociocultural context in which it is used. Indexicality is therefore a fundamental concept in understanding how slang—or indeed any linguistic form—comes to be associated with gender and other social categories.

Thus, to discover what is left out of metapragmatic representations of discourse and what is put in, it is necessary to examine linguistic items that index stances—and hence build styles and identities—in local interactional contexts. I offer two illustrations of how gendered youth styles are indexically built up in interaction in part through the use of slang: Kiesling's (2004) discussion of *dude* and my own analysis of the use of *güey* among Mexican immigrant youth in the United States. I then turn to how *güey* has been taken up ideologically through niche marketing within commodity capitalism in the U.S. context, which reproduces and reinforces the gendered dimensions of its semiotics.

Stance and Masculinity in the Use of *Dude*

Kiesling's (2004) analysis of the term *dude* offers a detailed example of how a slang form can operate at multiple levels of indexicality. Kiesling notes that the contemporary use of *dude* as an address term originated among African Americans and was later appropriated by European Americans, especially young men. Based on the distribution of the form in observational and self-report survey data, he argues that *dude* is currently used primarily (though not exclusively) by younger white male speakers. But unlike in most sociolinguistic studies of slang, Kiesling goes beyond an examination of the social patterning of the form across speakers to its use in interaction as well as its representation in the popular media. Drawing on discourse data among university fraternity members, he argues that interactionally *dude* creates an intersubjective alignment of friendly nonintimacy. Thus the direct indexicality of the term is to project a "stance of cool solidarity" (2004: 282), and this stance is often linked via indirect indexicality to masculinity and male speakers. As Kiesling puts it:

> The term is used mainly in situations in which a speaker takes a stance of solidarity or camaraderie, but crucially in a nonchalant, not-too-enthusiastic manner.... The reason young men use this term is precisely that *dude* indexes this stance of cool solidarity. Such a stance is especially valuable for young men as they navigate cultural Discourses of young masculinity, which simultaneously demand masculine solidarity, strict heterosexuality, and nonconformity. (2004: 282)

He goes on to argue that the term's indexical meaning in the social realm derives from its various discourse functions in the interactional realm, which include serving as a marker of discourse structure, an exclamation, a mitigator of confrontational stance, a marker of affiliation and connection, and an agreement marker.

Examples (1a) through (1c), which are taken from Kiesling's data on American fraternity men, illustrate some of these functions in the speech of a particular man, Pete. In example (1a), Pete and Hotdog, both European Americans, are conarrating a story about getting lost in an African American inner-city neighborhood. Pete uses *dude* in line 40 to introduce a high-affect exclamation in the evaluation of a key moment in the narrative:

(1a) *Dude* as exclamation (from Kiesling 2004: 294)

```
40   PETE:    Dude it was like boys in the hood man ai:n't no: lie:
41   HOTDOG:  And they're all they're fucked up on crack, wasted
42            they're all lookin' at us they start comin' to the car,
43            so Pete's like FLOOR IT.
44   ▷        so I take off (.) and (.)
```

In example (1b), Pete and Dave are playing the board game Monopoly. Pete uses the term *dude* first in line 44, to mitigate his initial unmitigated command to Dave to give him a piece of property, and then in line 47 as part of an improvised ditty that plays with the phonological similarity between *dude* and Dave's (real) name:

(1b) *Dude* as mitigator of conflict/marker of affiliation (from Kiesling 2004: 294)

```
44   PETE:   Fuckin' ay man.
45           Gimme the red Dave. Dude. (1.0)
46   DAVE:   No.
47   PETE:   Dave dude, dude Dave hm hm hm hm
48   DAVE:   I'll give you the purple one
49   PETE:   Oh that's a good trade
```

In example (1c), Dan offers a strongly affective evaluation of a drinking game he enjoys; Pete's response, using *dude*, undercuts Dan's enthusiasm by suggesting that the game is widespread and hence unremarkable:

(1c) *Dude* as part of a cool stance (from Kiesling 2004: 295)

```
DAN:    I love playin' caps.
        That's what did me in last-|      |last week.
PETE:                             |that's-|
        Everybody plays that damn game, dude.
```

As I demonstrate in the following analysis, a number of the characteristics of *dude* identified by Kiesling are shared by *güey*, although there are important differences as well. On the one hand, *güey* is not simply, as popular belief would have it, "the

Spanish word for *dude*." On the other hand, it is certainly true that both English-speaking and Spanish-speaking young people, especially but not exclusively young men, find that terms like these are vital to their interactional projects of stancetaking, style, and identity. I illustrate this point in detail with an analysis of ethnographic discourse data of Mexican immigrant teenagers at a California high school.

The Use of *Güey* in Interaction

In 2004–2005, I conducted a year of fieldwork in the Migrant Student Program at Orchard High School, a predominantly Latino public school in a traditionally agricultural community in Southern California.[2] The study yielded approximately 150 hours of video data involving over 40 students in beginning and advanced English as a Second Language (ESL) classes as well as a bilingual world history class. The data I analyze here are taken from a single day of fieldwork, a class field trip to the Museum of Tolerance in Los Angeles. The trip was part of a unit on the Holocaust in the world history class, but because beginning and advanced ESL were also taught by the same teacher, students in those classes were included as well. The data analyzed in the following examples are taken from interactions between three boys who were seated near each other on the bus on the drive down to Los Angeles from Orchard High. All three boys are from Mexico; two of them, Chris and Chilango, are close friends. The third, Dragon, who happened to be seated near them, is not part of their friendship group, although he is on friendly terms with both of the other two boys. (All three boys chose their own pseudonyms.)

My analytic decision to focus on *güey* was not an arbitrary one. In fact, I first heard about the term before I heard it in students' talk. On my first day of fieldwork, I explained to the primary ESL teacher, Ms. Rivera, and her classroom aide, Ms. Sánchez, the kinds of linguistic issues of interest to me. When I mentioned slang, both women reacted dramatically, jointly warning me against students' use of "bad words" from Mexican Spanish in the classroom. Ms. Rivera, a native speaker of Castilian Spanish, recounted how in her first days of teaching, students openly used "bad words" in the classroom but because she was not familiar with Mexican Spanish slang she did not recognize them; it was only when Ms. Sánchez, a native speaker of Mexican Spanish, overheard students using such words that Ms. Rivera learned what they meant and banned them from her classroom. The only example of a "bad word" from Mexican Spanish that the two women provided was *güey*; they explained to me that it originally meant 'ox' and that it functioned as a vulgar insult.

I was therefore primed to look for *güey*, but as it happened I did not need to exert myself very strenuously to find it. As the following data make abundantly clear, what is immediately striking about much of the peer interaction among migrant students at Orchard High School, and particularly boys, is the frequency with which *güey* occurs: a rough count of an hour's worth of recorded data from the interaction analyzed here, for instance, yielded 347 tokens of *güey*, or 1 nearly every 10 seconds. Much like other frequently used colloquial terms, such as *like* in English (D'Arcy 2007), *güey* is often perceived by its critics as being no more than verbal filler and hence as damning evidence of the inarticulateness of youth. However, the term is in fact highly expressive, performing a range of functions within discourse. Among other uses, it may act as an address term, as an insulting or noninsulting reference term, and as a discourse marker indicating emphasis or focus. In addition and related to these discourse functions, it also supports the performance of a stance of cool solidarity, especially during face-threatening social action such as self-aggrandizement or disagreement. Apart from referential uses of the term, in my data set *güey* overwhelmingly occurs at the ends of intonation units and thus also participates in the organization of discourse structure. The following analysis demonstrates each of these functions.[3]

The function of *güey* that is most widespread is its use as an affiliative address term, comparable to *dude*, *bro*, and similar slang items. This meaning is illustrated in example 2, in which *güey* is used as a noninsulting term for greeting a friend (see chapter appendix for transcription conventions):

(2) *Güey* as address term

<Chilango's phone rings. He takes it out of his pocket, puts it to his ear.>

1	CHILANGO:	¿Qué pedo, **güey**? (2 sec.)
		*What's going on, **güey**?*
2		¿Qué pedo, **güey**?
		*What's going on, **güey**?*
3		<Chilango lowers the phone.>
4	CHRIS:	¿Quién era?
		Who was that?
5		<Chilango switches to speaker phone and addresses the caller.>
6	CHILANGO:	¿Qué onda, **güey**?
		*What's up, **güey**?*
7	CALLER:	#
8	CHILANGO:	¿Qué onda?
		What's up?
9	CALLER:	(A::h,)

Chilango uses the term *güey* repeatedly in the initial greeting sequence of this phone call. Importantly, thanks to caller ID technology, he is aware of the identity of the caller from his very first utterance. Because cell phones establish person-to-person rather than station-to-station communication, they eliminate the identificatory preliminaries of the landline phone call openings that were analyzed in depth by conversation analysts before the advent of caller ID (e.g., Schegloff 1979). Thus Chilango's greeting is designed not simply for callers in general but for this caller in particular. It is evident that *güey* here operates primarily as an address term, both signaling Chilango's awareness of the caller's identity and inviting the initiation of the interaction. In line 2, Chilango's repetition of *¿Qué pedo, güey?* appears to be due to the caller's failure to respond to the question the first time, for in the repetition he uses the same intonational contour, as if uttering the question for the first time. Likewise, when he switches to speaker phone so that Chris can hear the caller, he again uses *güey* in line 6 to reestablish the interaction, which he has temporarily suspended in order to alter its participation framework. Once the caller produces a response to the greeting, Chilango abandons the address term, at least momentarily.

The use of *güey* as a friendly or neutral address term coexists with its function as an insult, although the pejorative meaning occurs typically (but not exclusively) in reference rather than address, for obvious reasons of face and social decorum. The use of *güey* in a negative context is seen in example (3), in which Chilango criticizes the poor driving of a motorist he spots through the bus window:

(3) *Güey* in insulting reference

1   CHILANGO: Ora, babo:so. (5 sec.)
                Hey, idiot.
2   Este **güey** no puede ir aquí:.
                *This **güey** can't go here.*
3   Debe de ir a la derecha.
                He has to go on the right.

Here *güey* is used in something closer to its derogatory sense of 'idiot'. In fact, in line 1 Chilango uses the term *baboso*, another term used to deride another's intelligence. The use of *güey* here may be understood at best as a noninsulting reference term; in any case, it clearly lacks any of the affiliative connotations it carries as an address term between friends.

If the insulting sense of *güey* may be less frequent among younger speakers, it may also be preserved in fixed idiomatic expressions, as in line 7 of example (4), *a lo güey*, 'like a *güey*; without thinking', in which the individual lexical item *güey* seems to retain the meaning 'idiot' but the expression as a whole generally has no negative connotations. In this example, Dragon is showing Chris his digital camera, and they are discussing how many photos its memory cards will hold:

(4) *Güey* as discourse marker

1   CHRIS: ¿Traes dos memorias?
              You have two memories?
2   DRAGON: ¿Y agarra cien, cien ocho, **güey**?
              *And it takes a hundred, a hundred and eight, **güey**?*
3   ¿Cada una, **güey**?
              *Each one, **güey**?*
4   Mira <[ira]>, **güey**.
              *Look, **güey**.*
5   <shows Chris the memory card>
6   CHRIS: Son como las que le caben a ésta.
              It's about as many as fit on this one.
7   DRAGON: Por eso voy a tomar a lo **güe:y**,
              *That's why I'm gonna take <pictures> like a **güey**,*
              <i.e., without thinking, automatically>
8   nomás.
              just like that.

In addition to this fixed expression, Dragon uses *güey* three times with nonreferential function in lines 2, 3, and 4. These uses resemble in structure the address-term function seen in example (2), but they are unlikely to be simple address terms given their repeated use in the middle of ongoing discourse. The function of *güey* here, as in several of the following examples, appears to be both to highlight important information and to maintain solidarity. This balancing of functions is especially important when taking a self-aggrandizing stance, as Dragon does here. Before this example begins, Chris has already indicated that he is impressed by the fact that Dragon has brought no fewer than three cameras on the field trip, and in line 1 he shows interest in the details of their capabilities. Thus Chris has invited Dragon to show off, which he willingly does in lines 2 through 5, culminating in a visual display of the camera's memory card. Each line is punctuated by *güey*, lest Chris fail to notice the impressive qualities of his camera; it also, and equally importantly, works to sustain interactional alignment. However, Chris soon ceases to act as a willing audience for Dragon's boasting; in line 6 he counters Dragon's claim that his memory card holds over a hundred photos by commenting that his own camera's memory holds the same amount.

A similar use of *güey* also occurs in example (5). In this interaction Chris has pulled out his own camera and is showing Chilango photos of members of his soccer team. What is immediately striking about the example is the heavy use of *güey* as a noninsulting term of reference, roughly equivalent to *guy* or to *dude* in its referential sense:

(5) Referential use of *güey*

1	TEACHER:	<to student teacher> Just keep an e:ye on tho:se ki:ds.
2	CHRIS:	<looking at his camera> ¿Este **güey**?
		*This **güey**?*
3	AIDE:	¡Los alum[nitos!]
		The students!
4	TEACHER:	[Those are] [[you:r]] ki:ds today.
5	CHRIS:	[No es] [[muy {bueno, el **güey**.}]] (creaky voice)
		*He's not very good, the **güey**.*
6	CHRIS:	Es pura banca.=
		He's total bench.
7		=¿Este **güey**?
		*This **güey**?*
8		Yo lo dejo en la banca,
		I leave him on the bench,
9		y me meten a mí, **güey**.
		*and they put me in, **güey**.*
10	CHILANGO:	<looking at Chris and smiling> <tongue click> <[æ̃::]>
11		<Chris looks at Chilango and smiles, then looks back down at camera.>
12	CHRIS:	Este **güe:y**,
		*This **güey**,*
13		está madreado,=
		he's fucked up,
14		=este **güey** es titular.
		*this **güey** is titular <i.e., a "chaired" player>.*

15	Este **güey** no está bien pesado,
	*This **güey** isn't very good <lit. 'heavy'>,*
16	este **güey** es bien bue:no, **güey**.
	*this **güey** is really good, **güey**.*
17	Buen<u>í</u>simo que es ese **güey**.
	*He's <u>very</u> good, that **güey**.*
18	Éste es el Alejandro, **güey**.
	*This is Alejandro, **güey**.*

The interpretation of this use of *güey* as noninsulting in valence is supported by the broad range of evaluations that Chris makes of the athletic abilities of each of the soccer players referred to as *este güey*. In addition to this referential function, Chris uses *güey* as a stance marker in lines 9, 16, and 18. In line 9 it is used in Chris's self-flattering evaluation of his own soccer talent, and Chilango responds to this blatant self-praise with playful derision. In the other two uses, it is more subtle. In line 16 Chris uses it in praising another player rather than himself, and in line 18 he uses it to introduce one of the players by name; in the interaction that follows the example Chilango claims to know the player as well. Thus even without openly boasting Chris is able to bask in the reflected glory of these two players: they are on *his* soccer team, captured on *his* camera, and he has primary epistemic authority (Heritage and Raymond 2005) in relation to them. As with Dragon in the previous example, Chris's use of *güey* to accomplish this boasting allows him to maintain a solidary alignment with his addressee, in this case relatively successfully.

The next two examples illustrate in greater detail the use of *güey* while taking a boastful stance, as well as offering additional insights into these boys' pragmatic deployment and metapragmatic understanding of the term. In each case, Chris is bragging to Chilango, who is variously receptive to and skeptical of some of Chris's wilder claims.

Example (6) finds Chris bragging once again, but this time, Chilango is more dubious, and in taking this stance he illustrates another interactional situation in which *güey* occurs in these data, in conjunction with a stance of mild disalignment. Whereas in previous examples *güey* worked to preserve intersubjective alignment during the self-elevation of the speaker, here its affiliative function also serves to counterbalance Chilango's disaligning stance toward Chris's claims. In both cases, the solidary stance indexed by *güey* has a mitigating function during a face-threatening moment that jeopardizes (albeit briefly and nonseriously) the friendly tenor of the interaction. Immediately before this example, Chris has been claiming that during one year of high school in Mexico he missed 360 classes:

(6) *Güey* in conjunction with a stance of disalignment

1	CHRIS:	Ahí tengo todavía la boleta, [**güey**.]
		*I still have the report card, **güey**.*
2	CHILANGO:	¿Trescientos se<u>sen</u>ta, **güey**?
		*Three hundred and sixty, **güey**?*
3	CHRIS:	Como lo de un año, {**güey**.}= <creaky voice>
		*About a year's worth, **güey**.*

4		=[Faltas.]

Absences.

5   CHILANGO: [Por eso] digo, **güey**.

*That's why I'm telling you, **güey**.*

6   No mames.

Come on. <lit., 'Don't suck'>

7   Ya casi— ¿Fuiste cinco días a clase, [o qué]?

Almost— Did you <only> go to class five days, or what?

8   CHRIS: [No, **güey**.]=

*No, **güey**.*

9   =Pero, ya ves que son ocho clases.=

But, you know there are eight classes.

10   =Osea, hay cuántas.=

Like, how many are there.

11   =Y en todas esas clases, en:—

And in all those classes, in—

12   Tuve trescientas y sesenta y algo faltas.

I had three hundred sixty something absences.

13   Pero iba a los concursos.=

But I used to go to the competitions.

14   =Y una clase, **güey**?=

*And one class, **güey**?*

15   =Iba a Puerto Valla:rta, **güey**,

*I used to go to Puerto Vallarta, **güey**,*

16   a, a las playas a concursar, **güey**.

*to, to the beaches to compete, **güey**.*

17   Y llegaba,

And I would get there,

18   y todos los profes me ponían mi {diez:, **güey**,} <creaky voice>

*and all the profs would give me my ten <points>, **güey**,*

19   bien chingón:.

really cool.

20   CHILANGO: @

As before, most of the boastful assertions—lines 1, 3, 15, 16, and 18—are fore-grounded with *güey*, and once again the audience for this braggadocio is not consistently admiring. In lines 2 and 5–7 Chilango openly and repeatedly challenges Chris's claim that he missed over 300 classes in a single school year, and he does so using the marker *güey*. Chris's response in line 8, which also involves disagreement, likewise includes *güey*. In such instances, as in some of the uses of *dude* analyzed by Kiesling (2004), the affiliative meaning of the term serves to soften the blow of disalignment.

In addition to the boastful and referential uses of *güey* already seen, example (7) features an illustration of metapragmatic commentary about the term emerging within interaction. Previous to this example, the two boys have been reminiscing

about the benefits of membership in soccer teams in Mexico. Here Chris is matching
one of Chilango's stories:

(7) Metapragmatic commentary on *güey*

1	CHRIS:	Pero, es que, esos **güeyes** tienen feria a lo {cabró:n, **güey**.} <creaky voice>
		*But, the thing is, those **güeys** had a lot of money, **güey**.*
2		Como el presidente,=
		Like the mayor,
3		=fíjate, **güey**,=
		*look, **güey**,*
4		=¿el pinche presidente?
		the freaking mayor?
5		Pagaba to:do, **güey**.
		*He paid everything, **güey**.*
6		¿Un pedo?=
		A problem?
7		=¿Te metían al bote?
		They threw you in jail?
8		Y, y salías a los diez minu:tos.=
		And, and you were out in ten minutes.
9		=Y a mí me metían #,
		And they used to throw me #,
10		¿me metieron dos veces?
		they threw me <in jail> twice.
11		Y {qué:.} <creaky voice>
		And what.
12		Pues <[pus]>, yo ando acá:, "Ay, usted me con-"=
		Well, I'm like this, "Oh, you <know> me"
13		=Le decíamos el Gordo, **güey**.
		*We called him Fatso, **güey**.*
14		Todos nos llevábamos bien chingón.
		We all got along really cool.
15		<smiling, putting hand on Chilango's shoulder>
16		Hasta le hablábamos de **güe:y**, **güey**.
		*We even called him **güey**, **güey**.*
17	CHILANGO:	<smiling> "¿Qué pe:do, **güey**?"
		*"What's going on, **güey**?"*
18	CHRIS:	"Ey, **güey**."
		*"Hey, **güey**."*

As shown in previous examples, Chris uses *güey* along with other linguistic resources
to mark for Chilango the parts of his narrative that are especially impressive: that the
mayor paid for the team's meals (lines 2–5), that the team members were on a nickname
basis with this distinguished personage (line 13), and, most importantly both for Chris

and for present purposes, that they "even called him *güey*" (*Hasta le hablábamos de güey*; line 16).[4] This latter statement, itself marked by *güey* and highlighted by Chris's friendly touch on Chilango's shoulder, both enacts and comments on the signification of *güey* as an affiliative term. Chilango offers uptake of Chris's claim by smiling and using quoted speech to imagine the improbable scenario in which a *presidente municipal* could be greeted with *¿Qué pedo, güey?*, and Chris joins in with his own enactment of hypothetical quoted speech addressed to the mayor.

As noted above, linguistic indices do not operate in isolation but as part of a cluster of semiotic resources that collectively create stances and styles. Chris's use of *güey* in this excerpt, as in several previous examples, co-occurs with extensive use of creaky voice and other expressive prosody, especially lengthening of the vowel of the penultimate stressed syllable of the intonation unit. In this context, Chris's voice quality and prosodic style seem to iconically contribute to the directly indexical stance of cool, casual nonchalance that he constructs both through the content of his talk and through the use of *güey* and other slang terms. This stance is closely akin to what Kiesling (2004) describes for *dude*. Moreover, as with *dude*, *güey* is used in my data set more often by and to male than female interlocutors, and it is often indirectly indexical of masculinity.[5]

Importantly, these two slang terms are tied not to a generalized version of masculinity but to particular gendered personas, especially within the ideologically saturated representations of each term as constructed in the popular media. These ideologized personas are not only gendered but often ethnoracially specific as well (although in the linguistic practices of ordinary speakers both terms transcend such categories). For its part, *dude* embodies what Kiesling calls "counter-culture, nonserious masculinity" (2004: 288), as seen in Hollywood in such iconic figures of white masculinity as the California surfer and the drug-addled slacker, an association that emerges both in his survey data and in media representations. By contrast, as I discuss further in the next section, to the extent that it features in U.S. media representations, *güey* is primarily associated with a hip urban Latino identity.

Metapragmatic Stereotypes in Media Representations of *Güey*

Ideologies about language circulate through both explicit metapragmatic commentary and implicit metapragmatic representation. Ideologies of *güey* and its (in)appropriateness in particular contexts are seen not only in Chris and Chilango's brief skit enacting the unlikely use of the term to a high-status official in example (7) but also in their teachers' admonishment to me to beware of this "bad word." These ideologies are indexically built on the use of *güey* in interaction; however, they oversimplify this interactional ground by regimenting the complexity of pragmatic practice—the diverse interactional uses and social meanings of *güey*—through metapragmatic typification (Agha 2007). The process of typification occurs not only in everyday interaction but also within wider-reaching cultural vehicles such as the media. Recent representations of *güey* in U.S. advertising reveal further ideologization of the term through the exploitation of the interactionally constructed stances and styles exemplified above. The typifications represented in these ads construct an idealized *güey* user along parameters of gender, age, ethnicity, and social class that restrict the broader semiotic field in which *güey* circulates in interaction. The ad campaign at issue projects a young, ethnicized yet safely upper-middle-class, urban masculinity to market a quintessential masculinized product, beer.

The media representations I examine below participate in a widespread marketing trend whereby heterosexual masculinity is reinscribed in the popular media but at a safely ironic distance (cf. Benwell 2003). This sort of marketing does not simply project a stance of cool solidarity onto the characters in ads but also claims it for companies themselves through its use of a deadpan cinéma vérité style that offers a humorously exaggerated representation of young masculinity rather than an earnest pitch for a product. At the same time, viewers are cast as knowing consumers who will catch and appreciate the ironic tone of such commercials and identify with the hipster world they portray, in a process of lifestyle branding that has been extensively analyzed and critiqued (e.g., Klein 2002; cf. Bucholtz 2007).

Both the direct and indirect indexicalities of *güey* make it particularly well suited for deployment in this sort of marketing. In May 2004, Bromley Communications, the self-described "country's largest Hispanic advertising agency" (Bromley Communications 2006), featured the term in a commercial for Coors Light beer produced on behalf of its client, Coors Brewing Company, and aimed at the Latino market as well as trendy urbanites more generally. The spot was an intertextual riff on Budweiser's award-winning "Whassup?" advertising campaign, which had already spawned a wealth of viral video parodies following the airing of the first ad, titled "Whassup?: True," during the 2000 Super Bowl. Featuring four young, hip, upper-middle-class African American men at leisure, the original "Whassup?" ad evoked the aimless linguistic interaction that stereotypically characterizes friendship among heterosexual American men:[6]

(8) Budweiser's "Whassup?: True" ad

1   <Male 1 is watching TV. Phone rings.>
2   MALE 1: Hello.
3   MALE 2: Hey hoo. 'Sup?
4   MALE 1: Nothin', B. Just watchin' the ga:me, havin' a Bu:d. Whassup wit'
             you? <[wɪtʃu]>
5   MALE 2: Nothin'. Watchin' game, havin' a Bud.
6   MALE 1: True. True.
7   MALE 3: <entering room behind Male 1> Whassu:::p!
8   MALE 1: Whassu:::h!
9   MALE 2: Yo, who's that?
10   MALE 1: Yo! Yo, pick up the phone.
11   MALE 3: <goes to kitchen, picks up phone> Hello?
12   MALE 2: Whassu:::h!
13   MALE 3: Whassu:::h!
14   MALE 1: U:::h!
15   MALE 3: Yo! Where's Dookie?

16   MALE 2: Yo, Dookie!

17   <cut to Male 4 at computer; he picks up phone>

18   MALE 4: Yo.

19   MALE 2: <higher pitch> Whassu::h!

20   MALE 4: Whassu:::h!

21   MALE 2: U:::h @!

22   <quick cuts to all four men, all shouting "U:::h!">

23   MALE 3: @@@

24   <intercom beeps>

25   MALE 3: Hold on. <presses intercom button> Hello?

26   MALE 5: Whassu:::p!

27   <quick cuts to all five men, all shouting "U:::h!"; then quick cuts to Male 2
      and Male 4 hanging up>

28   MALE 1: So whassup, B?

29   MALE 2: Watchin' the game, havin' a Bud.

30   <cut to black screen with Budweiser logo and the word "TRUE">
      MALE 1: <voice-over> True. True.

(Source: http://www.youtube.com/watch?v=ikkg4NobV_w&feature=relate)

As the campaign unfolded, Budweiser's ads created complex intertextual links to the original "Whassup?" ad, in the process demonstrating a remarkable metapragmatic sophistication, a savvy understanding of the American ideology of African American cultural authenticity that underwrites the campaign (cf. Cutler 2003), and an ironic stance toward masculine homosociality (for further discussion of the cultural significance of the "Whassup?" ad campaign, see Watts and Orbe 2002). As *Advertising Age* reporter Bob Garfield explained at the time: "'Whassssupppppp?' doesn't mean, 'Pray, have you any news you'd care to impart?' It means, 'You are my friend, and if you are doing anything interesting—interesting being defined as watching football and swilling beer—I'm in favor of doing it together.'"[7]

This parodic representation of inarticulate male bonding was also central to the Coors Light ad, which aimed at the same key young adult male demographic as the Budweiser commercials and echoed both their cool, casual style and their linguistic humor, but with a twist. The Coors Light spot did not hinge on the African American English greeting *Whassup?* (i.e., 'What's up?' or 'What's going on?'), the linguistic appropriation of which by young Americans of all races and ethnicities was fostered by the Budweiser ads. Rather, the Coors ad focused on the equally ubiquitous but less widely familiar *güey*, which was at the time and still remains much less well known outside the community in which it is used, even among Spanish speakers. The Bromley agency sought to bridge this linguistic gap with a brief gloss of the term at the end of the spot, which allowed versions of the commercial to play on both Spanish-language and English-language television. Example (9) is a transcript of the English-language version, which portrays the interlinked interactions among several casually but elegantly dressed light-skinned young men in a bar as they drink beer, play pool, and admire women:[8]

(9) Coors Light's "Güey" ad

1		<In a bar>
2	MALE 1:	¿Qué onda, **güe:::y**?
		What's up, güey?
3	MALE 2:	Nada, **güey**.
		Nothing, güey.
4		<They embrace; Male 2 sits at the bar next to a bucket of Coors Light bottles>
5	MALE 2:	¿Quieres una, **güey**?
		Do you want one, güey?
6	MALE 1:	**Güe::y.** <Male 2 passes him a bottle; he gestures across the room>
7		**¡Güey!**
8	MALE 3:	<glancing up from pool table> ¿Qué onda, **güey**?
		What's up, güey?
9	MALE 1:	<looking at his beer bottle, whispers> **¡Güe::y!**
10	MALE 4:	<at pool table, to Male 3> **Güey, güey, güey, güey, güey, güey!**
11		<Two women walk across the room>
12	(MALE 3?):	Ay.
13	(MALE 4?):	**¡Güey!**
14	MALE 3:	<looking up from pool table> ¡Ay, **güe:y**!
15		<Male 1 looks at Male 2, smiles, and raises his eyebrows; Male 3 moves to bar>
16	MALE 2:	<to Male 3> Agarra una, **güey**.
		Take one, güey.
17	MALE 3:	<taking a beer bottle, gestures with head, whispers> **¡Güey!**
18		<Two other women approach the pool table; Male 4 kisses each in greeting>
19	?:	¡Uu:::m:!
20	?:	<creaky> {**¡Güe:y!**}
21		<Male 1 lifts bottle in toast toward another pair of women, who look and smile>
22	MALE 2:	¡A[y, **güey:::!**]
23	MALE 1:	[¡Ay, **güey:::!**]
24		<Both men exchange glances and smile>
25		<Cut to black screen reading "GÜEY = DUDE">
26		<Cut to can of Coors Light being opened>
27	VOICE-OVER:	Unleash the Rocky Mountain cold taste of Coors Light.
28		<Cut to black screen with stylized mountain logo with the superimposed words "ROCK ON">

Although within the industry the commercial was quickly heralded as a master stroke in reaching its target demographic (Wentz 2004a), it stirred up negative reactions among some Spanish-speaking viewers, who complained, like the teachers at Orchard High School, that the term *güey* derives from the Spanish word *buey* ('ox') and is a derogatory term meaning 'idiot' (James 2005; Latino Pundit 2004; Sánchez 2006; Wentz 2004b). Indeed, the advertising agency was not unaware of this etymological account and even played on it in a separate billboard campaign in the Los Angeles area during the same period. The first billboards, reading simply, "What's the wave, ox?" generated considerable interest among non-Spanish-speaking motorists, who interpreted the question as a puzzle. Two weeks later, Bromley added to the billboards the Mexican Spanish colloquial greeting of which the English phrase is a calque: "¿Qué onda, güey?" This greeting is seen in example (2) above as well as in the Coors Light spot.

Although the *güey* billboards were generally considered clever, the *güey* television commercial drew complaints, especially from older Mexican American viewers who were familiar with the term only as an insult. Younger Chicano audience members, however, responded positively, apparently recognizing themselves in the linguistic practice represented in the ad. As the reporter for *Advertising Age* who covered the controversy noted, "For many young Hispanic males, 'güey' has crossed over into everyday speech between men. In the Coors Light spot, the word is delivered with different inflections and intonations that convey greetings, offers of beer and appreciation of attractive women" (Wentz 2004b).

This brief brouhaha (as it were) offers a clear illustration of the ideological dimension of indexicality as well as the complex relationship between stance and style constructed by the advertiser. To begin with, the commercial relies for audience recognition on metapragmatic stereotypes of *güey* use and *güey* users. These stereotypes include social categorization by age, gender, and ethnicity, as well as the social acts and interactional stances that can be performed through the use of *güey*, including greeting, agreeing, summoning, and conveying such affective states as satisfaction and lust, as well as the more enduring stance of casual hipness that accrues to *güey* users. Presumably recognizing that these ideologies would not be immediately shared by the largely monolingual English-speaking audience, the ad agency established intertextual links to Budweiser's earlier ad campaign via ironic representations of male bonding through linguistic minimalism. By means of such intertextuality, the semiotics if not the semantics of *güey* became intelligible to a wide range of media-saturated viewers, who could be expected to catch the allusion. Thus the stance of cool solidarity and upper-class urban sophistication displayed by the actors in the ad positioned viewers as likewise sophisticated and equipped with the semiotic resources to decode the message, even if they lacked the linguistic resources to interpret *güey* itself without assistance (and of course, the final "translation" of the term as 'dude' carries its own set of assumptions about viewers' familiarity with American English youth slang). At the same time, despite such measures, the intended metapragmatic stereotype was not in fact shared by the entire audience, and the lack of a shared interpretation of *güey* sparked controversy among Mexican Americans. In part this gap was due to the advertisers' focus on monolingual English speakers, rather than older Spanish speakers, as the group most in need of linguistic instruction.

In both the Coors Light ad and the Budweiser campaign, the linguistic practices of subordinated ethnoracial groups are used to sell products to speakers of the hegemonic language. The linguistic gap produced by such advertising techniques is bridged by inviting the audience's identification based on youth, hipness, urbanity, and masculinity, as well as by portraying idealized ethnic and racial minority speakers as comfortably middle-class—a representation that is quite remote from the working-class and underclass realities of Mexican migrant youth like Chris, Chilango, and Dragon.[9] However, such representations are by no means restricted to mass media corporate advertising. Even the niche advertising of small, politically progressive companies targeting Latinos may draw on many of the same indexicalities seen in the Coors Light ad to produce similar metapragmatic stereotypes, this time for consumption by Latinos rather than a wider market.

My final example of the indexical and ideological work accomplished by *güey* focuses on the term's circulation on a widely sold T-shirt produced by NaCo, an edgy California-based clothing company that bills itself as "the authentic Latino clothing brand." NaCo was founded by a pair of Mexican American art school graduates to produce casual clothing that combines a hipster sensibility with Latino pride; its name derives from the Mexican slang term *naco*, a derogatory term for a lower-class Mexican, and the company's founders' stated aim is to rehabilitate this term by celebrating "naconess" as an expression of nonconformist identity. The term *güey* appears on a popular NaCo T-shirt in which the bilingual pun *ONE GÜEY* is inscribed on the familiar logo of a "one-way" street sign.

Figure 7.1, which comes from an online distributor of NaCo's products that shares the company's commitment to making "authentic" urban Latino commodities

FIGURE 7.1 "One Güey" T-shirt produced by NaCo clothing company. (Source: Surropa.com.)

available to consumers, presents the imagined wearer of this shirt as a representative of the same cool masculinity seen to be associated with *güey* in other contexts. The model's pose and expression are cool and affectless, an embodied stance that corresponds with the interactional and ideological functions of *güey* seen above (not to mention the reigning aesthetic of high-fashion photography). This youthful representative of *güey*ness is light-skinned, and he sports an upper-middle-class urban bohemian bourgeois style, as evidenced by his retro soul patch and sideburns, his trendy distressed jeans, and the soulful-looking golden retriever that accompanies him. These signifiers stand not only in contrast to the decidedly lower-class aesthetic that the term *naco* often derides but also to the bodies and financial circumstances of the majority of Mexican Americans, who are generally darker-skinned and considerably less well-to-do than the idealized Latino represented in this ad. It is probable that this image, given its producer, is intended to foreground the diversity of Latino identities, yet the indexical embedding of *güey* in this version of cool, youthful, urban masculinity is more closely aligned with the representation in the Coors Light ad than with most real-world users of *güey*.

As these examples from advertising show, when indexicalities enter the highly ideologized space of the media, they rapidly undergo simplification and erasure. Thus although *güey* retains its directly indexical link to a stance of cool solidarity, its indirect indexical associations become restricted to a middle-class form of masculinity that excludes many of *güey*'s users. In this way, the youth-cultural style that Chris, Chilango, and Dragon enact through their use of *güey* and other semiotic resources becomes stylized as it enters the media domain. Coupland (2001: 345) defines stylization as "the knowing deployment of culturally familiar styles and identities that are marked as deviating from those predictably associated with the current speaking context." Although his analytic focus is on how stylization "dislocates" speakers and their utterances from the immediate discourse context, stylization, as a form of metapragmatic typification, also enables the displacement of some indexical associations in favor of others—a simplification of the indexical field, in Eckert's (2008) sense.

Yet despite the indexical narrowing that is characteristic of metapragmatic stereotypes, ideological representations are not entirely rigid. Indeed, advertisers often rely heavily on the indeterminacy and ambiguity of semiotic markers in order to reach the widest possible audience. In some cases, such as the outcry over the Coors Light ad, the multivalency of linguistic indices like *güey* may lead to outrage from nontarget viewers, but more often mediated ideologies depend on the flexibility and highly contextualized nature of indexicality for their success.

Conclusion

This chapter calls attention to the need for sociolinguists to examine both interactional practices and ideological representations in investigating the relationship between the linguistic and other semiotic features that directly index stances and the styles and identities—or personas or stereotypes—that they may also indirectly index. Much of the previous research on slang attempted to read off social meaning directly from the semantics or the demographic distribution of slang terms, but as the preceding analysis demonstrates, slang gains its semiotic value only within the socio-cultural context in which it is used. Indexicality is therefore a fundamental concept in understanding how slang and other semiotic resources come to be associated with social categories such as gender. As the work of Ochs and Kiesling shows in different ways, the indexicality of gender involves (at least) two semiotic levels: at the level of direct indexicality, linguistic forms are associated with interactional stances or ori-entations to ongoing talk, whereas at the level of indirect indexicality, these stances calcify into more enduring ways of being—that is, styles or identities—that are in turn ideologically associated with particular social groups (see also Inoue 2004). An indexical view of slang allows for a richer analysis than is possible in taxonomic or correlational approaches, by enabling researchers to link slang both to stancetaking and to other sociolinguistic and semiotic phenomena that cluster together as part of styles. Sociolinguists must therefore become more attentive to the contexts of slang's use and representation, including both interactionally grounded and ethnographically specific research and analyses of larger metapragmatic stereotypes. Such a dual per-spective allows analysts to take into account the narrowly regimented ideologies of slang that circulate via the media and other channels as well as the far more complex linguistic practices of stancetaking and stylistic display that speakers use in daily interaction to carry out their social goals.

As interactional and ethnographic analysis demonstrates, Chris, Chilango, Dragon, and other Spanish-speaking students at Orchard High School did not use *güey* because they were male, as correlational approaches to language and gender would argue. Nor did they use *güey* in order to directly construct a masculine identity, as many social constructionists would maintain. Rather, the term, in co-occurrence with other available semiotic resources, such as prosody, gesture, posture, clothing, topics of discourse, and material objects such as telephones and cameras, allowed these boys to do something of much greater immediate importance: to interact with one another, to greet their friends, to brag, to undercut a friend's boasting—in short, to establish both status and solidarity in relation to their social group—and to index a cool, nonchalant stance all the while. In turn, the habitual use of these practices by male speakers to perform these and other interactional and social actions could create an indirect indexical link to masculinity—and the evidence of advertising suggests that in some contexts, in fact, this is precisely what takes place. But not everyone who offers a metapragmatic stereotype regarding *güey* focuses on masculinity: for the ESL teachers at Orchard High, what was most salient was not the gender of the speaker but the perceived vulgarity of the term; for Chris and Chilango, imagining themselves addressing the *presidente municipal* as *güey*, what was most salient is the term's equalizing pragmatic force. Thus both interactional use and metapragmatic stereotypes work together to create styles as sets of indexical meanings that tie lin-guistic forms to the speakers who (are thought to) use them.

The introduction of stance into sociolinguistic analysis, especially in conjunction with the field's retheorizing of style, moves the sociolinguistic study of identity into fruit-ful new directions. As sociolinguistics increasingly shifts toward an indexical view of linguistic variation, the notion of stance becomes a critical mediating concept between linguistic forms and larger social structures. At the same time, sociolinguistics has a great deal to offer other scholars interested in stancetaking in discourse, through its careful attention to the range of linguistic resources available to mark speakers' interactional moves and their broader distribution across social categories and situations. These developments suggest on the one hand that the study of language variation must be equally attuned to the details of interactional context and to wider ideological formations, and on the other hand that the study of stance needs to consider not only the interactional subjectivities of interlocutors but also the more enduring subject positions and social categories they take up or have thrust upon them. By combining the insights of these complementary perspectives, the emerging sociolinguistics of stance provides a firm and fertile empirical ground for investigating the linguistic construction of social identity.

Acknowledgments

I am grateful to the Spencer Foundation for Educational Research as well as the Academic Senate and the Center for Chicano Studies at the University of California, Santa Barbara, for their financial support of the larger study from which these data originate. Thanks are also due to my research assistants Verónica Muñoz Ledo Yáñez and Erica Garcia for their invaluable help with transcription and translation, and to audiences at the Ohio State University, Stanford University, the University of California, San Diego, and Uppsala University for their comments and suggestions on this research. Finally, I deeply appreciate Misty Jaffe's insightful feedback on this chapter as well as her patience during its long gestation period. Of course, I alone am responsible for any weaknesses that remain.

Appendix: Transcription Conventions

.	end of intonation unit; falling intonation
,	end of intonation unit; fall-rise intonation
?	end of intonation unit; rising intonation
!	raised pitch and volume throughout the intonation unit
underline	emphatic stress; increased amplitude; careful articulation of a segment
:	length
=	latching; no pause between intonation units
—	self-interruption; break in the intonation unit
-	self-interruption; break in the word, sound abruptly cut off
@	laughter; each token marks one pulse
[ ]	overlapping speech
[[ ]]	overlapping speech in proximity to a previous overlap
( )	uncertain transcription
#	unintelligible; each token marks one syllable
< >	transcriber comment; nonvocal noise
{ }	stretch of talk to which transcriber comment applies
< [ ] >	phonetic transcription
" "	reported speech or thought

Notes

1. Ochs's framework focuses on two basic levels of indexicality in order to demonstrate the relationship between stance and social identity, an analytic convenience I follow here; however, it is clear that there are multiple levels of indexicality—what Silverstein (2003) calls "indexical orders"—each reliant on an ideologically "prior" level for its semiotic force.

2. All names and other identifying information have been changed.

3. It is important to note that this analysis is not exhaustive of *güey*'s function. For example, the fact that the boys are seated near one another and are constantly available as interlocutors means that the attention-getting functions of *güey* found in other interactional contexts are not seen here.

4. Interestingly, Chris's remarkable claim to have been in jail twice before the age of 15, his current age, is somewhat downplayed, perhaps to support the reenactment of his purported nonchalance at the time or perhaps to avoid a challenge from Chilango. As example (6) above demonstrates, such challenges are forthcoming when Chris's stories veer too directly into the realm of implausibility.

5. In fact, a number of Mexican and Mexican American girls and women use *güey* to varying degrees, but the particular styles of femininity displayed by most of the girls in the present study were incompatible with frequent *güey* use, and it rarely occurs among female speakers in my data.

6. The four men are in fact best friends in real life; one of them, Charles Stone III, is a filmmaker whose short film *True* was the inspiration for the ad campaign.

7. Cited in the Advertising Mascots feature of the TV Acres website (http://www.tvacres.com/admascots_whassup_guys.htm). I have been unable to locate the June 26, 2000, *Advertising Age* article to which the website refers.

8. I have not been able to obtain a copy or a description of the Spanish-language version, but it is likely that it omits the gloss and the use of English.

9. The fact that these teenagers, whose families faced often serious financial struggles, used and displayed to one another the latest electronic gadgets—cameras, cell phones—is indicative of the semiotic importance of such commodities in indexing contemporary youth styles.

References

Agha, Asif. 2007. *Language and social relations*. Cambridge: Cambridge University Press.

Benwell, Bethan, ed. 2003. *Masculinity and men's lifestyle magazines*. Oxford: Blackwell.

Braun, Virginia, and Celia Kitzinger. 2001. Telling it straight? Dictionary definitions of women's genitals. *Journal of Sociolinguistics* 5(2): 214–232.

Bromley Communications 2006. http://www.bromleyville.com.

Bucholtz, Mary. 2004. The appropriation of African American Vernacular English as European American youth slang. Paper presented at the annual conference on New Ways of Analyzing Variation, University of Michigan, Ann Arbor, October.

——. 2006. Word up: Social meanings of slang in California youth culture. In *A cultural approach to interpersonal communication: Essential readings,* ed. Jane Goodman and Leila Monaghan, 243–267. Malden, MA: Blackwell.

——. 2007. Shop talk: Branding, consumption, and gender in American middle-class youth interaction. In *Words, worlds, and material girls: Language, gender, globalization,* ed. Bonnie McElhinny, 371–402. Berlin: Mouton de Gruyter.

Bucholtz, Mary, and Kira Hall. 2005. Identity and interaction: A sociocultural linguistic approach. *Discourse Studies* 7(4–5): 585–614.

Cameron, Deborah. 1992. "Naming of parts": Gender, culture and terms for the penis among American college students. *American Speech* 67(3): 364–379.

Chun, Elaine. 2007. "Oh my god!": Stereotypical words at the intersection of sound, practice, and social meaning. Paper presented at the annual conference on New Ways of Analyzing Variation, Philadelphia, October.

Coupland, Nikolas. 2001. Dialect stylization in radio talk. *Language in Society* 30(3): 345–375.

——. 2007. *Style: Language variation and identity.* Cambridge: Cambridge University Press.

Cutler, Cecelia. 2003. "Keepin' it real": White hip-hoppers' discourses of language, race, and authenticity. *Journal of Linguistic Anthropology* 13(2): 211–233.

D'Arcy, Alex. 2007. *Like* and language ideology: Disentangling fact from fiction. *American Speech* 82(4): 386–419.

de Klerk, Vivian. 1990. Slang: A male domain? *Sex Roles* 22(9–10): 589–606.

——. 1992. How taboo are taboo words for girls? *Language in Society* 21(2): 277–289.

——. 1997. The role of expletives in the construction of masculinity. In *Language and masculinity*, ed. Sally Johnson and Ulrike Hanna Meinhof, 144–158. Oxford: Blackwell.

Du Bois, John W. 2007. The stance triangle. In *Stancetaking in discourse: Subjectivity, evaluation, interaction*, ed. Robert Englebretson, 139–182. Amsterdam: John Benjamins.

Eckert, Penelope. 2000. *Language variation as social practice.* Oxford: Blackwell.

——. 2003. The meaning of style. In *SALSA XI: Proceedings of the eleventh annual Symposium About Language and Society—Austin (Texas Linguistic Forum 47)*, ed. Wai Fong Chiang, Elaine Chun, Laura Mahalingappa, and Siri Mehus, 41–53. Austin: University of Texas Department of Linguistics.

——. (2008). Variation and the indexical field. *Journal of Sociolinguistics* 12(4): 453–476.

Eckert, Penelope, and John R. Rickford, eds. (2001). *Style and sociolinguistic variation.* Cambridge: Cambridge University Press.

Heritage, John, and Geoffrey Raymond. 2005. The terms of agreement: Indexing epistemic authority and subordination in talk-in-interaction. *Social Psychology Quarterly* 68(1): 15–38.

Hughes, Susan E. 1992. Expletives of lower working-class women. *Language in Society* 21(2): 291–303.

Inoue, Miyako 2004. What does language remember? Indexical inversion and the naturalized history of Japanese women. *Journal of Linguistic Anthropology* 14(1): 39–56.

Irvine, Judith T., and Susan Gal. 2000. Language ideology and linguistic differentiation. In *Regimes of language: Ideologies, polities, and identities*, ed. Paul V. Kroskrity, 35–84. Santa Fe, NM: School of American Research Press.

James, Deborah. 1998. Gender-linked derogatory terms and their use by women and men. *American Speech* 73(4): 399–420.

James, Jean-Paul. 2005. The multicultural paradigm. *Journal of Integrated Marketing Communications* 44–52. http://jimc.medill.northwestern.edu/JIMCWebsite/Archive2005/MulticulturalParadigm.pdf

Johnstone, Barbara. 2007. Linking identity and dialect through stancetaking. In *Stancetaking in discourse: Subjectivity, evaluation, interaction*, ed. Robert Englebretson, 49–68. Amsterdam: John Benjamins.

Kiesling, Scott F. 2004. Dude. *American Speech* 79(3): 281–305.

——. 2005. Variation, stance and style: Word-final -*er*, high rising tone, and ethnicity in Australian English. *English World-Wide* 26(1): 1–42.

Klein, Naomi. 2002. *No logo: No space, no choice, no jobs*. New York: Picador.

Labov, William. 1972. *Sociolinguistic patterns*. Philadelphia: University of Pennsylvania Press.

Lakoff, Robin Tolmach. 2004. *Language and woman's place: Text and commentaries*, ed. Mary Bucholtz. Revised and expanded edition. New York: Oxford University Press.

Latino Pundit. 2004. Coors guey. Latino Pundit: A Latino blog born out of underrepresentation. May 18. http://www.latinopundit.com/.

Mendoza-Denton, Norma. 2002. Language and identity. In *The handbook of language variation and change*, ed. J. K. Chambers, Peter Trudgill, and Natalie Schilling-Estes, 475–499. Oxford: Blackwell.

——. 2008. *Homegirls: Language and cultural practice among Latina youth gangs*. Malden, MA: Blackwell.

Miller, Jennifer. 2004. Identity and language use: The politics of speaking ESL in schools. In *Negotiation of identities in multilingual contexts,* ed. Aneta Pavlenko and Adrian Blackledge, 290–315. Clevedon: Multilingual Matters.

Miller, Laura. 2004. Those naughty teenage girls: Japanese Kogals, slang, and media assessments. *Journal of Linguistic Anthropology* 14(2): 225–247.

Ochs, Elinor. 1990. Indexicality and socialization. In *Cultural psychology: Essays on comparative human development*, ed. James W. Stigler, Richard A. Shweder, and Gilbert Herdt, 287–308. Cambridge: Cambridge University Press.

——. 1992. Indexing gender. In *Rethinking context: Language as an interactive phenomenon*, ed. Alessandro Duranti and Charles Goodwin, 335–358. Cambridge: Cambridge University Press.

——. 1993. Constructing social identity: A language socialization perspective. *Research on Language and Social Interaction* 26(3): 287–306.

——. 1996. Linguistic resources for socializing humanity. In *Rethinking linguistic relativity*, ed. John J. Gumperz and Stephen C. Levinson, 407–437. Cambridge: Cambridge University Press.

Risch, Barbara. 1987. Women's derogatory terms for men: That's right, "dirty" words. *Language in Society* 16(3): 353–358.

Sánchez, Melissa. 2006. Ads speak to young Latinos in two languages. *San Jose Mercury News*. February 12.

Schegloff, Emanuel A. 1979. Identification and recognition in telephone conversation openings. In *Everyday language: Studies in ethnomethodology*, ed. George Psathas, 23–78. New York: Irvington.

Schilling-Estes, Natalie. 2004. Constructing ethnicity in interaction. *Journal of Sociolinguistics* 8(2): 163–195.

Silverstein, Michael. 1976. Shifters, linguistic categories, and cultural description. In *Meaning in anthropology,* ed. Keith H. Basso and Henry A. Selby, 11–55. Albuquerque: University of New Mexico Press.

——. 1985. Language and the culture of gender: At the intersection of structure, usage, and ideology. In *Semiotic mediation: Sociocultural and psychological perspectives,* ed. Elizabeth Mertz and Richard J. Parmentier, 219–259. Orlando: Academic Press.

——. 2003. Indexical order and the dialectics of sociolinguistic life. *Language and Communication* 23(3–4): 193–229.

Stenström, Anna-Brita. 2003. "It's not that I really care, about him personally you know": The construction of gender identity in London teenage talk. In *Discourse constructions of youth identities*, Jannis K. Androutsopoulos and Alexandra Georgakopoulou, 93–117. Amsterdam: John Benjamins.

Sutton, Laurel A. 1995. Bitches and skankly hobags: The place of women in contemporary slang. In *Gender articulated: Language and the socially constructed self*, ed. Kira Hall and Mary Bucholtz, 279–296. New York: Routledge.

Watts, Eric King, and Orbe, Mark P. 2002. The spectacular consumption of "true" African American culture: "Whassup" with the Budweiser guys? *Critical Studies in Media Communication* 19(1): 1–20.

Wentz, Laurel. 2004a. Coors launches Hispanic version of a "Whassup" ad: Hey, dude, "guey" could become the latest barroom buzzword. *Advertising Age*. May 5.

——. 2004b. Coors Hispanic "Guey" ad sparks controversy: Slang meaning hotly debated: Creatively clever or derogatory? *Advertising Age*. May 17.

8

Style as Stance

Stance as the Explanation for Patterns
of Sociolinguistic Variation

Scott F. Kiesling

At the heart of the sociolinguistic enterprise is the search to explain why speakers choose one linguistic form over another. In the chapters in this volume, the focus of that explanation is stance: How do speakers use linguistic form to create stances, why do they take these stances up, and how are forms associated with stances? The search for the motivation of linguistic choices is also the focus of studies of variation and change, but whereas much of the focus on determining stance is more qualitative and syntax- and discourse-oriented, variationist studies are generally quantitative and focus on morphophonological phenomena. Variationist studies proceed mainly by finding correlations between a linguistic variable and either some other linguistic element (so-called internal factors) or some nonlinguistic factor (so-called external factors or sometimes, social factors). The kinds of factors included in the latter are almost always based on identity: age, gender, race, class, and so on. But Labov showed early on (1966) that there are other factors—which he placed under the general term "style"—that are not correlated with a speaker's identity, but rather with speech activity: careful and casual. In this chapter I explore how stance can be used in variationist sociolinguistics, specifically, how stance is related to the variationist conception of style.

The study of style in sociolinguistic variation has had renewed interest in recent years. Contemporary sociolinguistic work on style, including Schilling-Estes (1998), Eckert (2000), and the edited volume by Eckert and Rickford (2001), has explored style in a more speaker-centered, interactional vein than in much earlier style-focused analyses. Even so, the relationship between these style and identity meanings in variation has not been explored as much as we might expect. Rather, style and identity patterning have usually been seen as reflecting orthogonal meanings. In the earliest style work, Labov (1966) seems to suggest that it is the *social group meaning* (as I will call the gender, age, class, etc. meanings) that are primary. In this view, a linguistic form (that is, a variant) acquires a meaning of prestige because speakers perceive that it is used by the upper classes (and if a variant is used a lot by lower classes, it may have "covert prestige"). Similarly, Bell's (1984, 2001) model of audience design explicitly takes the view that stylistic variation is derivative of social group meaning. The meanings of the linguistic form within a particular inter-action (what I will call *interactional meaning*) in this view arise because speakers wish to adopt aspects of an identity category, or even claim that identity entirely.

As I discuss below, more recent conceptions of style do not share this view, and in this chapter I will extend these recent conceptions to argue that the premise that style derives from social group patterning should be reversed: I contend that stance is the main interactional meaning being created, and it is a precursor, or primitive, in sociolinguistic variation: that is, sociolinguistic variants are initially associated with interactional stances and these stances become in turn associated with a social group meaning in a community over time and repeated use (I will elaborate on what I mean by "associated with" below). In fact, I want to test the more extreme hypothesis that stancetaking is where indexicality in variation begins; stance is, in Silverstein's (2003) terms, where the "baptismal essentializations" of indexicality occur, and is the original first- (or, possibly, zero-)order indexicality (Silverstein 2003, Johnstone et al. 2006). I thus evaluate how far I can take the proposition that any choice of lin-guistic form made by a speakers is based ultimately on the interpersonal or epistemic stance they wish to take with their various interlocutors at a particular time, and that it is stances that become associated, through cultural models, with various identities (including particular speaking roles in specific situations).[1] The overall goal of this chapter is to connect the everyday use of language variation in discourse to the ways that it patterns on larger social scales, and to test the hypothesis that this connection can be made through the concept of stance.

In order to understand relationships between style, stance, and indexicality, we need to have some definitions and understandings of how these terms have been used, and how I will use them, which I address in the next section. I will then move on to discuss some examples of how stance can be seen to be driving the use of variants.

Style, Indexicality, and Stance

Stance

All linguistic patterns of use arise from decisions people make in interaction when they are talking to a real person and thinking about "who they are" in relation to that person or people.[2] I argue that people's primary way of organizing interaction (including and especially the language in interaction) is through stances. I define stance as a person's expression of their relationship to their talk (their epistemic stance—e.g., how certain they are about their assertions), and a person's expression of their relationship to their interlocutors (their interpersonal stance—e.g., friendly or dominating). Epistemic and interpersonal stance are often related: someone who is being patronizing (interpersonal stance) is usually expressing that they are also very certain (epistemic stance) about what they are saying, but they are also expressing something about that knowledge vis-à-vis their interlocutor, namely, that the interlocutor does not have the same knowledge. Stances are thus connected both to the ways we relate to the content of our talk and to the socialness of our talk.

Stances have been used extensively in the discourse analytic and linguistic anthropological literature (see Ochs 1992), but it is only recently that the interactional meanings arising from morphophonological variables have begun to be studied (see Benor 2001, Bucholtz 1999, Johnstone and Baumgardt 2004, Kiesling 1998). The work so far suggests that variants have very diffuse meanings (such as *casual* or *urban*) across interactions that are made specific in interaction to create stances in concert with other variables in talk, and that this meaning changes depending on the stability of the variable and the age of the change, if one is in progress.

There is a general problem in such work of *coding* stances. Variationist sociolinguistics requires that each variant be coded with certain characteristics so that it can be entered into a quantitative analysis. The main difficulty in coding for stance is that there is no single list of stances, and even one stance can be slightly different for different people. But we can notice that interactants are engaging in similar activities (such as *arguing* or *flirting*) in how they participate verbally (and nonverbally) in interactions, and we should be able to show some relationship between this participation and variation (see also DuBois this volume for some possibilities in encoding stance). In order to discern what kind of stance might be going on in an interaction (or text), we can use many features that discourse analysts have shown are used by speakers to indicate stances. In the examples below I will explain the specific steps taken in each study to code for stance. However, it should be noted here that there is no "automatic stance-recognition" that can be done (otherwise we could code for other linguistic features rather than stance), because the same linguistic features can be used to take up different stances depending on other elements of context (widely defined).

Approaches to Style in Variation

There is a rich literature on sociolinguistic style, which I will not attempt to completely review here. However, there are a few important points that need to be established. The first is how the term *style* is being used in this chapter. There are two main ways of thinking about style in variationist sociolinguistics. The first conception is similar to Labov's view: style is "intraspeaker variation." Individuals use variants at different rates depending on the situation, broadly speaking. The research on this type of style has the longest tradition, and the goal has been to account for the speech situation or activity so that we do not compare "a casual salesman and a careful pipefitter" (Labov 1972: 240) and conclude that they do not differ in the use of some variant. This is the way in which style has most often been considered in variationist work, including in Bell's (1984, 2001) audience design model.

Schilling-Estes's (1998) view of the "performance register" of style shifting also understands style to be intraspeaker variation. In this view, though, speakers are much more proactive in their style shifting. She notes (1998: 69) that "style-shifting is primarily a means whereby speakers alter the images of self which they project for others. Sometimes these alternations are triggered by changes in the conversational context, but more often they are not; in fact, they often serve, in and of themselves, to bring about contextual changes." Schilling-Estes's discussion of style as *altering* images of self aligns her interpretation with a stance-based approach.

Another definition of style focuses not on the use of a single variable by an individual speaker in different situations, but on the use of more than one linguistic variable by one speaker. This is the view discussed by Eckert and her students, which I will refer to as the Stanford group (see, for example, Benor 2001, Eckert 2000, Mendoza-Denton 2008, Podesva 2007, and Zhang 2008). In this view, a single variant is seen as part of a more complete *personal style* or *persona*: "While the individual variables available in a dialect may correlate with various aspects of social membership and practice, most of them take on interpretable social meaning only in the context of the broader linguistic styles to which they contribute" (Eckert 2000: 213). In this view, style is the product of the combination of a number of linguistic (and nonlinguistic) social practices, yielding a particular persona. It is a creative, negotiated process within a community of practice ("an aggregate of people who come together around some enterprise," which develops and shares practices "as a function of their joint engagement in activity" Eckert 2000: 35). "Stylistic practice is a process of *bricolage*, in which ways of being are transformed through the strategic re-use of meaningful resources" (Eckert 2002: 5). In her ethnographic sociolinguistic analysis of variation in a Detroit-area high school, Eckert shows how vowel variants covary with other aspects of social practice and style, such as "cruising" (driving around a particular route with friends without a destination) and pants cuff width. She shows that although the variables she analyzes have general meanings throughout the school (e.g., association with urban versus suburban areas of Detroit), they are used in specific ways to create personal styles by individuals.

Let me distinguish these two main views of style as "intraspeaker variation" and "personal style" in order to be more precise in my discussion. They are of course connected: the ways one individual shifts use of a single variant from situation to situation is related to that person's personal style and the other stylistic practices that shift in each situation. I will show that both of these conceptions of style are at heart talking about speaker stance. Schilling-Estes's is probably the most sophisticated understanding of intraspeaker variation because it understands that speakers actively use variants in situations for various ends. But she is clearly referring to stance in her claim that the performance of dialect is explained "in terms of the roles (both real and metaphorical) that conversational participants play with respect to one another during a given interaction" (1998: 72). It will also become clear that stances are taken not by using a single variant, but with a range of social practices in the manner that the Stanford group outlines for personal styles. However, they also argue that speakers take on or create relatively enduring *personas*, so that the style they discuss thus seems to be more a speaker's recurring set of linguistic practices. The view that stances underlay these personal styles and personae is completely compatible with this view of style: we simply understand the personal styles to be *repertoires of stances*. In Eckert's (2000) high school, she shows that burnout girls take on much more agentive and confrontational stances than the jock girls, who take up much more "smiley" personae; in other words, their personae match their "personalities," and the personalities are the same thing as regularly taken stances, or stances that generalize what is common to several stances regularly taken. The connection between stance and both personal style and intraspeaker variation will be noted throughout the rest of this chapter; the goal for variationist sociolinguistics is to produce an understanding of how this connection comes to be made and how such relationships affect language change.

Discussion of personae and personalities inevitably brings up the question of *identity*. Though variously defined, identity in one current of variationist work has to do with the ways in which individuals are similar to or different from other individuals in a particular social group—hence their grouping on characteristics such as gender and age. These kinds of identities have been shown since Labov (1963) to affect speakers' variation patterns. Eckert (2000) moved the discussion of identity forward by showing that individuals create personal styles and enact them linguistically; that is, they do not just play out social category memberships. Seeing stance as primary is compatible with both a focus on personal style and a focus on the role of census-like identity categories such as gender, race, class, sexuality, region, and so forth. First, personal style is often described by people (or novelists) in terms of their habitual stances: "she's very full of herself," "he's very touchy-feely," and so on. Second, we find that what tends to differentiate census-like groups—in the discourses of the society that define them, real or imagined—are the stances they habitually take. This is especially true with linguistic differences that are found between men and women (e.g., "men are confrontational," "women are servile"). Thus, identity and personal style are both ways of stereotyping habitual patterns of stancetaking, or repertoires of stance. This connection will be elaborated upon below.

The picture that emerges is that stancetaking is the main constitutive social activity that speakers engage in when both creating a style and "style-shifting." The Stanford group shows that personal style is similarly constitutive of more widespread social group variation patterns, and so by this logic, stance underpins social group variation as well as the two conceptions of style.

I also argue that stance underlies the acquisition of variation. First language development has long been seen, and still most often is, as a problem of how children take decontextualized "input" and create decontextualized grammars. But as Schieffelin and Ochs (1986) show, this is not how children learn language. Rather, they learn language in a rich contextual environment; they remember who said what and how, and what kinds of speech activity or stance work was taking place. The work on developmental pragmatics pioneered by Schieffelin and Ochs show that learning stances—how to take them and who normatively takes what stances—is an integral part of learning language. In their analysis of caregiver-child speech, they identify different normative stances associated with caregivers' accommodation to children. In some cases, it is the child's responsibility to speak so that he or she is understood (as in the Samoan culture observed by Ochs); in others, it is the caregiver's responsibility to repeat and guess what the child is saying (as in American middle-class white culture). Schieffelin and Ochs show that these different stancetakings by caregivers teach the children important lessons in how to orient themselves in talk in their societies, and that stance meanings are not separate from, but learned as part of, the grammar.

The limited work on sociolinguistic style and variation in young children provides evidence that style patterning is present early in the child's development of her or his adult grammar, and supports the view that children learn the stances of their caregivers and the variants that go with them before they learn other indexicalities in the speech community. Labov (1989) shows that distinct style patterns are present for children as young as seven, and generally pattern according to their parents' style shifting. We can thus conclude that children learn style variation before they are exposed to the full social variation present in their speech community. If this style variation is related to stance, then it can be argued that stance is what children learn first, and then generalize other meanings from these stance meanings.

A simple but elegant study performed by Smith, Durham, and Fortune (2007) provides evidence that it is stance the children are learning, or at least they are learning speech activities that entail stances. They analyzed talk from a corpus of recordings of caregiver-child dyads from the town of Buckie, Scotland, in which the children ranged from two to almost four years old. These recordings were made as caregivers carried the microphone and recorder throughout their day, so that a number of different speech activities and stylistic contexts were recorded. Smith et al. focus on the Buckie variable of (ou), the alternation between the more standard [ʌu] pronunciation and the local [u:] in words such as house and down. They find that caregiver talk is more nonstandard with older children, and that there is a strong correlation between caregiver rates and child rates: that is, older children use the more local variant more than younger children. Variation is thus conditioned by age (for the children) but not yet by sex, as is found in adult corpora on this variable. Finally, Smith and colleagues coded for four speech activities (what they call styles): playing, routine, teaching, and discipline. They find that the children mirror their caregivers' shifts in these speech activities almost exactly. There is thus evidence that children are learning what is appropriate in a speech activity before they learn social constraints like those related to gender.

Furthermore, Smith et al. found that playing and routine pattern together for most speakers, as do teaching and discipline. Teaching and discipline share a stance that focuses on hierarchy or power, and play and routine share a stance of connection or solidarity. By using stance, then, we can generalize the pattern found by Smith et al. further and more precisely. In other words, this study provides evidence that children are learning the stance (power and solidarity) indexicalities of the variants before they learn the social identity indexicalities such as gender (although they are likely learning about age indexicalities, as well, to the extent that they are developmentally capable of generalizing age categories from their experiences).

There is thus strong evidence from the few studies of the acquisition of variation in early childhood that stance is learned before many, if not all, other social constraints. This result is unsurprising, because the main differentiation a child is likely to hear is not among many different speakers, but different ways of interacting among the relatively few speakers (compared to adults) with whom she or he is in direct contact in early childhood. Even in extended families of more communal forms of childcare such as those described by Schieffelin and Ochs in the Kaluli and Samoan societies, the number of speakers a child is intensively exposed to is low. No matter who the child's primary caregiver or caregivers may be, it is crucial for that child to be able to interpret their stances; to tell, for example, whether a caregiver is giving important directions or playing (in fact, communication requires that the child be able to detect play, in the same way as described for primates by Bateson [1972]). Viewing stance as developmentally primary is thus not an unwarranted conclusion.

Indexicality

An index is a type of linguistic (or other) sign that takes its meaning from the context of an utterance, with context understood fairly broadly, including aspects of the speaker, hearer, and speaking situation. These issues are discussed in considerable detail by Silverstein (1976, 2003) and Agha (2003, 2007). Address terms (ATs) are a good example of such indexes: although they by definition identify a person being addressed, speakers always have a choice as to whether to use an AT or not, and which one to use; these choices both relate to cultural norms and have social and cultural implications. *Dude*, as used in North American English, is a good example of such an AT with indexical meaning. I will not explain all of its indexicalities here (see Kiesling 2004), but it does show how context can be encoded. Although this is changing, it most often identifies both speaker and addressee as male, and also may indicate the speaker's understanding of what kind of speech event is under way. Finally, *dude* expresses the speaker's interpersonal stance of "cool solidarity." Indexes thus both create and reflect context.

Indexical meaning is often taken to mean co-occurrence. That is, if a linguistic item co-occurs frequently in the speech of a particular person or kind of person, that linguistic item will be taken to index that group. In the case of *dude,* it has historically been used more by men to men, so it has taken on this indexicality. However, it is possible to have co-occurrence without indexical meaning. Johnstone and Kiesling (2008) show that in fact the people who use a particular feature of Pittsburgh speech (/aw/-monophthongization) do not necessarily understand that feature as indexing a Pittsburgh identity; rather, other aspects of social discourse must take up this possibility and "point out" to speakers in different ways that the form is local to Pittsburgh. Indexical meaning can thus arise out of statistical commonality or single instances of use that are salient enough to gain meaning for speakers.

Following Ochs (1992) we can also understand indexes to work both directly and indirectly. Indirect indices refer to a linguistic item which indexes a stance, act, or activity, which then acquires an indexical connection to something else, like gender, class, place, race, or age. I argue (Kiesling 2004) that *dude* is used this way, such that the cool solidarity stance it indexes also indexes masculinity. Analyzing the complex ways language indexes social identity in any instance thus requires a deep understanding of the social context of use because it is this context that structures speakers' models of indirect indexes.

In addition to direct and indirect indexicality, I would like to make a further distinction between interior and exterior indexicality. This is based on a spatial metaphor of the speech event, in which interior indexicality is indexical meaning created within, and particular to, the speech event, while exterior indexicality is indexical meaning that is transportable from one speech event to another, and connects to social contexts that perdure from one speech event to another, or at least change very slowly. Interior indexicality holds only at the moment of speaking, and creates local relationships with present interlocutors, such as stances, footings, and positions.

Let us consider the interior and exterior indexicalities of *dude*. The interior indexicality of a particular use of dude will depend on a host of factors that hold for a particular speech event. For example, in the middle of a confrontation between two men, the use of *dude* could diffuse the situation by indexically communicating that the speaker means no harm. A recent television advertisement for Bud Light is a good example of how an index can be used in a number of different situations and have different interior indexical meanings. This ad shows one man in several situations, and in each he utters simply the word *dude* with varying intonation. In each situation, it is not specific words that he is trying to communicate, but a stance, and these stances are clear from the situation, his intonation, facial expression, kinesics, and his use of the word *dude*. But the use of *dude* also has exterior indexicalities—it points to other levels of society beyond the immediate interaction. In each use, it retains some sort of solidarity meaning, but one that is not intimate. In addition, and through this more abstract and diffuse stance, it indexes masculinity (in fact, a certain kind of masculinity; see Kiesling 2004).

Interior and exterior indexicalities are connected. Meanings can flow from interior to exterior (as in the indirect indexicalities noted by Ochs), but they can also flow from exterior to interior. In the latter case, the exterior indexicalities are used in a "reverse indirect indexicality," such that the exterior indexicality (say, masculinity) is used to index an interior indexicality (a leadership role in a meeting, for example). Note that in this view, both interior and exterior indexes can be used to create stances within the speech event.

My claim is that the interior indexicalities of stance are the primary meanings of variables for children, and that they are generalized or "short-circuited" to groups who are thought to share these stances (and speech activities). In fact, the interior and exterior indexicalities become almost indistinguishable from one another: in Kiesling (2004), I show that this is exactly the path taken by *dude* in North America in the last two decades of the twentieth century: it was the counterculture, laid-back stance of so-called "surfers" and "stoners" that American men found attractive in the 1980s, and that as the word has become used less and less exclusively by young men the stance meaning has widened. Thus, it is the interior indexicality of *dude* that has been central to its spread—and the only consistent indexicality across time and speaker. Below, I pursue the argument that for second-order indexicals such as (ou) in Buckie Scots, (ING) in English, and (er) in Australia, stance is the primary social indexicality, both in terms of developmental primacy and social primacy.

The example of the spread of *dude* also shows that stance is implicated as one of the driving forces behind language change. In short, people adopt stances when they adopt ways of speaking, and changes spread (in part) because stances spread. This view is one that Eckert (2000) pursues in her work on a Detroit-area high school and the spread of the Northern Cities Chain Shift. In her study she shows that variables at different stages of shift have different local indexicalities for the students in the school. The differences in use are (to oversimplify) attributable to the students' different ideologies about what kind of person they want to be and what community of practice they want to be a part of. Much of this has to do with how they orient to the school and the urban area of Detroit, but even these are mediated by stances: boys avoid being "flamboyant," and the jock girls avoid being "loose." Although Eckert does not use the term *stance* to describe these, it is clear from her discussion that stance is what the students are taking into account when they are "deciding" about what variant to use—they are thinking about what stance to take, and their social practices (dress, walk, physical comportment), including their linguistic practices, are part of that stancetaking.

Eckert's work shows that to understand language change, we must understand how variation is used for speakers to create social meaning—what the processes of indexicality are, and how they are related to the patterning of linguistic variables. I have argued above that stance is primary in that social meaning, and Eckert's work supports the view that stance is at the basis of some of the patterns she finds. Of course, these stances are not isolated from the social landscape as seen by speakers; in fact, speakers rely on structured social knowledge—the ideologies and discourses of their community of practice, culture, and society—to give full meaning to the stances they take. As reported by Eckert (2000), in Belten High a jock girl may use (or avoid) a variant to maintain a "pure" image. A girl who does so would be relying on a cultural discourse of femininity in which the appearance of sexual chastity is hegemonic in order to create status in her community of practice. In the burnouts' community of practice, there is a different orientation to this discourse (perhaps one of rebellion), but the discourse is still there because to rebel against something is to acknowledge its presence. Thus, the stances indexed are still the interior indexicalities (what the speaker thinks she is doing at the time), but this focus on the interior indexicalities does not mean that they are not connected to the exterior indexicalities in a very salient way. So it is not the stances alone that account for their primacy in intraspeaker shifts, but how they fit into the total social landscape.

Finally and crucially, indexes do not work alone, but combine with other indexes and context to propose relationships among people, and these meanings are subsequently negotiated by the interactants. Stance is at the center of this process of indexicalization because it is not each individual linguistic and social practice that an interactant decides on, but what stance to take in a particular situation. I will illustrate these processes more fully through three examples.

Stance in Variation: Three Examples

The argument I am pursuing, then, is that stancetaking is always a speaker's primary concern in conversation; even in speech events in which we might think stance is peripheral, it is in fact of central importance. Explanations are made with stances that give cues that an explanation is taking place, that the speaker is taking an "explainer" role (perhaps even being identifiable as a "teacher" or "trainer"). To be effective, such explainers must take rather authoritative epistemic stances. So the informational function of language is subordinate to stancetaking: speakers ultimately make linguistic choices in order to take stances. Along with Eckert and others, I argue that linguistic features are resources that are deployed in concert with other resources; a variant, for example, does not have a necessary stance or social meaning, but rather several potential ones. New variants have a shifting indexicality, whereas older, more widespread and stable variants have an indexicality that looks more conventional, in that this indexicality is widely shared. It is the combination of linguistic features in conversation that gives any one instance of a feature a more precise stancetaking indexicality. I turn now to three examples of how this process works, and the primary role of stancetaking in each.

(ING) in a Fraternity

The first example is based on the data and argument in Kiesling (1998), and I refer the reader to that article for further details. In this work, I spent a little over a year recording interviews and interactions in a college fraternity in northern Virginia. In analyzing the variable (ING) (Houston 1985) among the men in this fraternity, I needed a way to control for what was usually called *style* in differing speech events; the attention-paid-to-speech model was impossible to use when analyzing interaction among members rather than just interviews. I therefore divided the data by speech activity, which fell into three broad categories:

1. *Interview speech*, which was all speech produced in the interviews
    I performed with the men, with the exception of word lists
    and other reading situations;
2. *Meeting speech*, which was all speech produced in the regular portion
    of meetings;[3]
3. *"Socializing" speech*, a residual category of speech of the men
    in "casual and spontaneous" conversation.

My goal in this research was to understand how men used this variable in the fraternity, with a view toward understanding why men might use higher rates of the "nonstandard" variant, as documented in every study of this variable. The results showed a strong consensus among the men in the rate of (ING) variation across individuals in the socializing situations, but in the interview and meeting situations individual differences appeared. Figure 8.1 shows this pattern.

The goal of variation studies is of course to explain such patterns. This one is not easily explained by the usual suspects of dialect, race, or class differences. Rather, I showed that the men who exhibit a higher rate of the alveolar variant (such as Speed, Waterson, and Mick) take very different kinds of stances in the meetings than the other men. The majority of men take stances that display their institutional power, or assume that power in some way. For example, Mack makes statements that are not marked epistemically, making them seem like "eternal truths" (see Agha 2007 and Scheibman 2007). On the other hand, Speed takes at one point a more laid-back approach, and later an oppositional stance. Saul and Mick both take stances that stress their hard-working identities and solidarity with the other members of the fraternity. The creation of laid-back, oppositional, and hard-working stances is aided by an increased use of -*in*': This variant has indexicalities that connect it to a stereotype of a hard-working masculinity, with an oppositional, practical stance and a particular kind of solidarity.

The indexicalities in this case are indirect in complex ways; this variable is old enough that it has short-circuited indexicalities with social categories like class and

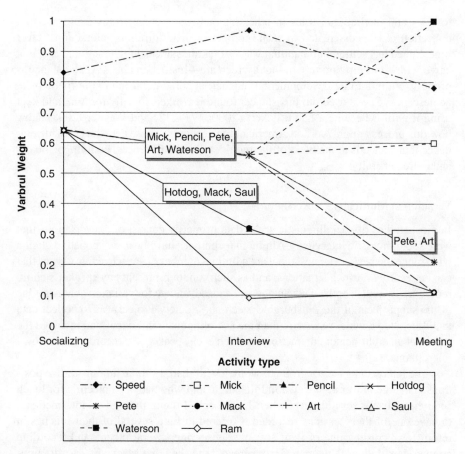

FIGURE 8.1 Varbrul results for the (ING) variable in the fraternity. Men are combined in groups when no significant differences were indicated. A varbrul weight above 0.5 indicates that the speaker is more likely to use the alveolar, or *-in'*, variant than the group. For details, see Kiesling (1998, in press).

gender. But the "nonstandard" is also used to represent informality, casualness, and opposition to formality or official power structures. These indexicalities mean that nonstandard speech can be used to create stances that emphasize solidarity and sub-versiveness. But it also is useful for men, because a casual power (that is, power exercised in a seemingly effortless manner) *and* cool solidarity is an ideal masculine trait for men in the United States (see Kiesling 2008). Thus, it is the stances that are ultimately at the heart of the indexicalities here: the men are unlikely to be thinking simply that they need to index masculinity, but rather that they need to create an impression of their persona and abilities for the audience, which they do by creating particular stances.

These stances are indeed parts of the men's individual styles. I show in Kiesling (1998) that Speed consistently maintains a laid-back style that expresses opposition to rules and institutional roles in other interactions. But this individual style is a collection of stances created in each moment of many different interactions. Over time, Speed has settled into habitual ways of taking stances in interaction, ways that agree with—or help him to continually recreate—his personality.[4] Again, stance is primary, but in a more developmental manner: at some point in his life (perhaps in adolescence) Speed tried out this stance, found it worked socially for him, and kept using it until it became a habit. Eckert (2000: 171–212) and Wagner (2008) show how this process might work in American high schools. These data thus provide evidence that stance is at the heart of the men's stylistic differences, both linguistically and more generally.

Variation in Multiparty Conversation

In most studies of sociolinguistic style, data primarily consist of conversations that were sociolinguistic interviews. Although techniques have been developed to elicit a wide range of speaker stances, there are a limited number of speech activity types that can be recorded in such situations, and as such cannot represent any speaker's entire repertoire (which is both an advantage and a disadvantage for variation analysis. One of the subprojects of the Pittsburgh Speech and Society Project was to collect data that illustrated a wider repertoire than the sociolinguistic interview, and involved the taping of an eight-person interaction in which each speaker was recorded on her own microphone.

The interactants were a group of women who shared similar administrative positions at a large university located in Pittsburgh, and who had been meeting for lunch semiregularly for several years when I approached them, through an intermediary, to have one of their sessions recorded. I offered to fund several of their lunches in return for recording one of their sessions, observing several others, and recording an interview with each woman. They agreed, but asked that Maeve Eberhardt, a linguistics graduate student at the University of Pittsburgh, and a research assistant for the project, be the one to observe the meetings because she is a woman. The women ranged in age from mid-20s to mid-50s, and were roughly of upper-working- to middle-class backgrounds.

Eberhardt observed three meetings before recording a fourth. Each person was recorded on a different track and transcribed separately. Eberhardt and I found that speakers engaged in many different genres and forms of participation in the recorded interaction. These included quasi-lectures, classic Labovian sociolinguistic narratives with a long monologue, short quips that barely counted as a turn, "byplay" (Goffman 1981: 133–134), and (in this conversation) simply an orientation to the management of the conversation itself. We chose to code "style" as "speech activity," similar to the way I did in the fraternity study, but with a stronger grounding in the features of the discourse itself. The speech activities in this study were as follows:

COMMISERATING: Alignment with other speakers but expertise not asserted
     (often complaining)
PROVIDING EXPERTISE: Instructional "how I do it" or "you can/can't do it this
     way"

FACILITATING: First pair parts that provide space for other speakers, without
   subordinating
GOSSIPING: Evaluative talk about nonpresent others
DISCUSSING LOCAL CONTEXT: Talk about current physical space/time
QUESTIONING: Alignment of other as expert, requests for advice, and
   admissions of uncertainty

We also coded three linguistic variables in one speaker's track throughout the
conversation. The three variables in question were all features of the local Pittsburgh
dialect that are not found in surrounding dialects (see Johnstone and Kiesling 2005):
(aw), or the monophthongization of /aw/, a local Pittsburgh dialect feature; (ay), the
monophthongization of /ay/, and (l-voc), the vocalization of /l/. Each of these variables has a different status in Pittsburgh, and potentially different indexicalities. The
main manner in which they differ in Pittsburgh is their place in the indexical order
(similar to their "level of awareness"—see Silverstein 2003, Johnstone et al. 2006,
and Johnstone and Kiesling 2008 for more on the indexical order and its importance
in Pittsburgh). The monophthongized variant of /aw/ is one that Pittsburghers are
most aware of, and typifies older working-class Pittsburghers. On the other hand,
/ay/-monophthongization shows much less awareness, although some people comment on it explicitly, and it also is used more by working-class Pittsburghers. Finally,
/l/-vocalization is a variable that Pittsburghers rarely talk about, or hear discussed as
part of their dialect; most cannot hear the difference between vocalized and nonvo-
calized variants. Given this distribution, we suspected that they would be used differently in the construction of stances in the conversation, and might pattern differently
statistically as well.

The results are shown in figure 8.2. Each line represents one variable, and the
y-axis charts the average percentage of the "nonstandard" variant used in a speech
activity. We can first note the wide variability of (aw). This was largely due to the fact
that there are not many tokens of this variable; words like *house* and *down* are surprisingly rare. An average for each thus does not necessarily represent many tokens.
However, because (aw) is a variable in wide metapragmatic circulation, it is logical
that it would be deployed differently in the conversation from (ay) and (l-voc), which
will be less overtly noticed by the interactants. Finally, we can see that "expert" is a
speech activity that shows a relatively low rate for all three variables, but especially
(ay). This is as we might expect, as experts are more likely to be indexed by the
"standard" diphthongal variant and an association with education, rather than with
the "nonstandard." Eberhardt then examined a more frequent and widely known variable: (ING), which has the variants [ɪŋ] (notated here as *-ing*), [ɪn] (*-in'*).

Eberhardt (2006) expanded the method for the stable variable (ING) coding all
(ING) tokens in the conversation for each speaker. She initially used the same set of
speech activities as above, but made some refinements as she found utterances that
were problematic to code in one of the existing speech activities. The final list is
shown in table 8.1.

The results were subjected to a varbrul analysis (see Tagliamonte 2006 and
Paolillo 2002). The speech activity factor group was significant, and the results are
shown in figure 8.3. However, we were interested in whether all speakers used this

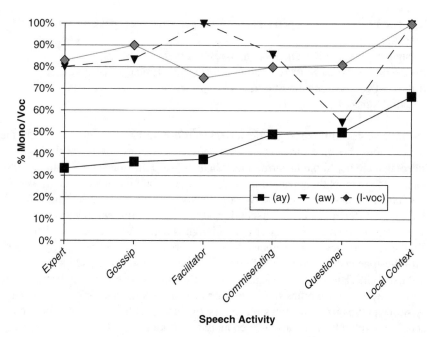

Speech Activity

FIGURE 8.2 Average use of the "nonstandard" variant for three variables in six speech activities, for all speakers in the women's conversation.

TABLE 8.1 Speech Activity and Description for Recorded Group Meeting

Speech Activity	Description
Commiserating	Alignment with other speakers but expertise not asserted (often complaining)
Expert Information	Information presented as "this is the way it is" or "this is how it's done"
Expert teaching	Instructional "how I do it" or "you can/can't do it this way"; often presented as the way things are.
Facilitator	First pair parts that provide space for other speakers, without subordinating
Gossip	Evaluative talk about nonpresent others
Local context	Talk about current physical space/time
Questioner	Alignment of other as expert, requests for advice, and admissions of uncertainty
Joking	Telling a joke or a funny story
Information sharing	Sharing information, but without asserting expertise; includes sharing how speaker does something, but not presented as "this is the way it should be done"
Clarification	Clarifying what someone else has said or clarifying for someone else what one has said
Personal evaluation	Expression of a personal opinion

TABLE 8.2 Collective Speech Activity Factors

Social	Informational	Discourse Management
Commiserating	Expert information	Local context
Gossip	Expert teaching	Clarification
Joking	Information question	Facilitator
Personal evaluation	Questioner	Other
	Information sharing	

variable at similar rates for similar speech activities. When cross-tabulated with speaker, however, there were not enough tokens for each speaker to find a discernible pattern. The decision was made to therefore group the speech activities into larger categories. This grouping is shown in Table 8.2. The "social" categories are those speech activities that have as their ends (in a Hymesian sense) social interaction, whereas the "informational" category comprises speech activities with ends that focus on information transfer and sharing (including aspects of the speaker's status as the giver of the information or the receiver). A third category, "discourse management," is composed of speech activities that focus on the discourse itself. This third category also did not have enough tokens to be meaningful in a cross-tabulation, but was included in the varbrul analysis. Although any such groupings obscure some of the complexities of speech acts that can have multiple functions (and thus require a qualitative analysis), this process nevertheless allows us to make a statistical analysis of the conversation that supports our claims about the role of variants in discourse and to explore if (and why) speakers take different epistemic and interpersonal stances in different speech activities, and the extent to which speakers exhibit a consensus as to how to use a particular variant in each speech activity.

The final analysis combined the collective speech activity factor group and speakers into a single factor group. For example, there was a single factor for "Debbie, social speech activity" (thus providing a method for determining interactions in varbrul). The model with this combined factor group proved to be a significantly better model for the data than the model with the factor groups separated, and the results are shown in figure 8.3.

The results show striking differences among all of the speakers, but that in general they are consistent in that they use less -in' in the informational speech activity type than in the social, which is consistent with findings in Labov (1972) and Trudgill (1972). It is clear that the majority of speakers agree on the general use of (ING) in these two speech activity categories. However, why is Marcie acting so differently? Does she not share the norms of the others in this community of practice? To answer these questions, Eberhardt carefully analyzed the stances adopted by Marcie and another speaker who shifts more standardly (Jane). Jane was chosen because both she and Marcie were named in the postrecording interviews as members of the group whom the interviewees viewed as leaders. Eberhardt's analysis shows that both women do significant amounts of informational work, but do so by taking up very different stances. Jane adopts what we might think of as a typical teacher-like

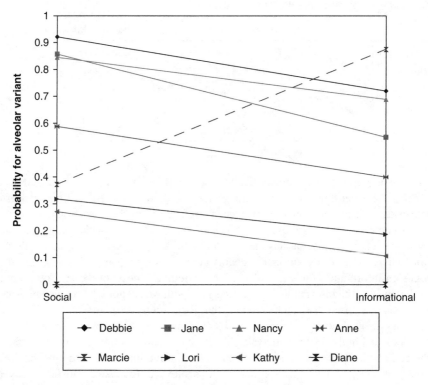

FIGURE 8.3 Varbrul results for the (ING) variable in the women's conversation for speaker and speech activity type combined factor group.

manner, taking epistemic stances of certainty, overtly displaying her knowledge and calling attention to it. She is in fact in a position to have more "inside" information about the organization, and often displays her knowledge from this kind of position, orienting to her privileged knowledge in the stances she takes. In fact, she sounds very much like Mack in the fraternity study described above.

Marcie, on the other hand, plays down her expertise, acting almost as if she is incompetent. This can be seen in excerpt 1.

Excerpt 1

1   ANNE: and I'm sometimes I'm sitting there till May
2   doing every
3   entry on my shadow system
4   which we're all supposed to get new ones
5   we're all supposed to start using
6   DIANE: well I called Tara to ask her
7   MARCIE: Is it ready
8   DIANE: yeah

9   she said it's not ready
10   because I'm not doing anything right now
11   except what I do on my indiv-
12   MARCIE: I just did it on Excel
13   I just started dumpin' everything in there
14   DIANE: but that's such a hassle on Excel
15   MARCIE: we're over so
16   ((laughs))
17   we're always over ((laughing))

Eberhardt notes the following:

> the hedges [*just* in lines 12 and 13], the lexical choice of "dumping," the laughter
> and the comment that her department is over budget, with the implication that it does
> not matter much how she does her budget report, all help Marcie create a stance of
> a non-expert when providing helpful information to the group members. It is not
> surprising to find that the token of (ING) present in this excerpt is realized as N and
> not G. In conjunction with the other features of Marcie's speech, N aids in the pre-
> sentation of Marcie as a casual bearer of information, not as an expert with advice
> that the rest ought to heed. (2006:21)

In sum, here again we find that the best way to explain Marcie's use of *-in'* is in terms
of the stances she takes in particular speech activities. Eberhardt shows that most of the
women switch from a more solidarity-focused stance in the social speech activities to
stances that emphasize their knowledge in the informational speech activities. This can
be explained by noting that (ING) can index both of these, with the *-ing* variant indexing
a more learned stance associated with formal education and positions of power, and the
-in' variant indexing a casual stance that can be deployed to specifically downplay positions of power and increase solidarity. There is thus a connection between the stances that
the variable indexes and the way it is used more generally in the speech community, and
in fact (ING) is such an established, stable variable that its indexicalities are very general
(solidarity, casualness, and possibly opposition) and can be deployed flexibly. The point
is that Marcie, is *actively and uniquely* (for this conversation) using the *-in'* variant to take
an interpersonal stance within a particular activity type. It is not only the norms of the
audience nor the norms of the speech activity that determine her use of (ING). Rather, it
is her stance; that she repeats such stances in similar activity types leads to her personal
style. But the association of this style with her person is based on her repeating similar
stances to the point that it appears to her regular interlocutors as a property of her as a person. So, the fact remains that the most satisfactory way to explain these data is through an
appeal to the different stances the speakers take in the conversation, just as was the case
for the fraternity data. The next case provides different kinds of data for this hypothesis.

Whatever and Ethnicity in Sydney

In her pathbreaking study of the Sydney speech community, Horvath (1985) showed
that both first- and second-generation migrants used a significantly different variety

of English than Anglo nonmigrants. In the mid-1990s, awareness grew of a variety of Australian English associated with the second generation of recent migrant groups (especially Greeks and Italians) in Sydney and Melbourne. In a paper based on interviews from 1998 (Kiesling 2005), I attempted to discover whether or not there is a "migrant" variety (which I referred to as "New Australian English," NAusE) of Australian English, and if so, how it might have developed. The variable in question was the lowering and backing of word-final -er, as in *brother* or *whatever* (I will refer to the lowest and most back pronunciations as "open"). Although I did find some intriguing correlations, these correlations are not necessarily indexical, and are unlikely to be second-order indexicals.

One important aspect of this study is that the interviews were performed by Ouranita, a second-generation Greek woman. This aspect of her identity may have been salient to the interviewees, but it is not *a priori* important, because she had other identities that may have increased distance, such as her role as a former teacher in a local high school. In fact, the analysis shows that those speakers who used the most NAusE tokens were those who were not only similar to her (and not differentiated by power in some way), but those who specifically oriented to their shared background in an authoritative way. That is, these speakers assumed or brought in shared second-generation migrant experiences in a stance of "authoritative connection."[5] I also show, through discourse analysis, that the more extreme new (er) is used in particular instances in interviews in which the stance of authoritative connection is being created. Further, *whatever* is the lexical item that consistently had the most open pronunciation. This lexical item, functioning as a general extender, is used by interviewees at the end of an utterance to mean something like "etcetera," and thus invites the interviewer to supply the missing information based on her own knowledge. *Whatever* thus lexifies the stance of authoritative connection because it displays (assumed) knowledge and connection simultaneously. Excerpt 2 shows a passage in which Ellie, a Greek woman, uses *whatever* and constructs the stance of authoritative connection (the "+" signals an HRT that does not rise as fully as clause-final HRT):

Excerpt 2

1	ELLIE:	Well I *remember*+... As kids we used to um... put um tobacco
2		I think my parents used to grow tobacco?
3		Do you remember that too? ...
4		And y'know we used to sit here
5	IVER:	No no no not me but but but tell me yeah
6	ELLIE:	Ye:s yes all like aunties or relatives or whatever+
7		I can't remember where we used todo this,
8		but you used to have like a needle?
9		Some sort of but they were flat needles.
10		And you had to hold it a certain way: and you put the tobacco?
11	IVER:	Mmm hmm
12	ELLIE:	And the kids used to help
13		everybody used to help+
14		and they used to my dad used to put them outside on a rack?

15		and let them dry out…
16		and he used to sell…that.
17		and he used to make money from that as well.
18		very tough life.
19	IVER:	tough life yeah
20	ELLIE:	but very h- I think it was a *harder* life on my *mother*.
21		because she had to…bring us up at the same time?

In this excerpt Ellie is recounting an experience from her childhood, and assumes that the interviewer shares much of this experience (even though in line 5 the interviewer says she does not actually share the experience). In line 6 Ellie uses *whatever* to stand for a list of relatives that the interviewer is also assumed to be able to fill in. Ellie is thus constructing a stance of authoritative connection. She succeeds in getting the interviewer to orient to this stance, as can be seen by the repetition in line 19, which references a tough life, not necessarily the details of tobacco growing.

The tokens that were measured in this section of the interview are in italics in the extract, and all of Ellie's measured tokens of (er) are plotted in figure 8.4 (not all instances of -*er* words were measured because there was a restriction on the number of tokens that could come from one lexical item; in this case *remember* and *whatever* had reached their quota).[6] The tokens shown in italics in excerpt 2 are also in italics in figure 8.4. These four tokens are clearly among the most back tokens in her set, showing a correlation between the stance of authoritative connection and a more open (er). I therefore argue that it is partially through this open (er) that Ellie creates this stance with respect to Ouranita. We might propose that the explanation can be made in terms of topic. But while the topic (such as narratives of migrant life) helps to predict the openness of (er), it does not explain why it is precisely these certain topics are the ones that trigger the open (er). Thus the explanation always leads to the stance the speaker is taking, and the uses she or he makes of linguistic resources to take this stance.

The results from both the entire corpus and Ellie's use of (er), in taking the stance of authoritative connection (along with other examples in Kiesling 2005), provide evidence that it is stance that speakers are orienting to. Thus, it is not an "automatic" process of talking the same as someone who appears to be similar to oneself, but, rather, using resources to take a particular stance toward someone who appears similar, and in fact fostering that similarity through language.

It is not hard now to see the connection and progression of the meaning of open (er) from interior to exterior indexicalities, and (in parallel, or perhaps necessarily) from first- to second-order indexicality. We can propose that open (er) would begin within non-Anglo communities as they took stances of authoritative connection with each other, and built solidarity through their shared experiences. As this stance became more widespread in the community, so would the open (er) become more widespread, providing the first-order indexicality that produces more non-Anglos using the open (er), but allowing for significant use in the Anglo community, as well, especially those Anglos with significant contact with non-Anglos. The use

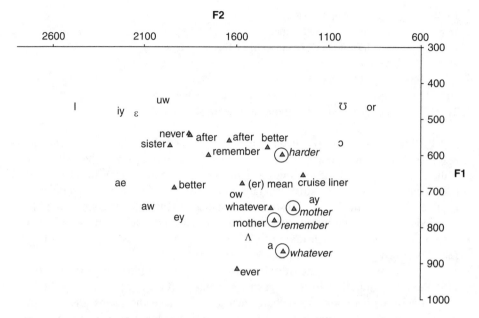

FIGURE 8.4 Plot of Ellie's tokens in an F2/F1 vowel space. The (er) tokens are triangles. The means for other vowels are plotted with their labels. The measured tokens in excerpt 2 (*remember, whatever, mother,* and *harder*) are circled.

of (er) thus becomes linked to any kind of authoritative connection, not just that focusing on the non-Anglo experience. Finally, it becomes enregistered (Agha 2007, Johnstone & Kiesling 2008) and becomes a second-order indexical marking a non-Anglo identity.

Summary and Unanswered Questions

In each of these three examples, local speaker relationships in the form of stance are the best explanations for the patterns found. In the (ING) examples, if we do not appeal to stance, we would have to assume that Speed and Marcie somehow have a different understanding of the indexicalities of (ING) than the other speakers in their communities. This seems unlikely because we find that the speakers are using the *-in'* variant strategically to create stances. This stancetaking is immediately relevant socially for the speakers. So it is logical to view these stances as motivating variation patterns that have social meaning. Finally, stance provides an explanation of variation use from the speaker's perspective that goes beyond a mere restatement of correlational patterns.

Stance also provides us with an improved way of understanding recent approaches to style, both those focusing on intraspeaker variation and personal style. All of these recent approaches share a focus on the agentive speaker; that is, a speaker who is actively managing his or her variable use in order to achieve socially meaningful impressions. Stance takes these ideas to their logical conclusion. Therefore, a personal style is created through habitual stancetakings (and in the case of innovative styles, in some cases defines the initial indexicalities of the variant).

There are two issues that I haven't had space to address here, and would constructively be the focus of future work: the role of the audience and "awareness." In the discussions above, and in most views of variation and some views of pragmatics, the intention of the speaker is taken to be equivalent to meaning. However, much work on discourse and interaction shows that this is not a warranted assumption (see, for example, the volume edited by Duranti and Goodwin 1992, as well as the chapters in this volume by Jaworski and Thurlow, Jaffe, and Coupland and Coupland). In other words, assuming that stance is a motivating factor in the choice of a linguistic variant, how does the response of an interlocutor to a speaker affect either subsequent uses of a particular variant or even what I have been arguing is the stance meaning of the variant? In fact, I believe that once we start going down this path, we find that stance is even more important. Assume, as with the authors just cited, that stances and meanings are negotiated in interaction. It would make sense then that social meanings in general are negotiated in interaction, and that would be the case for variants as well (at the specific interior indexicalities). But it is difficult to imagine this negotiation without reference to stancetaking: the use of a variant should elicit some stance in the interlocutor, and this stance will then be responded to by the original speaker of the variant. Thus if meanings of variables and variants are negotiated (as Eckert 2000 shows forcefully), then the way this must happen is through stancetaking.

However, the amount of negotiation available likely depends on the amount of enregisterment (Agha 2007, Johnstone et al. 2006, Johnstone and Kiesling 2008) that has taken place. That is, if a form's indexicalities have reached the second or third orders, then the possibility for negotiation is different. The interior indexicality is perhaps still open for negotiation, but because the indexicalities are so widely shared, the external indexicalities form the basis of the interior indexicalities—they are the resources upon which the interior indexicalities are built. For example, in Pittsburgh, some of the local variants are highly enregistered to the point that they appear to be third-order indexicals. This is the case with the second-person plural *yinz*. It is so readily indexed as "locally Pittsburgh" that a certain type of local identity is named after it: the *yinzer*. Thus one could use the term *yinz* for second-person plural reference, but in fact be recycling it so that the one is not necessarily making a claim about one's own ("authentic") identity, but rather building a solidary stance by a shared relationship to Pittsburgh. There is much we do not know about how these meanings circulate, relate, and feed into one another. Much more work is needed to understand the relationship between the stance indexicalities of variants and the social identity indexicalities, and how they change over the course of a linguistic change.

For example, in one of the fraternity meetings I analyzed (Kiesling 2001), one of the members (Pete) takes a very condescending and confrontational stance to the rest of the members in a meeting. The reaction is equally forceful, and pushes him to revise the stance he takes in the rest of his turn. Although he does not necessarily change his variable use, he does change his stance in reaction to the stance of his audience. We could also imagine more "overt" stances toward variable usage, for example, when someone repeats an utterance and shows skepticism about its use (for example when an Anglo might use *whatever* with a very open (er), and a non-Anglo repeats the usage in an exaggerated way with questioning intonation). It is through stances, then, that this meaning negotiation is generally going to take place.

Acknowledgments

Many people, including those whose voices are studied and representing in this chapter, deserve my thanks; this chapter is really a collaborative work. Most centrally, however, I would like to thank Maeve Eberhardt for her diligence, professionalism, and insights, without which this chapter would not have been possible. I also wish to thank Misty Jaffe for her sometimes-challenging comments which improved this chapter immeasureably. Of course, I alone am responsible for the claims in this work.

Notes

1. This claim is mainly for variables that end up with some kind of social meaning—so-called second-order indexicals. There are many variables that are much more conditioned by internal linguistic structural factors than social factors of any kind. Furthermore, there may be a distinction based on the linguistic complexity of the variable (although this influence may be also connected to awareness): the "short-a" pattern in Philadelphia (Labov et al. 2006) is subtle, as are the constraints on verbal -s in Buckie Scots (see Smith et al. 2007), and this may prevent speakers from exploiting the variation for stance. Other subtle sound changes similarly seem to show less social force. Mergers are one such class of changes that generally go unremarked, whereas lexical differences are almost always noticed. It may also be that some variables are not as cognitively available in some way for social work. Further research should focus not only on how social differentiation works, but on what variables are more likely to develop social meanings such as stance meanings.

2. These decisions are not necessarily "conscious" in the sense of being open to reflection, in the same way that we do not calculate all of the actions necessary and do calculus in order to catch a ball.

3. There was also a section after the regular meeting known as "gavel" that I did not include in these data; see Kiesling (2002).

4. By using this term I am not suggesting that actors have some stable personality that is simply expressed linguistically, but I am suggesting that because people tend to experience the self in this manner, we might try to understand how this consistent personality project is continually created.

5. The patterning of this variable—the migrant version of which I called "new (er)" —was complex, and there is not space here to recapitulate the entire analysis. However, there were linguistic constraints, including the length of the segment and its co-occurrence with phrase-final rising intonation in declarative clauses, called high rising tone (HRT) following Guy et al. (1986).

6. Ten instances of different words, if possible, were coded for each speaker. No more than three repetitions of the same word were used for any speaker. The first two formants were measured in the center of the vowel, using LPC analysis. The length of the (er) segment, and the preceding and following phonetic environments were also recorded. For more details, see Kiesling (2005).

References

Agha, Asif. 2003. The social life of cultural value. *Language and Communication* 23(3–4): 231–273.

——. 2007. *Language and social relations*. Cambridge: Cambridge University Press.

Bateson, Gregory. 1972. *Steps to an ecology of mind*. Chandler. San Francisco: Chandler.

Bell, Allan. 1984. Language style as audience design. *Language in Society* 13(2): 145–204.

——. 2001. Back in style: Reworking audience design. *Style and sociolinguistic variation*, ed. Penelope Eckert and John Rickford, 139–169. Cambridge: Cambridge University Press.

Benor, Sarah Bunin. 2001. The learned /t/: Phonological variation in Orthodox Jewish English. *University of Pennsylvania Working Papers in Linguistics* 7 (3): 1–16.

Bucholtz, M. 1999. You da man: Narrating the racial other in the production of white masculinity. *Journal of Sociolinguistics* 3(4): 443–460.

Duranti, Alessandro, and Charles Goodwin, eds. 1992. *Rethinking context: Language as an interactive phenomenon*. New York: Cambridge University Press.

Eberhardt, Maeve. 2006. Leadership and style-shifting: Women's use of (ING). Ph.D. comprehensive paper, University of Pittsburgh.

Eckert, Penelope. 2000. *Linguistic variation as social practice: The linguistic construction of identity in Belten High*. Malden, MA: Blackwell.

——. 2002. *Constructing social meaning in sociolinguistic variation*. Paper presented at American Anthropological society Annual Meeting, New Orleans.

Eckert, Penelope, and John R. Rickford, eds. 2001. *Style and sociolinguistic variation*. Cambridge: Cambridge University Press.

Goffman, Erving. 1981. *Forms of talk*. Philadelphia: University of Pennsylvania Press.

Guy, Gregory, Barbara Horvath, Julia Vonwiller, Elaine Daisley, and Inge Rogers. 1986. An intonational change in progress in Australian English. *Language in Society* 15(1): 23–51.

Horvath, Barbara M. 1985. *Variation in Australian English: The sociolects of Sydney*. Cambridge: Cambridge University Press.

Houston, Ann Celeste. 1985. Continuity and change in English morphology: The variable (ing). Ph.D. diss., University of Pennsylvania.

Johnstone, Barbara, Jennifer Andrus, and Andrew E. Danielson. 2006. Mobility, indexicality, and the enregisterment of "Pittsburghese." *Journal of English Linguistics* 34(2): 77–104.

Johnstone, Barbara, and Dan Baumgardt. 2004. "Pittsburghese" online: Vernacular norming in conversation. *American Speech* 79(2): 115–145.

Johnstone, Barbara, and Scott F. Kiesling. 2005. Steel town speak. In *American voices: How dialects differ from coast to coast*, ed. Walt Wolfram and Ben Ward, 77–81. Malden, MA: Blackwell.

——. 2008. Indexicality and experience: Exploring the meanings of/aw/-monophthongization in Pittsburgh. *Journal of Sociolinguistics* 12(1): 5–33.

Kiesling, Scott. 1998. Men's identities and sociolinguistic variation: The case of fraternity men. *Journal of Sociolinguistics* 2(1): 69–99.

——. 2001. "Now I gotta watch what I say": Shifting constructions of masculinity in discourse. *Journal of Linguistic Anthropology* 11(2): 250–273.

——. 2002. Playing the straight man: Displaying and maintaining male heterosexuality in discourse. In *Language and sexuality: Contesting meaning in theory and practice*, ed. Kathryn Campbell-Kibler, Robert J. Podesva, Sarah J. Roberts, and Andrew Wong, 249–266. Stanford, CA: CSLI Publications.

——. 2004. Dude. *American Speech* 79(3): 281–305.

——. 2005. Variation, stance and style: Word-final -er, high rising tone, and ethnicity in Australian English. *English World-Wide* 26(1): 1–42.

——. 2008. Recasting language and masculinities in the age of desire. *Indiana University Linguistics Club working papers*. Department of Linguistics, Indiana University Bloomington, IN.

Labov, William. 1963. *The social motivation of a sound change*. Word 19(3): 273–309.

——. 1966. *The social stratification of English in New York City*. Washington, DC: Center for Applied Linguistics.

——. 1972. *Sociolinguistic patterns*. Philadelphia: University of Pennsylvania Press.

——. 1989. The child as linguistic historian. *Language Variation and Change* 1(1): 85–97.

——. 2001. *Principles of linguistic change: Social factors*. Malden, MA: Blackwell.

Labov, William, Sharon Ash, and Charles Boberg. 2006. *The Atlas of North American English*. New York: Mouton deGruyter.

Mendoza-Denton, Norma. 2008. *Homegirls: Language and cultural practice among Latina youth gangs*. Malden, MA: Blackwell.

Ochs, Elinor. 1992. Indexing gender. In *Rethinking context*, ed. Alessandro Duranti and Charles Goodwin, 335–358. Cambridge: Cambridge University Press.

Paolillo, John. C. 2002. *Analyzing linguistic variation: Statistical models and methods*. Stanford, CA: CSLI Publications.

Podesva, Robert. 2007. Phonation type as a stylistic variable: The use of falsetto in constructing a persona. *Journal of Sociolinguistics* 11(4): 478–504.

Scheibman, Joanne. 2007. Subjective and intersubjective uses of generalizations in English conversations. In *Stancetaking in discourse*, ed. Robert Englebretson, 111–138. Amsterdam: John Benjamins.

Schieffelin, Bambi B., and Elinor Ochs. 1986. *Language socialization across cultures*. Cambridge: Cambridge University Press.

Schilling-Estes, Natalie. 1998. Investigating "self-conscious" speech: The performance register in Ocracoke English. *Language in Society* 27(1): 53–83.

Silverstein, Michael. 1976. Shifters, linguistic categories, and cultural description. In *Meaning in anthropology*, ed. Keith H. Basso and Henry A. Selby, 11–55. Albuquerque: University of New Mexico Press.

——. 2003. Indexical order and the dialectics of sociolinguistic life. *Language and Communication* 23(3–4): 193–229.

Smith, Jennifer, Mercedes Durham, and Liane Fortune. 2007. "Mam, my trousers is fa'in doon!": Community, caregiver, and child in the acquisition of variation in a Scottish dialect. *Language Variation and Change* 19(1): 63–99.

Tagliamonte, Sali. 2006. *Analysing sociolinguistic variation*. Cambridge: Cambridge University Press.

Trudgill, Peter. 1972. Sex, covert prestige and linguistic change in the urban British English of Norwich. *Language in Society* 1(2): 179–195.

Wagner, Suzanne Evans. 2008. *Language change and stabilization in the transition from adolescence to adulthood*. Ph.D. diss., University of Pennsylvania.

Zhang, Qing. 2008. Rhotacization and the "Beijing smooth operator": The social meaning of a linguistic variable. *Journal of Sociolinguistics* 12(2): 201–222.

9

Taking an Elitist Stance

Ideology and the Discursive Production of Social Distinction

Adam Jaworski and Crispin Thurlow

The Discursivity of Elitism

This chapter examines elitism as an everyday discursive accomplishment in the light of a critique of contemporary class privilege and social inequality. Empirically and conceptually it complements our earlier study of identity *stylization* in airline fre-quent-flyer programs (Thurlow and Jaworski, 2006). Our approach to stylization traces its origins to the work of Bakhtin (1981, 1986) on multivoicing, as well as of Austin (1961), Bauman and Briggs (1990), and Butler (1990) on performative lan-guage use and performativity, and follows Rampton's (1995) and Coupland's (2001, 2007) views of stylization as a knowing display of language style(s) deemed in a par-ticular situation to be nonnormative, unpredictable, or "as if." According to Bakhtin, language is never monologic but always dialogic, which presupposes a rich mixing and multiplicity of "voices," or "heteroglossia," in all texts. Thus, "acts of identity" (Le Page and Tabouret-Keller, 1985) involving stylized talk are not autonomous and separate but involve intercorporeal appropriation, reworking, and subversion of different social voices. In her discussion of how style may be used as a linguistic resource for performing an identity (*styling*), Cameron (2000) refers to Bell's (1997) "initiative shift" and Rampton's (1995) "crossing," both of which refer to speakers adopting a way of speaking that is not their own—in other words, putting on a voice (Coupland's *stylization*). These sociolinguistic approaches align with the broader framework of Fairclough's (2003: 159) notion of *style* as the discursive enactment of identity: "Styles are the discoursal aspect of ways of being, identities. Who you are is partly a matter of how you speak, how you write, as well as a matter of embodi-ment—how you look, how you hold yourself, how you move, and so forth."

Thus we take stylization to be the strategic (re)presentation, promotion, and imposition of particular ways of being (or styles) involving language, image, social practice, and material culture. Over time, if these different identificational meanings endure through repetition and routinization, they may become habituated and "structurated" (Giddens, 1991) into a more extensive narrative of self and a *lifestyle* that in turn forms (or reshapes) one's *habitus* (Bourdieu, 1990). As we will suggest here, stance and style are themselves ideologically and interactionally coconstitutive. To start, however, we offer our general perspective on elitism.

For our purposes, we define elitism as a person's orientation or making a claim to exclusivity, superiority, and/or distinctiveness on the grounds of status, knowledge, authenticity, taste, erudition, experience, insight, wealth, or any other quality warranting the speaker/author to take a higher moral, aesthetic, intellectual, material, or any other form of standing in relation to another subject (individual or group). Elitism then is a claim or bid for an enduring identity position that requires constant, momentary, and interactive enactment. In this sense, too, we distinguish *elitism* as a discursively achieved identity and subject position from *elite* that, as it has typically been discussed in sociological literatures (e.g., Carlton, 1996; Field and Higley, 1980; Dogan, 2003), is usually conceived of as a material, social category describing those who rule or lead through instrumental, political power. We are thus more concerned—in this chapter and elsewhere—with the consensual power of cultural, nongoverning elites whose investment in systems of governance may be more hegemonic than directly political. (Both types of elite status are of course heavily implicated in economic privileging.) Through our interest in elitist stancetaking, we are also concerned less with any objective or descriptive categorization of elite groups per se, and more with individual subjectivities, passing acts of identity, and processes of self- and other-attribution by which people may appeal to the notion or "ideal" of, for example, exclusivity, superiority, or distinction.

Numerically and, to some extent, descriptively, the notion of "elite" is notoriously hard to define. It is far easier and, we suggest, more accurate, to examine elitism as part of Raymond Williams's *structures of feeling*, "meanings and values as they are actively lived and felt" (Williams, 1977: 132). Such structures of feeling are analytically accessible through discourse, in particular when members of a culture try to articulate or understand their experiences as they are changing at a particular time, for example, within a generation or period. Understood in this way, this feeling gives rise to discourse whereby an elite status/identity is *enacted*; in other words, it is talked into existence and otherwise semiotically achieved. In these terms, elite status is never allowed to be simply a marker of political status, economic affluence, or heritage. This has important political implications for the general critique we are advancing. Assigning elite behavior only to the obviously rich and powerful overlooks two things. First, social hierarchies are mutually (which is not to say equally) established; hegemonic order is maintained through the socially consensual, constant promotion and uptake of symbolic and material markers of privilege and status (Gramsci, 1971). Second, any assumption that elitism is done only by elites also tends to obscure wider global inequalities by which all "Western" consumption patterns can be viewed as elitist. Specifically, and in the context of our analysis here, it can be argued that all tourism, all travel-for-leisure, is elite—be it vacationing on Mustique, touring Italy with the kids, partying on the Costa del Sol, or backpacking through Thailand. It is for this reason that much of what we are currently examining we deliberately characterize as *superelite* travel (see also Thurlow and Jaworski, 2009).

In this chapter, we focus on the linguistic (and to some extent visual) manifestations of taking an elitist stance in the travel sections of newspapers. As we
have stated, elitism is premised on the semiotic achievement of superiority, which
is a specific instance of what Gunther Kress (1995) refers to as the production of
social difference in texts. Drawing on the concepts of dialogism, heteroglossia, and
intertextuality (Voloshinov, 1973; Bakhtin, 1981, 1986), Kress argues that all text
production relies on past or current, recognizable or imperceptible contributions by
copresent or absent speakers and takes place within social structures characterized
by the unequal distribution of power. The production of different texts reinforces
these structures, and social actors are then assumed and trained to adopt unequal
positions of power in particular types of texts and interactions. These text types, or
genres, are relatively stable and persistent encodings of social power relations "and
are reproduced in the social structurings of occasions of linguistic (inter)action"
(Kress, 1995: 121). However, in the production of texts, the interaction of participants with different subject positions or coding orientations results in struggle and
contestation focusing on a particular set of the system of cultural classifications and
representations, or what M. A. K. Halliday (1978) refers to as *field of discourse*:
the social action, or the nature of the activity in which the text is embedded and the
participants are engaged in doing.

Thus, text producers, their interpreters, and the social actors represented in these
texts may differ with regard to their relative places in the political and economic hierarchy, mutual distance, and power relations, but the differences produced by these
texts are never stable and incontestable. Stuart Hall's (1980 [1973]) model of three
reading positions of texts—dominant (or "hegemonic"), negotiated, and oppositional
("counter-hegemonic")—is a useful heuristic in conceptualizing the dynamics of difference production in texts, as it suggests that stancetaking, understood here as production of difference, is a collaborative processes achieved (or rejected, contested,
subverted, etc.) by coparticipants in a communicative act (cf. Du Bois, 2007).

Following Pierre Bourdieu (1977, 1984, 1991), we view communication as fundamentally about the pursuit of symbolic profit and that cultural capital achieved through
language is simultaneously material, social, and economic. All spoken and written texts
are thus ideological in that they (a) constitute identities and relationships; (b) reproduce
systems of belief and power; and (c) maintain structures of inequality and privilege. In
the texts we want to examine here, each of these ideological functions is in evidence in
the stances taken up by authors and projected onto the implied reader.

Theorizing Stance: Evaluation, Relation, and Identification

Stance has many cognate terms in the (socio)linguistic literature. In their overview, Thompson and Hunston (2000) subsume stance under *evaluation* (cf. also
Labov and Waletzky, 1976) as a superordinate term (see Jaffe's overview in the
introduction to this volume). Consequently, the stance-evaluation nexus appears
to permeate all aspects of meaning making, all communicative functions, and all
levels of linguistic production. In our own view of stance, we start with Kress's
view of texts as the site for the construction of subject positions and social difference (see above). We further align ourselves with the critical discourse analytic

approach to evaluation and modality. For example, Fairclough (2003) considers how people "commit" themselves in texts, distinguishing between *modality* (i.e., commitments to what is true or what is necessary) and *evaluation* (i.e., commitments to what is desirable/undesirable or good/bad). He also aligns his notion of modality to Halliday's (1994) and Verschueren's (1999), as well as to Hodge and Kress's (1988) rather wide-ranging treatment of *modality*, by which they mean a particular *stance*, expressed as a degree of *affinity* (expressed in terms of "power" or "solidarity") between participants in a communicative situation and their (participants') perspective on the message in terms of its status, authority, reliability, ontological status, and truth value. Furthermore, Hodge and Kress argue that the significance of modality is that it constitutes an essential site of political struggle, in other words, modality is a means of constructing and contesting knowledge systems, enforcing classifications, establishing one's preferred version of social reality as "knowledge" or "fact," as well as being a means of resistance and contestation (cf. also Foucault, 1978, 1980, on discourse/counterdiscourse, "regimes of truth," and "knowledge/power"):

> Modality is consequently one of the crucial indicators of political struggle. It is a central means of contestation, and the site of the working out, whether by negotiation or imposition, of ideological systems. It provides a crucial component of the complex process of the establishment of hegemonic systems, a hegemony established as much through the active participation of social agents as through sheer "imposition" of meaning by the more powerful on the less powerful participant. (Hodge and Kress, 1988: 123)

Furthermore, Fairclough (2003) links modality and evaluation to the process of self-identification of social actors:

> Modality is important in the texturing of identities, both personal ("personalities") and social, in the sense that what you commit yourself to is a significant part of what you are—so modality choices in texts can be seen as part of the process of texturing self identity. But this goes on in the course of social processes, so that the process of identification is inevitably inflected by the process of social relation.... The texturing of identity is thoroughly embedded in the texturing of social relations. (2003: 166)

Conceived of as Fairclough's (2003) "social relations," or Hodge and Kress's (1998) relations of power and solidarity between social actors, social identities or personas are shaped through the deployment of specific linguistic resources, in other words, the constitutive "work" of direct or indirect indexing of self or other in a rather complex matrix of linguistic forms and conventional associations linked to them (Ochs, 1992; cf. Fairclough's 2003 "relations of equivalence and difference"). These resources, including styles of speaking, gesturing, and dressing, taste, and so on, result in the production of a particular *styling* of self or the stylizing of other (see above).

Du Bois (2007) refers to stance as possibly "the smallest unit of social action" (p. 173) that he conceives of:

as a public act by a social actor, achieved dialogically through overt communicative means (language, gesture, and other symbolic forms), through which social actors simultaneously evaluate objects, position subjects (themselves and others), and align with other subjects, with respect to any salient dimension of the sociocultural field. (p. 163)

There are a number of analogies and parallels in Du Bois's (2007) and Kress's (1995; Hodge and Kress, 1998) approaches to stance and the social production of language. Both find dialogicality a key, underlying concept in the production of meaning; Du Bois's notion of "sociocultural field" corresponds to Kress's use of Halliday's "field"; both view stance (Du Bois)/modality (Kress) as coconstructed by the participants, located intersubjectively between them. Social actors' convergent or divergent alignment positions proposed by Du Bois are reminiscent of Kress's theorizing of the acceptance or contestation of the dominant cultural classifications of the other, and constitutive of their identities emergent through the convergent or divergent alignment positions/relations. However, one seeming difference between the two approaches to stance is the explicit orientation to power and inequality by Kress (and other *critical* discourse analysts), although in his final characterization of stance, Du Bois emphasizes that it comprises "three key aspects of social life: act, responsibility, and value" (p. 173). By these, he means

1. the public enactment of stance, its cumulative effect and consequences for all possible domains of sociocultural life (act);
2. ownership of stance once taken by a speaker and accountability to self and others (responsibility);
3. "what stance is all about—literally" (p. 173), invoking, directly or indirectly systems of value (cf. ideology above), their enactment and reproduction (value).

It is precisely in these three key aspects of social life that the everyday enactments of power take place and its effects are rendered visible (cf. Blommaert, 2005). And herein, we think, lies the ideological nature of stancetaking, which brings us to our data examples and, eventually, to our own conceptualization of stance.

Taking an Elitist Stance: The Case of Travelogues

Not unlike many other newspapers around the world, the weekend editions of two national British papers, the *Guardian* (published on Saturdays) and the *Sunday Times*, include dedicated travel sections, with features, information, interviews, and advertisements on tourism-related themes. In particular, these two newspapers are often referred to as "broadsheet" or "quality" papers, the *Guardian* being known as more liberal and progressive than the *Sunday Times*, which is associated with a more conservative, right-wing, and affluent readership. Accordingly, the tone and, to some extent, content of their respective travel sections reflect these primary demographics in terms of education and class. The *Guardian* displays unquestionably better credentials in dealing with environmental issues than the *Sunday Times*, for example, carrying a weekly note about all of the journeys taken by its writers being offset by paying a carbon emission fee to Climate Care, and encouraging the readers to follow suit and, if possible, to avoid flying when going on holiday. The *Guardian* also runs a regular "guilt-free" column, in which the environmental implications of travel and "eco-friendly" travel options are discussed. However, despite the *Guardian*'s folding of environmentalism into the attribution of elitism to its "progressive" middle-class readership, both newspapers pander to the pursuit of a consumerist lifestyle and plea-sure (with their glossy magazines covering "style," property, food and drink, culture, and so on) and promote high-end, conspicuous consumption and leisure for their readers (even if only aspirational), allowing them to fantasize about joining the ranks of the "leisure class" (Veblen, 1979 [1899]; De Garzia, 1964; MacCannell, 1999), or espousing what we call here the elitist stance.

We now turn to our data to illustrate a number of key formal and semantic fea-tures through which stance is enacted and cumulatively established in this particular travel writing genre. The examples cut across epistemological and affective stances in Du Bois's (2007) sense, and they show overlap across the ideational, interpersonal, and textual functions outlined above. Moreover, by illustrating basic principles of stancetaking, they confirm the particularly ideological nature of this process. In each case, we focus on the thematic and lexico-grammatical forms used and the evaluated object chosen; ultimately, however, what interests us more are the identities and rela-tionships being realized and the ideologies being promoted.[1]

Evaluation: Disdain for "Mass" Tourists (and Locals)

"Tourists dislike tourists. God is dead, but man's need to appear holier than his fellow lives" (MacCannell, 1999: 10). This sentiment is very prominent in tourism discourse (scholarly and lay), most typically expressed when the distinction is drawn between "tourists" and "travelers," between escapist, mass vacationers and those who travel more "independently" and with "serious" intercultural intent (see Cohen, 2004). Although scholars are critical of their own tendency to perpetuate specious tourist typologies (Franklin and Crang, 2001), this crude status hierarchy is one heard often from tourists/travelers themselves, for whom it clearly continues to have significance (McCabe, 2005). Not surprisingly, therefore, we find instances in the travelogues of stancetaking that plays on the simple, binary distinction between "good" (elite) and "bad" (nonelite) tourists. Importantly, this is a distinction that can cut across conventional markers of class status such as wealth and education—even if these are simultaneously invoked in the performance of the distinction:

Extract 1

(*Guardian Travel*, January 31, 2004. pp. 2–3)

Barbados is one of those places that doesn't demand but eventually requires that you relax. For men, this tends to mean undoing that extra button on their short-sleeve shirt *without feeling a sleaze;* for women (though not, *she has asked me to emphasize*, my girlfriend), thinking they *might actually* look *chic* in a batik.... After three days relaxing, we moved hotel, not because of any problems, but just to see somewhere else. The Colony Club is, *or hopes to be,* a little more *upmarket* than

Tamarind Cove. The guests, in other words, may read the same papers (the *Mail* is very popular), but at the Colony *they start from the front, not the back*. (Emphasis added by authors here and in subsequent extracts.)

Extract 2

(*Sunday Times Travel*, July 16, 2006, p. 26)

Mass tourism is horrible. I hate arriving somewhere to find a horde of barbarians who've had that operation to weld a camera to their eyelids: they don't *really* see things, they *just* photograph them and get back on the *coach*.... Wherever I go, I try to mix with the locals, assimilate myself. That can backfire, of course. My car got broken into in Tunisia, and the policeman was so chatty, he ended up inviting us to supper at his home. What a nice idea, I thought: but we arrived to find a really *grim* police barracks, where he was cooking up *vile-looking* goat stew *over a Bunsen burner*.

In both of these extracts (by different authors) we see a range of objects—things and behaviors—evaluated: ways of dressing, ways of reading, ways of seeing (or photographing), and ways of eating or preparing food. Each of these is, of course, a common cultural marker and also a common marker of class (cf., respectively, Crane, 2000; Bourdieu, 1984; Sontag, 1977; Lévi-Strauss, 1966). The stances taken in extract 1, encode "undoing that extra button" as *sleazy* and batik as *not chic*, as well as the *Daily Mail* (a conservative, tabloidesque, national paper), and people who read the sports section first as *downmarket*. In extract 2, it is mass tourists' inability to see things "really" that is appraised as undesirable, as are snapshot photography and coach travel. The same author then expresses his distaste for not only the food being prepared but also the mode of preparation.

Clearly, in both extracts the authors position themselves as arbiters of good taste through their various evaluative, stancetaking acts. This subject position augments itself the more such stances are taken; that is, stancetaking is both reiterative and self-sustaining (see above). In each case, what strikes us is less the direct adjectival opinion markers (e.g., "grim," "vile-looking," "barbarians," "horrible," "upmarket," "chic," and "sleaze") but the evaluative force of a more indirect, deeply coded, fleeting stancetaking. In extract 1, we note the girlfriend's implied distress at possibly being thought of as a batik-wearer, the hedging of "might actually" and "or hopes to be," the parenthetical insinuation of the *Mail* as downmarket, and the metaphoric privileging of politics/issues over sports. In extract 2, meanwhile, it is the assumption that things may be truly or properly known that is noteworthy, as is the inappropriate use of a Bunsen burner for cooking, which arguably promotes "uneducated" before "poor" as a preferred interpretation.

Taking a stance of superiority through positive self- and negative other-evaluation is only superficially mitigated by understatement and hedging here (see especially extract 1). The former allows the author to "invite" the reader to take up these evaluations and collude in the coconstruction of this particular stance. Furthermore, these preferred readings are based on the assumption of shared attitudes and values between the author and the reader, creating a sense of in-group membership (hence, the reader is also positioned as "elite") (cf. Brown and Levinson, 1987). The use of positive politeness between authors and readers is also evident in the parenthetical references in extract 1. They both introduce information extraneous to the evaluation at hand, and their main purpose appears to be providing the reader with additional interpretive work for establishing the boundaries of in-groupness that is meant to include the author, his girlfriend, the implied *Sunday Times* reader, but not the *Mail* readers.

Taken as a whole, one of the dimensions of an *elite* identity (i.e., the elitist stance) being created in both these texts is that of the seasoned, worldly traveler. This is most apparent in extract 2, where the author claims for himself the cultural capital of the "cosmopolitan" in the way Hannerz (1996: 103) defines cosmopolitanism:

> ...an orientation, a willingness to engage with the Other. It entails an intellectual and aesthetic openness toward divergent cultural experiences, a search for contrasts rather than uniformity. To become acquainted with more cultures is to turn into an *aficionado*, to view them as artworks. At the same time, however, cosmopolitanism can be a matter of competence, and competence of both a generalized and a more specialized kind. There is the aspect of a state of readiness, a personal ability to make one's way into other cultures, though listening, looking, intuiting, and reflecting. And there is cultural competence in the stricter sense of the term, a built up skill in manoeuvring more or less expertly with a particular system of meanings.

The author may indeed display an *orientation* to engage with local people and cultures, but his text also displays lack of *willingness* and *competence* in doing so, when circumstances do not conform to his idea of travel as "home plus" (Theroux, 1986). We see this very clearly in his negative description of the Tunisian policeman's living quarters and food, where there is no shade of sympathy and understanding of how global inequalities may structure his host's lifestyle. Such displays of "liberalism" (e.g., hedging racist remarks or claiming nonprejudicial intent, see Coupland, 1999), although simultaneously othering and eroticizing local people, emphasize the relational nature of stance.[2] An elitist stance here is being built on a contrast with both bad "tourists" and exotic "locals," albeit with the overtly negative evaluation of the "locals" mitigated/masked by a liberal rhetoric.

On the elitist theme of avoiding the "wrong" kinds of tourists, we also have a third extract that returns us to the underlying social judgment of mass tourists:

Extract 3

(*Sunday Times Travel,* July 2, 2006, p. 14)

The Last Bit of *Brit-free* France. Winding valleys, wooden hilltops, sleepy hamlets: Corréze has all the charm of the Dordogne, but without the GB-plated *tailbacks*. Go before the *invasion*, says Stephen Clarke.

As before, the author/writer selects a specific object as a vehicle (in this case, also literally so: "tailbacks"—U.S. "gridlock"), for expressing his more general, ideologically motivated evaluation of mass tourism. Extract 3 is in fact an extended headline for the author's article, which paraphrases its content in the form of constructed reported speech (Tannen, 1986) focusing specifically on the article's mention of British tourists and second-home–owners identified as a separate "species" ("*Britannicus countryhousis*") spoiling the authenticity of rural France. The byline is a "stance follow" (Du Bois, 2007: 161) to that of the author's (Clarke) demonstrating the participants' inferencing with regard to one another and to stance object's "positioning, alignment, and evaluation" (Du Bois, 2007: 165). That is, the subeditor's voicing of the author's stance aligns them both in sharing their subjective orientation to the stance object (i.e., "mass British tourist"). Just as in extract 2, "mass tourism" appears to work metaphorically as a marker of class and education; in extract 3 it is additionally framed as an "invasion" (see also "horde" in extract 2) with all of its quantitative denotation and negative connotation. The phrase "Brit-free" relies on exaggeration of quantity (because the British journalist himself is there) and indirectly indexes and operationalizes a distinction between "desirable/acceptable Brits" and "undesirable/unacceptable Brits" (creating social differentiation, see Kress above). The author's/newspaper's stance therefore expresses disdain for bad tourists and places the author on the "right" side of the distinction. As in our discussion of the previous two extracts, we assume that the text's preferred reading position (interpretation of stance) is for the readers to align themselves with the elitist stance of the author, although, of course, the reader may reject the preferred reading and adopt a contested reading (or counterstance), or, in Du Bois's terms again (see above), the reader may or may not "take ownership" of the stance with the author and the newspaper. Either way, the reader is obliged to respond.

Celebrity Cachet

Of course, stancetaking is not only expressed through the lens of the negative. Much of it occurs through association with positively valued stance objects (positive affinity) that are exploited for their existing cultural capital. In this regard, a particularly productive link exists between "celebrity" and newspaper travel sections that typically include features on destinations used as locations in recent Hollywood blockbusters, often mentioning gossip from the life of famous actors on and off the filming set. Whereas traditional notions of class and elite status were based on heritage and breeding (note, however, the use of the word "stable" in extract 7), nowadays cinematic celebrity invariably trumps all (Turner, 2004).[3] In this regard, the first of our examples comes from an article featuring the Dominican Republic as the set for Cuba in *The Lost City*, a film starring Hollywood actor Andy Garcia and, less well known to British audiences, international model Inés Sastre.

Extract 4

(*Guardian Travel*, July 15, 2006, p. 3)

Havana's domestic interiors were found in the privately owned homes in Santo Domingo's colonial district (visitors can wander along Calle Hostos to *sneak a view* of the *fronded* botanical splendour of their courtyards).

As sister countries in the Caribbean's Greater Antilles island group (the Dominican Republic shares an island mass with Haiti, to the east of Cuba and to the west of Puerto Rico), the landscapes (*sierras*, mountains, tobacco and cane) and brightly lit tropical climate were almost indistinguishable. Ideal for bagging those sweeping, scene setting *vistas* of old Cuba, then? Well yes, except for *a few human-sized flies in the tanning ointment.*

"There's a montage in the middle of the film where Fico [Garcia's character] and Inés's [Sastre] character Aurora go to the idyllic beach to get away from the city," said Garcia. "The beaches are pretty busy in the Dominican, but we eventually found Macao, on the eastern part of the island in the Punta Cana Region. It was perfect until 3 PM, when a hotel *dropped a busload of guests*—we had to film the most romantic shots of the day without sound, because just off-screen there were 50 tourists *partying* to a *portable system."* ...

After a hard day of filming, Garcia would unwind in the bar of the Santo Domingo's Renaissance Jaragua Hotel, listening to the house band play a *bachata* and indulging in a *fine cigar*—one thing, he says, that the Cubans will always do better.

The piece relies first and foremost on glamorizing quotations from an interview with the Andy Garcia reporting the detail of his preferred ways to "unwind" and "indulgencies" he enjoys. Stance is therefore taken through the celebrity-embodied vehicle of Garcia himself. That Garcia's stancetaking can be quoted directly serves to augment the journalist's own stancetaking. In this sense, the article also demonstrates the typical paradox of the travelogues mentioned above: resentment of (mass) tourists whose presence "spoils" "unspoiled" destinations accessed by (elite) tourists (e.g., travelogue authors). The paradox lies in the fact that the travelogues are in fact veiled advertisements for the destinations, as well as for the tour operators, airlines, and other agents of the tourist industry sponsoring the authors' travels. Notwithstanding the actual problems for the filming a romantic scene caused by noisy company, the reference to "a busload of guests" and "50 tourists partying to a portable system," represents Garcia not only as a privileged Hollywood celebrity, but also as a tourist attributing a desire for exclusivity at a destination. This stance is taken up and amplified by the author in his depiction of other tourists as unwanted: "human-sized flies in the tanning ointment."

In addition to channeling Garcia and his antitourist stancetaking, the journalist's stancetaking also includes a register claiming the symbolic capital of an "expert" on the destination, and of a Hollywood "insider" and skilled writer commanding an elevated style that is at once poetic and polyglot (e.g., "fronded," "sierras," "vistas," "bachata") including the punning fly-in-the-ointment reference itself (see *intertextuality* below). It is these performative allusions that realize not only the ideologies of elite tourism but also of education and class. The positive evaluation underpinning these stances is established and clarified through the embedding of Garcia's own disapproving evaluation of the "partying" and "portable system" of the (mass) tourists.[4]

A similar sentiment is expressed in the next extract from the "on location" feature in the *Guardian*, inspired by the Disney production *Pirates of the Caribbean: Dead Man's Chest*, starring Johnny Depp, filmed on the Caribbean island of Dominica.

As the film's producer explains in the extract below, the island was chosen for its beauty and because it is "virtually untouched" and "totally undiscovered" (the latter claim being challenged by the author of the article in a section not reproduced here). Once again, also note the poetic register (e.g., "clothed," "veined," "glittering fairy glade"):

Extract 5

(*Guardian Travel,* July 8, 2006, p. 3)

Lying between Guadeloupe and Martinique, Dominica, with its volcanic mountains clothed in rainforest and veined with rivers and waterfalls, in fact, not unlike Depp's Sparrow: charismatic, beguiling, *unknowable.* And for just those reasons, it was chosen as a location for both Pirates 2, which opened this week, and, coming next year, Pirates 3. "We selected Dominica because it's beautiful and *virtually untouched*—and *totally undiscovered* by film makers," said producer Jerry Bruckheimer....

Disney brought a bit of its own treasure to Dominica, an island struggling in the wake of globalisation and the collapse of its banana industry: at least some of the film's US$300m budget—three times more than the government's annual expenditure—went on the logistics of housing, feeding and servicing an army of actors and technicians. Depp, meanwhile, *stayed on his yacht.* Yet gossip has it that he was seen as an *affable figure* among the locals. For example, he chilled out at Indigo Cottages, perched on a steep slope three miles from Portsmouth—and *did the washing up.* Owned by Clem Frederick, a Rastafarian, and his French-born artist wife, Marie, its buildings, including an *open-sided art gallery* with furniture made of driftwood, are set in a *glittering fairy glade* of tropical plants. Depp was generous with his time; and many a home can boast a photograph of Depp shoulder to shoulder with a Dominican extra, both grinning like old mates at the camera.

The second part of the extract continues to present the destination by retracing, at least in part, the footsteps of its celebrity visitor (Depp), and providing the reader with information on his accommodation and his contacts with the locals. Unlike in the Garcia/Dominican Republic extract above, the only other people mentioned in the text are the locals: two named hotel owners and unnamed extras, all seemingly adding "color" to Depp's experience of the island and mediating its exoticism for the reader. The name-dropping use of celebrities as stancetaking vehicles is also seen in extract 6 and, with the added traditional cachet of royalty and "A-listers," in extract 7.

Of greater interest than the fairly obvious objects of celebrity, poetic register, money ($300m budget), and fine art ("open-sided art gallery") is the way stance is expressed through the totalizing phrases "virtually untouched" and "totally undiscovered," as well as the personalizing "stayed on his yacht," "affable figure," and "did the washing up" in extract 5 (see also extract 7's "private island"). To begin, the elitism that underpins these particular acts of stancetaking relies on the favorable evaluation of newness and of excessive and exclusive space that together communicate the consumerist idealization of the new and unused (McCracken, 1988), coupled with the neocolonial reevaluation of supposedly undiscovered, virgin territories as a hallmark of luxury tourism (see Thurlow and Jaworski, 2009; also extract 7 and the next section). Then, with regard to Depp's perceived friendliness ("affable figure"), the journalist's stance emphasizes not so much his personality as the relation between Depp and the "locals"—as well as his deigning to do the washing up himself. The interesting ideological work being done relates, therefore, to the rewarding of an "egalitarian elitism" expressed in part through understatement, and a kind of "inconspicuous conspicuous consumption" (cf. Veblen, 1979). As Bourdieu points out, however, this kind of linguistic maneuver can be read as a form of condescension: a move by a high-status individual to style him- or herself in the language or social practices of a subordinate group (Bourdieu, 1991). Invariably, argues Bourdieu, the condescension serves only to reinscribe hierarchical relations of inequality.

This paradoxical reframing of elitism is also evidenced in the "laid-back, low-rise glamour" and the characterization of elites as "regulars" in extracts 6 and 7.

Extract 6

(*Guardian Travel,* October 29, 2003, p. 8)

The atmosphere at Camps Bay, Cape Town's most *fashionable* beach resort, has something of the *laid-back, low-rise glamour* of Los Angeles about it, a feeling only heightened when the waiter mentions that Tiger Woods dined here the previous night, Vinnie Jones was a frequent visitor the week before and Jean-Claude Van Damme is currently relaxing between shoots on his latest movie at a *luxury* hotel a mile or so down the road.... *The list of celebrity visitors has been growing* ever since the Western Cape became a favourite location for filmmakers and commercials directors, and it comes as no surprise to learn that Cape Town is a regular body double for LA, Monterey and San Francisco.

Extract 7

(*Sunday Times Travel,* June 25, 2006, p. 2)

Who's the *Coolest* of them all? The Turks and Caicos, favourite *A-list* sun spot, has a new Aman resort. Can it knock Parrot Cay off its perch, asks Susan d'Arcy.... Parrot Cay, a half hour boat ride north of Providenciales *on its own private island*, is the hotel that brought the Turks and Caicos to international attention back in 1998, and it's far less expensive proposition. From the same *stable* as London's *ever-trendy* Metropolitan, it is Princess Stephanie to Amanyara's Princess Caroline: less serious, but no less attractive, especially if you like the circus. The celebrity circus, I mean. The main pool is so *packed with A-listers*, it looks like a 3-D version of Heat Magazine. Regulars include Julia Roberts, Matt Damon, Cindy Crawford and Bruce Willis.

In the short space of these two extracts, both authors manage to enact the positive-affinity stance reiteratively by their mention of the repeated return and appearance of celebrities. The value of the destination is established metonymically in relation to the visiting celebrities, and the authors use these references to establish their own stance credentials as well. However, the authors' commitment to the veracity of these extracts is vague (note the hyperbole "the main pool is so packed with A-listers", and humour "it looks like a 3-D version of Heat Magazine" in extract 7) and suggests that encounters with celebrities are not part of the authors' personal experiences but imaginary associations with place and elite vacationing style. The characterization of celebrities as "regulars" in extract 7 claims a reduction of difference and distance between the celebrities, locals, and the author-tourist, but there is no "evidence" of contact other than secondhand gossip from a waiter (extract 6).

Stancetaking in these extracts and throughout our sample appears also to manage the tension between evaluating quality and quantity. Much of the time, contemporary elitism is predicated on comparative quality often expressed through the ambiguous lexicon of "fashionable," "luxurious," and "coolest." However, the traditional discourse of quantity (e.g., measurable wealth) is persistent and perpetuated through, for example, the growing list of celebrity visitors (extract 6) and "packed with A-listers" (extract 7). As with the promise of endless choice (see Schwartz, 2004), untamed exclusivity quickly begins to undermine itself. This tension is often managed most effectively through the use of lexicogrammatical superlatives (see below).

Empty Spaces, Silent Places

In our analysis of the representations of luxury tourist spaces in magazine advertisements (Thurlow and Jaworski, 2009), we have suggested that the visual linguistic landscape of the photographs depicting "high-end" travel destinations are frequently realized discursively by the mutual concepts of space and silence. Generally, these ads promise the superelite traveler vast, empty indoor and outdoor spaces, an escape from talk or noise, and exclusion of the babble of local people and the "drivel" of the masses (including other mass tourists). Thus "silence" (or the promise of silence) and "emptiness" become key symbolic resources for performing/promoting superelite travel and elitism. As we have already indicated, the same tropes are present in newspaper travelogues, whether in the visual representations of travel destinations or authors' accounts of various locations' desirability. Just a few examples from the reader-led section "Readers' Guide to..." on European beaches illustrate this point. Of the 25 beaches mentioned on a two-page spread, over half are described in a variety of ways as quiet, secluded, empty, vast, and so on.

Extract 8

(*Guardian Travel*, June 10, 2006, pp. 8–9)

One of the most beautiful and secluded beaches on the island...you'll be very unlikely to find *noisy gangs* of Brits....Camping out over night on one of the otherwise *deserted beaches* to await sunrise is a truly wonderful experience....The sand *squeaks* beneath your toes and the atmosphere is Mediterranean and *peaceful*....It's *inaccessible by road*....There's an imposing bay, with steep, pine-forested mountains and the ruins of ancient Aigosthena immediately behind the largest beach.... You should feel aggrieved if you can't find *10 acres of empty space* to put your beach towel on.... A *pristine* National Trust beach... it's popular but *still undeveloped*, thankfully... with *huge sweeps of sand and dunes*... If you aim for the middle section, you'll avoid the *boy racers* (they're not intimidating—just a bit annoying). Out of season, you can rent a dinghy for a reasonable price and *have the place (almost) to yourself.* A village *tucked away....* A *huge beach....* Just a short bus ride or walk further up the coast from the town's main beach... but usually *a lot less crowded.* This sandy beach is *surprisingly quiet.*

Cutting across the discourse in extract 8, we note the repetitive and consistent evaluation of "acres of empty space," "huge sweeps of sand and dunes," and "huge beach." These topographical markers of exclusivity are in turn linked to social makers as in "deserted beaches," "inaccessible by road," and "tucked away." We also note again the neocolonial appraisals inherent in "pristine" and "undeveloped." Finally, we are brought to the explicit appreciation of quietude in "unlikely to find noisy gangs," "peaceful," and "surprisingly quiet" and the (relative) absence of others: "have the place (almost) to yourself" and "a lot less crowded." Silence is also implicit in being able to hear the squeaking sand beneath one's feet. In extracts 9 to 11, this general evaluation of social isolation/exclusivity is realized in stancetaking acts that combine the range of different objects listed thus far:

Extract 9

(*Sunday Times Travel,* May 28, 2006, p. 1)

Hide from the World: *Ten Islands You Can Have to Yourself.*

Extract 10

(*Sunday Times Travel,* April 30, 2006, p. 6)

Mine, ALL MINE. An *uncrowded island, a beach to call your own*—in the Med? In summer? It can be done, says Jeremy Lazell.

Extract 11

(*Sunday Times Travel,* July 9, 2006, p. 5)

Q: I am planning our first family trip to Disney World and would like to know how to *avoid the crowds.* Ian Haddon, Dundee

The appeal to/for exclusivity (expressed through the negatively evaluated object "crowds") in Disney World strikes us as highly unrealistic or just very optimistic. In either case, the validity or likelihood—in other words, the modality—of the claim is not what is at stake in stancetaking that centers on the underlying appraisal of crowds as undesirable. It is possible also that the aspirational stance of extract 11 reveals the uptake of the elitism that runs through more obviously "luxurious" elite destinations and modes of contemporary travel. It is also the very unrealizability of the aspiration that marks its elitist ethos. As we have noted before, "The goal is to keep people covetous of their ideal by carefully balancing opportunities for its realization (e.g., by acquiring or possessing a concrete manifestation of the ideal) and sustaining the impossibility of its attainment" (Thurlow and Jaworski, 2006: 115).

Secrets, Hot Tips, and Insider Information

Our next set of stancetaking acts is closely allied to the illusory nature of exclusivity just discussed. In this case, one hallmarked value in tourism is being able to go "backstage" and behind the scenes for a glimpse (see, for example, "sneak a view" in extract 4) of local life that is perceived, or staged, as "real" or "authentic" (MacCannell, 1999). In this regard, we find a number of related stancetaking acts that inflect this general tourist trope with the added promise of its being privileged information or insight. Once again, the implication here is that the "secrets" (extract 14, 16, and 17) are to be had only by the knowledgeable, well-traveled person. Others would simply "never guess" (extract 13). Of course, a key feature of these commercial travelogues has to be the promise, as in extract 12, of an authoritative heads-up on "where to go and where not to go" that carries the same implication of discernment.

Extract 12

(*Sunday Times Travel,* April 16, 2006, p. 1)

Welcome to the South Pacific. *Where to go and where not to* for the ultimate tropical adventure

Extract 13

(*Sunday Times Travel,* June 11, 2006, p. 1)

Europe's new hot spots. *You'll never guess.*

Extract 14

(*Sunday Times Travel*, July 23, 2006, p. 1)

France's *best kept secret.*

Extract 15

(*Guardian Travel,* May 20, 2006, p. 1)

Look where you can go without flying. *We show you* how.

Extract 16

(*Sunday Times Travel,* July 9, 2006, p. 1)

The *secrets* of the Lake District.

Extract 17

(*Sunday Times Travel,* May 21, 2006, p. 26)

The island made for the weekend. Any plans for the weekend? How about a quick hop to Trogir, Croatia's *bite-size secret,* suggests Fiona Watson.

In positioning themselves as knowledgeable of the useful tips and information about tourist destinations, these journalists claim exclusivity and superiority of status by virtue of their having visited, experienced, and familiarized themselves with the places desired by their readers. This is the power/knowledge principle to be found across the whole spectrum of "lifestyle" magazines concerned with advising their readers on personal relationships, sex, beauty, work, leisure, and travel. As such features are premised on the "problem-solution" discourse schema (Machin and van Leeuwen, 2007), posing the problem of the most desirable tourist destinations as "secrets" is a necessary gambit for the travelogues from which they can establish their superior "expert" stance. In other words, it is not the inside knowledge itself that is of value but being in the know and performing this knowing. The *object* of the stance is thus exclusive knowledge per se and not the specifics of that knowledge.

Claiming the Superlative: "Best of…" Lists

In another type of lexico-grammatical marking, one form of stancetaking is achieved through superlative claims. One obvious example of this is the *Guardian*'s regular feature "Five Best…," examples of which we show in extract 18. In this case, the categories covered are not always particularly luxurious or glamorous in themselves, but the features imply a high degree of "expertness" and suggest that the authors have traveled to the locations to test them, reiterating the elitist claim to cosmopolitan status in itself (see above).

Extract 18

(in order, all *Guardian Travel:* April 1, 2006, p. 9; April 15, 2006, p. 10; April 22, 2006, p. 10; May 13, 2006, p. 10; May 20, 2006, p. 12; May 27, 2006, p. 10; June 3, 2006, p. 10; June 10, 2006, p. 10; July 8, 2006, p. 10; July 15, 2006, p. 10)

*Five Best…*Road Trips; Riverside Pubs; Rooms over the Channel; Cool Beach Hotels; Green Hotels; Summer Solstice Parties; Hostels in Europe; Beach Campsites; Rooftops; Lakeside Hotels

Of course, claiming a superlative ranking is a fairly obvious tactic, especially for a promotional genre; however, what makes this particular type of stancetaking remarkable is the largely unwarranted nature of those claims and the absence of any clear substantiation. Claims to being the best are impossible to prove or to disprove and so must be taken at face value. This is not to say that elitist claims to superiority are always as straightforward as "We're the best." In fact, they can be made with a host of oxymoronic rhetorical moves that, on the one hand, intensify the claim, and, on the other hand, hedge the claim—or at least appear to. Take the following slogan promoting the island of Mustique: *Unquestionably one of the most exclusive islands in the world.*[5] This sweeping superlative claim ("most exclusive in the world") is modified doubly by the intensifier "unquestionably" and the qualifier "one of." Whereas the former strengthens the boldness of the claim, the latter adds a pretense of modesty, while at the same time presupposing its membership in a necessarily small club of equally exclusive destinations. To challenge the preeminence of Mustique automatically positions the reader as the kind of person clearly not qualified to make the judgment.

Other examples of the "best of..." lists/features include the following:

Extract 19

(*Sunday Times Travel,* May 28, 2006, p. 6)

Crusoe Deluxe. Lots of resorts can offer luxury. Seclusion's harder to find. To get both, you want a hotel on its private island—and Susan d'Arcy has *10 of the best.*

Extract 20

(*Sunday Times Travel,* June 30, 2006, p. 1)

India's *Finest.* Alastair Sawday picks the *best* hotels on the subcontinent.

Extract 21

(*Sunday Times Travel,* June 25, 2006, p. 6)

Late Getaways: Summer's Sorted. Are there any great family holidays left this summer? You bet—and Stephen Bleach has *20 of the best.*

Extract 22

(*Sunday Times Travel,* June 11, 2006, p. 1)

Beat the Daily Grind. *The world's best* rut-busting holidays.

Extract 23

(*Guardian Travel,* April 15, 2006, p. 10)

World's best on a plate. Restaurant magazine editor Joe Warwick on five favourites from the *World's 50 best* restaurants list.

The same types of claims can, of course, also be made with grammatical superlatives:

Extract 24

(*Guardian Travel*, July 8, 2006, p. 1)

Jazz on a summer's evening. New York's *coolest* clubs.

Extract 25

(*Guardian Travel,* April 1, 2006, p. 1)

Planet Earth's *greatest* hits.

Extract 26

(*Guardian Travel,* June 10, 2006, p. 1)

Beach special. From Europe's *finest* to an American beauty.

Whether the authors of these lists are named (extracts 19, 20, 21, and 23) or anonymous, the precise criteria for these judgments are not always clear. It's also unclear why these cutoff points are chosen—why, for example, the "*five best*," why specifically 20 or 50, and so on? We suspect none of the details really matters. To some extent, the display of narrative detail simply works to legitimize the travel narrative or account as a whole—to establish the stance as somehow quantifiably accurate or valid (cf. Tannen 1989). In this sense, the evaluation has the added appeal of high modality. The important identificational and relational work being done in these acts of stancetaking positions the writer (first party) as the person who knows best—has access to privileged information—and implies that the reader (second party) deserves the best and should want the best. Lists then are a powerful subgenre in that they include only allowable items within agreed categories (e.g., private islands, beaches, and hotels) (cf. Sacks, 1992), and they conform to the marketing and consumerist ethos of the travel sections by providing their readers with a sense of endless choice (whether real or imaginary) from among equivalent products. These are not "to-do lists," like shopping lists (although they are not uncommon in travel writing), which allows the reader to aim or dream of visiting only one of the destinations to attain elite status.

Excess, (Self-)Indulgence, and Service

Not surprisingly, elitist stancetaking in the context of tourism also entails the positive evaluation of excess—a comparative judgment of having more than normal and/or having more than others. We have shown how this conspicuous performance of the have/have-not boundary is key to the maintenance of elite status in frequent-flyer programs and airline business-class services (Thurlow and Jaworski, 2006). In extracts 27 to 31 we see a number of different ways in which excess and indulgence is appraised as desirable and, we note, acceptable. In each case, what is important is that the primary objects being evaluated "indulgence," "gastronomy," "hedonists," "a party you'll never remember," and being "very, very drunk" are carefully qualified with "follows tough adventure," "Michelin-starred," "the handbook of," and "suffering from Glastonbury withdrawal."

Extract 27

(*Sunday Times Travel,* April 9, 2006, p. 1)

Travel...and relax. *Sheer indulgence* follows *tough* adventure on our perfect two-part breaks.

Extract 28

(*Sunday Times Travel,* June 6, 2006, p. 2)

Corking companions. Antony Sher is lightly fermented by Richard Wilson's company, *Michelin-starred gastronomy* and some vintage Burgundy wine.

Extract 29

(*Sunday Times Travel,* May 28, 2006, p. 2)

The handbook of hedonists. Katie Brown put on her dancing shoes, party frock and lucky knickers to road-test the wildest guidebook ever to hit London.

Extract 30

(*Sunday Times Travel,* July 16, 2006, p. 2)

Vodka with ice, and fire. *Suffering* from Glastonbury withdrawal? Head to the Westman Islands for *a party you'll never remember*, says Graham Little.

Extract 31

(*Sunday Times Travel,* July 30, 2006, p. 2)

...and I was very, very drunk. Each June, in the beautiful hills of Tuscany, the locals welcome in the new vintage. Vincent Crump helps them celebrate.

One available interpretation here is that elitist stancetaking needs justification; this is why there is the added evaluation that excess/indulgence is rendered acceptable if it is in some way earned or deserving (e.g., through effort or hard work—"tough" and "suffering"—or through spiritual growth; see below). Whether or not these references are made ironically, the implication is being made and the ideological work is being done. Incidentally, but not without significance, the phrase "...and I was very, very drunk" would be recognizable to many British readers as an intertextual reference to the "13th Duke of Wybourne," a caricature of aristocratic excess from the very popular BBC comedy program *The Fast Show.* In much the same way, references to codified/standardized markers of acceptance ("Michelin-starred" and "handbook") arguably serve to mitigate social sanctions toward greed and self-indulgence. In so much of what we have been seeing in tourism discourse, travel for leisure is often justified by an underlying "because I deserve it," "I owe it to myself" presumption of privilege. (As the clichéd L'Oreal cosmetics commercial catchphrase has it, "Because I'm worth it.") Motivated, at least in part, by the Weberian, work-related anxieties that both motivate and constrain the pursuit of leisure, a substantial part of "tourist talk" likewise involves stories that frame travel as labor (e.g., the trials of booking a holiday and the tribulations of airplane journeys).

Extract 32

(*Guardian Travel,* May 27, 2006, p. 6)

So *hip* it hurts. A luxury *hand-crafted tent with a king-sized bed*—it's camping but not as we know it in the Archede.

Extract 33

(*Guardian Travel,* April 22, 2006, p. 4)

Self-catering—but not as you know it. In fact *you don't even have to cook for yourself,* because these Kenyan beach houses even *come with a chef.* Nick Maes can't believe such *glamour* can be had for £20 a night.

Extract 34

(*Sunday Times Travel,* May 12, 2006, p. 29)

Would sir care for a body sculpt? *Country-house posh* meets *spa chic* in deepest New Forestshire—*spiffing*, says Vincent Crump.

Closely related to the mitigated but ultimately positive evaluation of excess and (self-) indulgence is the particular stance taken toward the labor and preparation of tourism professionals in the shaping of the elite tourist experience. Key to management of the host-tourist encounter is the double bind demanded by such tourists of local people: that they be both friend and servant (Jaworski et al., 2003a). In luxury travel especially, this tension is managed through the complex presentation and performance of labor that must be simultaneously unobtrusive and apparent—what we might call "visibly invisible labor" (cf. Sherman, 2007). In extract 34, the body sculpt is clearly an evaluated object but, perhaps more important, it is the ingratiating tone expressed (however ironically) by "would sir care for" that is upheld as desirable. The spoof-like use of "spiffing" also offers the author a chance to disassociate himself slightly from the anachronistic elitism indexed by the image of the butler (or any other clearly labeled *servant*).

Elite (or superelite) travelers are therefore reassured constantly of the effort in preparing their experience but in ways that do not discomfort them. This is why luxury tourism promotion, including luxury hotel Web sites, shows endless images of highly manicured lawns, immaculately made beds, ornately arranged flowers, elaborately laid tables, and fastidiously prepared (*haute/nouvelle cuisine*) meals. In precisely the same way, it is not the deliberately mundane objects in extracts 32 and 33 ("tent," "self-catering") that are evaluated per se, but more so "handcrafted" and "chef" and the oxymoronic significance of self-catering with a hired chef and of "handcrafting" an object that typically signifies no-frills "roughing it." The king-size bed merely adds to this.[6] In fact, we would suggest that one rhetorical feature that characterizes (contemporary?) elitist stancetaking is the oxymoron and, in particular, the degree of oxymoron such that the greater the incongruity the more luxurious or elite. For example, we see this principle applied in luxury tourism advertising that continually juxtaposes ordered (or manicured) spaces and disordered ("natural") spaces, and commonly promotes itself in terms of casual elegance, affordable exclusivity, or contemporary tradition (see Thurlow and Jaworski, 2009). It is the performance of these contrasts that offers superelite tourists another resource for knowing themselves as elites.

Fashionable (but Affordable) Good Taste

Without going so far as to express a high-modality opinion or attitudinal evaluation (see our discussion of stance below), the stancetaking we see in our sample of travelogues is sometimes done through explicit adjectival markers that appraise any number of objects as desirable or undesirable—usually the first. In other words, without making an explicit claim to superiority, superiority is encoded in a more indirect lexicon. In extracts 35 to 40, this elitist lexicon collectively establishes the value of being "cool," "stylish," "designer," "new wave," "newly revamped," and "chic." As before, what ultimately gets evaluated is the latest, the newfangled, the *en vogue*—but *not*, it seems, the trendy or popular that would work against the requisite exclusivity. Nor should the *avant garde* come at the expense of authenticity. Elitist stancetaking insists on having its cake and eating it.

Extract 35

(*Guardian Travel,* April 22, 2006, p. 1)

Kenya gets *cool*. Chill out *in style* on the Indian Ocean.

Extract 36

(*Guardian Travel,* June 24, 2006, p. 1)

All over for *design* hotels? Try telling the Italians.

Extract 37

(*Guardian Travel,* April 15, 2006, p. 1)

Mexican *new wave*. How Acapulco regained its sparkle.

Extract 38

(*Guardian Travel,* June 10, 2006, p. 4)

Cape cool. Cape May was the Hamptons of the 19th century, then forgotten for about 100 years. Now the *newly revamped* beach town is *more stylish than ever*, says Douglas Rogers.

Extract 39

(*Sunday Times Travel,* May 21, 2006, p. 24)

Bargains *with class*. This June, it's not just the Costas that are cutting prices—Mark Hodson finds *chic* trips *going cheap*.

Extract 40

(*Guardian Travel,* July 22, 2006, p. 1)

Raw Africa. How Zambia manages to keep it *real*.

Extract 41

(*Sunday Times Travel,* April 23, 2006, p. 1)

The naked Truth. You *don't have to spend a fortune* on a spa break.

Extract 42

(*Guardian Travel,* June 10, 2006, p. 6)

Beach *therapy*. A spa resort on the stunning Baltic coast mixes traditional and modern treatments at *ludicrously cheap prices*.

In keeping with the reference to "class" in extract 39, another set of adjectival stance markers includes those that index tradition and/or authenticity (extract 42). In this sense, we see how contemporary notions of elite status (e.g., the appreciation of newness) continue to be infused with old-fashioned ideas of status (e.g., the royalty reference in extract 7). See, for example, the coupling and positive appraisal of "country-house posh" and "spa chic" in extract 34. Once again, the stance(s) being taken here evaluate(s) not only country houses and spas, but also the combination of the two.

It is for this reason precisely that journalists can also afford to condescend to "good value," "affordable," and even "cheap" recommendations because what they ultimately uphold is the elitist notion of exclusivity, superiority, and distinction. By the same token, the ambiguity of any stancetaking act is easily resolved in the context of (a) tourism discourse generally, and (b) the promotional discourse of the travelogue. In this way, the apparent oxymorons of "bargains with class" and "cheap chic" (extract 39) are resolved through the presumed knowledge that the evaluated objects are worth more—whether in economic or symbolic terms. One may not have to spend a "fortune" (extract 41), but the "spa break" is *worth* a fortune and/or is what those who have a fortune do. These complex significations remind us why the "elite = rich" formula is too simplistic (see p. 196 above).

It is also important to remember that all the references in these travelogues have to be interpreted within the broader, elitist discourse of tourism. As such, many of the objects evaluated in the stancetaking we have looked at end up being doubly encoded as elite or superelite. Furthermore, because these are commercial travelogues (i.e., typically sponsored by travel organizations), the default appraisal of the stancetaking is favorable. In other words, unless specifically characterized as undesirable (e.g., extract 1's "might actually look chic in batik"), the promotional discourse of the travelogues assumes a positive evaluation—even if some things must be dismissed along the way. By the same token, the general stance of travelers presupposes an elitism, as does the general stance of the *Guardian* and the *Sunday Times*, as well as that of journalists or celebrity writers. In effect, therefore, stancetaking acts may indeed be small ones, but they appear to function collectively and cumulatively.

Spirituality and Transcendence

Another way in which the elitism of contemporary tourism arguably mitigates and justifies itself is through appeals to the high moral ground of quasi-religious spirituality. Although pilgrimage has always been an important part—a key precursor even—of tourism (MacCannell, 1999), it appears that the promise of things transcendental is becoming an increasing feature of contemporary, luxury travel. In this case, the spiritual/transcendental is itself appraised as a desirable aspect of the general elitist stance of tourism.

Extract 43

(*Guardian Travel,* July 22, 2006, p. 4)

Falls *paradise*. When Douglas Rogers was growing up in Zimbabwe, Zambia was considered a wild and under-developed neighbour—precisely what makes it such a *hot* safari ticket today.

Extract 44

(*Sunday Times Travel,* July 23, 2006, p. 1)

The Island of the Sun: A *magical pilgrimage* across Lake Titicaca.

Extract 45

(*Sunday Times Travel,* May 14, 2006, p. 10)

The hard way to *heaven.* If Rosie Thomas can get to Pakistan's Hunza valley in one piece, there'll be a *spiritual reward,* spectacular views and all the fruit she can eat.

Extract 46

(*Sunday Times Travel,* July 30, 2006, p. 1)

Paradiso! Italy's sexiest islands.

The stancetaking acts in extracts 43 to 46 (see also "idyllic" in extract 4) that reference "paradise," "paradiso," "heaven," "pilgrimage," and "spiritual reward" not only shore up the cultural capital of spirituality but, more important, deploy this capital in the service of framing many of the privileged activities of tourism as somehow more acceptable and/or worthy. The representation of spa treatment, which is at the heart of so much "luxury travel," and, in a similar way, the framing of the beach—or, more probably, lounging on the beach—as "therapy" achieves a similar end (see extract 42). In the historical context of Roman Catholic alms-giving and indulgences, buying one's way into heaven and to spiritual grace is certainly not new; what is new, however, is the New Age aestheticization and life stylization of spirituality; this is spirituality without dogma, transcendence with a cocktail. What is also noticeable sometimes is the dovetailing of tourism and Eastern religious or healing practices that evidences a renewed Orientalism (Said, 1978) in keeping perhaps with the neocolonialist reinvention of, say, the grand tour and elite travel in general.

Intertextual Cultural Capital

True to their reader demographic perhaps, the underlying (or cumulative) stance taken with respect to tourism is that of the educated, discerning educated classes. A frequently evaluated object—and one working arguably at an even more subtle level—occurs in the intertextual play that we found a number of times (recall the fly-in-the-ointment pun in extract 4). In almost tabloidesque style, these "witty" references are almost always located at the start of feature articles, in headers or sub-headers such as those in extracts 47 to 52.

Extract 47

(*Sunday Times Travel,* June 25, 2006, p. 1)

Into Africa: by foot, by boat, by starlight—the safari that gets you up close and personal.

Extract 48

(*Guardian Travel,* May 13, 2006, p. 3)

The unbearable lightness of Barnsley. An extraordinary work of art in a Yorkshire field brings the sky almost close enough to touch.

Extract 49

(*Sunday Times Travel,* June 4, 2006, p. 10)

Walk on the mild side. You don't have to be super fit or rough to walk in the Himalayas. Stick to the foothills and enjoy the mountains from afar.

Extract 50

(*Guardian Travel,* July 1, 2006, p. 6)

Children and the revolution. Cuba with kids needs a bit of planning, but get it right and it offers far more than other Caribbean islands.

Extract 51

(*Sunday Times Travel,* April 23, 2006, p. 10)

Mission impassable. For most of the year, the Himalayan valley of Spiti is cut off from the world. Duncan Sprott climbs into a part of Tibet where life is harsh, but the locals still know how to party.

Extract 52

(*Sunday Times Travel,* May 28, 2006, p. 1)

They eat horses, don't they? In the obscure cluster of central Asian nations, Kazakhstan stands out for its fine art, naked choristry and equestrian recipes. Waldemar Januszczak investigates.

Elsewhere, other examples of this exploitation of cultural capital included "Walk on the wild side," "The greatest show on earth," "A star is reborn," "Natural thrillers," and "Laird of the Fairways." In the case of extracts 47–52, the range of cultural references made include Hollywood blockbusters (Brian De Palma's *Mission Impossible*) and Oscar-winning adaptations (Sydney Pollack's *Out of Africa*, also a novel, and *They Shoot Horses, Don't They?*), rock/pop songs (T-Rex's "Children of the Revolution," Lou Reed's "Walk on the Wild Side"), and novels (Milan Kundera's *The Unbearable Lightness of Being*).

Of course, the reader doesn't really have to know where a particular reference comes from; he or she has only to recognize the phrase just enough to be able to know that it indexes some kind of shared cultural capital. Once again, the cachet lies in the knowing rather than the knowledge. The possibility exists that these moments of formulaic wordplay also serve to ridicule and/or frame as frivolous the significance of the destination culture; if not, their primary function is nonetheless the elevation of "people like us" or, rather, people who get the joke (see Jaworski et al., 2003b, on *linguascaping*). In many respects, these last examples best exemplify the kind of strategies of social control that privilege dominant cultural capital and in ways that, as Bourdieu (1990: 127) notes, are not overt but usually "gentle, invisible [and] unrecognized"—and, it has to be said, often "misrecognized" by the writers themselves. In fact, we believe that it is precisely this kind of "symbolic violence" that characterizes all of the elitist stancetaking acts we have considered here. These fleeting, but performatively accreting, moments of elitist stancetaking reinscribe not only the cultural capital of the object being evaluated but also the notion of cultural capital per se as a necessary or sufficient marker of class status. We are also left wondering if this is not true of the inherent ideological evaluation that underscores all acts of stancetaking. Which brings us to our own conceptualization of stance, based on what we have seen here and with a view to elitism in particular.

Rethinking Stance: Ideology, Symbolic Order, and Social Control

> What thus seems to take place outside ideology, in reality
> takes place in ideology.... That is why those who are in
> ideology believe themselves by definition outside ideology:
> one of the effects of ideology is the practical denegation of
> the ideological character of ideology by ideology: ideology
> never says, "I am ideological."
>
> —Althusser, 1972: 118

Following Thompson and Hunston, and Du Bois, we view stance as an *evaluation* or appraisal of an *object* (whether a thing, a person, an event, a behavior, or an idea) as being somehow desirable/undesirable or good/bad. As we have seen above, in the case of *elitist* stancetaking the evaluation is made partly on the basis of the evaluated object but always through a claim to both distinction and superiority. So, where a stance might express the judgment "this is good," an elitist stance carries the added or specific implication of "this is better," or even "this is the best." In either case, the object is evaluated in its own right, but primarily as a *vehicle* for expressing a relational, identificational, and, most important for our purposes here, ideological orientation.[7]

Ideology, as the collective imaginary, is characterized chiefly by its capacity to persuade us of its obviousness and its neutrality (Althusser, 1972). Stancetaking likewise often seeks to obfuscate and obscure itself. Typically, stancetaking obscures itself as judgment and conceals its evaluation as "neutral" and "normal." It is this that often gives stancetaking its power—the production and naturalization of knowledge without our being aware of it (Foucault, 1980). For Bourdieu (1977), the logic of self-interest that drives power relations is rendered all the more effective through the appearance of disinterest. Here is how Swartz (1997: 43) describes Bourdieu's position:

> Activities and resources gain symbolic power, or legitimacy, to the extent that they
> become separated from underlying material interests and hence go misrecognized as

representing disinterested forms of activities and resources....Symbolic capital is a form of power that is not perceived as power but as legitimate demands for recognition, deference, obedience, or the service of others.

It is no coincidence perhaps that, in contexts of luxury, the performance of disinterest, of a studied insouciance, should itself come to be coded as "classy." All of which also leaves the presumed outsider in something of a double bind: either collude with the act of stancetaking or call it out as reprehensible and run the risk of marking oneself out as déclassé.

What gives stances their inherently ideological significance, then, is that they are less likely—relatively speaking—to draw attention to themselves. As with ideology, some claim to knowledge-about-the-world is made but in a way that is *apparently* less "committed" and therefore presented as more of a commonsensical taken-for-granted. In other words, the stances we have analyzed in this corpus do not often have the modal conviction of *attitudinal* statements flagged by phrases such as "I believe," "I think," "I feel," "I hate," "I agree," and so on. Rather, stancetaking tends to be subtle and is premised on inference rather than assertion of evaluation (Du Bois, 2007), as in extract 1, for example, "(the *Mail* is very popular), but at the Colony they start from the front, not the back."

In functional terms, we would therefore define stancetaking as simultaneously instantiating *ideology*, establishing interpersonal *footing*, *styling* the speaker/writer, and *stylizing* the second party hearer/reader and sometimes a third party who may or may not be present. Stance is thus an act of self-identification and social identification by which I say something not only about myself and my view of the world, but by which I also make a judgment about you and about others as being like me or unlike me. In the case of elitist stancetaking, this evaluation presumes that "we" are better than or superior to "they." Whether the immediate addressee (the second party) agrees with the appraisal or not, they are subjected to it. They must respond by agreeing or disagreeing, by affirming or disaffirming, or merely acquiescing. Stance is thus always interpellative (Althusser, 1972), a view that is consistent with social identity theory:

> Social identities are not only descriptive and prescriptive; they are also *evaluative*. They furnish an evaluation...of a social category, and thus of its members, relative to other relevant social categories. Because social identities have these important *self-evaluative consequences*, groups and their members are strongly motivated to adopt behavioural strategies for achieving or maintaining ingroup/outgroup comparisons that favour the ingroup, and thus of course the self. (Hogg et al., 1995: 260, emphasis ours; see also Tajfel and Turner, 1979)

Thus we suggest that stancetaking is the *primary* discursive mechanism by which social identity is realized, through the shifting of footing (i.e., one's alignment to the addressee/audience) (Goffman, 1981), the positioning of self relationally (i.e., simultaneously styling oneself and stylizing others), and taking an orientation toward or affinity with the extralinguistic reality, in other words, the physical, social, and mental referents and their discursive representations. Stance may be predicated on intellectual, moral, or affective grounds, but always indexes a particular ideological position—political, social, cultural, economic, religious, and so on. Rather than being equivalent to ideology, we view stancetaking as instances of activating or actualizing particular aspects of ideology. In keeping with Hodge and Kress's (1988, cited above) views of modality, stancetaking evaluations are unavoidably sites of ideological construction and contestation. (This allows both modality and evaluation to function ideologically.)

By extension, new, often subversive stancetaking may eventually filter through and become accepted as part of the collective ideology if its underlying associations between linguistic (semiotic) forms and social meanings, or relations of equivalence and difference, become sufficiently conventionalized. These small (see Du Bois, above) discursive moments partly derive their influence through being small, subtle, unobtrusive, and fleeting, yet normative. Their formulation, especially expressed by inference rather than assertion (see Du Bois, above) is sometimes ambiguous and artful. It is precisely through their constant repetition that these momentary, performative evaluations constellate and "solidify" (cf. Butler, 1990; also Giddens, 1984, on *structuration*). Just as a passing alignment or *footing* may over time persist as a *relationship,* and a *style* become an identity or even a *lifestyle,* innocuous moments of stancetaking endure as personal *stands* and, eventually, as collective ideologies. These fleeting alignments, orientations and adjustments also become habituated and "hidden."

In sum, we see the relationship between stancetaking and ideology as dialectical. The term *ideology* is understood here as a general and abstract set of social representations shared by members of a group and used by them to accomplish everyday social practices: acting and communicating (cf. Van Dijk, 1998; Billig et al., 1988; Fowler, 1985). These representations are organized into systems that are deployed by social classes and other groups "in order to make sense of, figure out and render intelligible the way society works" (Hall, 1996: 26). Instances of the deployment of such representations are referred here to as *stancetaking.* Widespread adoption and conventionalization of particular stances turns them into an *ideology.*

Herein too lies the social control. Ideology understood as a shared system of values and beliefs is articulated through acts of stancetaking. Whereas ideology favors the social order of class dominance and subordination, or privilege and disadvantage, stancetaking becomes a force of social, cultural, political, and economic control and class inequality—a hegemony: "the whole lived social process as practically organized by specific and dominant meanings and values" (Williams, 1997: 109). The reiterative, self-sustaining, and solidifying capacity of stancetaking discussed above is crucial here, as hegemony is not a passive form of dominance. "It has continually to be renewed, recreated, defended, and modified," and it is continually confronted, resisted, limited, altered, and challenged by counter- and alternative hegemonies (ibid., pp. 112–113).

In the case of our focus on elitist stancetaking, especially in the context of the consumption of leisure as an identity resource, we have been interested here in the way that elite subjectivities and feelings are enacted and are structured by

what Rampton (2003: 68) calls "processes of symbolic differentiation" and, specifically, "dualities of high-low" (though in our case, the duality is perhaps more
accurately one of "superior-inferior"). As our analysis suggests, elite subjectivity of newspaper travelogue writers and their implied readers adheres to and
reproduces the "cultural semantic" of class contrast (cf. Stallybrass and White,
1996), through the reiterative, affective process of stancetaking. Rather than
some essentialist fixity, it is a "structure of feeling" whose nature is, according
to Williams (1977), always captured through ever-changing styles of speaking
and writing, physical demeanor, dress, and so on (cf. Bourdieu's 1977 notion of
"habitus"). Hence, in our data we see a clustering of slightly hedged, somewhat
ludic or humorous ("I'm only joking..." cf. Billig, 1999), and apparently "liberal" discourses attempting to deflect accusations of outright arrogance or snob-
bery, but whose overall effect is that of othering local people and other tourists
who fall short of partaking in exclusive modes of travel. The cumulative effect
of conveying the social and material experience of elitism is thus achieved by
invoking a range of different discourses or sets of representation. In no particular
order, in our data we have identified the discourse of the "superlative," "celebrity" discourse, "silence and quietude," "excess and self-indulgence," "good
taste," "power/knowledge," "intertextual knowingness," "disdain for others," and
"repression of the miseries of service." No doubt, there are others.

In a world in which identity is supposedly indexed more by consumption-led
lifestyle choices (Giddens, 1991; Featherstone, 1991) and self- and other-styliza-
tion (Rampton, 1995, 1999; Cameron, 2000; Coupland, 2007), the allegiances and
identities are built around sets of stancetaking positions social actors as members
or aspiring members of particular groups. Thus, reading stories about elite holidays
(luxury or otherwise) may be seen as an ersatz form of consumption of such highly
desirable *products* that position us as "modern," international," even "global" (Urry,
2002), but it remains an important semiotic resource for identifying (or not) with
those who do the consuming. Furthermore, as we demonstrate in our analyses above,
the media sources from which we quote engage in more or less subtle rhetorical work
that allows the readers to orient to these stances in specific ways. In some respects,
of course, the selection of which destination to cover or whose piece to feature is
itself an act of editorial or journalistic stancetaking. Journalists and editors who position themselves as traveling elites claim knowledge and authority authenticating and
legitimating their experience, potentially allowing them to produce more believable
and amusing stories, and to sell more newspapers. But equally, the reader's act of
purchasing a particular newspaper is an act of stancetaking and an identity resource
(Scollon, 1997). In this sense, we might think of stancetaking as a multilayered,
chain-like series of acts in the way that Fairclough (2003) talks of genres and discourses being networked into more complex "orders of discourse."

Acknowledgment

We thank the editor of this volume, Alexandra Jaffe, for her useful comments on
earlier drafts of this chapter.

Notes

1. In each extract, we highlight the main stancetaking acts that we discuss either immediately or elsewhere in the chapter.

2. On the "denial of racism" as gambits for expressing prejudice see also Billig (1991, 1998), Wetherell and Potter (1992), and Van Dijk (1992).

3. On the celebrity-centered representation of tourism in British TV holiday programs and their foregrounding of "first-person narratives," see Dunn (2005, 2006), Jaworski et al. (2003a).

4. Certainly, partying on an exotic beach to a portable system may well be a sign of elite consumption to others. Tourism, not unlike other areas of high consumerism, creates hierarchies of values and tiers within tiers of elitist identities (Thurlow and Jaworski, 2006).

5. Source: http://www.mustique-island.com/.

6. That the author (extract 33) also "cannot believe such glamour can be had for £20 a night" says a lot about his grasp of foreign exchange or global inequality! In the same extract, the cook is slotted in the "amenity" position usually reserved for inanimate things—a typical trope for representing servers/helpers in travel journalism (Jaworski et al., 2003a).

7. The term *vehicle,* as used here, is chosen deliberately because the act of stancetaking typically has a metaphorical quality about it, expressing in figurative, familiar terms a more abstract notion (or "tenor").

References

Althusser, Louis. 1972. *Lenin and philosophy, and other essays.* New York: Monthly Review Press.

Austin, J. L. 1961. *How to do things with words.* Oxford: Clarendon Press.

Bakhtin, Mikhail M. 1981. *The dialogic imagination: Four essays*, ed. Michael Holquist. Translated by Vern W. McGee. Austin, TX: University of Texas Press.

——. 1986. *Speech genres and other late essays.* Translated by Vern W. McGee. Austin, TX: University of Texas Press.

Bauman, Richard and Charles Briggs. 1990. Poetics and performance as critical perspectives on language and social life. *Annual Review of Anthropology* 19: 59–88.

Bell, Allan. 1997. Language style as audience design. In *Sociolinguistics: A reader and coursebook*, ed. Nikolas Coupland and Adam Jaworski, 240–250. Basingstoke: Palgrave Macmillan.

Billig, Michael. 1991. *Ideology and opinions.* London: Sage.

——. 1998. Dialogic repression and the Oedipus complex: Reinterpreting the Little Hans Case. *Culture and Psychology* 4: 11–47.

——. 1999. Freudian repression: Conversation creating the unconscious. Cambridge: Cambridge University Press.

Billig, Michael, Susan Condor, Derek Edwards, Mike Gane, David Middleton, and Alan Radley. 1988. *Ideological dilemmas.* London: Sage.

Blommaert, Jan. (2005). *Discourse: A critical introduction.* Cambridge: Cambridge University Press.

Bourdieu, Pierre. 1977. *Outline of the theory of practice.* Cambridge: Cambridge University Press.

——. 1984. *Distinction: A social critique of the judgement of taste.* Translated by Richard Nice. Cambridge, MA: Harvard University Press.

——. 1990. *The logic of practice*. Translated by Richard Nice. Cambridge: Polity.

——. 1991. *Language and symbolic power*. Edited and introduction by John B. Thompson. Translated by Gino Raymond and Matthew Adamson. Cambridge: Polity.

Brown, Penelope, and Stephen C. Levinson. 1987. *Politeness: Some universals in language usage*. Cambridge: Cambridge University Press. [Originally published in 1978.]

Butler, Judith. 1990. *Gender trouble: Feminism and the subversion of identity*. New York: Routledge.

Cameron, Deborah. 2000. Styling the worker: Gender and the commodification of language in the globalized service economy. *Journal of Sociolinguistics* 4: 323–347.

Carlton, Eric. 1996. *The few and the many: A typology of elites*. Aldershot: Scolar Press.

Cohen, Erik. 2004. Who is a tourist? A conceptual clarification. In *Contemporary tourism: Diversity and change*, 17–36. Amsterdam: Elsevier. [Originally published in *Sociological Review* 22: 527–555, 1974].

Coupland, Nikolas. 1999. "Other" representation. In *Handbook of pragmatics 1999*, ed. Jef Verschueren, Jan-Ola Östman, and Chris Bulcean, 1–24. Amsterdam/Philadelphia: John Benjamins.

——. 2001. Age in social and sociolinguistic theory. In *Sociolinguistics and social theory*, ed. Nikolas Coupland, Srikant Sarangi, and Christopher N. Candlin, 185–211. Harlow, Essex: Pearson Education.

——. 2007. *Style: Language variation and identity*. Cambridge: Cambridge University Press.

Crane, Diana. 2000. *Fashion and its social agendas: Class, gender, and identity in clothing*. Chicago: University of Chicago Press.

De Garzia, Sebastian. 1964. *Of time, work and leisure*. Garden City, NY: Anchor Books.

Dogan, Mattei. 2003. Introduction: Diversity of elite configurations and clusters of power. In *Elite configurations at the apex of power*, ed. Mattei Dogan, 1–15. Leiden: Brill.

Du Bois, John W. 2007. The stance triangle. In *Stancetaking in discourse: Subjectivity, evaluation, interaction*, ed. Robert Englebreston, 139–182. Amsterdam: John Benjamins.

Dunn, David. 2005. "We are not here to make a film about Italy, we are here to make a film about ME..." British television holiday programmes' representations of the tourist destination. In *The Media and the tourist imagination: Converging cultures*, ed. David Crouch, Felix Thompson, and Rona Jackson, 154–169. London: Routledge.

——. 2006. Singular encounters: Mediating the tourist destination in British television holiday programmes. *Tourist Studies* 6: 37–58.

Fairclough, Norman. 2003. *Analysing discourse: Textual analysis for social research*. London: Routledge.

Featherstone, Mike. 1991. *Consumer culture and postmodernism*. London: Sage.

Field, G. Lowell, and John Higley. 1980. *Elitism*. London: Routledge & Kegan Paul.

Foucault, Michel. 1978. *The history of sexuality*, Vol. I. New York: Random House.

——. 1980. *Power/knowledge: Selected interviews and other writings 1972–1977*. Harlow, Essex: Pearson Education.

Fowler, Roger. 1985. Power. In *Handbook of discourse analysis*, vol. 4, ed. Teun van Dijk, 61–82. London: Academic Press.

Franklin, Adrian, and Mike Crang. 2001. Editorial: The trouble with tourism and travel theory. *Tourist Studies* 1: 5–22.

Giddens, Anthony. 1984. *The constitution of society: Outline of the theory of structuration*. Cambridge: Polity.

——. 1991. *Modernity and self-identity: Self and society in the late modern age*. Cambridge: Polity.

Goffman, Erving. 1981. Footing. In *Forms of talk,* 124–159. Oxford: Blackwell. [Originally published in 1973.]

Gramsci, Antonio. 1971. *Selections from the prison notebooks.* London: Lawrence & Wishart.

Hall, Stuart. 1980. Encoding/decoding. In *Culture, media, language: Working papers in cultural studies, 1972–79,* ed. Centre for Contemporary Cultural Studies, 128–138. London: Hutchinson. [Originally published in 1973.]

——. 1996. The problem of ideology: Marxism without guarantees. In *Stuart Hall: Critical dialogues in cultural studies,* David Morley and Kuan-Hsing Chen, 25–46. London: Routledge.

Halliday, M. A. K. 1978. *Language as social semiotic: The social interpretation of language and meaning.* London: Edward Arnold.

——. 1994. *An introduction to functional grammar,* 2nd ed. London: Edward Arnold.

Hannerz, Ulf. 1996. *Transnational connections.* London: Routledge.

Hodge, Robert, and Gunther and Kress. 1988. *Social semiotics.* Cambridge: Polity.

Hogg, Michael A., Deborah J. Terry, and Katherine M. White. 1995. A tale of two theories: A critical comparison of identity theory with social identity theory. *Social Psychology Quarterly* 5: 255–269.

Jaworski, Adam, Virpi Ylänne-McEwen, Crispin Thurlow, and Sarah Lawson. 2003a. Social roles and negotiation of status in host-tourist interaction: A view from British TV holiday programmes. *Journal of Sociolinguistics* 7: 135–163.

Jaworski Adam, Crispin Thurlow, Sarah Lawson, and Virpi Ylänne-McEwen. 2003b. The uses and representations of host languages in tourist destinations: A view from British TV holiday programmes. *Language Awareness* 12: 5–29.

Kress, Gunther. 1995. The social production of language: History and structures of domination. In *Discourse in society: Systemic functional perspectives. Meaning and choice in language: Studies for Michael Halliday,* ed. Peter H. Fries and Michael Gregory, 115–140. Westport, CT: Ablex Publishing.

Labov, William, and Joshua Waletzky. 1967. Narrative analysis: Oral versions of personal experience. In *Essays on the verbal and visual arts,* ed. June Helm, 12–44. Seattle: American Ethnological Society.

LePage, Robert and Andrée Tabouret-Keller. 1985. *Acts of identity.* Cambridge: Cambridge University Press.

Lévi-Strauss, Claude. 1966. The culinary triangle. *Partisan Review* 33: 586–595.

MacCannell, Dean. 1999. *The tourist: A new theory of the leisure class.* Berkeley: University of California Press. [Originally published in 1976.]

Machin, David, and Theo van Leeuwen. 2007. *Global media discourse.* London: Routledge.

McCabe, Scott. 2005. "Who is a tourist?": A critical review. *Tourist Studies,* 5(1): 85–106.

McCracken, Grant. 1988. *Culture and consumption: New approaches to the symbolic character of consumer goods and activities.* Bloomington, IN: Indiana University Press.

Ochs, Elinor. 1992. Indexing gender. In *Rethinking context: Language as an interactive phenomenon,* ed. Alessandro Duranti and Charles Goodwin, 335–358. Cambridge: Cambridge University Press.

Rampton, Ben. 1995. *Crossing: Language and ethnicity among adolescents.* London: Longman.

——, ed. 1999. *Styling the other.* Special issue of the *Journal of Sociolinguistics* 3/4.

——. 2003. Hegemony, social class and stylisation. *Pragmatics* 13: 49–83.

——. 2006. *Language in late modernity: Interaction in an urban school.* Cambridge: Cambridge University Press.

Sacks, Harvey. 1992. *Lectures on conversation,* vols. 1 and 2. Edited by Gail Jefferson. Oxford: Blackwell.

Said, Edward W. 1978. *Orientalism.* New York: Pantheon Books.

Schwartz, Barry. 2004. *The paradox of choice: Why less is more.* New York: Harper Collins.

Scollon, Ron. 1997. Handbills, tissues and condoms: A site of engagement for the construction of identity in public discourse. *Journal of Sociolinguistics* 1: 39–61.

Sherman, Rachel. 2007. *Class acts: Service and inequality in luxury hotels.* Berkeley, CA: University of California Press.

Sontag, Susan. 1977. *On photography.* New York: Farrar, Straus and Giroux.

Stallybrass, Peter, and Allon White. 1996. *The politics and poetics of transgression.* London: Methuen.

Swartz, David. 1997. *Culture and power: The sociology of Pierre Bourdieu.* Chicago: Chicago University Press.

Tajfel, Henri, and John C. Turner. 1979. An integrative theory of intergroup conflict. In *The social psychology of intergroup relations*, ed. William G. Austin and Stephen Worchel, 33–47. Monterey, CA: Brooks/Cole.

Tannen, Deborah. 1986. Introducing constructed dialogue in Greek and American conversation and literary narrative. In *Direct and indirect speech*, ed. Florian Coulmas, 311–332. Berlin: Mouton de Gruyter.

———. 1989. *Talking voices: Repetition, dialogue, and imagery in conversational discourse.* Cambridge: Cambridge University Press.

Theroux, Paul. 1986. *Sunrise with seamonsters.* Harmondsworth: Penguin.

Thompson, Geoff, and Susan Hunston. 2000. Evaluation: An introduction. In *Evaluation in text: Authorial stance and the construction of discourse*, ed. Susan Hunston and Geoff Thompson, 1–27. Oxford: Oxford University Press.

Thurlow, Crispin, and Adam Jaworski. 2006. The Alchemy of the upwardly mobile: Symbolic capital and the stylization of elites in frequent-flyer programs. *Discourse & Society* 17: 131–167.

———. 2009. Silence is golden: Elitism, linguascaping, and "anti-communication" in luxury tourism. In *Semiotic landscapes: Language, image, space,* ed. Adam Jaworski and Crispin Thurlow. London: Continuum.

Turner, Graeme. 2004. *Understanding celebrity.* London: Sage.

Urry, John. 2002. *The tourist gaze,* 2nd ed. London: Sage.

Van Dijk, Teun A. 1992. Discourse and the denial of racism. *Discourse & Society* 3: 87–118.

———. 1998. *Ideology.* London: Sage.

Veblen, Thorstein. 1979. *The theory of the leisure class.* New York: Penguin. [Originally published in 1899.]

Verschueren, Jeff. 1999. *Understanding pragmatics.* London: Arnold.

Voloshinov, Valentin Nikolaevich. 1973. *Marxism and the philosophy of language.* Translated by L. Matejka and I. R. Titunik. Cambridge, MA: Harvard University Press. [Originally published in Russian in 1929.]

Wetherell, Margaret, and Jonathan Potter. 1992. *Mapping the language of racism.* Hemel Hempstead: Harvester/Wheatsheaf.

Williams, Raymond. 1977. *Marxism and literature.* Oxford: Oxford University Press.

10

Attributing Stance in Discourses of Body Shape and Weight Loss

Justine Coupland and Nikolas Coupland

The Stance Family

Stance, and concepts closely related to it, generally point to an ordering of social meaning between forms of talk and some higher order construct such as "identity." To take just a few instances, Elinor Ochs (1992) argued that speakers take up stances in talk—say a woman being supportive or consultative to a listener—which then, at a higher order of interpretation, can be construed as indexing the social category "feminine." Barbara Johnstone (1995, this volume) defends the concept of "mode of ethos," which might be thought of as a variable orientation toward being open versus strategic in talk, and which plays a role in indexing personal identity. Erving Goffman's (1981) notion of footing refers to a negotiated relational basis on which social interaction proceeds, fully recognizing that footings are potentially ephemeral and do not define "the relationships" among participants in any consolidated way. In the sociolinguistics of style, the concept of persona (N. Coupland 2007) refers to a socially constructed person-image, which may well be a strategic projection rather than a reliable index of the speaker's "real identity." Stance and these other concepts mark constructionist sociolinguistics' retreat from an essentialized view of identity and relationships, toward the view that language plays a constitutive role in social life. In fact Bronwen Davies and Rom Harré (1990) argued that "who we are" is not necessarily a coherent notion. What we work with is a set of autobiographical fragments linked to how we position ourselves and are positioned by others in conversation, so positioning is another term in the stance family of mediating concepts.

It is difficult to find much consensus in this wide-ranging and evolving theoretical field (though see Berman et al. 2002), but there is some. Stancetaking is agreed to be dialogic, in the sense that stances are taken in alignment with or in opposition to other possible stances and other people who hold them (Du Bois 2007, White 2003). For Ochs, stance is a socially recognized disposition, and there is some agreement that many and probably all of the social orderings that we want to analyze as stances, personas, positionings, and so on will have a known typological history behind them, and will have social meaning in that sense. Individuals of course can and do adopt idiosyncratic and very local evaluative and attitudinal stances to things. But some stancetaking has acute sociocultural significance when we are dealing with stances that are, in one way or another, clearly hooked into wider social discourses and ideologies, or are contextualized in important ways by them. Those discourses and ideologies can be more general or more specific. For example, speakers universally have the option of constructing the relational stance of "closeness" with a speaking partner. But particular values attach to a closeness stance if, say, it is constructed by a young adult in her first meeting with an elderly person. In this case, stancetaking is embedded in, and we might say saturated in, culture-specific ideologies of personal autonomy and face in relation to aging and the politics of intergenerational relationships (Giles et al. 1993). It will link through to understandings of the status and entitlements of older people in a particular society in a given epoch, and interactional norms for intergenerational encounters structured by those understandings (Coupland, Coupland, and Giles 1991). This example also makes it clear that the social value of a stance relates to its context of situation and genre, because intergenerational relationships are sensitive to how individuals are positioned institutionally or in family relationships, and in different modes and stages of acquaintance. Furthermore, it shows that the meaning of adopting a particular stance in a particular context is filled out contrastively—in reference to other culturally familiar stances that could have been but were *not* been adopted. The younger adult could, for example, have taken a stance informed by the norms of same-age first encounters.

Stances are taken in relation *to* things (Du Bois's "stance objects"), which include a speaker or writer's stance toward his or her own utterances (truth value, generality of application, emotional orientation, and so on) as well as toward listeners/readers, with whom the speaker/writer may establish different sorts of relational engagement (Martin 1997). Many other sorts of orientation are relevant, though. A stance can be a communicator's orientation to his or her own persona, as in the case when a speaker deauthenticates that persona by stylizing it. For example, a radio presenter might exaggerate his own local vernacular dialect, or use linguistic features stereotypically associated with out-groups, to generate humor and/or metacultural reflexivity (N. Coupland 2001, 2007). In more everyday uses of the term *stance,* people are recognized to adopt stances toward social issues and controversies. These may be moral or political stances, which surface, in whole or more likely in part, as rhetorical stances in specific discussions or arguments. Evaluation and appraisal are core dimensions of stancetaking, and linguistic resources for expressing evaluation or appraisal (Hunston and Thompson 2000) are often deployed in relation to social and moral debates. The particular theme of our chapter is stance in relation to body shape, weight and weight loss, the clearly different personal, public, and institutional "takes" we document on body size and shape, and the different ideologies of personal autonomy, control, and obligation in relation to one's body that these discourses display. Stance in local discourses around body weight inevitably connects through to wider sociocultural discourses; one of our main motivations is to track these connections between local contexts of talk and more global discourses. Our chapter continues a tradition of research on the body as a moral site, and we engage with some of that research in the next section.

Although stancetaking is known to be a fundamentally intersubjective process in which speakers construct relational orientations with other participants or targets (Kiesling 2001, White 2003), stance has usually been analyzed from a predominantly *authorial* perspective, focusing on how stance is implicated in a speaker or writer's projection of his or her *own* evaluative, epistemic, or other orientation and how this is worked into discourse. Dubois argues that all acts of stancetaking are simultaneously acts of evaluation, positioning, and alignment (2007: 168) and alignment, once again, is inherently a matter of relational design. There is an important distinction to be made, however, between the act of endorsing, validating, or sharing another person's known or witnessed stance and the act of projecting a stance onto someone else—specifying what the other person's stance is, was, will be, or should be. In the first case, social interaction is loaded up with devices for marking shared stance, including what Du Bois, taking at this point a narrow view of the dialogic, calls "the diagraph," when one speaker aligns syntactically and in stance terms with a cospeaker's just-previous stance act, as in the following:

A: I don't know if she'd do it.
B: I don't know if she'd do it either. (Du Bois 2007: 22)

This sort of stance alignment is quite routine in social interaction, described as communicative convergence in accommodation theory (Giles, Coupland, and Coupland 1991). But *other stance attribution*—the attributing of stances to others—is not so routine, and has been less frequently studied in the literature. In social encounters there is a preference for *avoiding* attributing stances to others. Expressions like "You're lying" and "You don't know what you're talking about" attribute epistemic stances to addressees, and they are characteristic of conflict talk. Expressions like "You must be thinking..." are often less antagonistic, but are often require relational delicacy and some reflexive awareness of what the evidence base is for making that sort of attribution. With "You must be thinking...," the speaker might believe s/he has sufficient local evidence to make that attribution, perhaps based on stances she has experienced the other person taking in the past. Or s/he might be invoking some social consensus about what is a reasonable stance for anyone to take under this particular set of circumstances.

But the relational politics of stance generally require a speaker to show respect for the other person's entitlement to construct their own stances, rather than have them constructed for them. Stance attribution can put an addressee into the position of having to struggle against a socially attributed and possibly normative orientation. It can also use the addressee's attributed orientation in the service of the speaker's own agenda. Even when an attributed stance is "correct," in the sense that it reflects what a listener would concede actually is his or her own stance, the listener might well be uncomfortable to have that stance articulated on his or her behalf. These principles are evident in metadiscourse around stance attribution: we speak of "being patronized" when others "speak for" us.

At the same time, levels of presumed entitlement to "speak for" another vary across social situations, and not least across institutional settings. Medical discourse has often been characterized as asymmetrical, and asymmetry between doctors and patients (notwithstanding recent trends toward "shared decision making") can be realized in acts of "speaking for." One of the two data contexts we consider below is geriatric medicine, in which doctors negotiate problems of being overweight with older patients. The other context is magazine features, also relating to weight and body shape issues. The discourse of both contexts is distinctive in that authoritative, institutional voices attribute stances to laypeople (as patients or magazine readers) in relation to their body weight, and this is the main focus of our analysis. Before turning to the data, we need to characterize the ideological climate in which such discourses surface.

A Big Fat Problem?

Personal body weight is a burgeoning but complex moral and social policy arena in Britain and the United States. We start from the observation that, in relation to the size and weight of bodies, public discourse in these two countries reflects increasingly entrenched but nonuniform sociocultural values. People are often positioned as needing to adopt particular personal stances toward their weight. Stances are attributed to and to some extent imposed on people discursively, but in ways that realize different ideologies.

In the United Kingdom, a press release from the National Audit Office (NAO 2001) claimed that most adults in England were overweight and that one in five was "obese," with an estimated cost to the National Health Service of £500 million a year. The text of the full report prepared by NAO had a cover showing an engraving of a fat, smiling man, captioned with the Shakespearean quotation, "Thou see'st that I have more flesh than another man and therefore more frailty."[1] In Wales in 2004, the Welsh Assembly Government launched their *Big Fat Problem* campaign in partnership with the BBC. During its launch, the minister for Health and Social Services was cited as saying that "physical activity and a healthy balanced diet are known to have substantial health benefits in terms of general well-being. They are also recognized as key factors in the prevention of obesity and related illnesses such as coronary heart disease, colorectal cancer, hypertension and diabetes" (WAG 2004). On January 24, 2008, the (London) *Telegraph* and *Daily Mail* both headlined stories— "Obesity Crisis: Get Paid to Lose Weight"; "We'll Pay You to Lose Weight"—about government plans to issue vouchers for healthy food and cash reward for people who succeed in their attempts to lose weight. A front cover story in the (London) *Times* on February 7, 2008, reported, "Almost a third of children in Britain are obese or overweight."

Even in these headlines, sound bites, and other preliminaries, we get a clear sense not only of the evaluative tone of the dominant British discourse, but also of its impositional force. The fat, smiling man is apologizing for his adjudged "frailty," seemingly in response to being "seen" ("Thou see'st") to be overweight. The headline "We'll Pay You to Lose Weight" formulates a deal between aberrant and problem-causing overweight people and an unspecified (voice of the majority) "we." It proposes and perhaps anticipates people's compliance with a new regime of imposed weight loss. Quite significantly, there is an assumption that people have agentive control over their own actions toward losing weight; this provides a basis for censuring them when they fail to exercise that control. The minister's comments on the benefits of healthy living are thus embedded in a moral discourse about well and badly lived lives, and by implication people's responsibilities, not only to themselves but to the state. The state (or, again, an unspecified "we") is identified as needing to bear the substantial costs occasioned by people's failure to lose weight.

Many of the other key social and moral elements associated with body weight in recent discourses surface in these reports, too. Scale, for example, matters, as we see in the numerical accounts of the perceived problem—"almost a third" and "one in five." The term "epidemic" is not used in the examples we mentioned, although it is used elsewhere and it is consistent with the notion of "crisis" and the catalogue of general health problems said to be associated with being overweight. "Obesity" is itself also a scaled concept and in fact it is given a numerical definition in clinical discourse: a person having a body mass index of 30.0–39.9 is clinically obese. Note that the minister and the newspaper headlines use "obese" as an unmarked category, naturalizing it as a familiar and commonsensical notion that we are already aware of (cf. Scheibman 2007). "Obesity" is therefore ideologized as an extreme, big-scale issue, both biologically and socially, and one that all of must deal with.

Health and risks to health enter into a complex relationship with moral elements of these discourses. Good health is important, at one and the same time, for the individual (the minister's phrase is "health benefits in terms of general well-being") and for the state (specifically again in relation to costs to the National Health Service in Britain). Identifying benefits to the individual can make stance attribution more warranted, in the sense that the state's impositions are cast as being "in your own interests." Age is very often implicated, because weight problems are commonly associated either with children (raising issues of responsible parenting, socialization, lifestyles, diet regimes, and so on) or with older people (referring to predominantly later-life health issues like heart disease and cancer). For younger adults the problem is represented as being mainly one of personal body aesthetics, appearance, and control (and the aesthetic dimension surfaces in the visual image accompanying the Shakespeare quote, above). The "big fat problem," as we see below, takes on different qualities and emphases when different parts of the lifespan are in question.

Like Rich and Evans (2005) in their critique of "fat ethics," our point is not to disavow the epidemiological basis of excessive weight or to deny the reality of the social problem addressed in these reports and media headlines. Rather, we want to expose the ideological bases of public discourses about obesity and being overweight and to make the point that these discourses have real-life consequences for people's social and psychological well-being. We need to develop critical analyses of discourses around bodily weight because the social experience of bodily weight and obesity is mediated by those discourses (cf. J. Coupland, forthcoming, 2007; J. Coupland and Gwyn 2003; J. Coupland and Williams 2002). Rich and Evans point to the potentially damaging role of mass media in relation to health issues in general (cf. Lupton 1994, 1996). Media reports of the "obesity crisis" can trigger senses of shame and guilt (Gard and Wright 2005) as well as poor body image, which can be as psychologically risky as the physiological condition of being overweight. Societal discourses about obesity can also legitimate prejudicial attitudes and even discriminatory practices against fat people (Schwartz and Brownell 2004), who are "thought to be weak willed, lazy, sloppy, incompetent, emotionally unstable, and even defective as people" (204: 44).

It is crucial for discourse analyses to tease out the complex and variable relationships between discourse, the body, and aging. Prejudicial discourse about the body, as Julia Twigg (2004) points out, relates systematically to prejudicial discourse about aging itself, and in fact the ideology realized in these discourses might be largely a unitary one. Aging, like being fat, is inherently "bad"; undesirable aging is inscribed on the body and a "bad body" betrays a person's out-of-control aging. The more specific point we hope to make here is that the impositional "weight" of body discourse can be analyzed, in part, as patterns of stance attribution. If a culture promotes some body configurations over others and urges its members to conform, in specific discursive frames and genres, then stance work is likely to be key to the constitution of body-age ideological discourse. Below, we will see that different stance types are attributed to potential weight-losers. As in the above fragments, listeners and readers can be attributed the stance of being in agentive control of their own weight or, in a moralistic discourse, the stance of needing to have that control. Attributing stances around people's desires, efforts, and emotions surrounding losing weight are other parts of a rich repertoire of public discourse. Age is systematically implicated in these stance attributions, in the presupposition that needing to control one's weight in particular ways and toward particular targeted outcomes is a normal requirement at particular life stages.

First, we focus on extracts from lifestyle magazine features dealing with weight and weight loss. The second context, as indicated above, is geriatric medicine, in which we analyze sequences of talk from geriatrician/older patient consultations in which themes of body weight arise. These contexts take us into very different social arenas, and of course into discourse addressed to people of different ages, although "the problem of being overweight" is the concern in each case. We are interested in both the similarities and the differences between the two contexts. Our main question is how stances are attributed discursively by authoritative institutional voices to people who are in contact with those institutions, as readers or patients. We will see that a speaker or writer attributing a stance to someone in discourse necessarily entails that author taking particular stances in his or her own right. So, in fact, we will be dealing with "stance dances" rather than a straightforward and unidirectional process of attribution.

Body-Weight Stance in Lifestyle Magazine Texts

We compiled an informal corpus of 15 women's magazines sold in the United Kingdom in March 2004. All magazines were high circulation and at least partly concerned with bodily and other appearance and style issues, targeted at a range of readership ages but principally young to middle-aged adult women.[2] Extracts 1, 2, and 3 are from typical feature articles in the corpus that dealt with women's body size and shape; every magazine in the corpus contained features of this sort. Feature articles in the corpus do not generally address the specific theme of weight *loss* (although extract 1 does), but they refer to the visible semiotic spaces of the body where weight impinges. Lexical items such as *shape, curves, tummy, thighs,* and *rear* are very common. Age is very commonly implicated in the extracts, where it is associated with visible, incremental changes in body size and shape over time as weight is (in these projections) predictably gained. Bodily shape and appearance are construed as particular problems in midlife.

Extract 1 (from *Zest* magazine)
(The original source has photos of high-calorie meals or snacks juxtaposed with lower calorie suggestions for "swaps." Precise calorie counts are given for each item of food and drink in each case.)[3]

1	EAT MORE, lose weight
2	Sticking to small portions but still can't lose weight? Then learn to swap
3	calorie-dense foods for bigger portions of naturally low-calorie foods that will
4	help you shed pounds without going hungry. You'll feel fuller for longer and
5	you won't want to snack, and in many cases you get a whole meal's worth of
6	food for the same number of calories in just one of your old choices. To get
7	calorie smart, check out these startling comparisons, taken from Dr. Shapiro's
8	"Picture Perfect Weight Loss: The Visual Programme for Permanent Weight
9	Loss" (Rodale, £14.99).
	(Photos of the relevant meals appear under the headings SWAP STEAK AND CHIPS...FOR A FISH SUPPER...)
10	Would you rather have a steak and chips or a three course meal with wine?
11	(Total = 650 calories) The latter is a far healthier option...Tuna is rich in
12	Omega 3 fatty acids which help lower cholesterol and blood pressure...The
13	broccoli, tomatoes and peppers are packed full of antioxidants including
14	Vitamin C and with the fruit dessert make up 3 of your 5 a day portions of
15	fruit and veg.

Extract 2 (from *Essentials* and *Woman's Own* magazine, a copublished supplement titled *Dream Bodies Diet Special*)
(Each day has three sections, diet, beauty, and exercise. Only the first sections are reproduced here. The text is examined in full in J. Coupland, forthcoming.)

1   Dump a decade in a week
2   Want a younger-looking face? A svelte body and glossy hair? Follow our
3   guide to knock 10 years off your looks in just seven days.
4   Saturday
5   Diet: Start a detox
6   The first few days of a detox diet (while you're eliminating toxins and
7   boosting cell renewal) can be tough. You may suffer from mood swings,
8   headaches, tiredness and aching muscles, but these side effects will subside.
9   On the first day of your detox you shouldn't eat anything. Instead, drink plenty
10   of water, adding a squeeze of fresh lemon to cleanse and stimulate the bowels.
11   To quell hunger pangs, drink herbal tea. Three glasses of fresh fruit and
12   vegetable juice are also allowed...
13   Sunday
14   Diet: Add fruit
15   Continue to drink plenty of water and juices, but now introduce small portions
16   of fruit whenever you feel hungry...
17   Monday
18   Diet: Add raw, unsalted vegetables
19   Have a raw vegetable salad for lunch and dinner—do not add salt. Continue to
20   eat fruit for breakfast and for snacks...
21   Tuesday
22   Diet: Add brown rice and cooked vegetables...
(The week's regime continues with "Wednesday—Add lentils, beans, nuts and seeds...";
"Thursday—Add grains or live yogurt..."; "Friday—Add grilled fish, chicken or tofu...")

Extract 3 (from *Woman and Home* magazine)

1   Take control of your curves
2   The results of your body survey in February's issue revealed some surprising
3   facts about you and the shape you're in. You definitely don't want to be ultra-
4   slim, but while you love the look of curvier gals like Catherine Zeta Jones and
5   Halle Berry, you often feel that your curves are a touch out of control. To help
6   you tighten, flatten, tone and generally smooth out all those less than perfect
7   bits often pointed out by partners (who seem to enjoy telling it like it is!) we
8   have pulled together the best spot toning ideas and diet moves to help you
9   keep those sometimes dangerous curves under control...
10   Smooth out those thighs
11   14% of us are unhappy with the tops of our legs. Saddlebags on the outer
12   curves, soft and ever-increasing inner thighs can be a real problem duo that
13   gets worse as we age.
14   The answer? A canny mix of exercise and maybe a little deep and meaningful
15   massage.
16   Lift up your rear
17   10% of us are less than thrilled with our rear. The obsession with our rears
18   is definitely an age thing. Kiss goodbye to 45 and your waist becomes the

19   focus. The answer? A regime of tightening spot exercises and a diet rethink.
20   Tighten up your tum
21   46% of us are frantic about an expanding waist and pouty tum…
22   If you're 40 or less and that middle isn't as shapely as it should be, the cure is
23   simple—eat less and exercise more. If you're 45 or more, things get more
24   complex. Much as we'd love to deny it, middle-age spread is a reality. The
25   result? Surplus calories get stored as fat and decreased exercise means the
26   pounds creep on. The answer? Rev up your metabolism with fewer
27   calories, aerobic moves, weight training, and some de-puffing tricks.
28   Jiggle proof your arms
29   6% of us are not at all happy about those jiggly arms
30   Nothing knocks off the years better than smooth, highly-toned arms and
31   shoulders. The answer? A daily regime of just one or two focussed load
32   bearing exercises really does the biz.

The dialogic character of written texts is well established, for example, in academic writing (Hyland 2005) and in newspaper texts (White 2003). The three magazine extracts above have some particularly obvious dialogic elements, such as addressing readers as "you" and putting questions directly to them. In extract 2, lines 2 and 3, there is a closely sequenced conjunction of "our" and "your," and similarly with "you" and "we" in lines 6–8 of extract 3. The third extract in fact conflates "you" and "we" in describing the survey it has conducted as "your body survey" (line 2), which it then interprets in terms of "us," "we," and "our": what certain percentages "of us" think (lines 11, 17, 21, and 29), problems that worsen "as we age" (line 13), and "the obsession with our rears" (line 17). But the extracts do intersubjective positioning in more implicit ways, too. They display understanding of readers' experiences and problems. For example, the reference to partners "who seem to enjoy telling it like it is!" (extract 3, line 7) in-groups women readers with the knowing authorial voice and out-groups men who pass judgment. Authorial voices across the extracts generally rhetorically frame certain issues as shared by and problematic for readers, whether or not these exist in reality. One of very many instances is "Nothing knocks off the years better" (extract 3, line 30), in which the concept of looking younger ("knocking off years") is embedded as a given and shared goal and value.

The interpersonal tenor of the texts is, up to a point, one of shared perspective—shared experiences, feelings, judgments, and aspirations—although there is an important and recurrent difference of perspective, too. The voice of the text in each case takes an authoritative and indeed an authoritarian stance. It displays appreciation (Martin 2000) of body problems, but also control over the manner of their resolution. Lifestyle magazine features are heavy users of the two-part problem-solution format (Machin and van Leeuwen 2003). This rhetorical structure is sometimes syntactically encoded as interrogative + imperative (see extract 1, lines 2–4; extract 2, lines 2–3). Extract 3 uses a slightly different syntactic pattern to encode the same problem-solution format when it establishes the problems reported in the "body survey" at length, then repeatedly prefaces its solution elements with the phrase "The answer?" (lines 14, 19, 26, and 31). In each extract, authoritarian stance is carried by the textual voice's very frequent use of imperatives ("learn" (extract 1), "follow" (2), "drink" (2), "lift up" (3), etc.) but also by its familiarity with expert scientific knowledge and its self-aggrandizing claims to be promoting what it would consider to be "best practice." The textual voice positions itself as doing teaching (because readers must "learn"—extract 1, line 2), helping (extract 3, line 8), leading (because readers must "follow"—extract 2, line 2), disallowing (because readers "shouldn't eat"—extract 2, line 9), and allowing (extract 2, line 12).

But a particularly interesting aspect of textual authoritarianism here is stance attribution. The textual voice claims to do more than generally appreciate readers' concerns. It claims insider status in knowing and representing readers' stances, sometimes explicitly and sometimes implicitly. "You'll feel fuller for longer and you won't want to snack" (extract 1, lines 4–5) is a prediction of readers' affective and motivational stances under the circumstances of eating larger quantities of lower calorie food. This isn't a particularly presumptive prediction, because it relies on a "commonsense" reading of physical consequences. However, (as Alexandra Jaffe points out in a personal note) it locates control over weight as being "about" the physiological (feeling hungry or not) more then the psychological. So if the fat person would "just" eat the right things, he or she would be able to lose weight. By erasing other causes of overeating, it renders them morally suspect. The problem-solution format at the head of extract 1 is arguably even more presumptive, first because it attributes to readers the affective stance of past and current concern about "sticking to small portions but not losing weight." The presupposition that a problem exists ("your old choices," line 6) is in fact supported by the problem-solution discourse format itself. Also, the solution element is cast in terms of "learning," which implies that the readers' epistemic stance had been one of relative ignorance (see also "get calorie smart," lines 6–7).

Extract 2 attributes readers' feelings of discomfort and hunger ("a detox diet... can be tough," lines 6–7); it predicts "mood swings" and so on. Again, if readers find the textual voice's own stance to be credible, they might consider these attributions to themselves warranted—the text voice "knows about this from experience" because she is "someone like them." However, the listing of possible "side effects" shifts into medical discourse and claims its authority now from that different source. In extract 3, though, the voice confidently asserts readers' evaluations of their own body shape preferences, both for themselves—"you definitely don't want to be ultra-slim" (lines 3–4); "you often feel that your curves are a touch out of control" (line 5)—and for others as models for their own appearance—"you love the look of curvier gals" (line 4). There is an interesting element of syntactic ambiguity with "you don't want to be...," which is being regrammaticalized in contemporary informal talk into meaning "do not," but still from the stance of "common sense." In terms of stance attribution the difference is a subtle one, between "I say that you already do not want to..." and "Common sense and I tell you not to...." As the extract proceeds, the expert voice explicitly aligns with readers in the use of inclusive "us" (lines 11, 17, 21, and 29) and links "an expanding waist and pouty tum" to (middle) age, a lifespan incumbency that "we" would "love to deny."

This very detailed profiling of readers' stances is to some extent validated by the "body survey," and to some extent by the empathetic emotional stance selectively adopted by the writer ("46% of us are frantic..."). From the point of view of stance-taking, surveys provide simple, cheap warrants for a magazine to claim it has valid access to the feelings and knowledge of its readers. Details of particular survey methods and findings are usually very sparse in magazine features. Even if those details could be given (assuming surveys actually had been conducted and assuming they actually had some validity in research terms), they would pull texts into an objectivist and scientistic genre that would conflict with the chatty and intimate relational tenor that lifestyle magazines mainly employ. Also, survey questions may create as much as reflect readers' concerns. Surveys promote the idea that issues emanate from readers, even though they are constructed by the magazines themselves. For all of these reasons magazine surveys are therefore best seen as rhetorical stance-warranting devices rather than substantive efforts to gather data.

Body-Weight Stance in Geriatric Medicine

In medical contexts body weight is a relatively frequent theme, but it is almost always framed in reference to ideologies of health and well-being rather than personal body aesthetics. We saw earlier that broad current concerns about body weight, at least in relation to "the obesity crisis," attach some special salience to the extremities of the lifespan. Our earlier ethnographic work on geriatric medical discourse focused on various different identity concerns but not on body weight itself.[4] In this section we revisit some of our earlier clinic data to see how geriatricians and elderly patients negotiate stance in relation to bodies perceived to be overweight.

The patient ("Pat") in extract 4 is a 76-year-old woman.[5] She walks into the consulting room with difficulty. She appears overweight, and leans heavily on a walking stick. She is accompanied by her daughter-in-law ("Da"). The doctor ("Dr. E") is a senior geriatrician his 60s. He later tells the researcher that the patient has angina, high blood pressure, and arthritis. The patient is attending the clinic for a regular checkup. Extracts 4a, b, and c are not continuous.

Extract 4a

```
1    Dr. E:  now you've certainly managed to get a little bit of weight down
2            haven't you which
                     [
3    Pat:             yes yes
4    Dr. E:  is great (.) because I think we had a long chat about that some time ago
5            how important this was because this is quite crucial to those nasty
6            pains in your knees=
7    Pat:    =yeah=
8    Dr. E:  =to get the load off your joints=
9    Pat:    =yes=
10   Dr. E:  =um (.) are you still sticking fairly strictly to your diet?
11   Pat:    yes (to daughter-in-law) aren't I? but I haven't (.) yeah
                             [
12   Dr. E:                      good good
13   Da:     (loudly) yes and we've really tried this time=
14   Dr. E:  =I'm sure well er it's clearly being successful
                     [        ]    [   ]
```

```
15   PAT:               yes              but
                          [
16   DA:               we really have tried but
17   DR. E: I can see that by the different weight
                                [
18   DA:                     yes I wish I could get her to do a bit more exercise
19            doctor but I can't she'll come down to the shops with me one time
                          [
20   DR. E:           yes yes
21   DA:    fine she'll go all the way back and when she comes back it might be
22            a month again before she'll=
23   DR. E: =yes=
24   DA:    =make the effort to go back down again
25   DR. E: yes
26   PAT:   I get so out of breath like you know walking
                                [
27   DR. E:                   do you?
28   PAT:   yes
                 [
29   DA:    perspires a lot she does
                 [
30   DR. E: yes
31   PAT:   and er the perspiration pours off me then
                                      [
32   DR. E:                         yes yes (.) you see really what
33            it's best to do is (.) er kind of little and often (.) erm it's obvious that
34            while your weight is what it is you can't do large amounts of exercise
35   PAT:   no
36   DR. E: but if you could do small amounts of exercise often then it would help you
37            greatly to get your weight down because I don't think you can do it
38            wholly by diet (.) becau- you can but it would mean such a restrictive
39            diet that it would make life a bit of a misery (.) and so I think you should
40            try a combination of exercise and diet and in that way you can eat a
41            reasonable diet without being terri- (.) over strict
42   PAT:   yes
43   DR. E: er but er being careful and um yet still lose weight but (.) so the exercise side
44            of it is quite important.
```

Extract 4b

```
1    DR. E: um (.) so I think it (.) also your blood pressure I must
2            check it now again (.) but the last few times we've checked
3            it it has remained high (.) and that's something else we're
4            concerned about and weight (.) does push up the blood pressure
5            (.) and er (.) a lot (.) and er again it may actually mean if your
6            blood pressure today is as it's been for the last two or three
7            occasions (.) we might have to give you some tablets to get that down
```

8	PAT:	yes

9   DR. E: but um (.) for your other symptoms it will be much better if you could
10   try and get- (.) you've done well mind you don't let me complain at
11   you because you've actually managed to lose since you were last here
12   something er (.) <u>eight</u> pounds in actual fact (.) which is good going (.)
13   so you can be pretty pleased with that (.) and proud of yourself that
14   you've got that much down
          (The patient smiles, nods, blushes; the doctor continues to praise the
          patient for the weight loss she has achieved over the past six months.)
15   -and you can be very proud of yourself on achieving that (.)
16   and it's just that we'd like to con<u>tin</u>ue the good work and make it easier
17   on you for you you to cope with it
18   PAT: yes yes
19   DR. E: <u>o</u>kay (.) so (.) may I just check your blood pressure dear so if you slip
20   your coat off
21   DA: excuse me doctor (.) but how about my mother-in-law's angina?
22   DR. E: well (.) again all (.) all these um (.) conditions (.) er angina
23   osteoarthritis and blood pressure (.) are very <u>weight</u> related
24   DA: I see yes
25   DR. E: and so (.) really it's almost a a <u>ma</u>jor key to solving er <u>many</u> problems
26   DA: I see.

Extract 4c

1   PAT: when I went to walk (coughs) excuse me (.) when I walk down
2   to the shops
3   DR. E: yes
4   PAT: and coming back I thought I was going to <u>die</u>
5   DR. E: yeah well maybe you're setting yourself (.) those- very
6   occasionally a very <u>heavy</u> task (.) whereas if you <u>regularly</u> set
7   yourself a very <u>small</u> task (.) that is going to the corner (.)
8   however far the corner is and back again (.) but do it <u>every</u> day
9   DA: yes
10   DR. E: and sometimes when the weather is <u>really</u> nice (.) maybe a <u>couple</u>
11   of times a day
12   PAT: yes
13   DR. E: and you'll be able to achieve that because it's not too far (.) and it
14   won't make you feel un<u>well</u>
15   PAT: yes
16   DR. E: those are the ways to think about it (.) okay (.) let's have a look
17   (taking blood pressure) (4.0) (quietly) that's right (11.0) now just
18   relax.

In some ways like the authorial voice in the magazine features, the doctor in extract 4 constructs an authoritative stance around weight issues, but it is bolstered by his institutional role and professional credentials. He is arbiter of the health problems associated with the patient's weight (he lists them in lines 22–23 of extract 4b), and also of her relative success in bringing down her weight in pounds (4b, lines 11–12). He refers to the impact of weight on health (4b, lines 4, 22–23) and deploys the technology of measuring her blood pressure to make some assessment of this (4c, lines 16–18). But he also attributes stances to the patient with respect of how she experiences and reacts to her weight problem, and how she will do in the future. These stances mainly relate to the two themes of *feeling* (affective stance) and *trying* (motivational stance). When the doctor refers to "those nasty pains in your knees" (extract 4a, lines 5–6), he is voicing the patient's own (presumably current) evaluation of the "nastiness" of her condition. Because it is pain that is being thematized here, the condition is attributionally "nasty" (painful) for the patient, not in any more general sense (such as "very serious"). Similarly at line 39, the doctor projects that dieting "would make life a bit of a misery." In various other utterances he projects how the patient will experience the treatment regime—he says it will be "easier... for... you to cope with" (4b, lines 16–17).

The caring function of the doctor role requires empathy and perhaps sympathy, and these are terms that many would use to describe the doctor's modeling of the patient's affective stances in the extract. He signals an awareness of what the patient is going through and projects better stances for her in the future. The sequence in 4b at lines 13–15 involves a different sort of attribution, through repeated formulations of "you can be... proud of yourself" (line 13). Here the doctor is, we might say, *donating* a new stance to the patient—giving her entitlement to "feel proud," a gift whose value is underwritten by his professional authority.

The "trying" theme works relationally in much the same way, and the extract is peppered with both the doctor's and the daughter-in-law's mentions of how much or how little the patient has "tried" to keep to her regime of taking exercise and eating less (4a, lines 13, 16, 18, 24; 4b, lines 10–11, 16; 4c, lines 5–7, 8, 13). At one point (4a, line 13—"we've really tried this time") the patient's daughter-in-law constructs a stance that includes herself as well as her mother-in-law in agentively and collaboratively "trying" to keep within the bounds of the regime. But moments later she excludes the patient and stances herself as having been in charge of the patient's trying ("I wish I could get her to do a bit more exercise," line 18). But the doctor consistently works to validate the suggestion that the patient (with help or on her own) has indeed tried (see 4a, lines 14–17: "I'm sure well er it's clearly being successful"; "I can see that by the different weight"). By repeatedly praising the patient for having "managed" to lose some weight, he recognizes her motivational stance as positive. At one point the doctor even models a positive epistemic stance for the patient—a global orientation to her regime and its associated demands—by saying "those are the ways to think about it" (4c, line 16).

Going back to our earlier brief discussion of "talking for," the stance attributions in extract 4 inevitably raise the question whether the patient feels patronized. Sociopsychological research on patronizing speech suggests that older people's reactions to "overaccommodated" styles of talk vary systematically with their "functional capacity" (Hummert and Ryan 1996, Kemper 2001). Less resourceful and more vulnerable older people, that is, are less likely to feel patronized, and more likely to infer nurturing and endearment. The elderly patient says rather little across the turns of extract 4, and there is no discursive evidence of her resisting or seeming threatened by the stance attributions that the doctor makes. Apart from the unfulfilled "but" clause in line 15 of 4a, she mainly offers tokens of agreement and assent. It is the daughter-in-law who does the most striking "talking for" her, particularly in extract 4a, although even there the patient seems to be actively inviting the daughter-in-law to do this ("aren't I?," 4a, line 11). At line 26 the patient's account of getting out of breath confirms that her daughter-in-law's attribution just before—that she doesn't often "make the effort"—was correct and warranted. The delicacy that, as we mentioned earlier, attaches to attributing stance to others is nevertheless highly relevant in this pattern of exchange. It is easy to imagine how stance attributions intended to be nurturing could miscarry in other contexts.

If extract 4 mainly illustrates the caring functions of geriatric medical discourse, involving morale-boosting stance attribution and shaping, extract 5 shows a very different set of professional strategies, though again centering on stance work. In this case, another experienced clinician quite directly engages with and sometimes articulates the patient's stances, but focuses specifically on his *ideological* stances, trying to bring them more into line with the doctor's own stances, and perhaps with the preponderant stances of modern geriatric medicine. Extract 5 is again in three parts, this time with a male patient, aged 81, attending the clinic alone. The doctor is female and in her 50s. She tells the researcher that the patient suffered from blackouts three years previously, and that he may have had a small cerebral embolism. He is attending the clinic for a regular checkup. In the first segment doctor and patient have been talking about the patient's wife, who has recently had a heart operation, and how the two of them share domestic jobs at home—she cooks, and he cleans.

Extract 5a

1	Dr. C:	any problem? (.) anything that you think that (.) erm
2	Pat:	oh about myself you mean?
3	Dr. C:	yes yes
4	Pat:	well (.) er (.) I get tired (.) rather quickly but I (.) course I (.) I'm not
5		getting any younger am I? I mean er
6	Dr. C:	well nobody gets any younger but that's not the reason that you
7		should get tired
8	Pat:	well I'm hoping it is (laughs briefly)
		[
9	Dr. C:	(laughs briefly)
10	Pat:	er well I (.) now and again I very very rarely I get shortness of breath
11		and that's-
12	Dr. C:	wh- what kind of situation by the way how much do you drink?
13	Pat:	nothing…(Six turns are omitted.)
14	Dr. C:	the point which I'm trying to make that you should lose a bit of weight
		(2.0) (The doctor leans toward patient and looks intently at him.)
15		I know you are you will say not in my age but eighty-one is not that
16		old and you are otherwise a very fit gentleman if you can reduce
17		your tummy a bit it will help you in breathing
18	Pat:	mhm I know I know

19	Dr. C:	you know you see my point and the way you can do that and this
20		would be helpful to your wife because she had an operation isn't it
21		(breathes) em if you cut down certain foods like sweets butters (.)
22		breads
23	Pat:	I try to use er=
24	Dr. C:	=use your <u>comm</u>on sense=
		[
25	Pat:	who- wholemeal bread
26	Dr. C:	yes
27	Pat:	and er I (.) I got a sweet tooth I got to admit that I mean
28		[
29	Dr. C:	cut down all the fats in your food
30	Dr. C:	yes I think she makes a lot of cakes and pastries
31	Pat:	well she looks after me yes
	Dr. C:	yes I can see it on you you know it shows (laughs heartily)
		[
32	Pat:	(laughs)
33	Dr. C:	I'm sure she's a super cook you know (laughs).

Extract 5b (The patient has been telling the doctor that he no longer has a problem with swelling and discomfort in his ankles.)

1	Pat:	they're really good (.) well that's the only thing that is er (.) and it's
2		not very often I get that shortness of breath
3	Dr. C:	mhm (breathes)
4	Pat:	and er
5	Dr. C:	this is what I'm trying to say that this shortness of breath which comes
6		when you are a bit- (.) doing something
7	Pat:	yeah
8	Dr. C:	you it will be helped if you can get rid of that tummy little bit
9	Pat:	I'll do my best
10	Dr. C:	I'm not saying that you should cut down all your food and go on a diet
11		I'm not saying that but use your discretion and ask your wife not to
12		make any cakes and pastries (.) cream cakes things like that that's not a
13		lot to give up for a good life (patient smiles, and does a "visual tut")... (Two turns are omitted. The doctor suggests a compromise— eating cakes only once a week.)
14	Dr. C:	I <u>do</u> appreciate that if you love something you know how hard it <u>is</u> to
15		give up
16	Pat:	yes
17	Dr. C:	you know and I'm not asking you to change your lifestyle all of a
18		sudden at this age but what I'm trying to say is use your common sense (Three turns are omitted. The doctor advises eating lots of chicken, fish, and vegetables.)
19	Dr. C:	you know in many ways you are a very fortunate gentleman because
20		you are otherwise very fit your mind is very clear (.) a and why

```
                                        [
21   PAT:                                oh yes I'm fairly fit
22   DR. C:  ruining it by eating too many sweets
23   PAT:    right
24   DR. C:  use your common sense
                       [
25   PAT:                       yeah so er=
26   DR. C:  =I would say this very strongly right now I'm going to go through
27           these tablets now
28   PAT:    I I yes yes.
```

Extract 5c (The patient has been describing how he has felt a slight pain in his chest on a couple of occasions when rushing for a bus.)

```
1    DR. C:  the important thing is that to (.) not to create a situation to have that
2            happen again
3    PAT:    mm
4    DR. C:  and you said you were rushing for the bus
5    PAT:    well yes I was walking very fast
6    DR. C:  yeah yeah yes and also weight reduction will help you you know
7    PAT:    mhm
8    DR. C:  you know
9    PAT:    yes I must try to ((get over)) that…(Six turns are omitted. The doctor
10           advises the patient to slow down.)
11   DR. C:  so don't rush into things take your time plenty of time if you have
12           missed your bus there will be another bus (.) nothing is more precious
             than your own life.
```

We noted in our initial review that stances will often connect through to, and articulate (parts of), ideological discourses. But we also suggested that a constructed stance might in fact be *toward* an ideological discourse. This will be a characteristic of ideology-laden contexts of talk, and geriatric medicine is one of those contexts. This is partly because of its avowedly anti-ageist orientation, at least in Britain, and its recognition that holistic care for older people inevitably includes challenging the low health expectations that many patients bring to the clinic (N. Coupland and J. Coupland 1999). Early in extract 5a, the doctor and the patient are negotiating stances toward health in aging (J. Coupland and N. Coupland 1994). The patient's utterance "I get tired (.) rather quickly but of course I (.) I'm not getting any younger am I?" may sound conventional, and in fact we have found in earlier work that making own-health assessments is often done conversationally in causal relation to age. The patient is implying that his getting tired is a *consequence* of his age, and understandable or normal in that context. The expression "I'm not getting any younger" is itself a conventional self-oriented stance taken by many older people, and it means that a person is not only "getting old," but "getting old along with all that that naturally brings, health-wise."

Dr. C takes issue with this stance, seeking to falsify it in the following turn. Notice how she brings the causal relation implicit in the patient's turn to the surface in her own turn—she mentions "the reason" (extract 5a, line 6), and refutes the implication that the patient's health status is causally determined by age itself. In fact, she goes further than this by generalizing the principle out to everyone's circumstances—"nobody gets any younger"—and in so doing she undermines the conventional but arguably auto-ageist reading of "I'm not getting any younger." She is taking a stance against the punitively deterministic ideology of health in aging (which we referred to in earlier work as "normal decrement") and in favor of a more open and literal understanding of the fact that "nobody gets any younger." Very interestingly, though, in his next turn, "well I'm hoping it is" (line 8), the patient talks back against the doctor's own ideological stance. He makes a countermove by allowing the inference that, if age alone were not the cause of his getting tired (as in the doctor's version), then there might be some more specific health problem to be addressed, which he doesn't want to be the case. The exchange of laughter that follows this exchange might indicate that the two speakers are aware of and somehow enjoying the complex, oppositional stance games that they are working through, and how they relate to ideological formations around health in aging. But undaunted, the doctor reinstates her medical agenda, asking about drinking alcohol (5a, line 12) and suggesting some weight loss (5a, line 14).

Dr. C makes several further attempts to fracture the patient's ideological stances, as she perceives them. She urges him to be rational (according to her own sense of what is rational) when three times she says "use your common sense" (5a, line 24; 5b, lines 18, 24). She constructs a version of the patient's own unspoken ideological reasoning in response to her suggestion that he should lose weight ("you will say not in my age," 5a, line 15), prefiguring that he will again put his age into a causal relationship, this time with his weight. And then she immediately refutes the validity of that projected stance as her turn continues ("but eighty-one is not that old," lines 15–16). She asserts her own ideological position, partly through the device of telling the patient that *he* is already converted to *her* own stance—"you know you see my point" (5a, line 19). This attributes to the patient not only the epistemic stance of "seeing her point" but also the higher-order epistemic stance of him "knowing that he sees it." In 5b she offers him a reasoning configuration—an epistemic schema for not eating cream cakes—that will bring his ideological stance into line with her own—"that's not a lot to give up for a good life" (lines 12–13), and very similarly, at the end of 5c, along the lines of "don't rush, keep perspective on your weight and your aging, and value your life."

Discussion

Extract 5 is one of the clearest examples in our geriatrics data of interactive discourse overtly referencing ideological stances and sustaining contests between them, although there are very many instances in which related undercurrents can be detected. As we noted earlier, geriatric medicine can sometimes seem to be as much a matter of challenging restrictive ideologies as a matter of providing health care itself to older people. Considerable emphasis is nowadays put on body weight as a health indicator, and excessive weight is known to be a significant risk factor, particularly among the elderly, so geriatricians inevitably have to encourage their patients to control their weight. But body weight is *ideologically* relevant in geriatric medicine when doctors perceive that their patients are overweight through insufficient self-control and self-regard. Excessive weight can be taken as an index of "letting oneself go," and this stance might itself be part of an auto-ageist ideology—that declining health is inevitable or that the older person's body is not worth controlling. As we have seen, some geriatricians then try to challenge these assumptions, on occasions very overtly, mobilizing their own anti-ageist ideology. Stance attribution in geriatrics is a rhetorical device by which doctors can empathize with patients' feelings and ambitions, but also subtly mold them into healthier, more positive, and perhaps less ageist orientations.

Similarly to the geriatrics data, the magazine texts proceed on the assumption that the body is a locus for significant work and management—the body viewed as a project and in need of controlling. Feature writers invoke technologies and regimes to counter an assumed threat to readers' bodies. In the magazine context the emphasis is less concertedly on health and very intensively on bodily appearance. The bodily insecurities and quests that are promoted in the magazine features mainly have to do with issues such as having "a svelte body and glossy hair" or "knocking ten years off your looks" (text 2), or "being happy with the tops of our legs" (text 3). The magazines quite ruthlessly expound ideological values that equate midlife, especially (in the present data, at least) for women, with declining bodily attractiveness, *unless* hapless women take the steps they advocate to alleviate the effects of what they might construe as "slippage" or, once again, "letting oneself go." Like the geriatricians, the feature writers use stance attribution to mold their targets' subjective orientations, but this time attributing feelings of bodily inadequacy and aspirations for aesthetic improvement.

Ageism is an important aspect of the ideological framework in which these discourses function. In each of the two contexts we have examined here, prejudicial assumptions about aging impinge on discourses of body weight, but in different ways. As we suggested earlier, the body and human aging are, ideologically, closely entwined. The most obvious and crass forms of ageism reference aspects of physical appearance; revulsion at age, gerontophobia (Woodward 1991, 1999), is primarily a reaction to visible aging. As Twigg says, "Dominant culture teaches us to feel bad about ageing and to start this early, reading our bodies anxiously for signs of decay and decline" (2004: 61). These are the anxieties modeled as stances in the magazine texts, which then offer the "solution" of disciplining the body through regimes for losing weight. Weight is just one dimension of bodility, and it is by no means the most immediate bodily index of aging. But it is "age-sensitive," and this is a sensitivity that appears to sell magazine copy.

Body-ageism in the context of mid-adulthood is inculcated anxiety over the loss of youth (cf. Gullette 1997). This is the territory in which mass market initiatives to do with dieting, face creams, face lifts, and so on operate (J. Coupland 2007, forthcoming). In late life, body-ageism is far less clear cut. Twigg (2004) points out that the discipline of social gerontology itself has been reticent to engage critically with the theme of aging bodies, possibly because a liberal politics of bodily self-determination is considered harder to apply. Do we think that, in late life, we actually can make choices about our own size, shape, and appearance? The geriatricians in our clinic data orient very specifically to the health implications of patients' weight, and not to any wider considerations, which might, for example, include making assessments of the trade-off between health (losing weight) and enjoying high-calorie food. The doctors define what form of body control is necessary and how success will be measured. Although the doctors' overt ideological commitment is to anti-ageism, in some respects they begin to seem rather like the magazine feature writers, who set bodily agendas and targets for readers and define criteria for successful weight loss.

Stance attribution is a discursive resource for speakers or writers to map their own evaluations, attitudes, and aspirations onto other people. It provides opportunities for ideological transfer. This transfer is far from automatic or inevitable, and there are many instances when transfer is not the intended outcome. In relation to stance attribution in media texts, there is the important argument that mass media tend to address "ideal subjects" (Fairclough 1989) rather than individual recipients, who may be skeptical and to some extent immune. In fact, we take it as axiomatic that audiences do not, inevitably and uncritically, accept or implement the stances created for them in the media (see also Talbot 1995, Thornborrow 1994), any more than elderly patients, inevitably and definitively, have Damascene age-ideological conversions in geriatric clinics. On the other hand, authoritative stances offered in both of these contexts inevitably create reference points for whatever stances readers or patients actually take up. Stance attribution is not stance inculcation, but it contributes to defining the field of possible stances and, more important, is able to suggest that particular stances are normative and not to be ignored.

We would expect the normativeness of an attributed stance to relate to its distribution. It may or may not be demonstrably true that many women, for example, "feel that their curves are out of control." But the *act* of attributing this stance (in extract 2) contains within it the claim that it *is* normative. Claims of this sort are implicit in the use of "you" and inclusive "we," and explicit in the account of the readers' survey. Again, a stance is inferably normative by virtue of its *contextualization*, for example, if it is attributed by an authority figure or institution. We saw how the textual voices of the magazine features encoded their own authority through the use of imperatives, but also through occasional use of warrants inherited from scientific research. In the geriatrics data the doctors sometimes assert their own (professional) logic over that of their patients and urge their patients to use "common sense." Their institutional authority underpins the "correctness" of their acts of attribution, either in particular (e.g., in the observation that a patient has recently "tried hard") or in general (in the universalist aphorism "nothing is more precious than your own life").

Intersubjectivity, glossed by Du Bois (2007: 140) as "the relation between one actor's subjectivity and another's," is recognized to be a focal concern in the analysis of stance. The term *alignment* is used to refer to different intersubjective relations between speakers and between stances. To this extent, the processes we have been concerned with in this chapter are familiar ones in stance research. But, paradoxical as it sounds, perspectives on intersubjectivity in this literature have been author-bound. Stance alignment is understood to be one speaker's reaction to another's, and there is the more general assumption that stances are constructed and in a sense owned by individuals, albeit relative to other stances. The phrase "stancetaking in discourse" (Englebretson 2007) captures these assumptions well. We hope to have shown that personal stances are not fully within the authorial control of individuals, and that people's stances are sometimes made for them. But this technical observation is far less important than the observation, if it can be confirmed in other work, that stance attribution plays a key role in the dissemination of normative ideologies, such as those relating to aging, health and the body.

Acknowledgments

We are grateful to Alexandra Jaffe for generously helping us formulate this point and many others later in the chapter. As it is necessary if conventional to say, we alone are responsible for remaining shortcomings.

Notes

1. The image is a representation of Falstaff from *Henry IV*, speaking words from Part 1, Act 3, Scene 3.

2. The magazines were *Boots Health and Beauty, Cosmopolitan, Essentials, Eve, Good Housekeeping, Marie-Claire, New Woman, Real, Red, Saga, She, Vogue, Woman's Own, Woman and Home,* and *Zest.*

3. We are unable to reproduce original magazine pages for copyright reasons. Our transcripts capture only very rudimentary aspects of the typographical and text-alignment details of the originals, and none of the visual elements. Upper- and lowercase in the transcripts reflect the same in the original sources. Boldface reflects larger font in the originals. Three dots indicate that some text has been omitted.

4. See J. Coupland and N. Coupland 1994; J. Coupland, N. Coupland, and Robinson 1992; J. Coupland, Robinson, and N. Coupland 1994; N. Coupland and J. Coupland 1997; N. Coupland and J. Coupland 1999, N. Coupland and J. Coupland 2000. Details of the geriatric clinic setting in which our ethnographic work was done can be found in these sources.

5. Transcribing conventions show simultaneous speech vertically aligned and linked by square brackets; closely "latched" turns are conjoined by equals signs; short, untimed pauses are represented by (.) and longer pauses, times in seconds, by, for example, (4.0). Heavily stressed syllables are underlined. Our own interpretive comments are enclosed in parentheses.

References

Berman, Ruth, Hrafnhildur Ragnarsdóttir, and Sven Strömqvist. 2002. Discourse stance: written and spoken language. *Written Language and Literacy* 5(2): 255–289.

Coupland, Justine, ed. Forthcoming. Discourse, the body, and the reversibility of ageing: Commodifying the decade. *Ageing and Society* (Special issue on *Identity and change in mid-to-late-lifespan*, ed. J. Coupland).

——. 2007. Gendered discourses on the "problem" of aging: Consumerised solutions. *Discourse and Communication* 1(1): 37–61.

Coupland, Justine, and Nikolas Coupland. 1994. "Old age doesn't come alone": Discursive representations of health-in-ageing in geriatric medicine. *International Journal of Aging and Human Development* 39(1): 81–95.

Coupland, Justine, Nikolas Coupland and Jeffrey Robinson. 1992. "How are you?": Negotiating phatic communion. *Language in Society* 21: 201–230.

Coupland, Justine, and Richard Gwyn, eds. 2003. *Discourse, the body and identity.* London: Palgrave Macmillan.

Coupland, Justine, Jeffrey Robinson, and Nikolas Coupland. 1994. Frame negotiation in doctor-elderly patient consultations. *Discourse and Society* 5(1): 89–124.

Coupland, Justine, and Angie Williams. 2002. Conflicting discourses, shifting ideologies: Pharmaceutical, "alternative" and feminist emancipatory texts on the menopause. *Discourse and Society* 13(4): 419–446.

Coupland, Nikolas. 2001. Language, situation, and the relational self: Theorising dialect-style in sociolinguistics. In *Style and sociolinguistic variation,* ed. Penelope Eckert and John R. Rickford, 185–210. Cambridge: Cambridge University Press.

———. 2007. *Style: Language, variation and identity.* Cambridge: Cambridge University Press.

Coupland, Nikolas, and Justine Coupland. 1997. Discourses of the unsayable: Death-implicative talk in geriatric medical consultations. In *Silence: Interdisciplinary perspectives,* ed. Adam Jaworski, 117–152. Berlin: Mouton de Gruyter.

Coupland, Nikolas, and Justine Coupland. 1999. Ageing, ageism and anti-ageism: Moral stance in geriatric medical discourse. In *Language and communication in old age: Multidisciplinary perspectives,* ed. Heidi Hamilton, 177–208. New York: Garland Publishing Inc.

Coupland, Nikolas, and Coupland, Justine. 2000. Relational frames and pronominal address/reference: The discourse of geriatric medical triads. In *Discourse and social life,* ed. Srikant Sarangi and Malcolm Coulthard, 207–229. London: Longman.

Coupland, Nikolas, Justine Coupland, and Howard Giles. 1991. *Language, society and the elderly: Discourse, identity and ageing.* Oxford: Blackwell.

Davies, Bronwen, and Horace Romano (Rom) Harré. 1990. Positioning: The discursive production of selves. *Journal for the Theory of Social Behaviour* 20(1): 44–63.

Du Bois, John. 2007. The stance triangle. In *Stancetaking in discourse: Subjectivity, evaluation, interaction,* ed. Robert Englebretson, 139–182. Amsterdam: John Benjamins.

Englebretson, Robert, ed. 2007. *Stancetaking in discourse.* Amsterdam: John Benjamins.

Fairclough, Norman. 1989. *Language and power.* London: Longman.

Gard, Michael, and Jan Wright. 2005. *The obesity epidemic: Science, morality and ideology.* London: Routledge.

Giles, Howard, Justine Coupland, and Nikolas Coupland, eds. 1991. *Contexts of accommodation: Developments in applied sociolinguistics.* Cambridge: Cambridge University Press.

Giles, Howard, Susan Fox, and Eliza Smith. 1993. Patronizing the elderly: Intergenerational evaluations. *Research in Language and Social Interaction* 26: 129–149.

Goffman, Erving. 1981. *Forms of talk.* Philadelphia: University of Pennsylvania Press.

Gullette, Margaret M. 1997. *Declining to decline: Cultural combat and the politics of midlife.* Charlottesville: University of Virginia Press.

Hummert, Mary Lee, and Ellen B. Ryan. 1996. Toward understanding variations in patronizing talk addressed to older adults: Psycholinguistic features of care and control. *International Journal of Psycholinguistics* 12(2): 149–169.

Hunston, Susan, and Geoff Thompson, eds. 2000. *Evaluation in text.* Oxford: Oxford University Press.

Hyland, Ken. 2005. Stance and engagement: A model of interaction in academic discourse. *Discourse Studies* 7(2): 173–192.

Johnstone, Barbara. 1995. Sociolinguistic resources, individual identities and the public speech styles of Texas women. *Journal of Linguistic Anthropology* 5(2): 1–20.

Kemper, Susan. 2001. Over-accommodations and under-accommodations to aging. In *Communication, technology and aging: Opportunities and challenges for the future*, ed. Neil Charness, Denise C. Parks, and Bernhard A. Sabel, 30–46. New York: Springer.

Kiesling, Scott. 2001. Stances of whiteness and hegemony in fraternity men's discourse. *Journal of Linguistic Anthropology* 11(1): 101–115.

Lupton, Deborah. 1994. *Medicine as culture: Illness, disease and the body in Western cultures.* London: Sage.

———. 1996. Constructing the menopausal body: The discourses on HRT. *Body and Society* 2(1): 91–97.

Machin, David, and Theo van Leeuwen. 2003. Global schemas and local discourses in *Cosmopolitan. Journal of Sociolinguistics* 7(4): 493–512.

Martin, Jim R. 1997. Analysing genre: Functional parameters. In *Genres and institutions: Social processes in the workplace and school*, ed. Frances Christie and Jim R. Martin, 3–39. London: Cassell.

———. 2000. Beyond exchange: APPRAISAL systems in English. In *Evaluation in text*, ed. Susan Hunston and Geoff Thompson, 275–303. Oxford: Oxford University Press.

NAO. 2001. http://www.nao.org.uk/publications/nao_reports/00–01/0001220.pdf (accessed July 26, 2007).

Ochs, Elinor. 1992. Indexing gender. In *Rethinking context: Language as an interactive phenomenon*, ed. Alessandro Duranti and Charles Goodwin, 335–358. Cambridge: Cambridge University Press.

Rich, Emma, and John Evans. 2005. "Fat ethics": The obesity discourse and body politics. *Social Theory and Health* 3: 341–358.

Scheibman, Joanne. 2007. Subjective and intersubjective uses of generalizations in English conversations. In *Stancetaking in Discourse,* ed. Robert Englebretson, 111–138. Amsterdam: John Benjamins.

Schwartz, Marlene B., and Kelly D. Brownell. 2004. Obesity and body image. *Body Image* 1: 43–56.

Talbot, Mary. 1995. A synthetic sisterhood. In *Gender articulated: Language and the socially constructed self,* ed. Kira Hall and Mary Bucholtz, 143–65. London: Routledge.

Thornborrow, Joanna. 1994. The woman, the man and the Filofax: Gender positions in advertising. In *Gendering the reader,* ed. Sara Mills, 128–151. London: Harvester Wheatsheaf.

Twigg, Julia. 2004. The body, gender and age: Feminist insights in social gerontology. *Journal of Aging Studies* 18: 59–73.

WAG. 2004. http://new.wales.gov.uk/news/archivepress/healthpress/healthpress2004/708436/?lang=en (accessed July 26, 2007).

White, Peter R. R. 2003. Beyond modality and hedging: A dialogic view of the language of interactive stance. *Text* 23(2): 259–284.

Woodward, Kathleen. 1991. *Aging and its discontents: Freud and other fictions.* Bloomington: Indiana University Press.

———, ed. 1999. *Figuring age: Women, bodies, generations.* Bloomington: Indiana University Press.

INDEX